"X/1999 DEMANDS YOUR ATTENTION…THIS TITLE IS A SELF-CONTAINED, INTELLECTUAL SERIES THAT, WHILE BEGRUDGINGLY GIVES THE READER PLENTY OF GRATUITOUS ACTION AND VIOLENCE, MANAGES TO STAND APART FROM THAT AND ENTICE READERS WITH THE BEAUTY OF ITS ART AND THE SERIOUSNESS OF THE STORY."

—EX: THE ONLINE WORLD OF ANIME & MANGA

This volume contains the X/1999 installments from Animerica Extra, the Anime Fans's Comic Magazine, Vol. 2, No. 6 through Vol. 2, No. 12 in their entirety.

STORY & ART BY CLAMP

ENGLISH ADAPTATION BY FRED BURKE

Translation/Lillian Olsen
Touch-Up Art & Lettering/Wayne Truman
Cover Design/Hidemi Sahara
Layout and Graphics/Carolina Ugalde
Editor/Julie Davis

Director of Sales & Marketing/Dallas Middaugh
Senior Marketing Manager/Renée Solberg
Senior Sales Manager/Mike Roberson
Assitant Sales Manager/Denya S. Jur
Assitant Marketing Manager/Jaime Starling
Editor-in-Chief/Hyoe Narita
Publisher/Seiji Horibuchi

Printed in Canada

Published by Viz Communications, Inc.
P.O. Box 77010 • San Francisco, CA 94107

10 9 8 7 6 5 4 3
First printing, April 2000
Third printing, June 2001

X/1999 GRAPHIC NOVELS TO DATE

PRELUDE
OVERTURE
SONATA
INTERMEZZO
SERENADE
DUET
RHAPSODY

ANIMERICA EXTRA GRAPHIC NOVEL

X/1999™
DUET

BY CLAMP

X/1999
THE STORY THUS FAR

The End of the World has been prophesied…and
time is running out. Kamui Shiro is a young man
who was born with a special power—the power to
decide the fate of the Earth itself.

Kamui had grown up in Tokyo, but had fled
with his mother after the suspicious death of a
family friend. Six year later, his mother too, dies
under suspicious circumstances, engulfed in
flames. Her last words to him are that he should
return to Tokyo…that his destiny awaits.

Kamui obeys his mother's words, but almost
immediately upon his arrival, he's challenged to a
psychic duel—a first warning that others know of
his power, and of his return.

Kamui is also reunited with his childhood
friends, Fuma and Kotori Monou. Although
Kamui attempts to push his friends away, hoping
to protect them, they too are soon drawn into the
web of destiny that surrounds him.

Meanwhile, two sides to the great conflict to
come are being drawn. On one side is the dream-
seer Hinoto, a blind princess who lives beneath's
Japan's seat of government, the Diet Building. On
the other side is Kanoe, Hinoto's dark sister with
similar powers, but a different vision of Earth's
ultimate future. Around these two women are
gather the Dragons of Heaven and the Dragons of
Earth, the forces that will fight to decide the fate
of the planet. The only variable in the equation is
Kamui, whose fate it is to choose which side he
will join.

Although not all the Dragons have yet
assembled, the battle has already begun. Fuma
and Kotori's father, priest of the Togakushi shrine,
is killed by the Dragon of Earth, Nataku, for the
sacred sword kept in the shrine. Tokiko Magami,
Kamui's aunt, mysteriously disappears before she
can fully explain the secrets of Kamui's birth.

Now, as the time of decision draws closer,
Kamui begins to feel the pull of destiny from
both sides.…

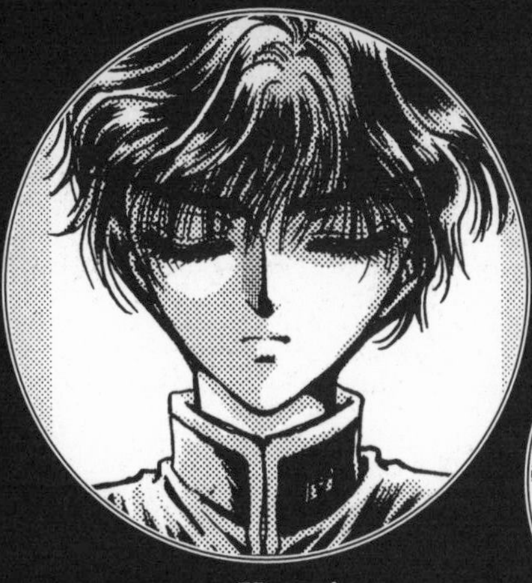

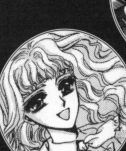

Kamui

A young man with psychic powers whose destiny will decide the fate of the world.

Fuma

Kotori's brother, and Kamui's childhood friend.

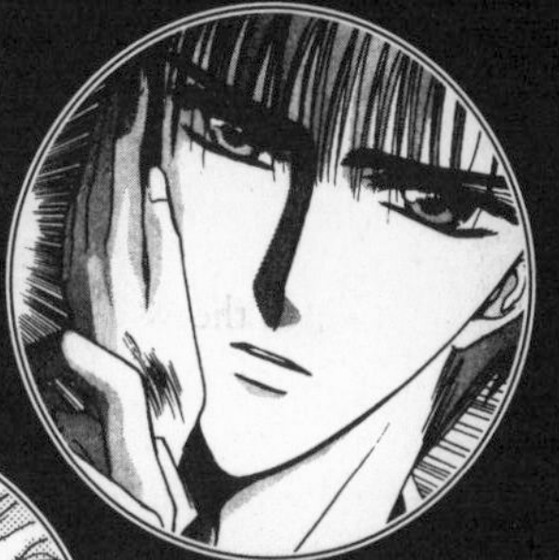

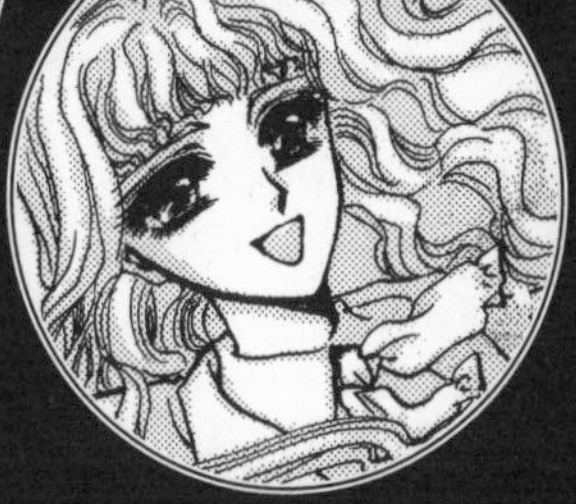

Kotori

A delicate girl with a heart condition, Kotori was Kamui's childhood friend. She is deeply in love with Kamui.

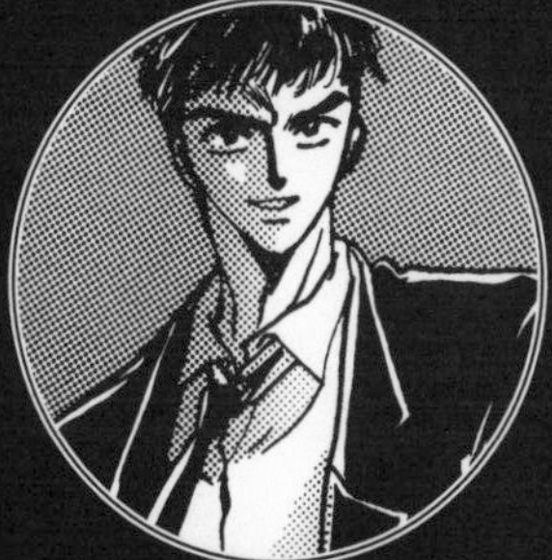

Sorata

A brash, but good-natured young Buddhist priest of the Mt. Koya shrine.

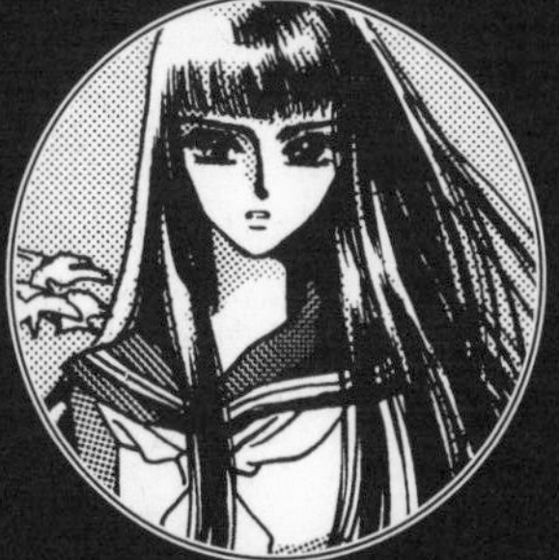

Arashi

Priestess of the Ise Shrine, Arashi can materialize a sword from the palm of her hand.

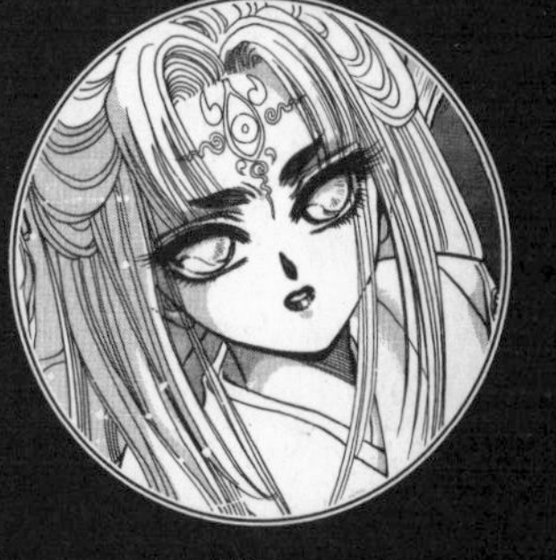

Hinoto

Blind, unable to speak or walk, Hinoto is a fragile, but powerful prophetess, far older than she looks. Atttended by her two maid-servants, Sohi and Hien, she lives in a secret shrine located beneath Tokyo's Diet Building, and is often called upon to advise the Japanese government with her visions.

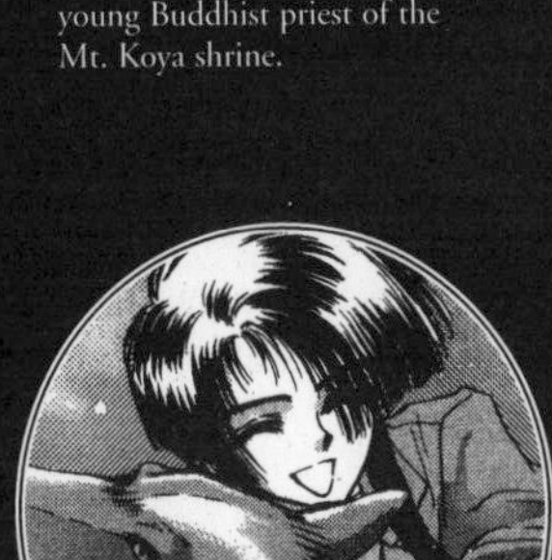

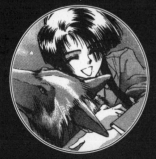

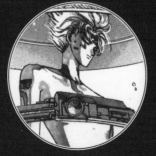

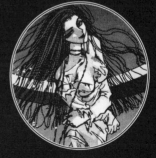

Yuzuriha Nekoi

The 14-year-old Nekoi is the youngest of the Dragons. She is always accompanied by a spirit dog, Inuki, that only she and others with psychic powers can see.

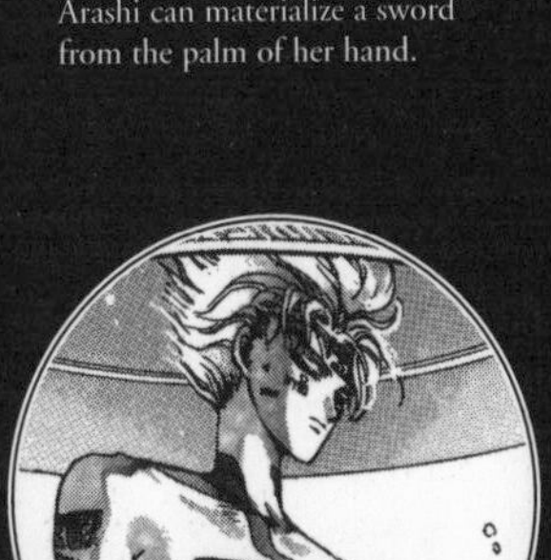

Nataku

A genetically engineered human, Nataku wields a ribbonlike piece of cloth as his weapon.

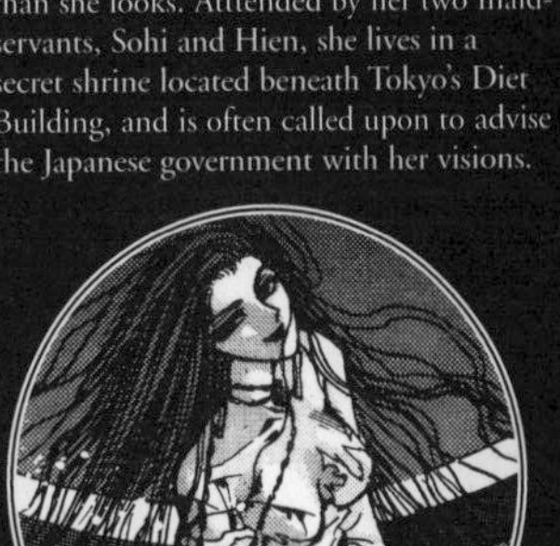

Kanoe

Hinoto's sister shares her ability to see the future…but Kanoe has predicted a different final result.

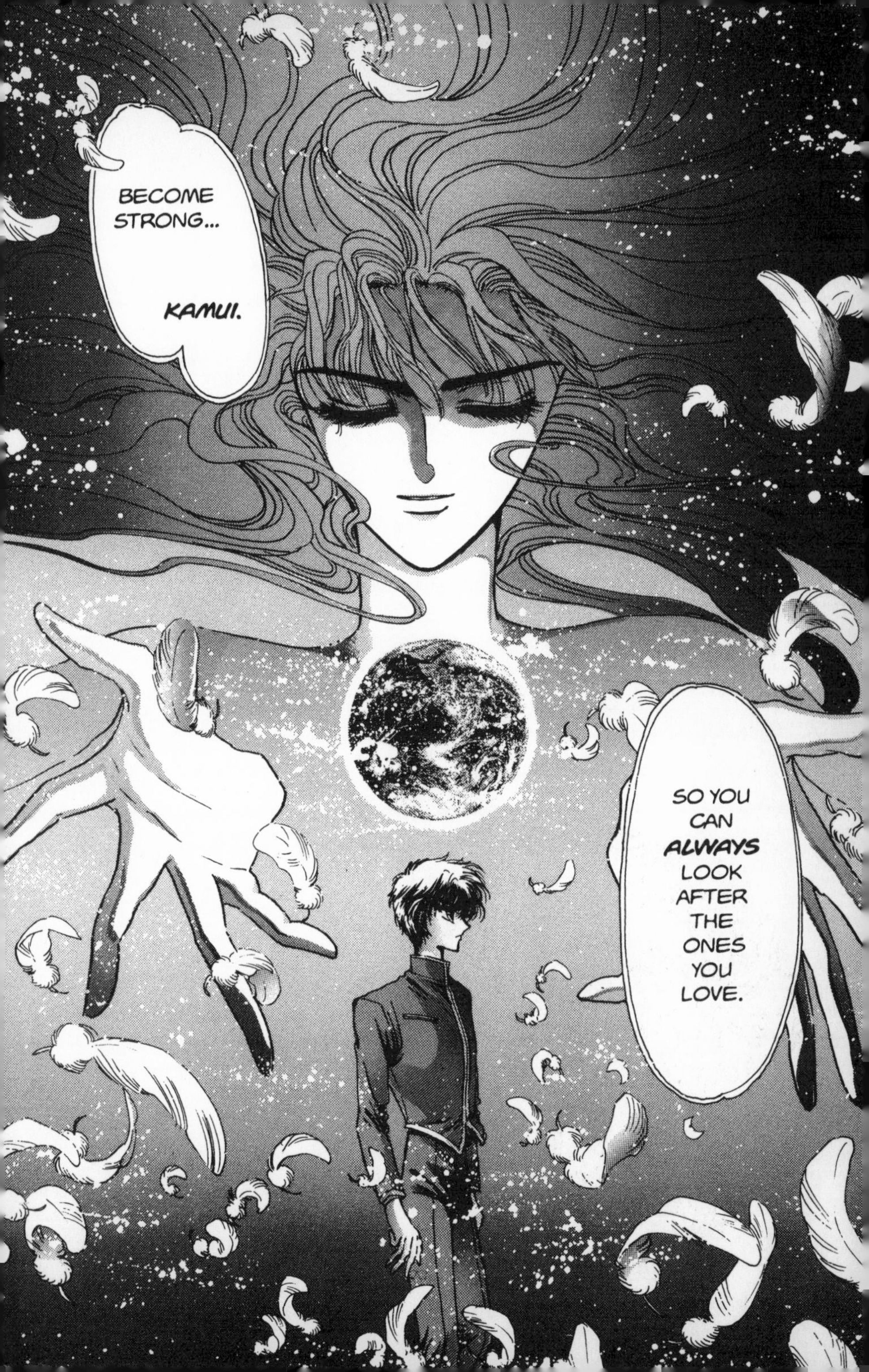
BECOME STRONG...
KAMUI.
SO YOU CAN ALWAYS LOOK AFTER THE ONES YOU LOVE.

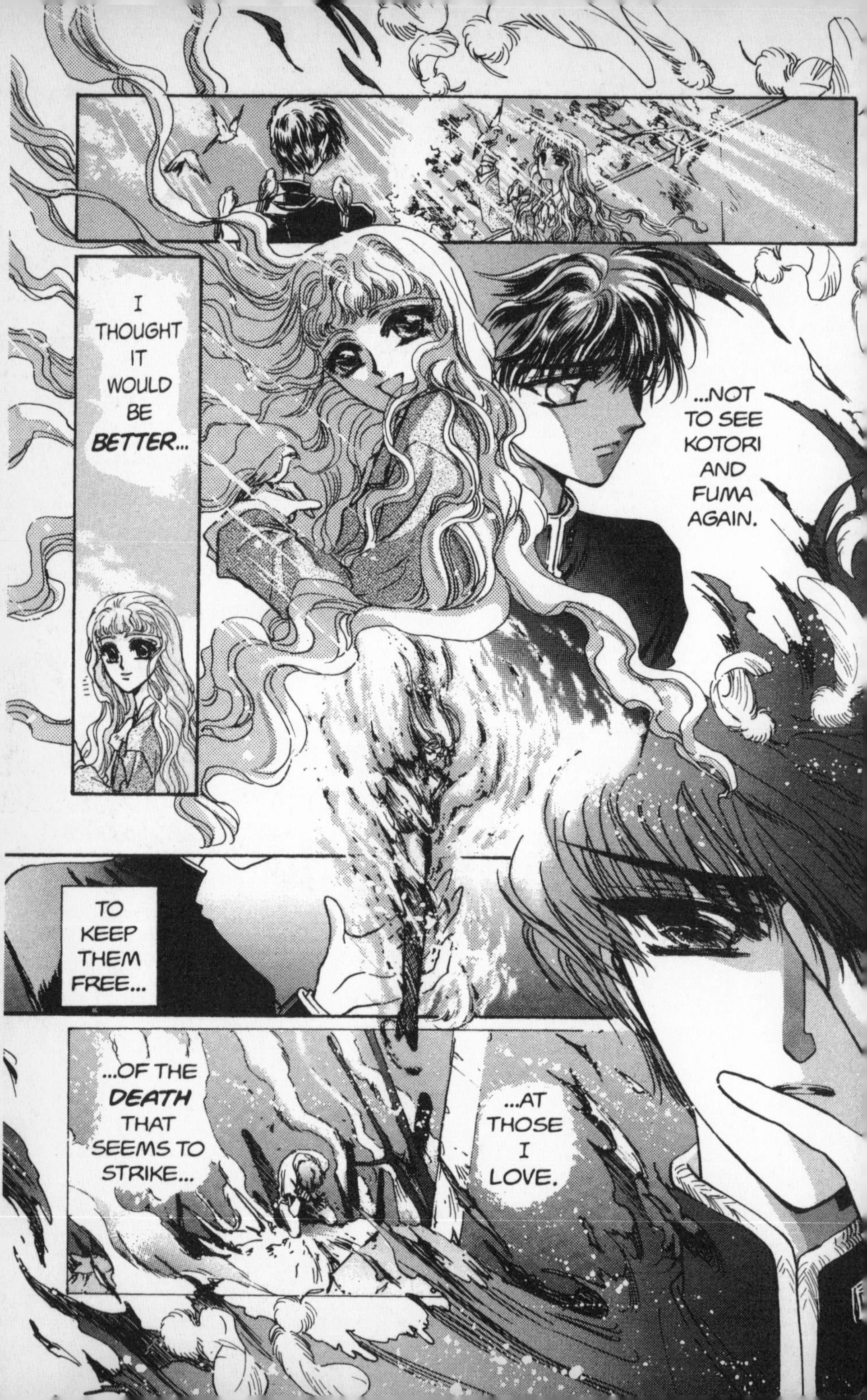
I THOUGHT IT WOULD BE **BETTER...**
...NOT TO SEE KOTORI AND FUMA AGAIN.
TO KEEP THEM FREE...
...OF THE **DEATH** THAT SEEMS TO STRIKE...
...AT THOSE I LOVE.

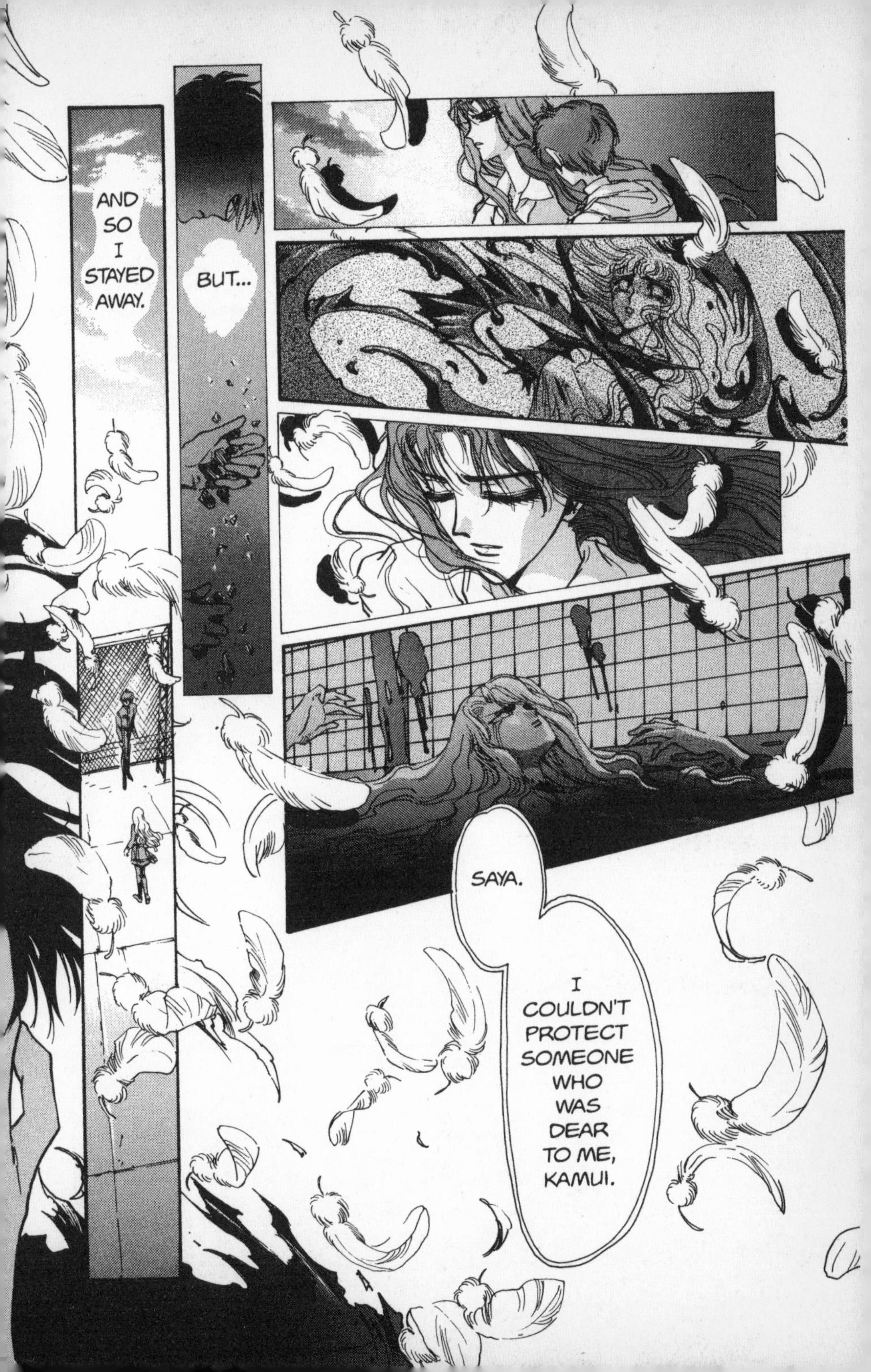
AND SO I STAYED AWAY.
BUT...
SAYA.
I COULDN'T PROTECT SOMEONE WHO WAS DEAR TO ME, KAMUI.

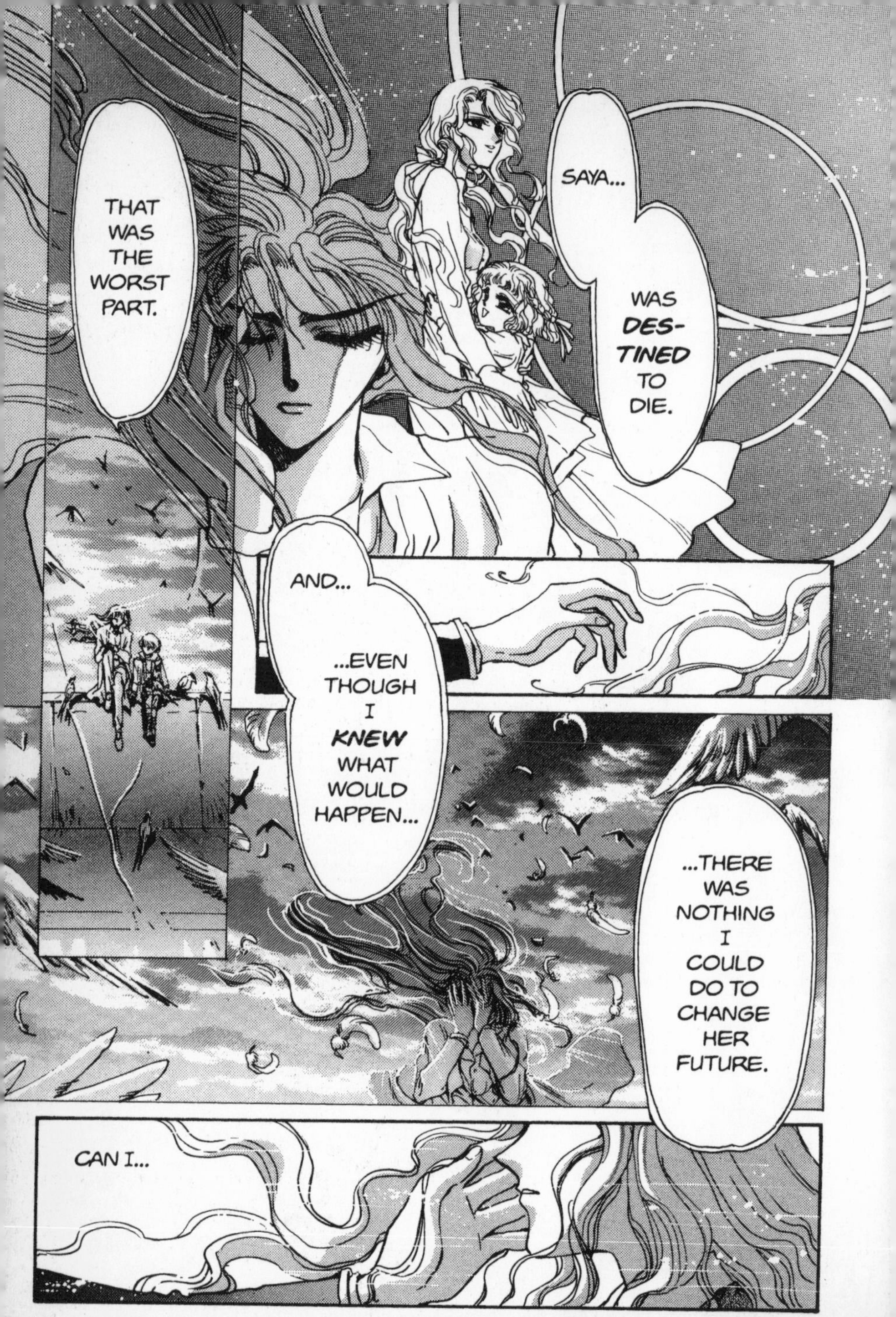
THAT WAS THE WORST PART.
SAYA...
WAS DESTINED TO DIE.
AND...
...EVEN THOUGH I KNEW WHAT WOULD HAPPEN...
...THERE WAS NOTHING I COULD DO TO CHANGE HER FUTURE.
CAN I...

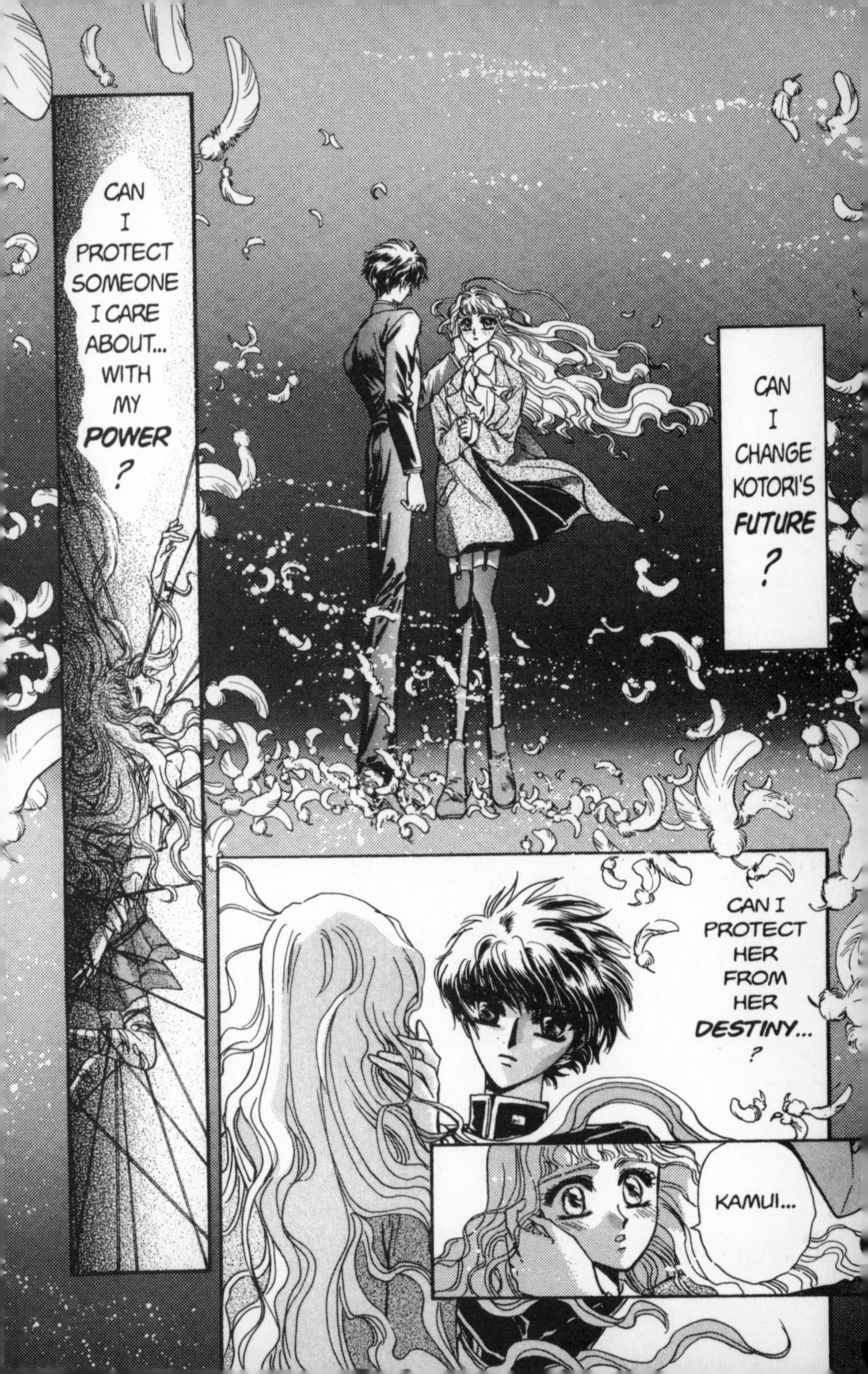

CAN I PROTECT SOMEONE I CARE ABOUT... WITH MY POWER ?
CAN I CHANGE KOTORI'S FUTURE ?
CAN I PROTECT HER FROM HER DESTINY... ?
KAMUI...

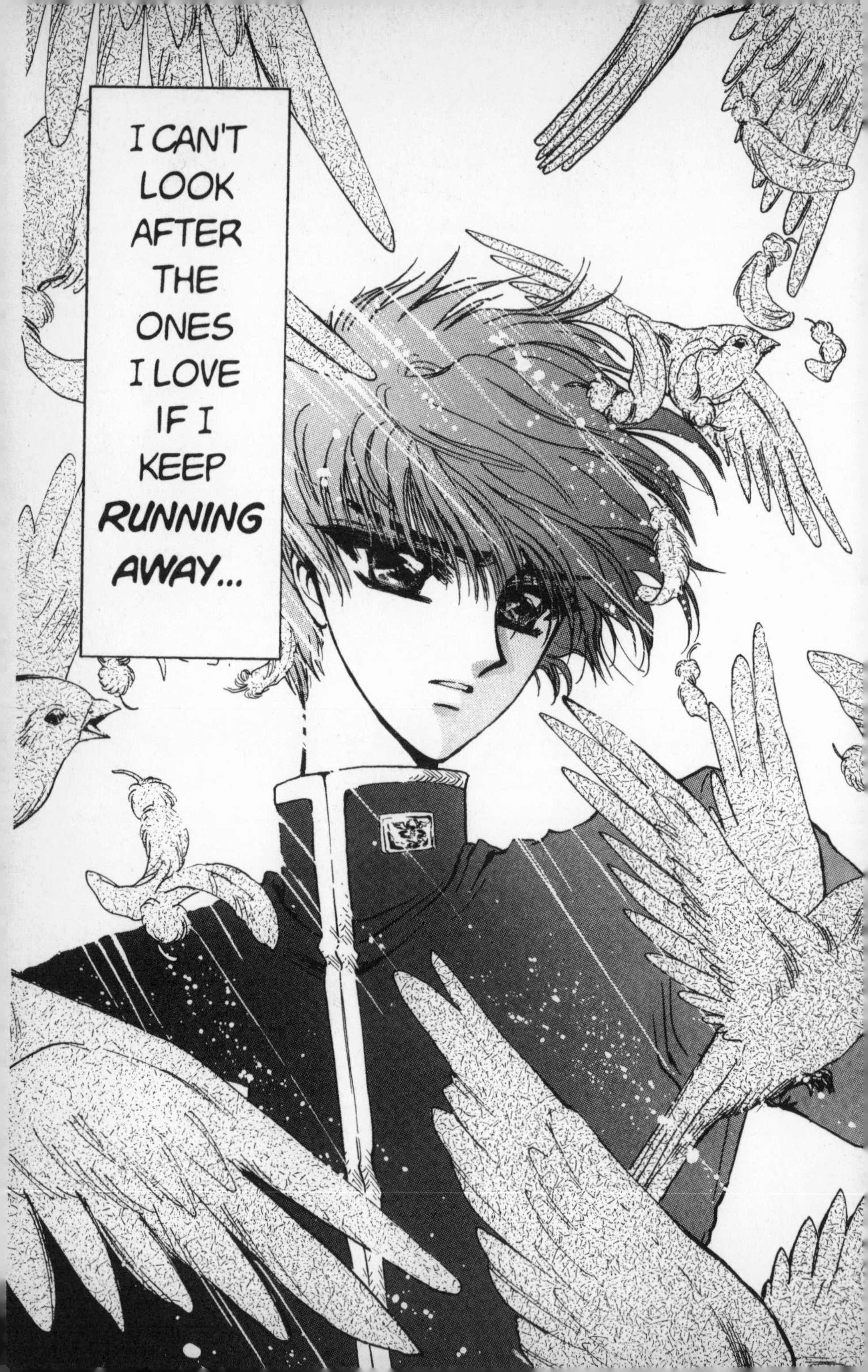
I CAN'T LOOK AFTER THE ONES I LOVE IF I KEEP RUNNING AWAY...

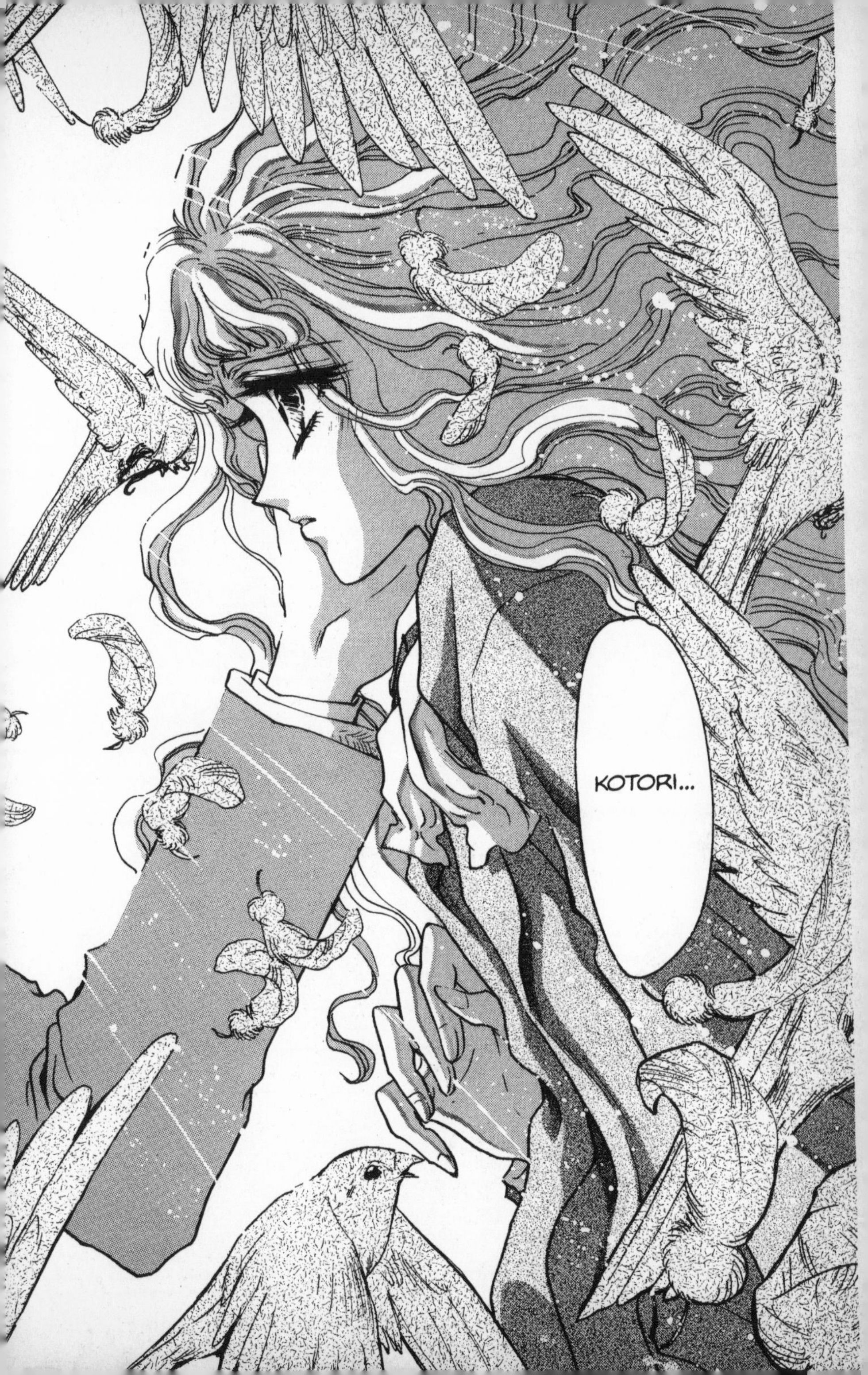
KOTORI...

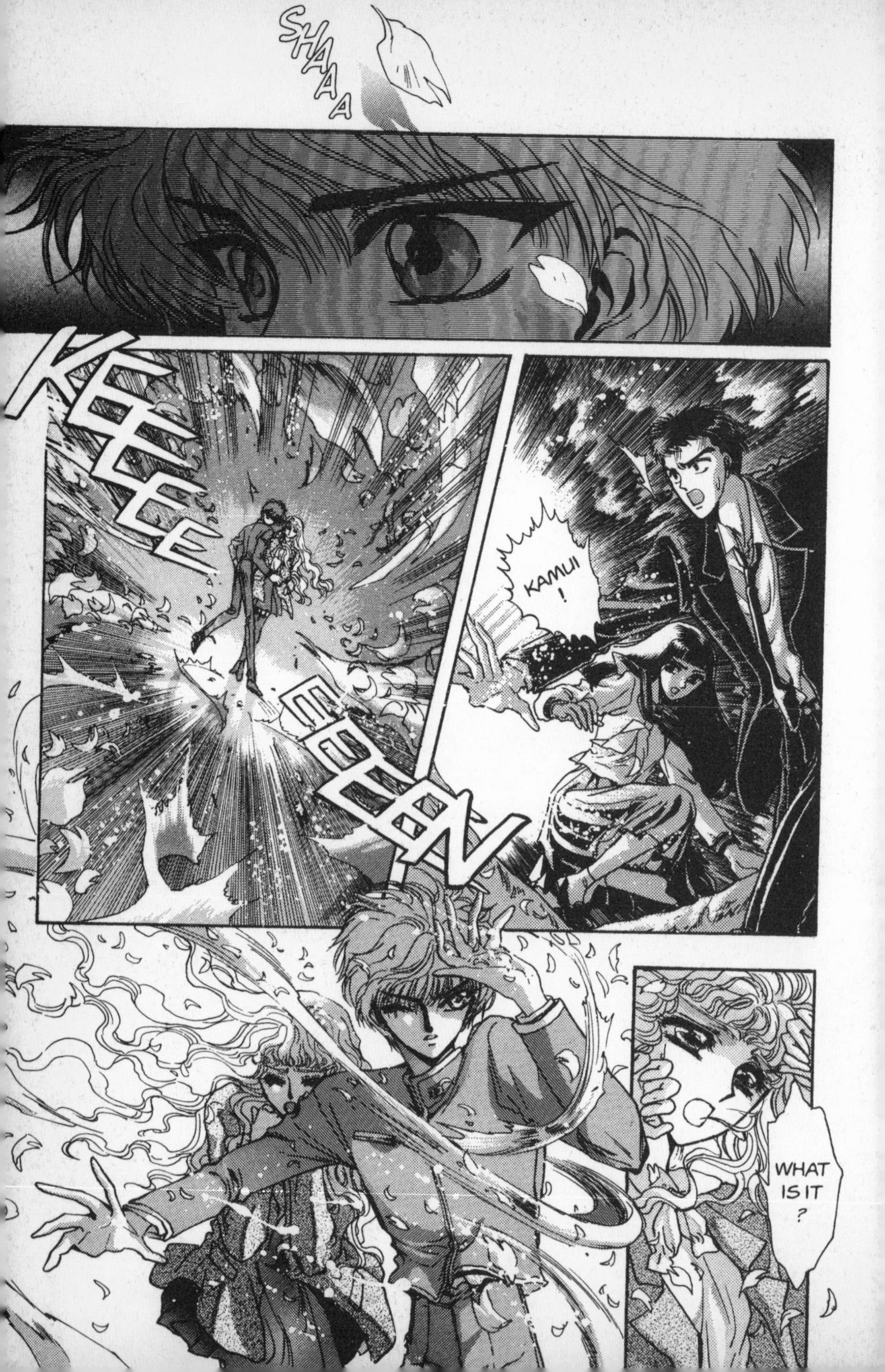
SHAAAA
KEEEEEEEEN
KAMUI!
WHAT IS IT?

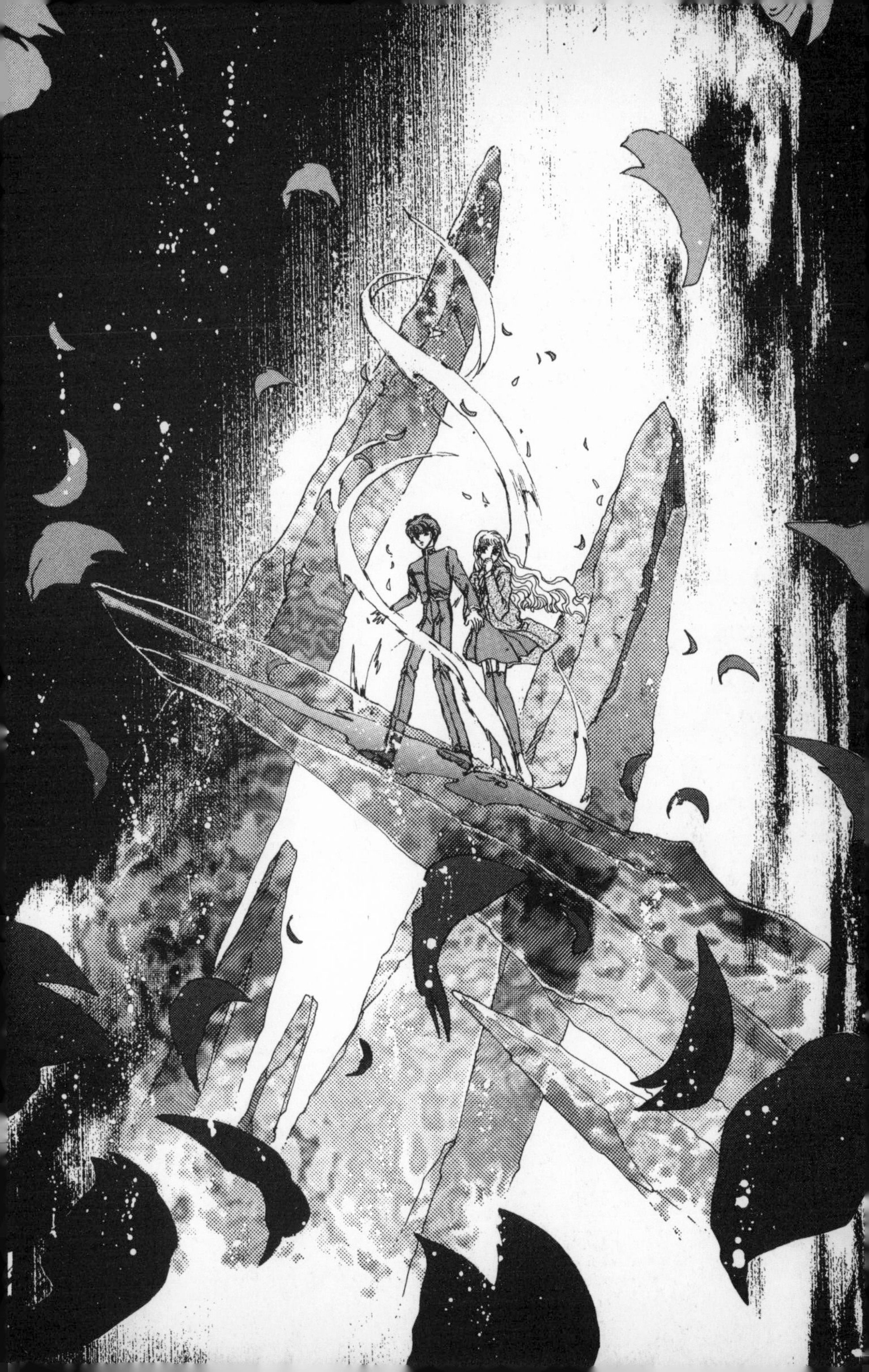

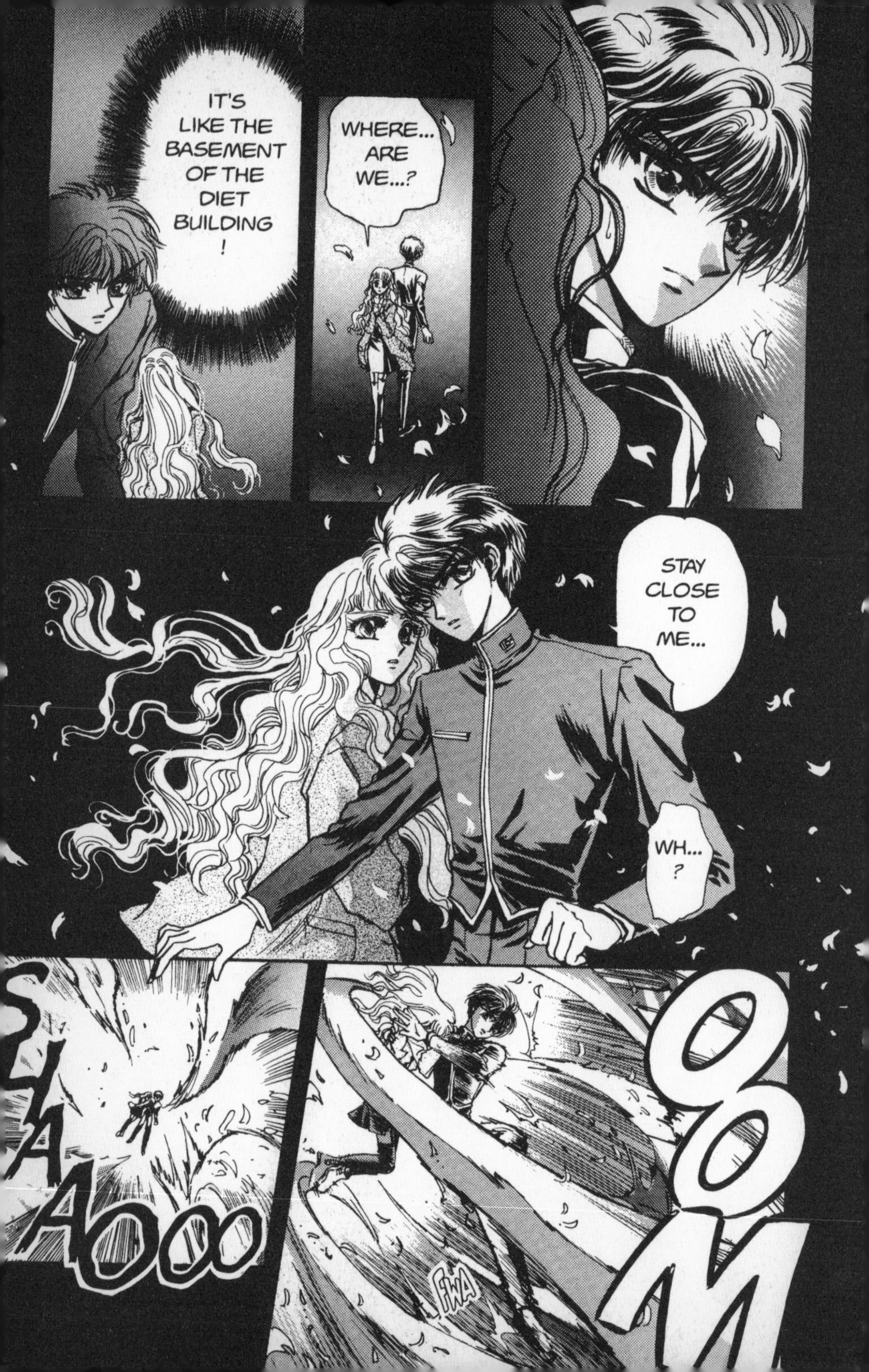

IT'S LIKE THE BASEMENT OF THE DIET BUILDING!
WHERE... ARE WE...?
STAY CLOSE TO ME...
WH...?
AOOO
FWA
OOOM

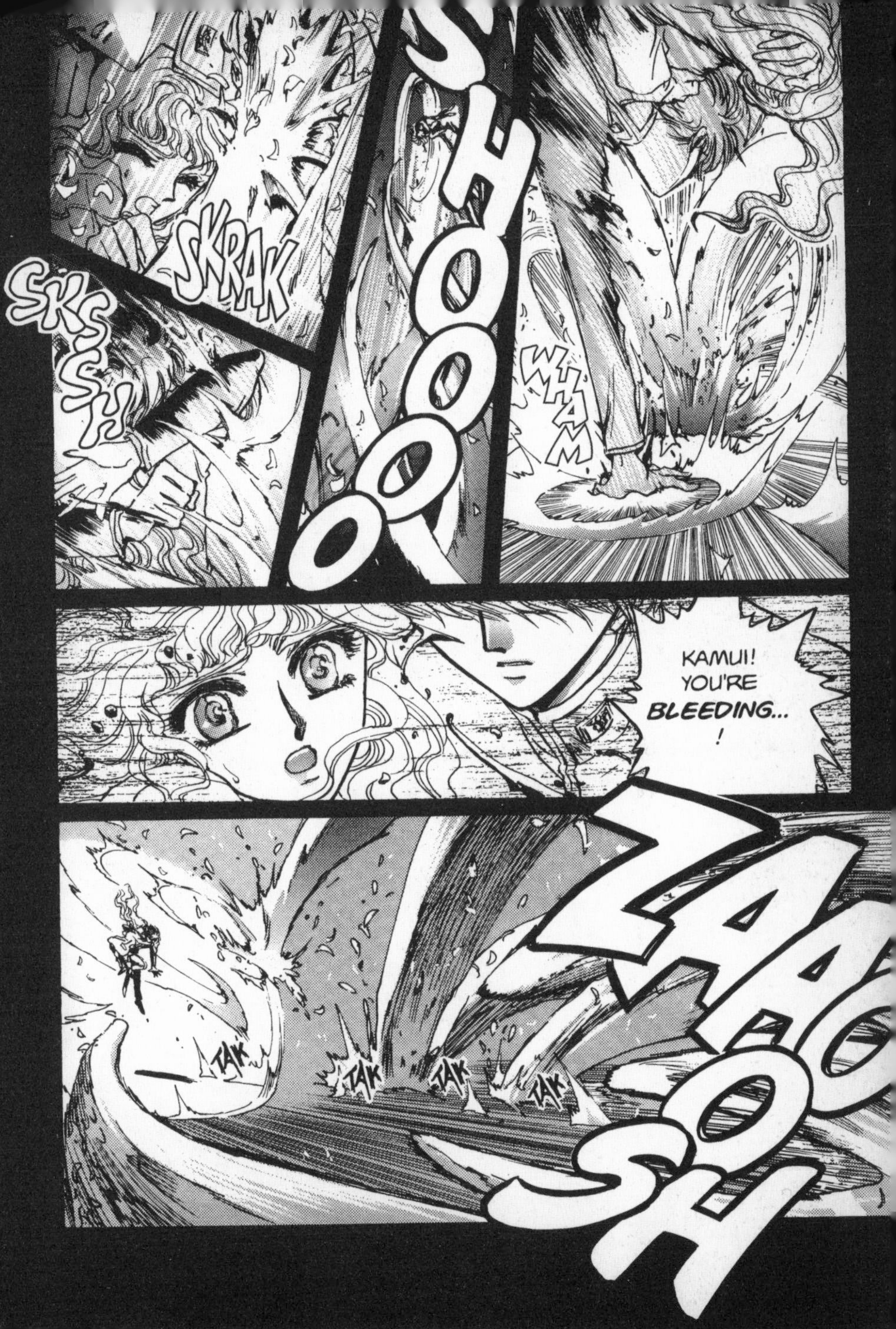
SKRAK
SKSSSH
SHOOOOO
WHAM
KAMUI! YOU'RE BLEEDING... !
TAK
TAK
TAK
TAK
ZAAOOSH

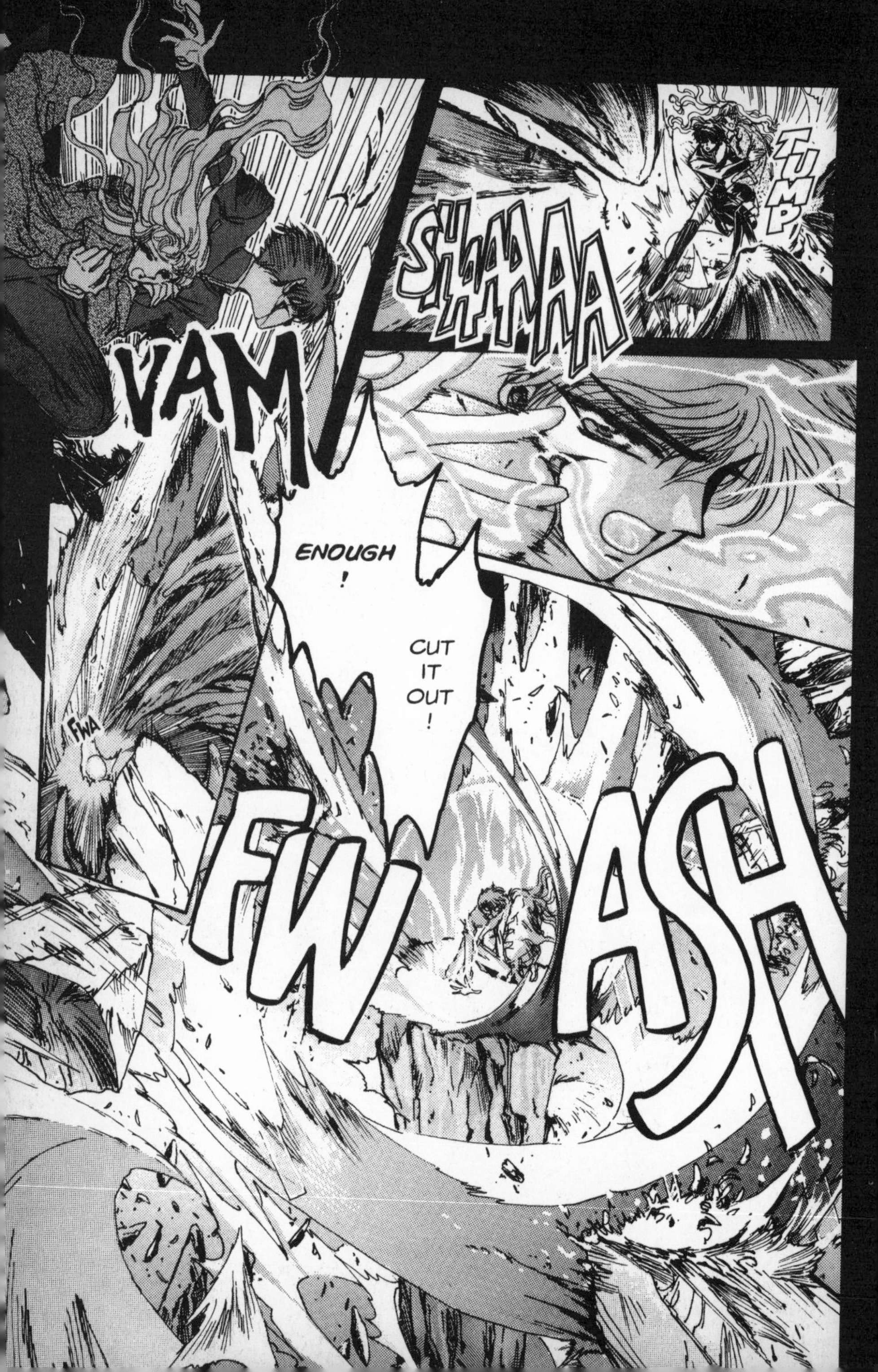
VAM
SHAAAA
TUMP
ENOUGH!
CUT IT OUT!
FWA
FWAASH

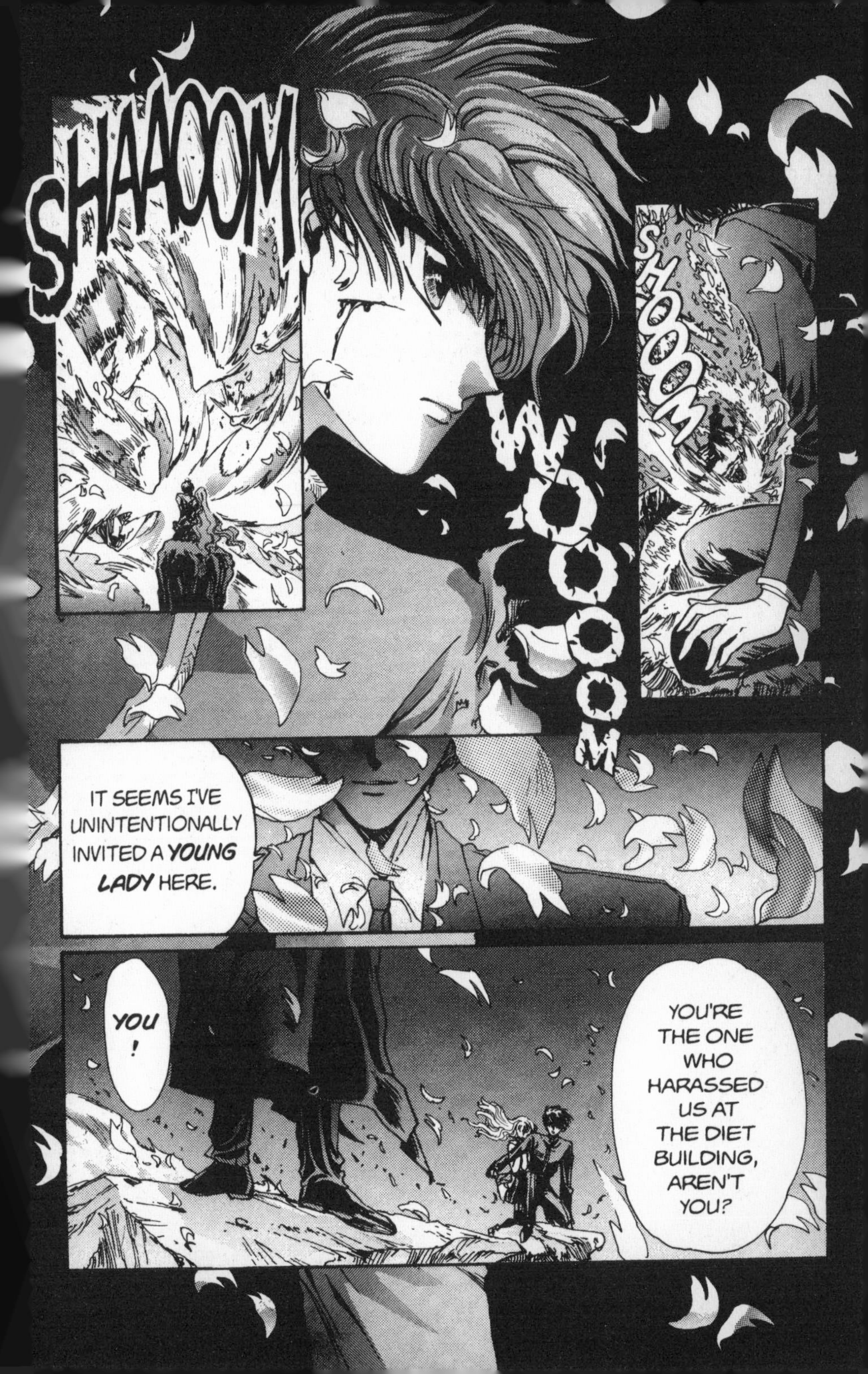
SHAAOOM
SHOOOM
WOOOOOM
IT SEEMS I'VE UNINTENTIONALLY INVITED A YOUNG LADY HERE.
YOU!
YOU'RE THE ONE WHO HARASSED US AT THE DIET BUILDING, AREN'T YOU?

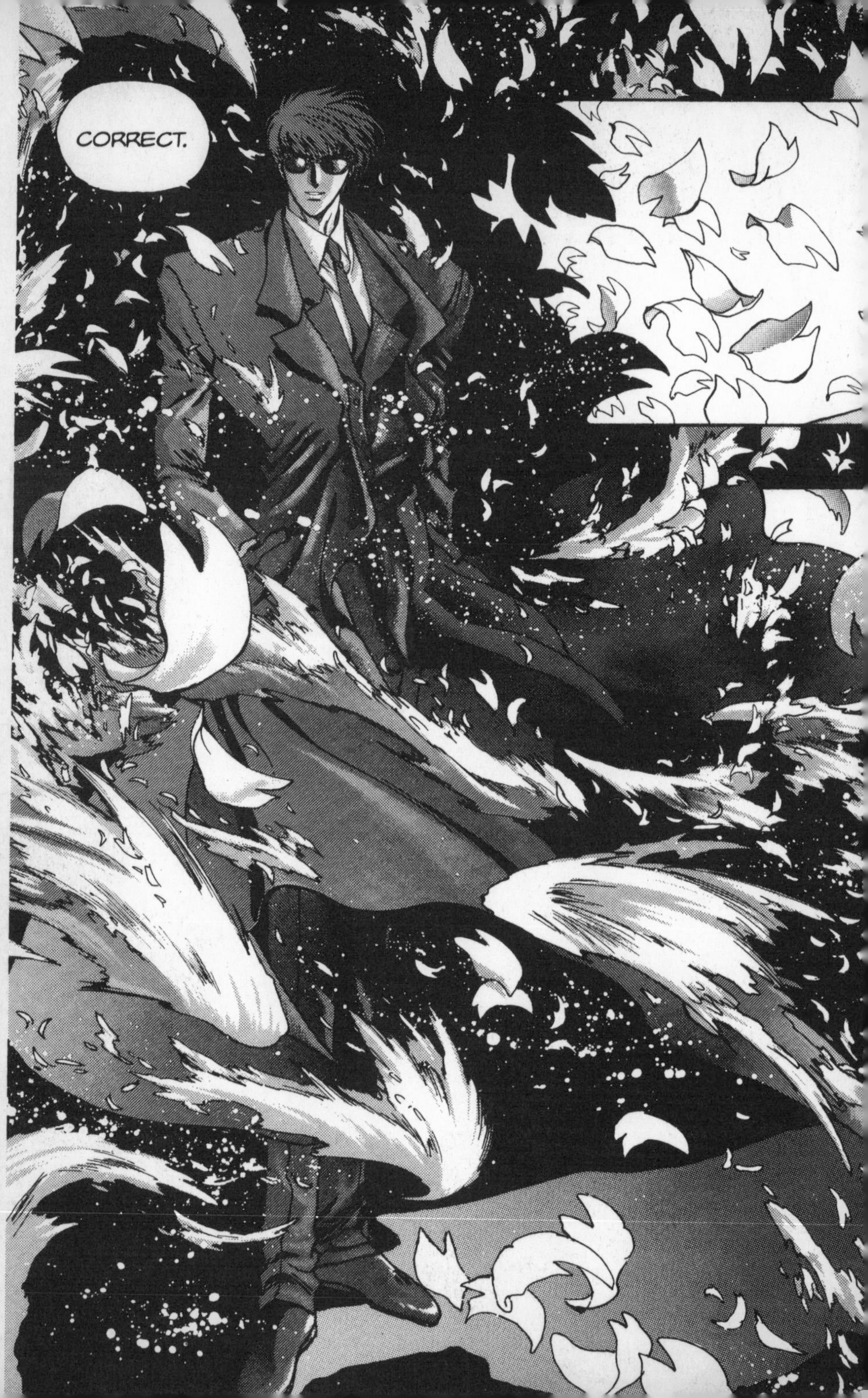
CORRECT.

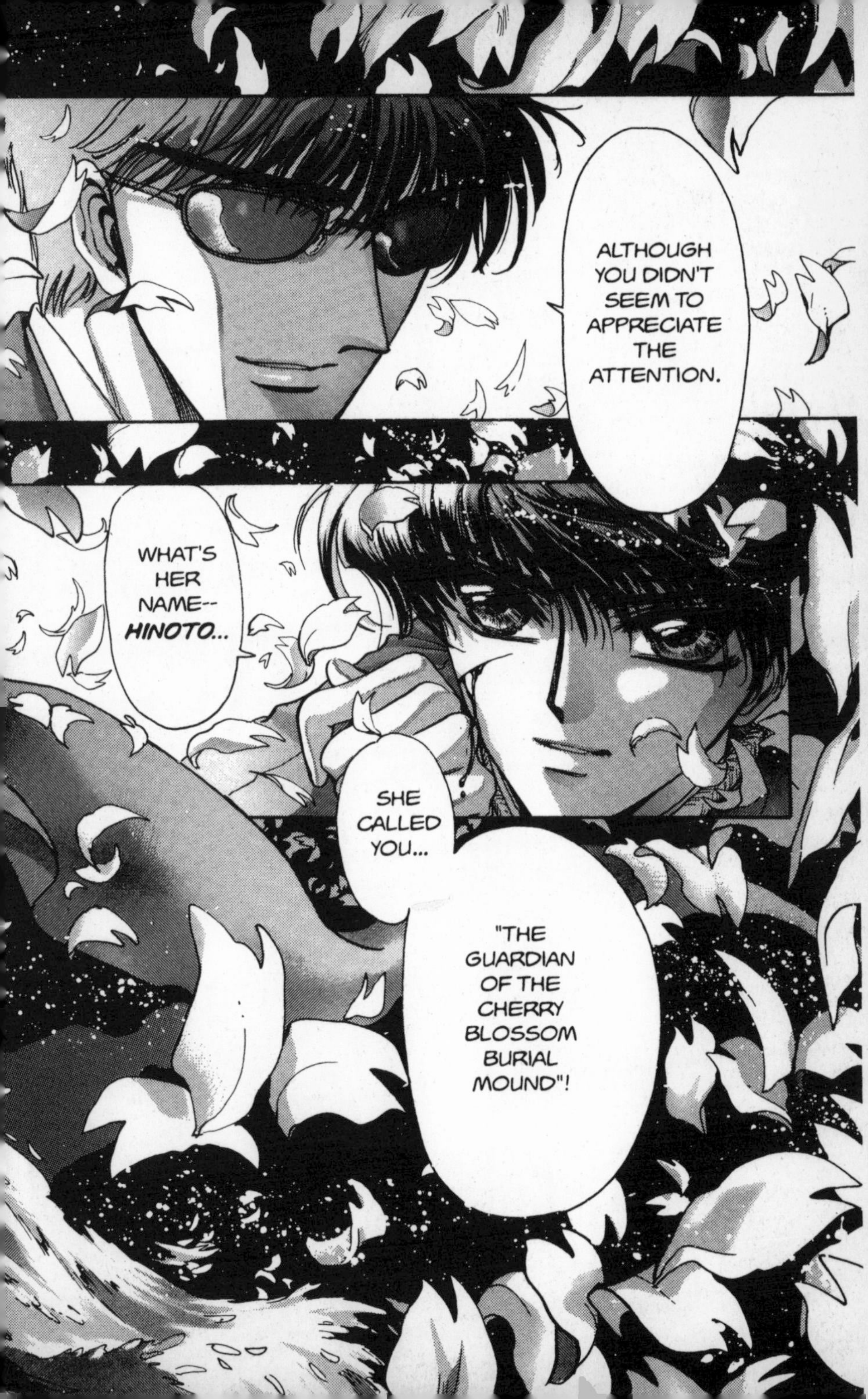
ALTHOUGH YOU DIDN'T SEEM TO APPRECIATE THE ATTENTION.
WHAT'S HER NAME--
HINOTO...
SHE CALLED YOU...
"THE GUARDIAN OF THE CHERRY BLOSSOM BURIAL MOUND"!

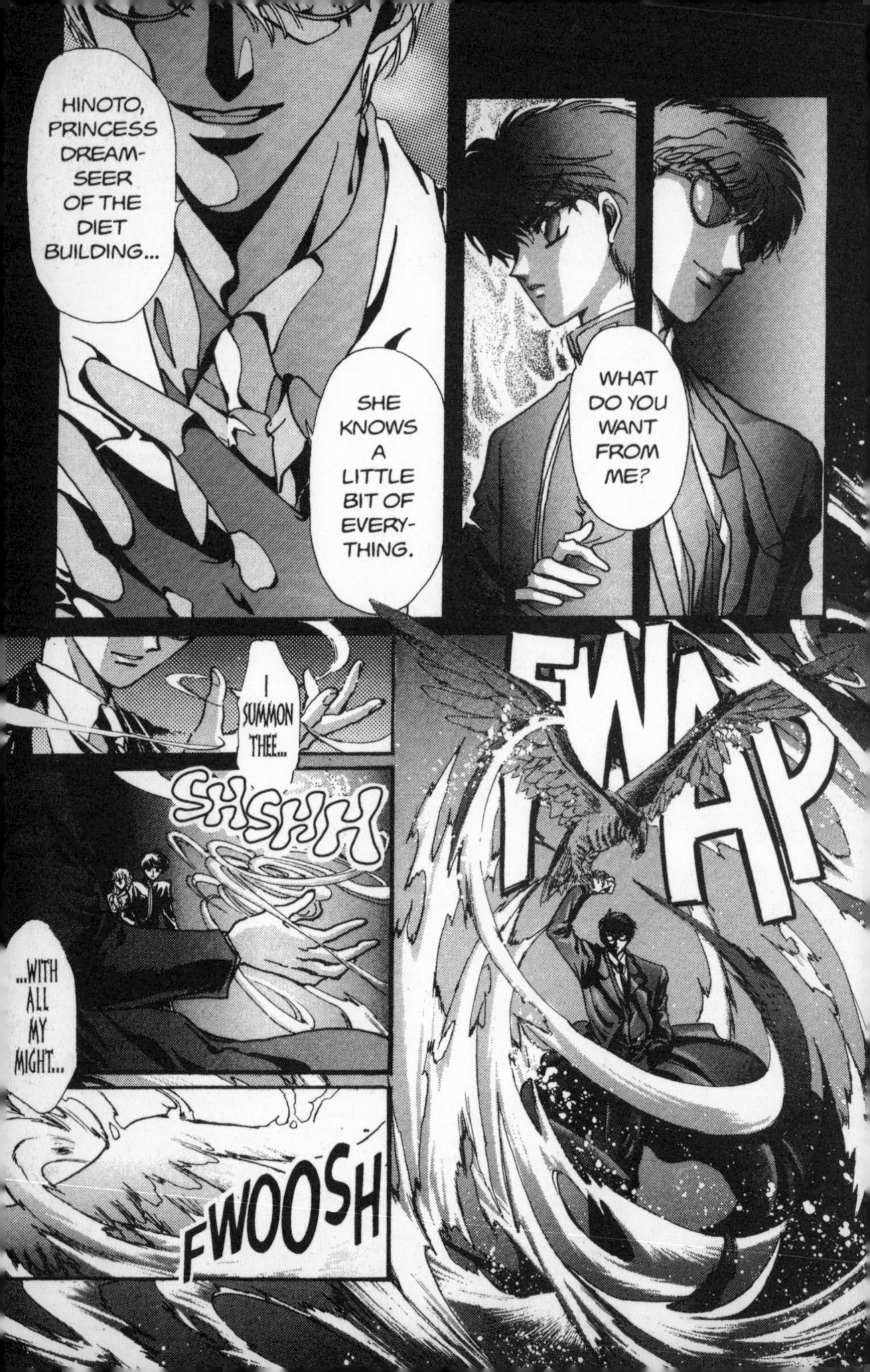
HINOTO, PRINCESS DREAM-SEER OF THE DIET BUILDING...
SHE KNOWS A LITTLE BIT OF EVERY-THING.
WHAT DO YOU WANT FROM ME?
I SUMMON THEE...
SHSHH
...WITH ALL MY MIGHT...
FWOOSH
FWAP

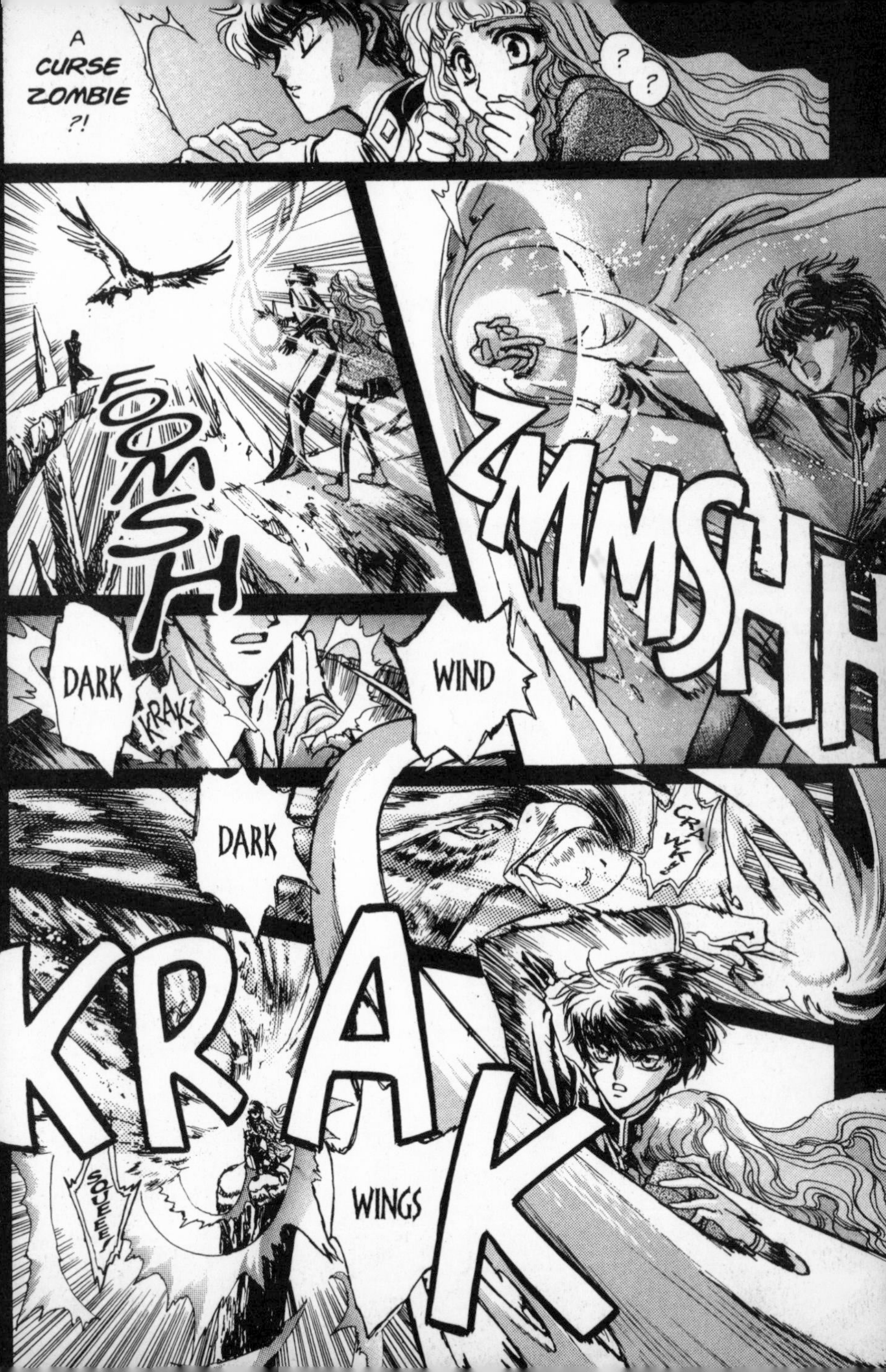
A CURSE ZOMBIE ?!
? ?
FOOMSH
ZMMSHH
DARK
KRAK!
WIND
DARK
CRAWK!
KRAK
SQUEEE!
WINGS

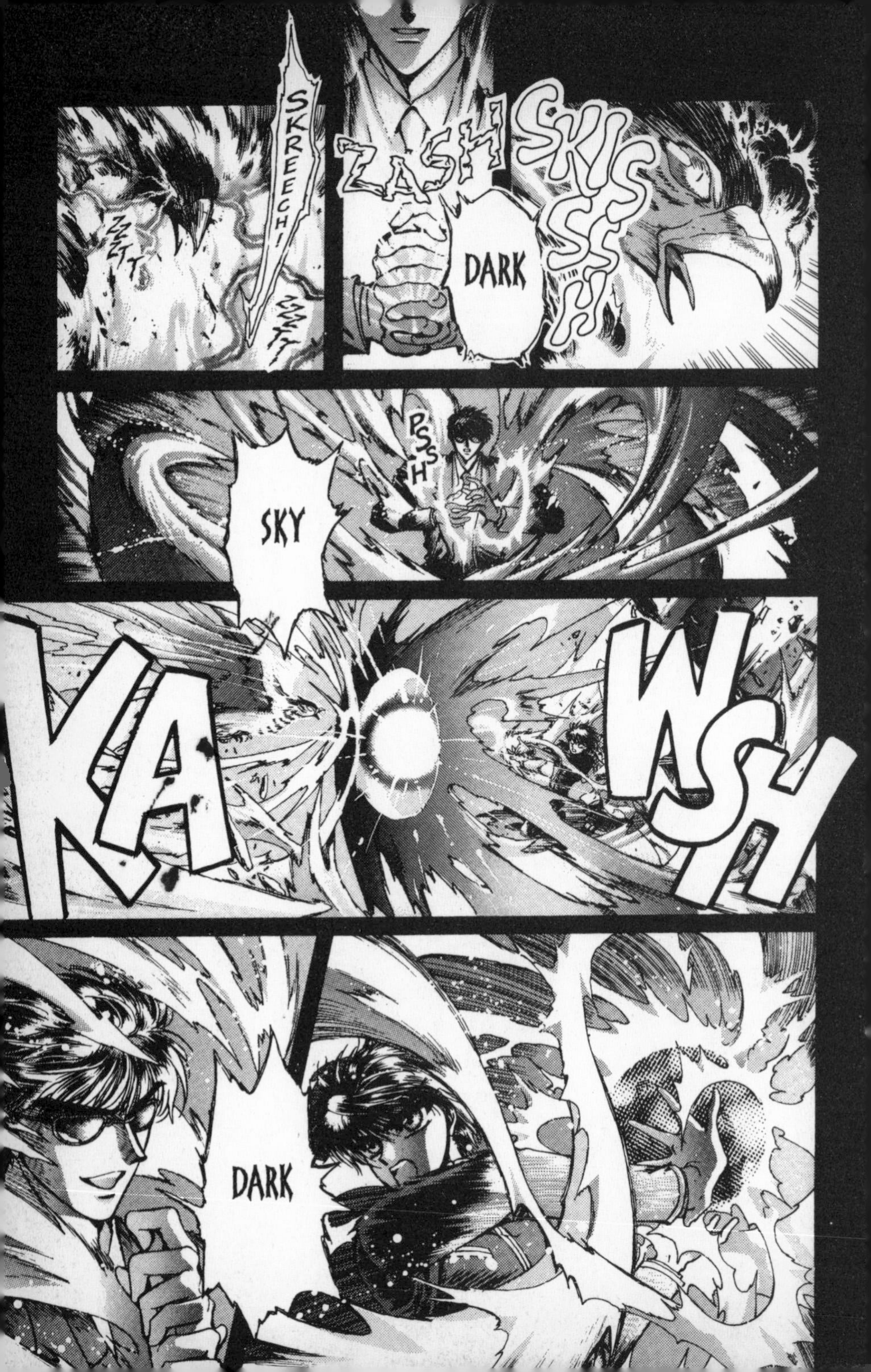
ZZZTT
SKREECH!
ZZZTT
ZASH
DARK
SKISSSH
SKY
PSSSH
KA
WSH
DARK

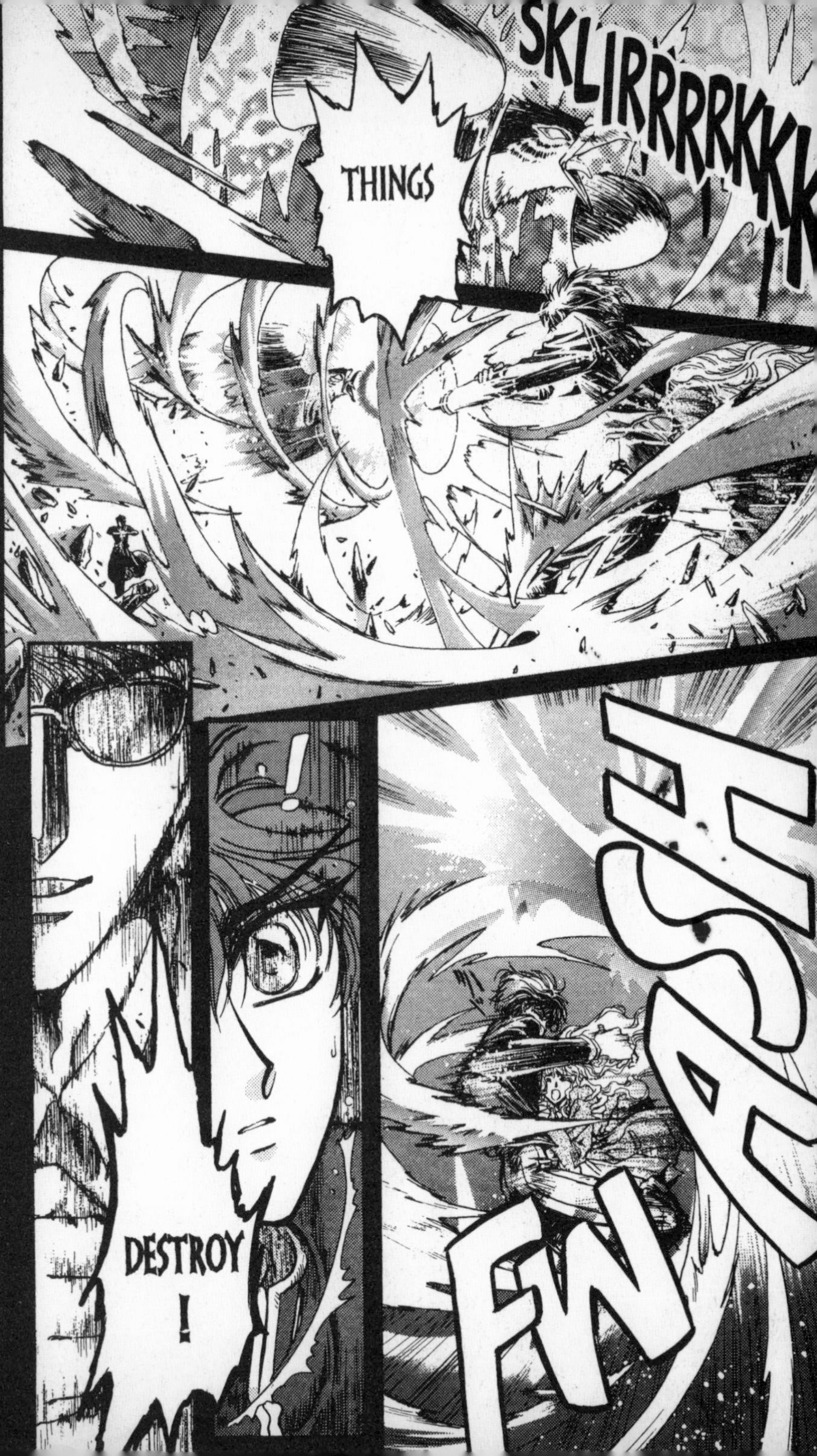
THINGS
SKLIRRRRKKKK
!
DESTROY
!
FWASH

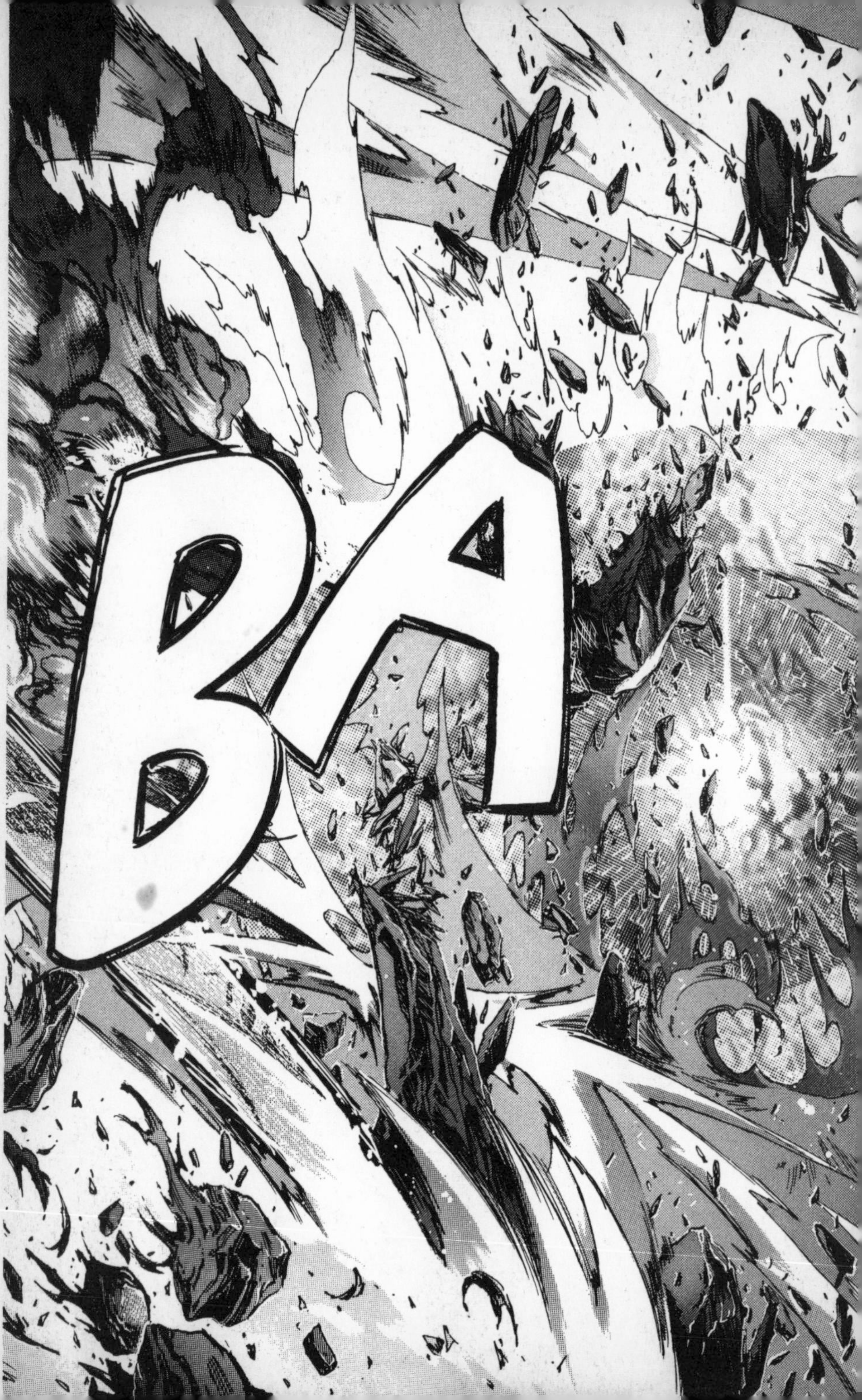
BA

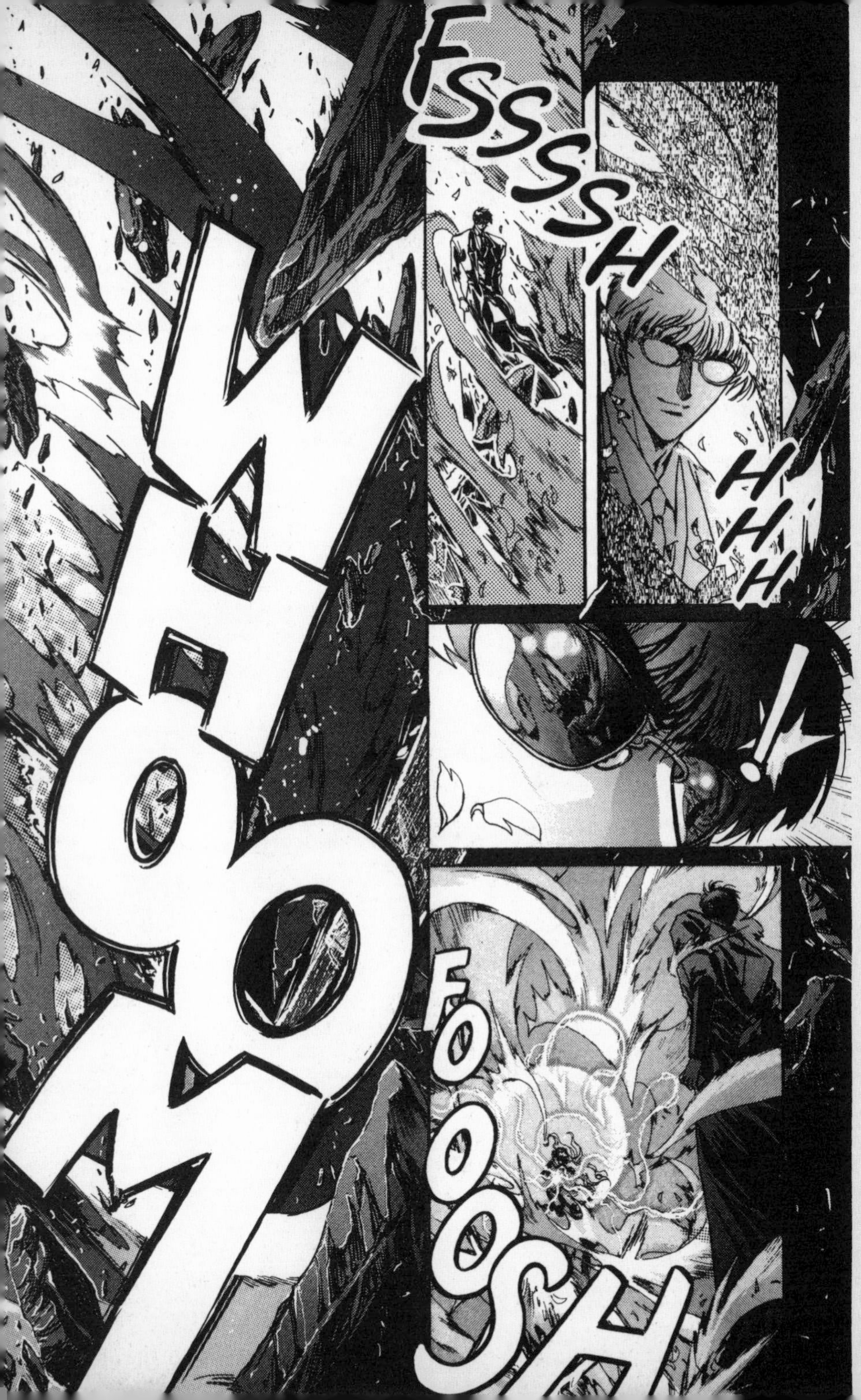
WHOOM
FSSSSH
HHHH
!
FOOOOSH

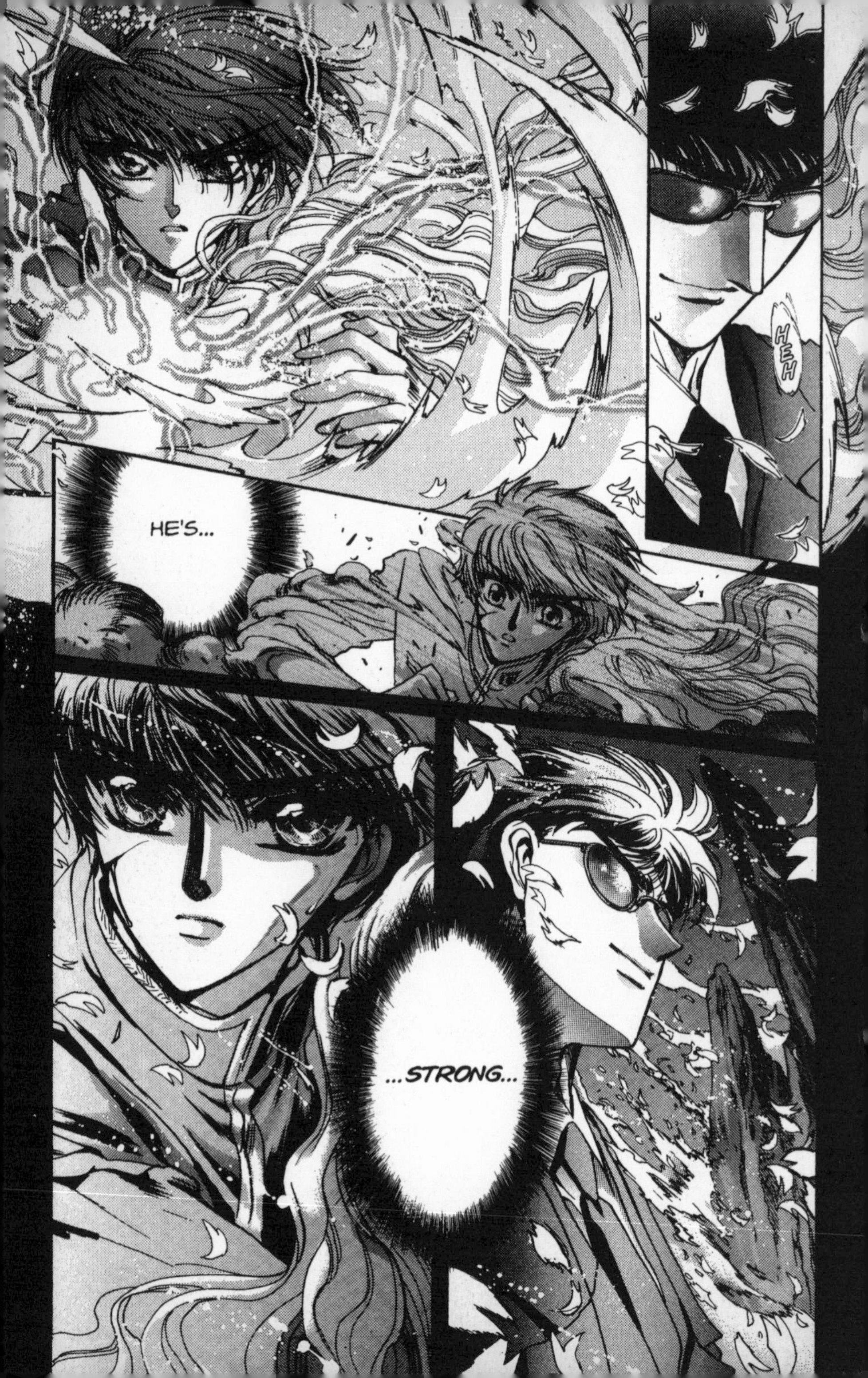
HEH
HE'S...
...STRONG...

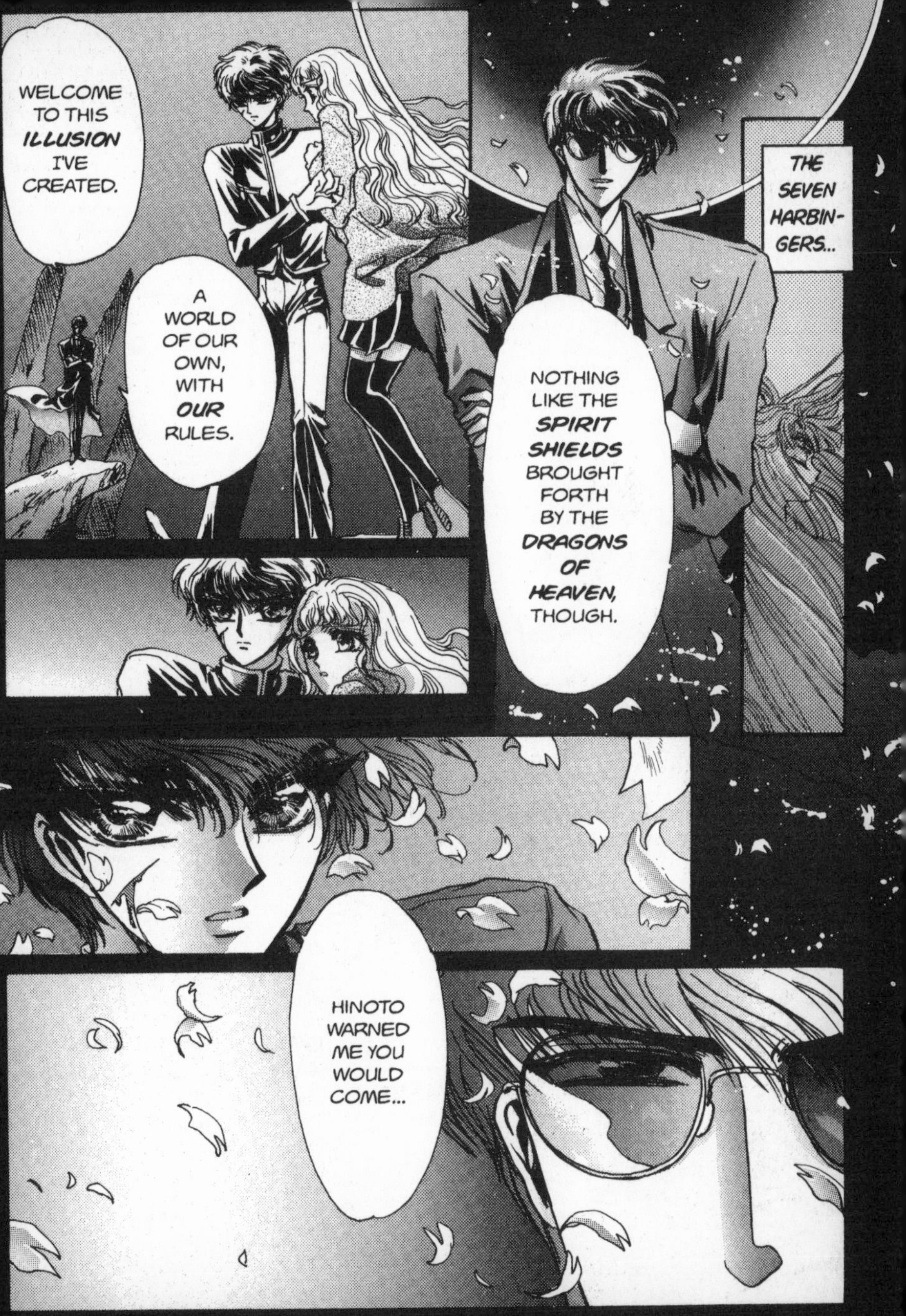
WELCOME TO THIS ILLUSION I'VE CREATED.
A WORLD OF OUR OWN, WITH OUR RULES.
THE SEVEN HARBINGERS...
NOTHING LIKE THE SPIRIT SHIELDS BROUGHT FORTH BY THE DRAGONS OF HEAVEN, THOUGH.
HINOTO WARNED ME YOU WOULD COME...

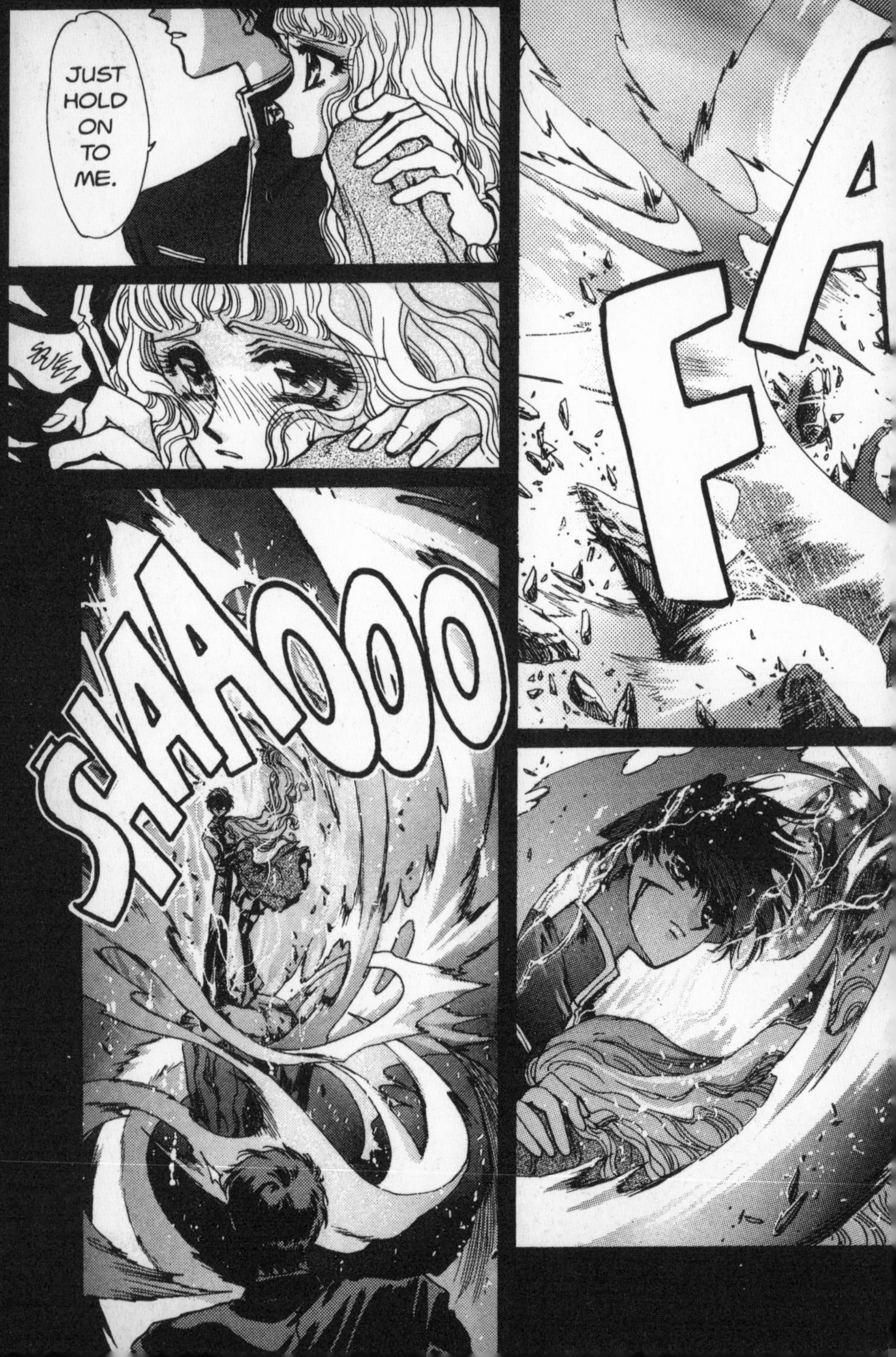
JUST HOLD ON TO ME.
SQUEEZ
SHAOOO
FA

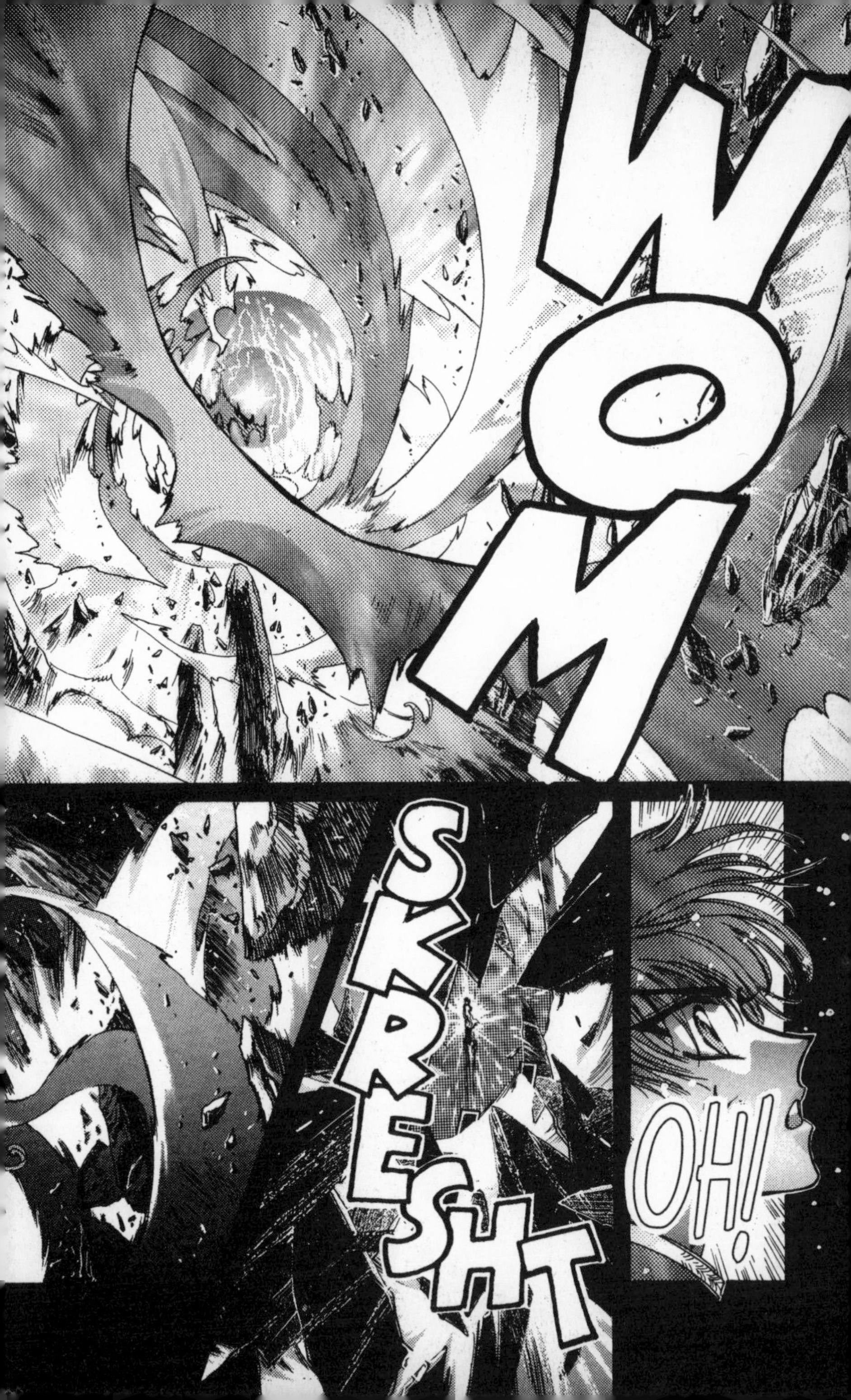
WOM
SKRESHT
OH!

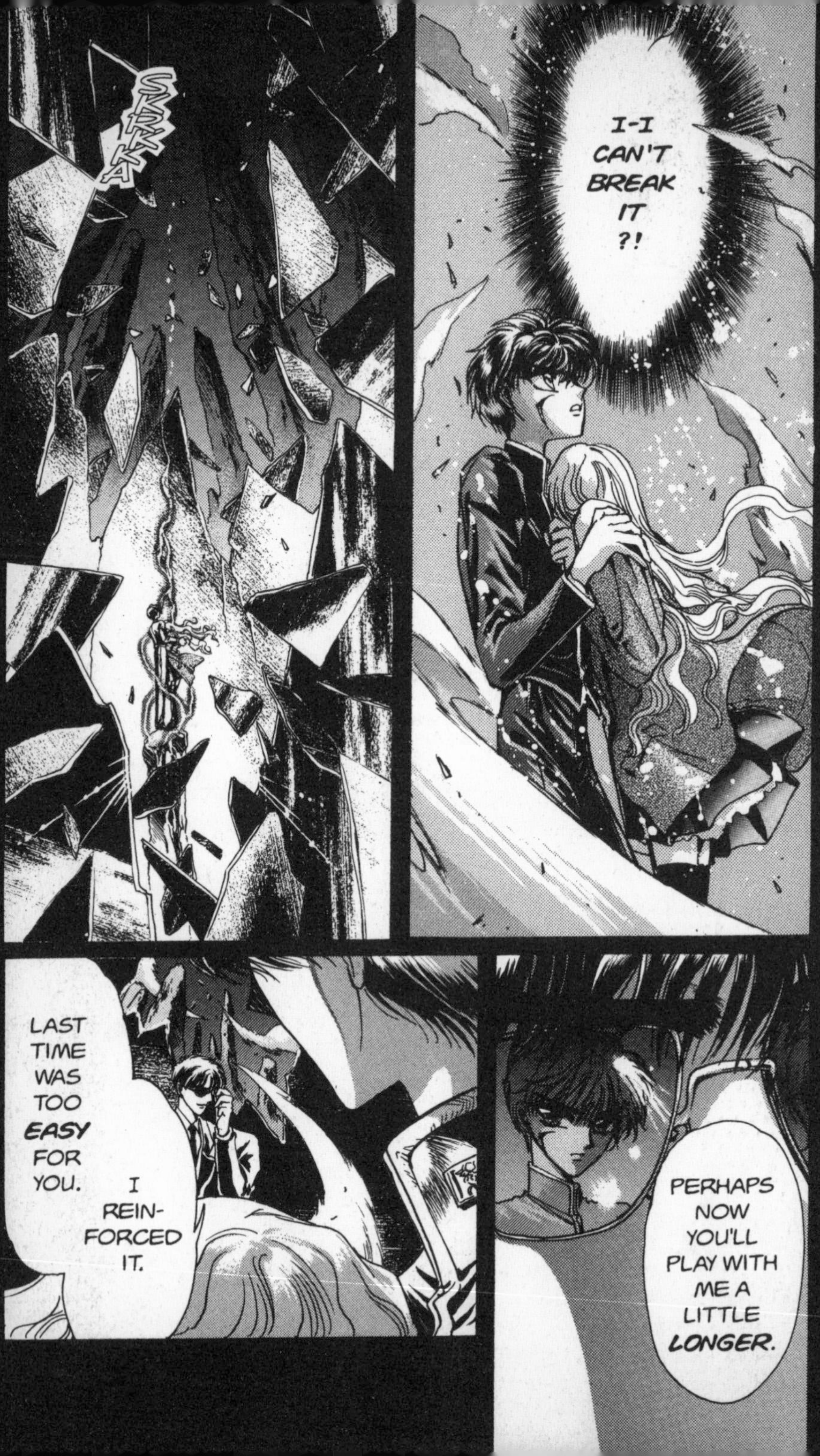
SKRKA
I-I CAN'T BREAK IT ?!
LAST TIME WAS TOO EASY FOR YOU.
I REIN-FORCED IT.
PERHAPS NOW YOU'LL PLAY WITH ME A LITTLE LONGER.

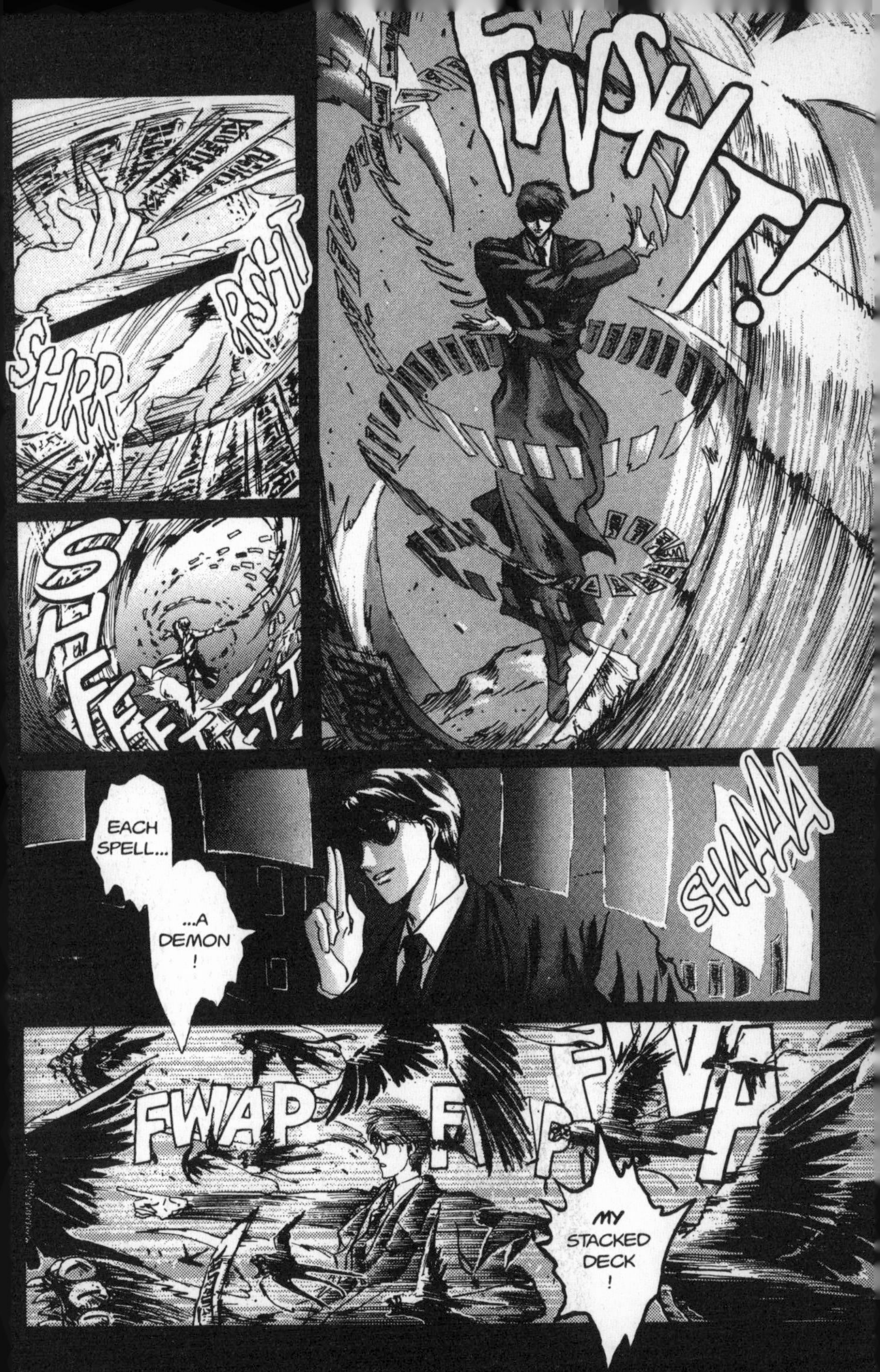
SHRR
RSHT
FWSHT!
EACH SPELL...
...A DEMON!
SHAAAA
FWAP
MY STACKED DECK!

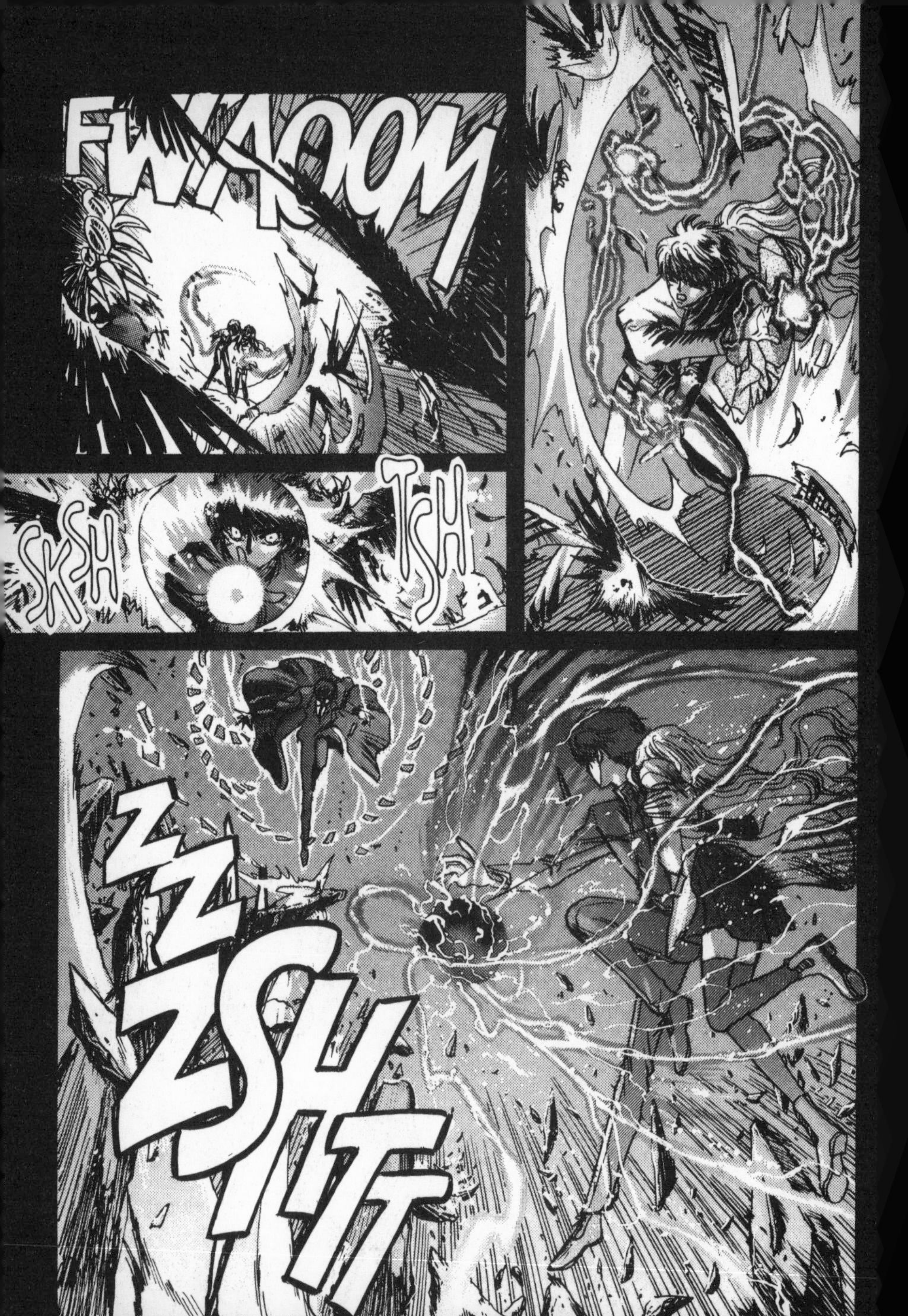
FWAOOM
SKSH
TSH
ZZZSHHT

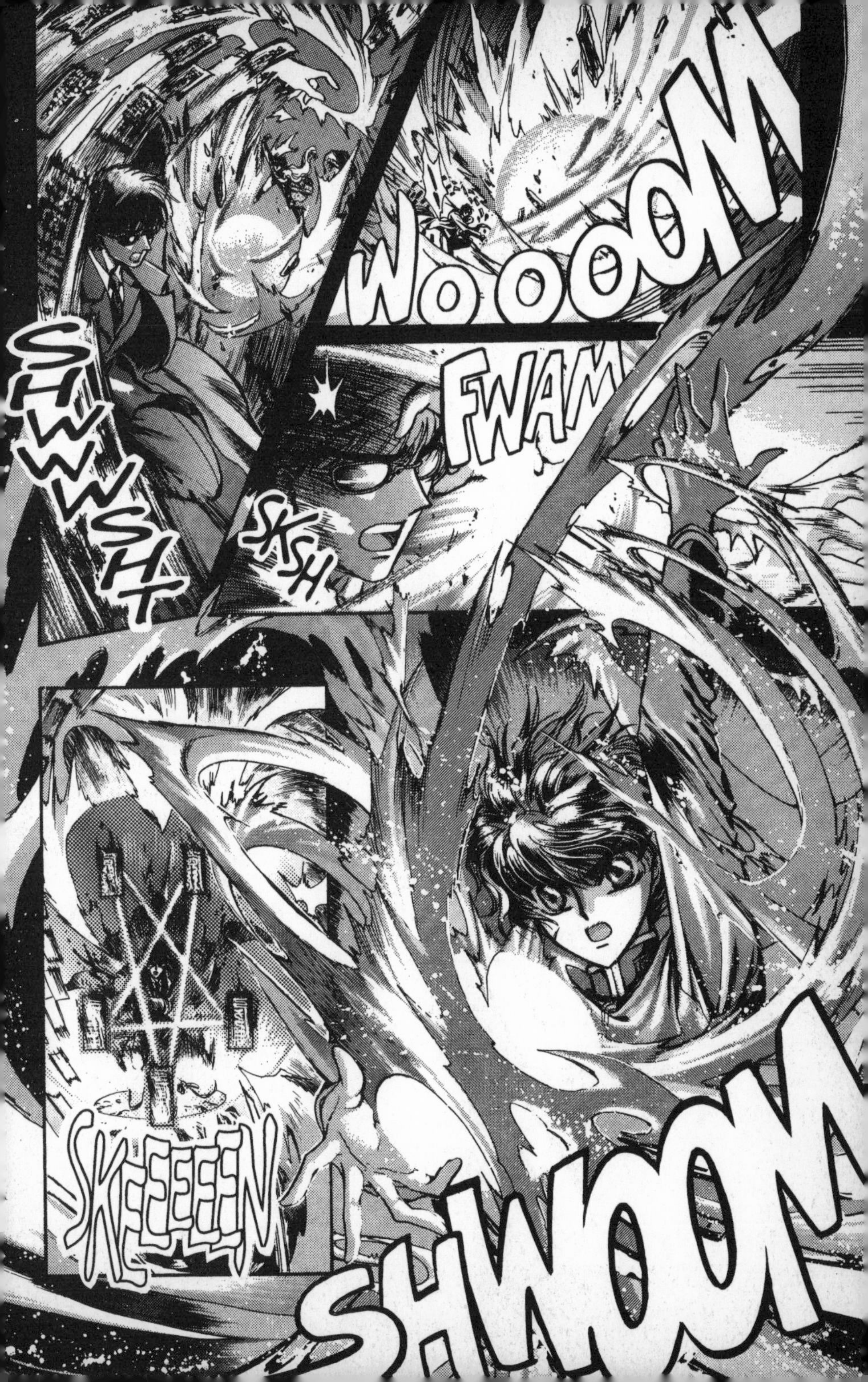
SHWWWSHT
WOOOOM
FWAM
SKSH
SKEEEEN
SHWOOM

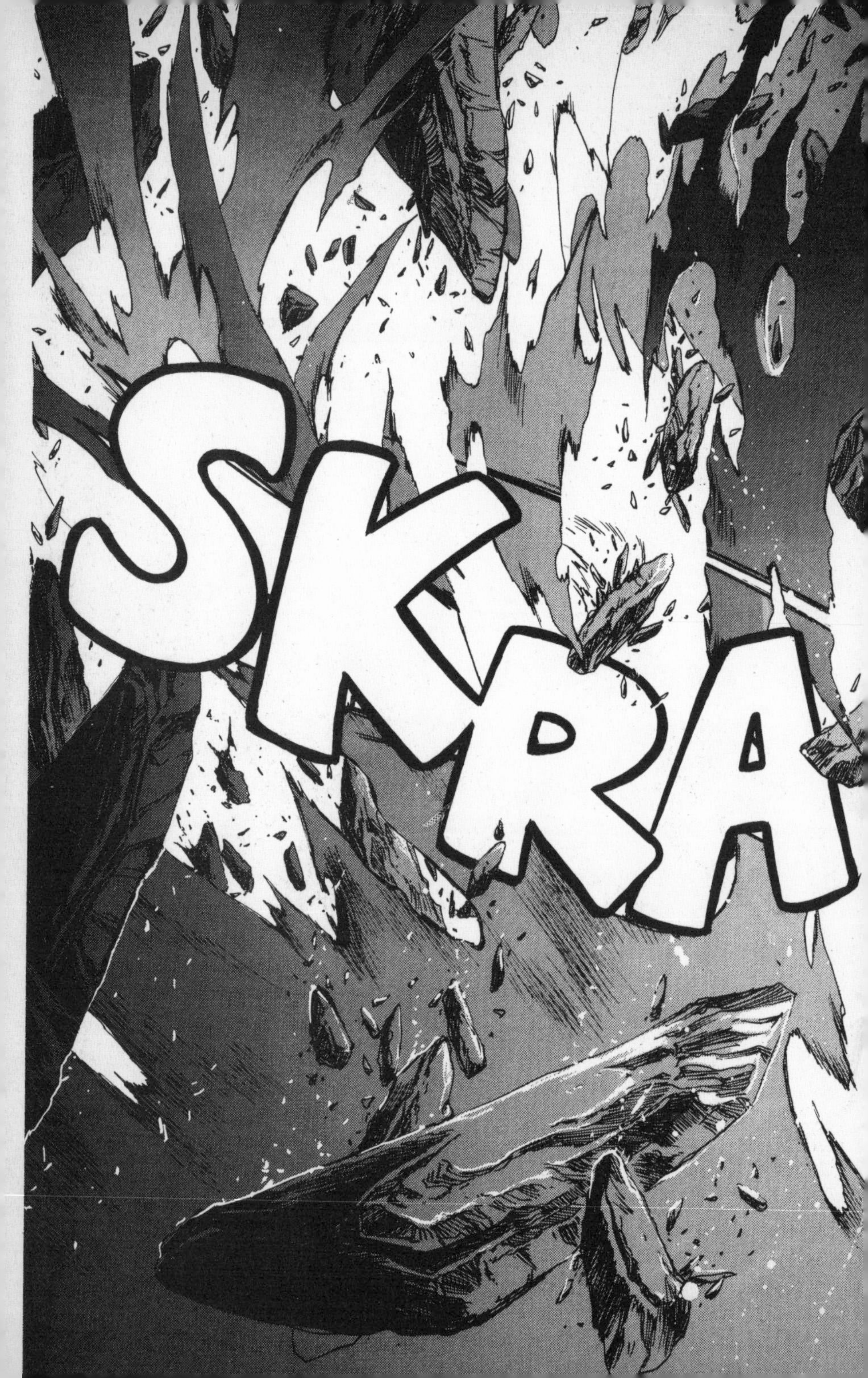
SKRA

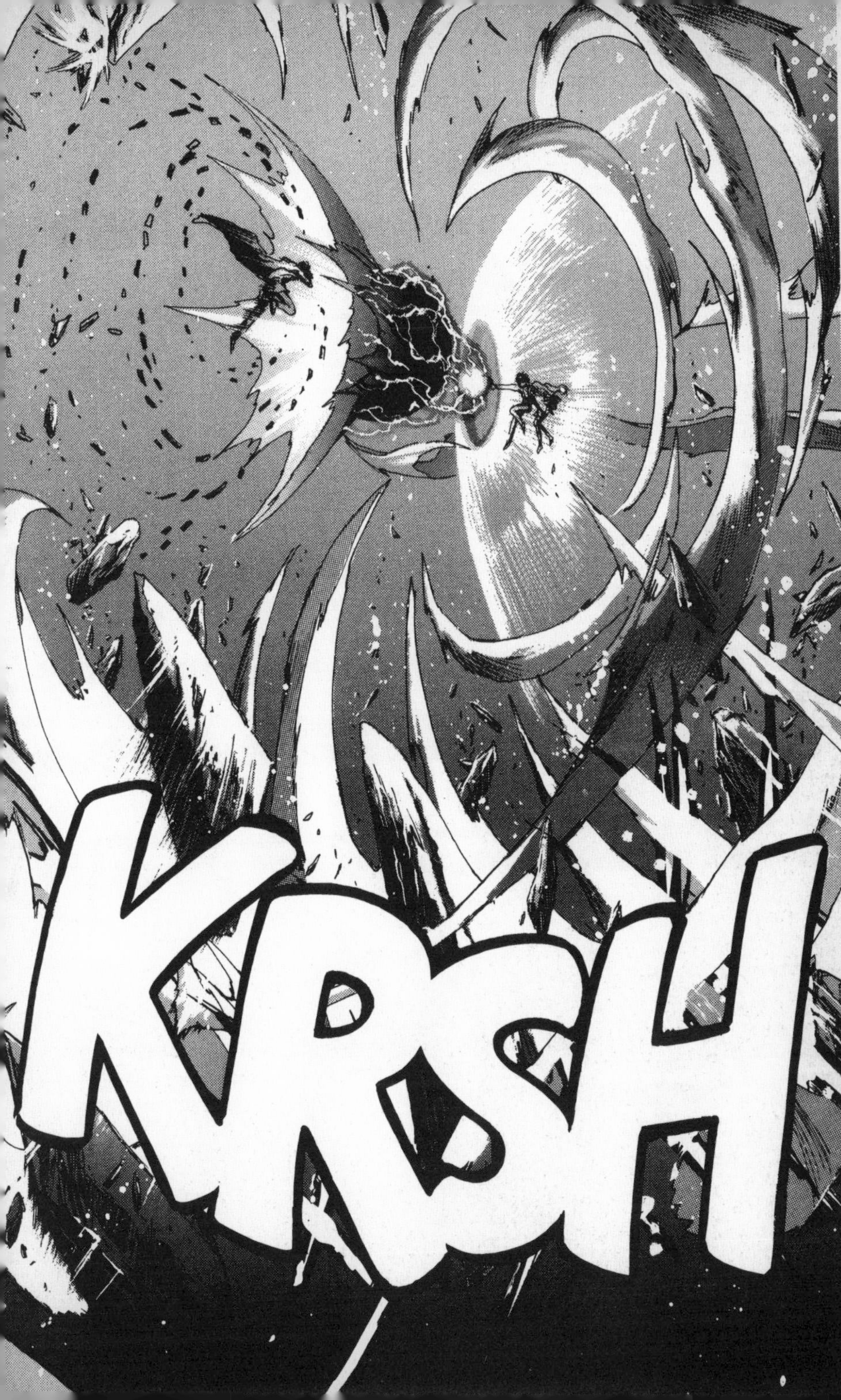
KRSH

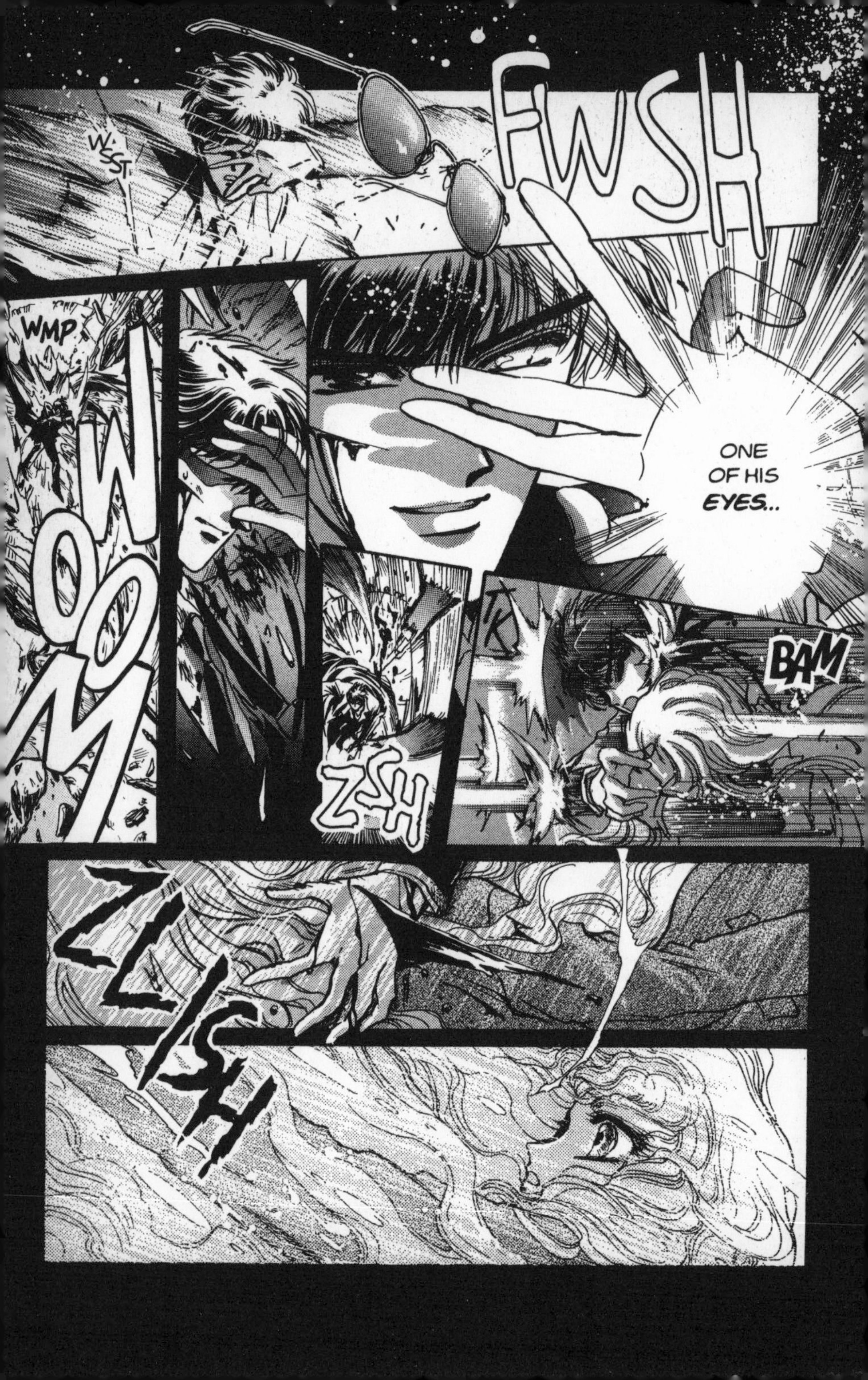
WSST
FWSH
WMP
WOOM
ONE OF HIS EYES...
ZSH
TK
BAM
ZZISH

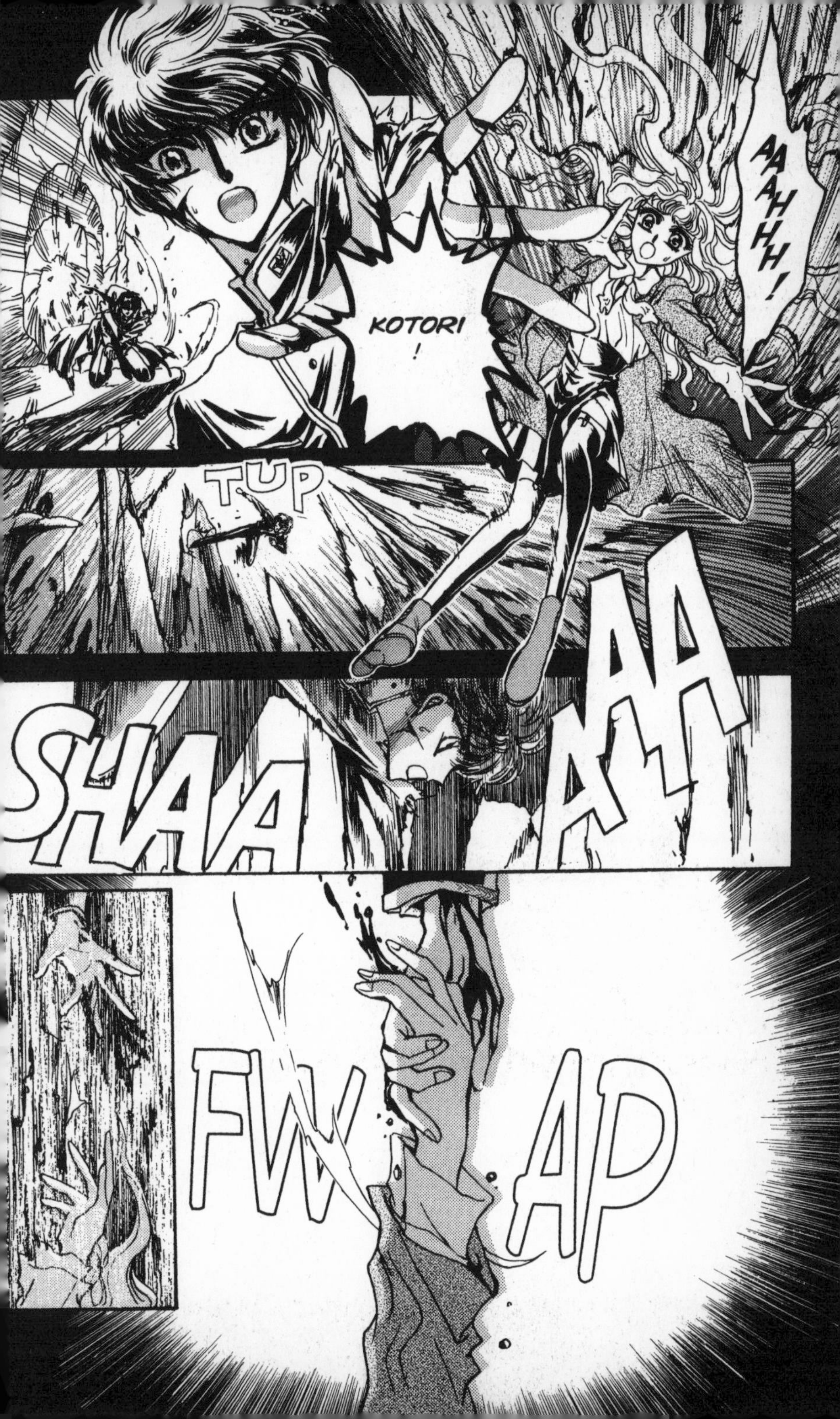
KOTORI!
AAAHHH!
TUP
SHAAAA
FWAP

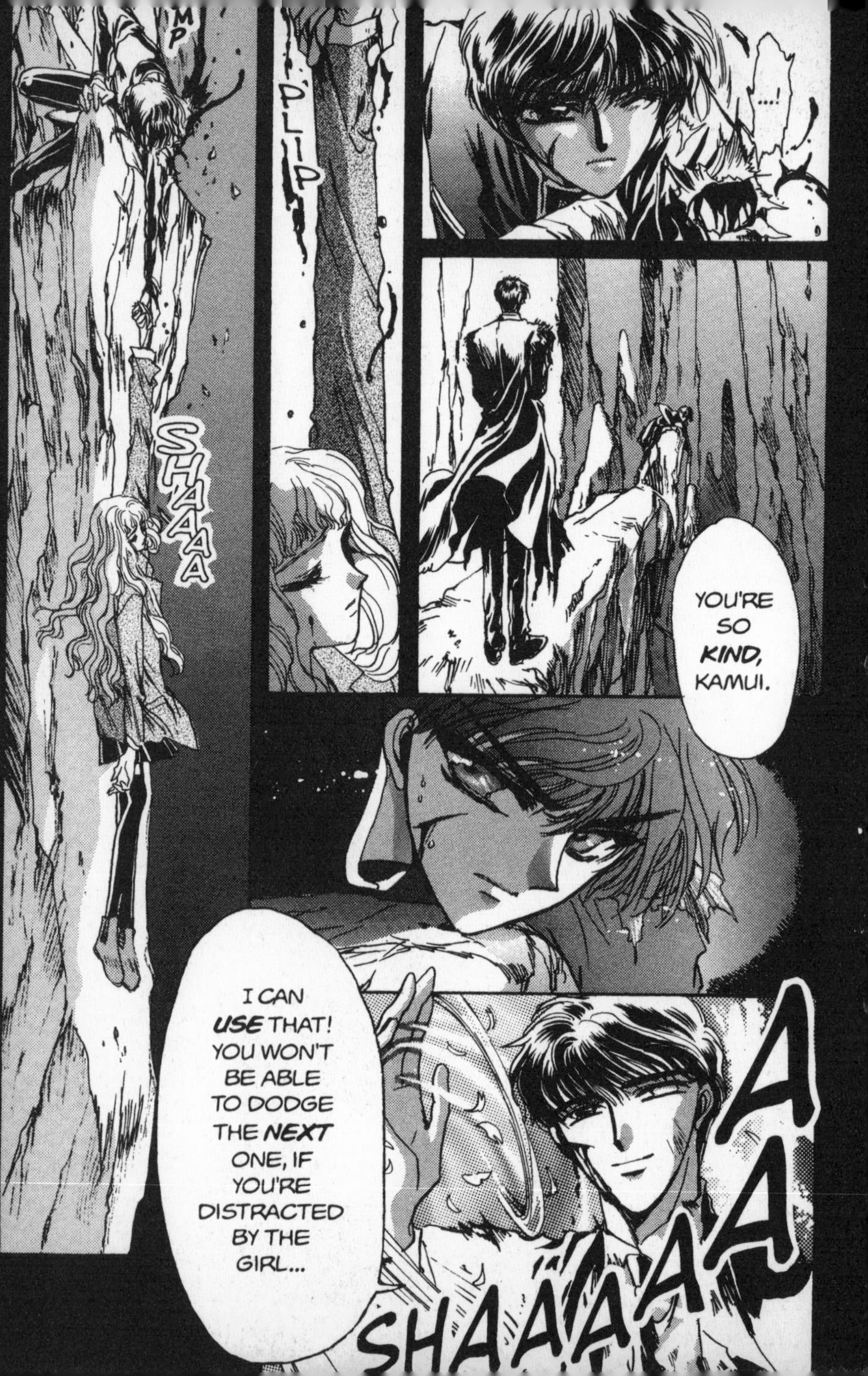
MP
SHAAAA
PLIP
...!
YOU'RE SO KIND, KAMUI.
I CAN USE THAT! YOU WON'T BE ABLE TO DODGE THE NEXT ONE, IF YOU'RE DISTRACTED BY THE GIRL...
SHAAAAAAA

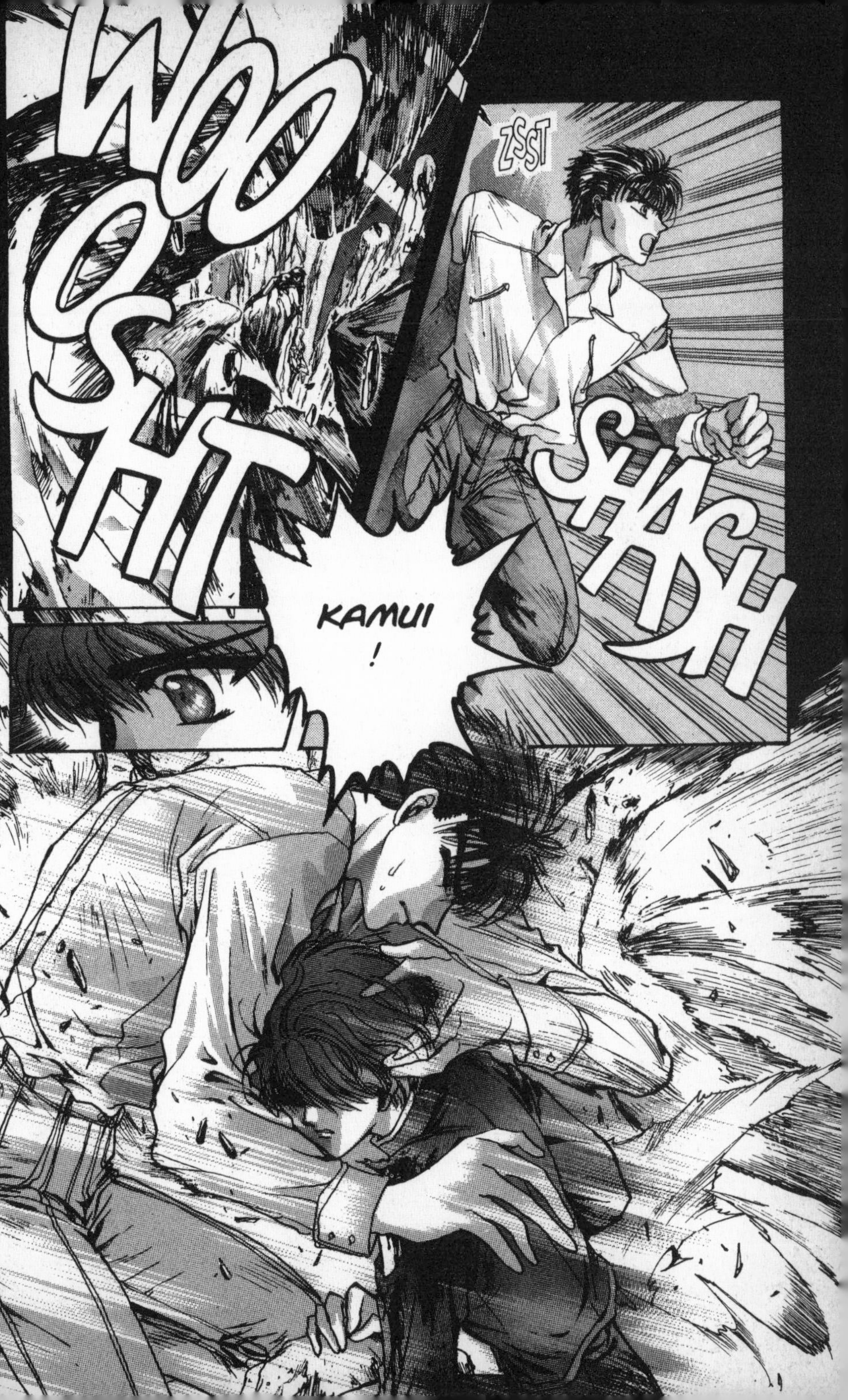
WOOSHT
ZSST
SHACH
KAMUI
!

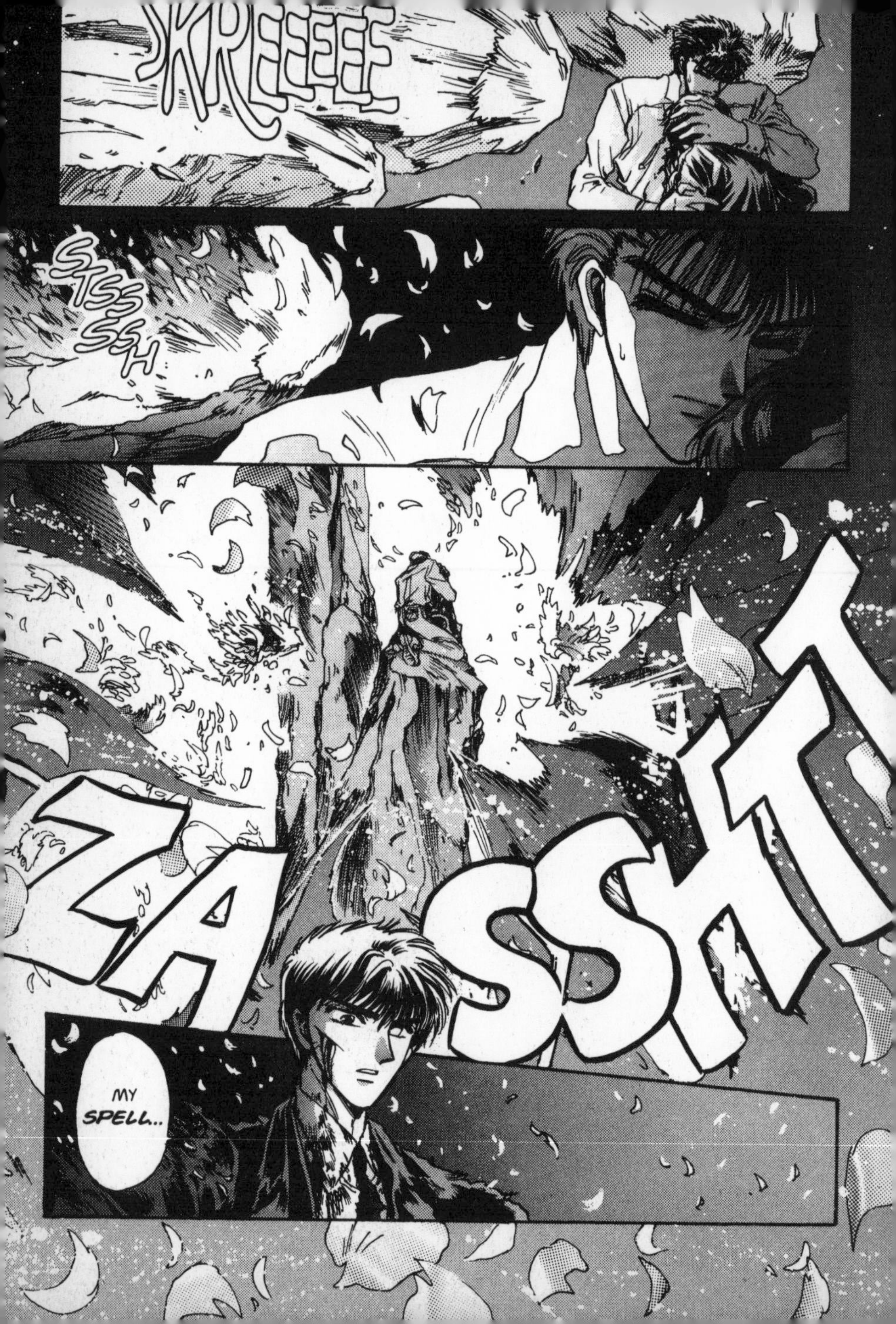
SKREEEEEE
STSSSSH...
ZASSH
MY SPELL...

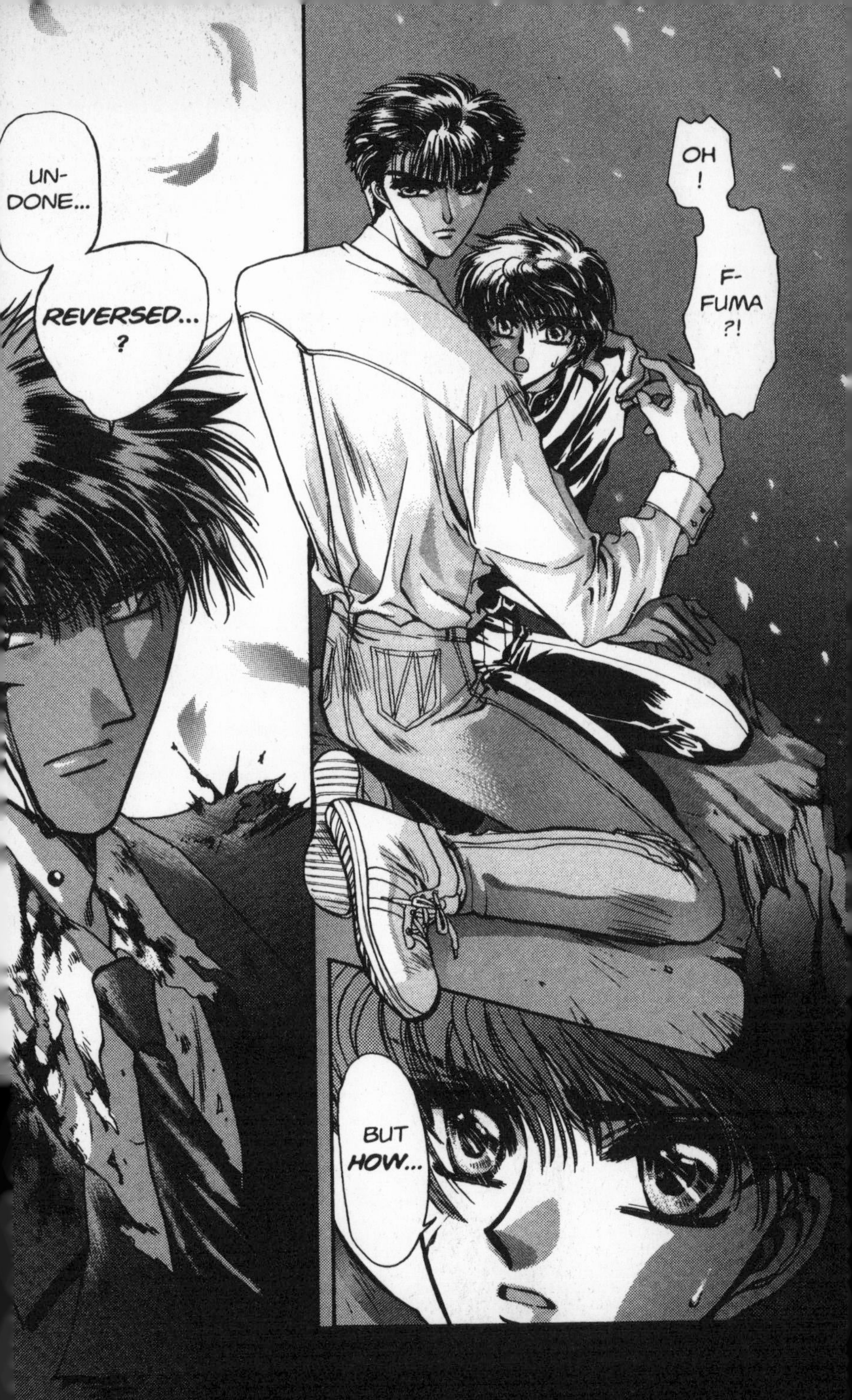
UN-DONE...
REVERSED...?
OH! F-FUMA?!
BUT HOW...

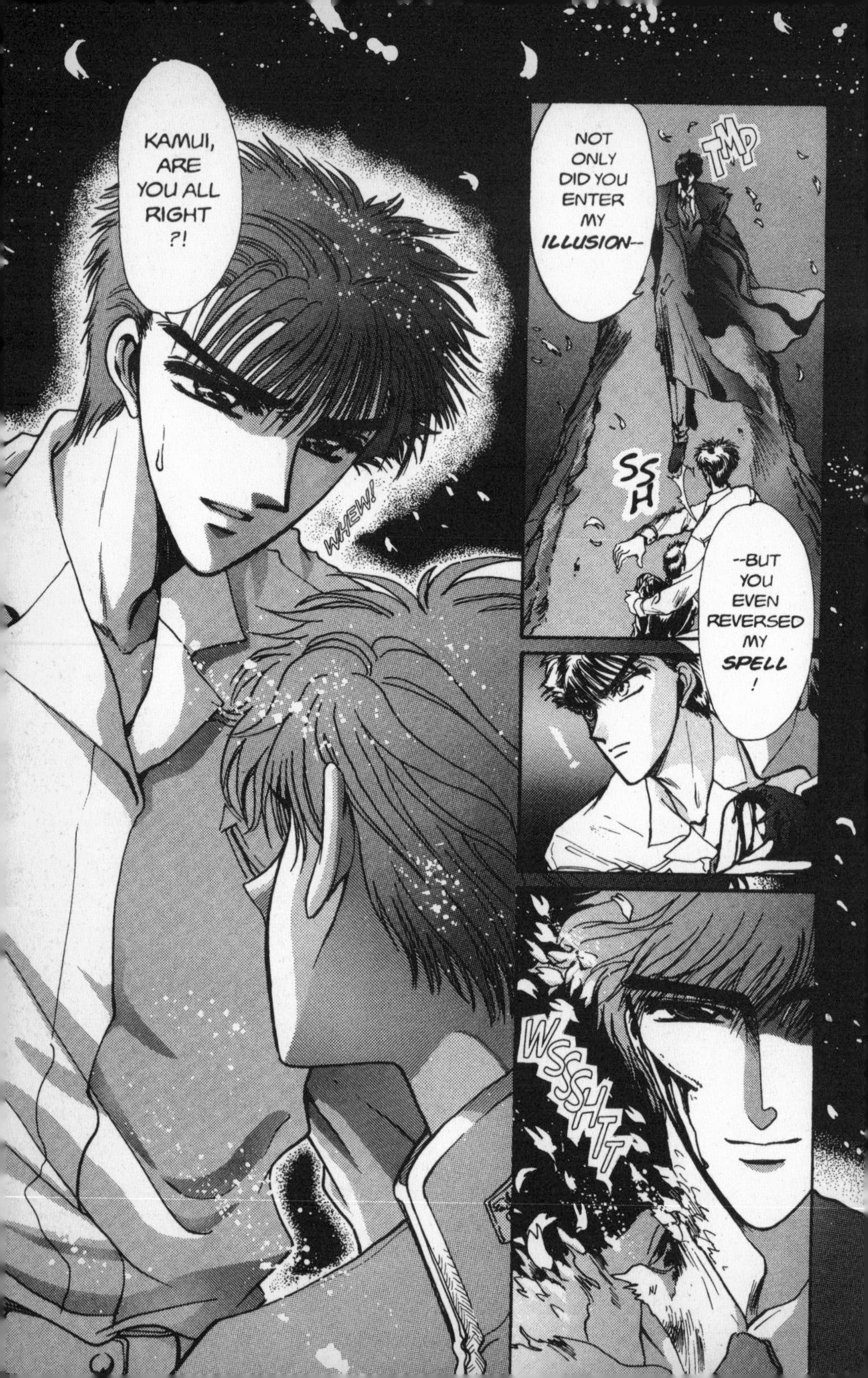
KAMUI, ARE YOU ALL RIGHT ?!
WHEW!
NOT ONLY DID YOU ENTER MY ILLUSION--
TMP
SSH
--BUT YOU EVEN REVERSED MY SPELL !
WSSSHTT

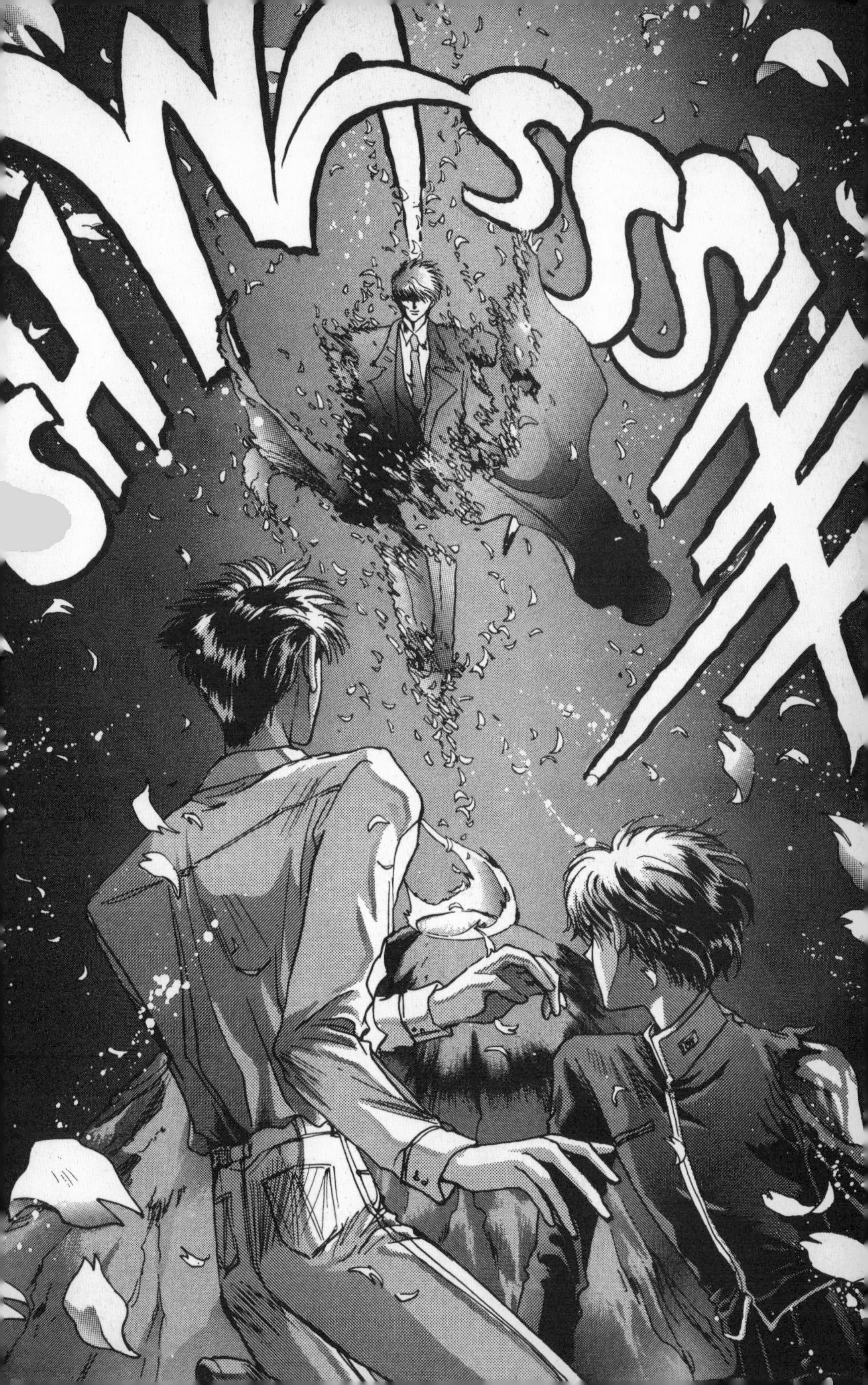

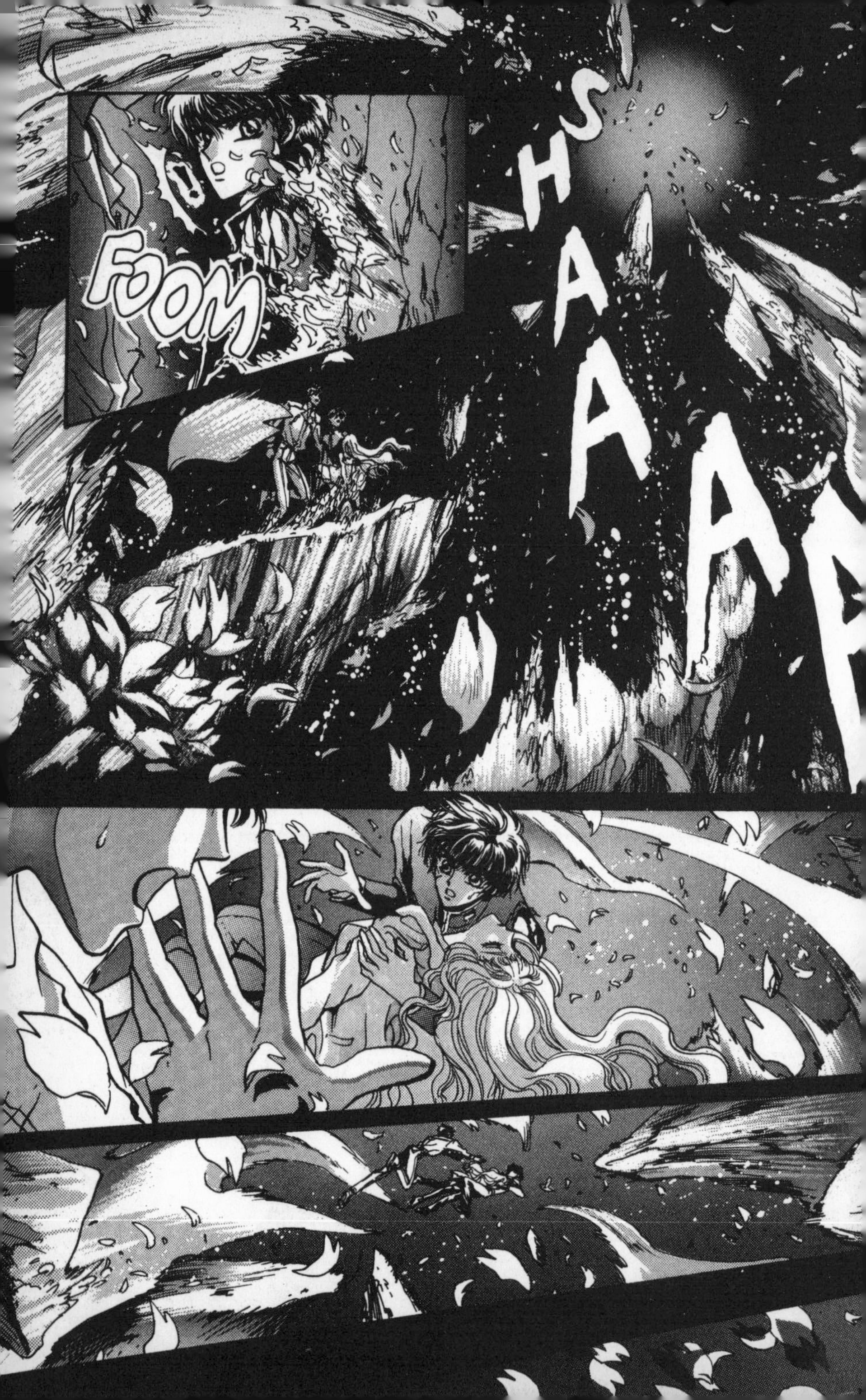
!
FOOM
SHAAAA

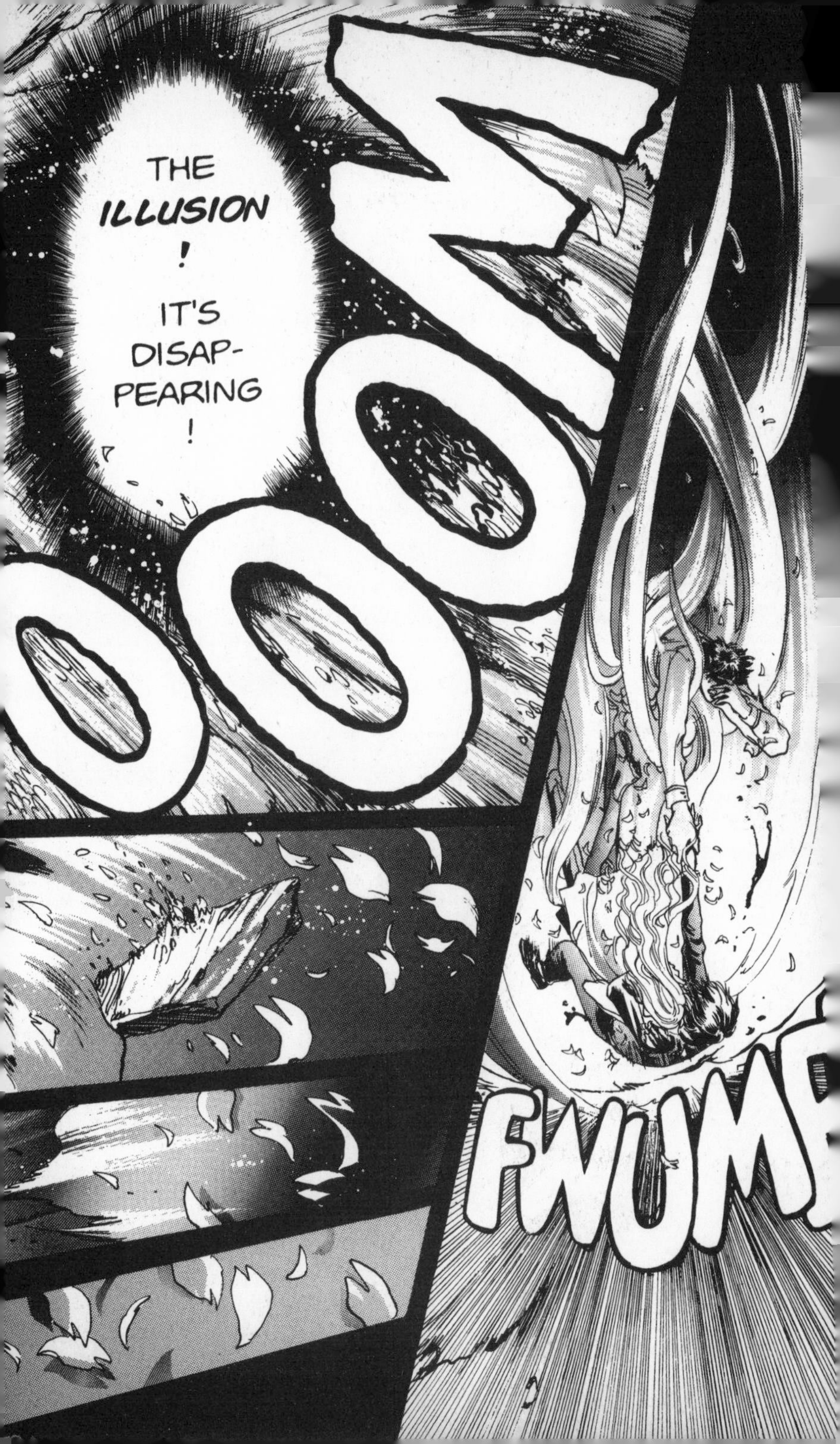

THE ILLUSION!
IT'S DISAP-PEARING!
BOOOOM
FWUMP

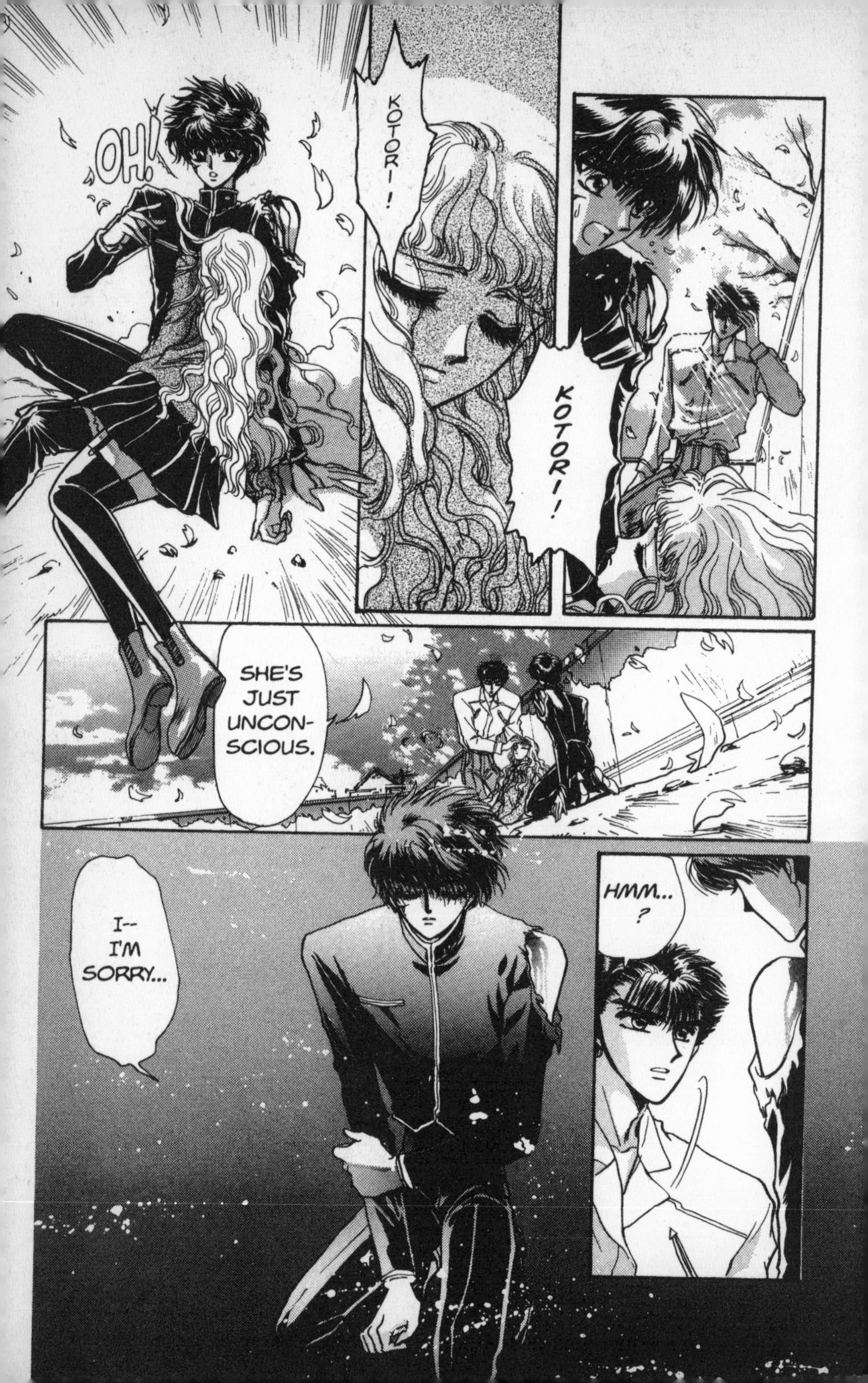
OH!
KOTORI!
KOTORI!
SHE'S JUST UNCONSCIOUS.
I-- I'M SORRY...
HMM...?

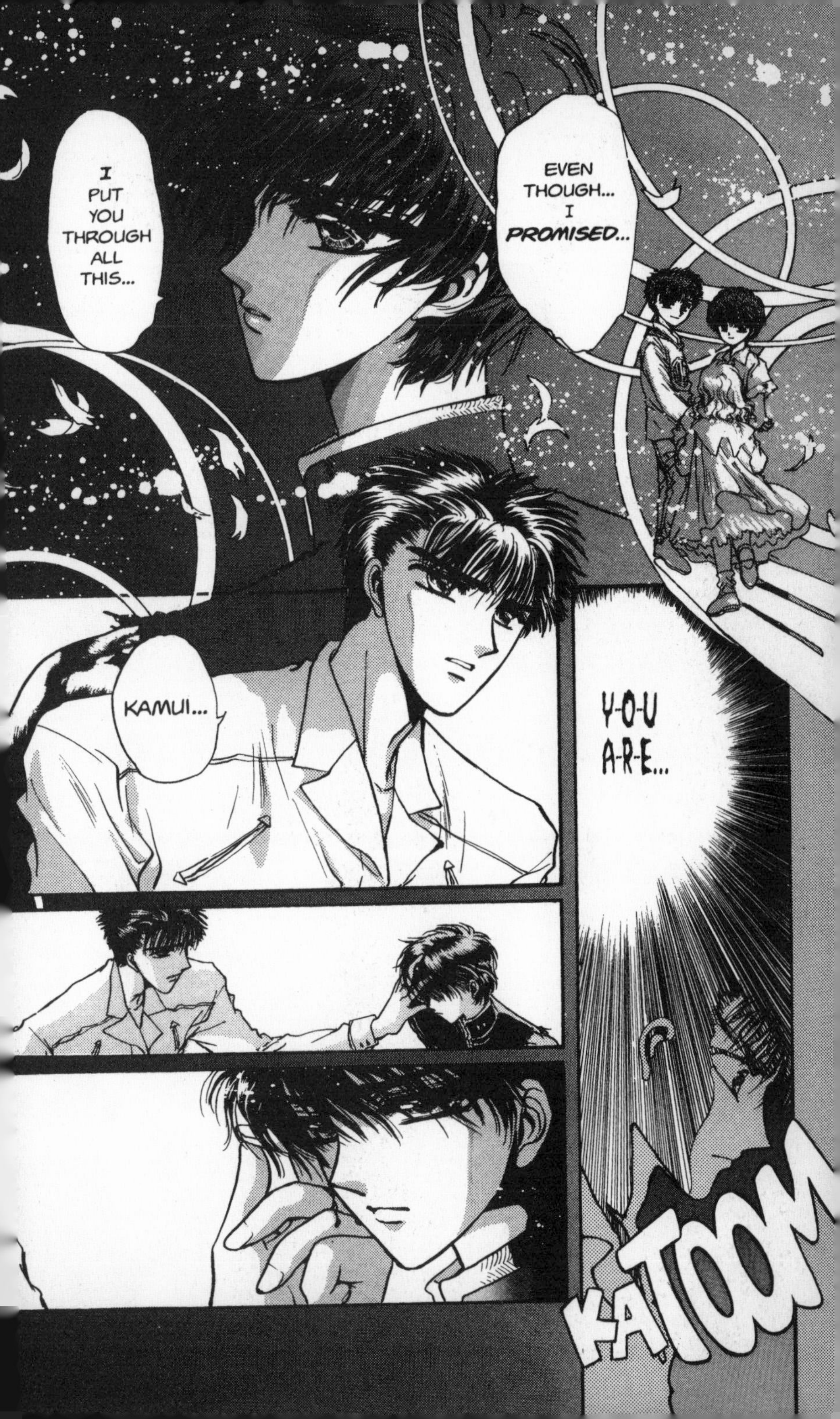
I PUT YOU THROUGH ALL THIS...
EVEN THOUGH... I PROMISED...
KAMUI...
Y-O-U A-R-E...
KATOOM

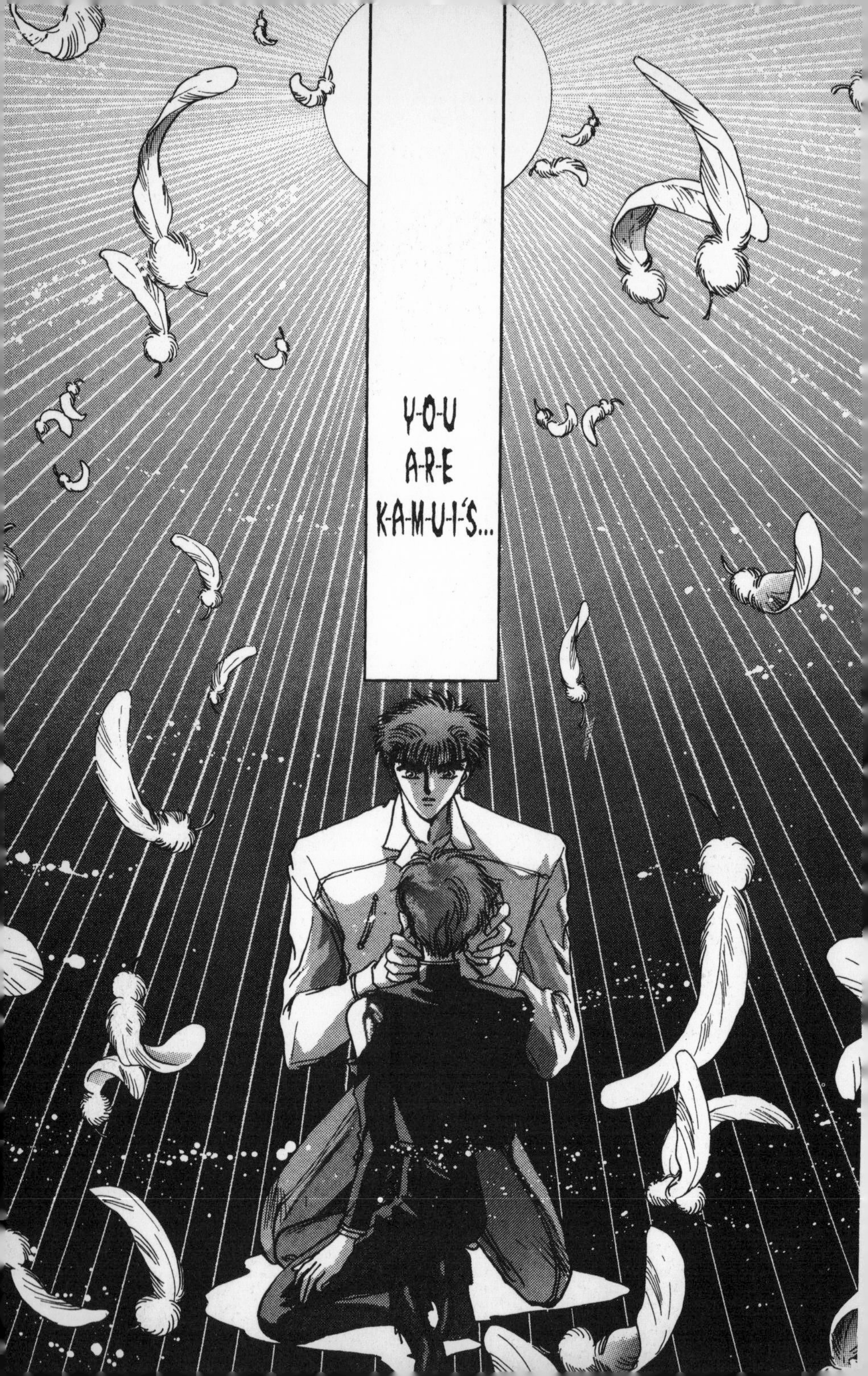
Y-O-U
A-R-E
K-A-M-U-I-'S...

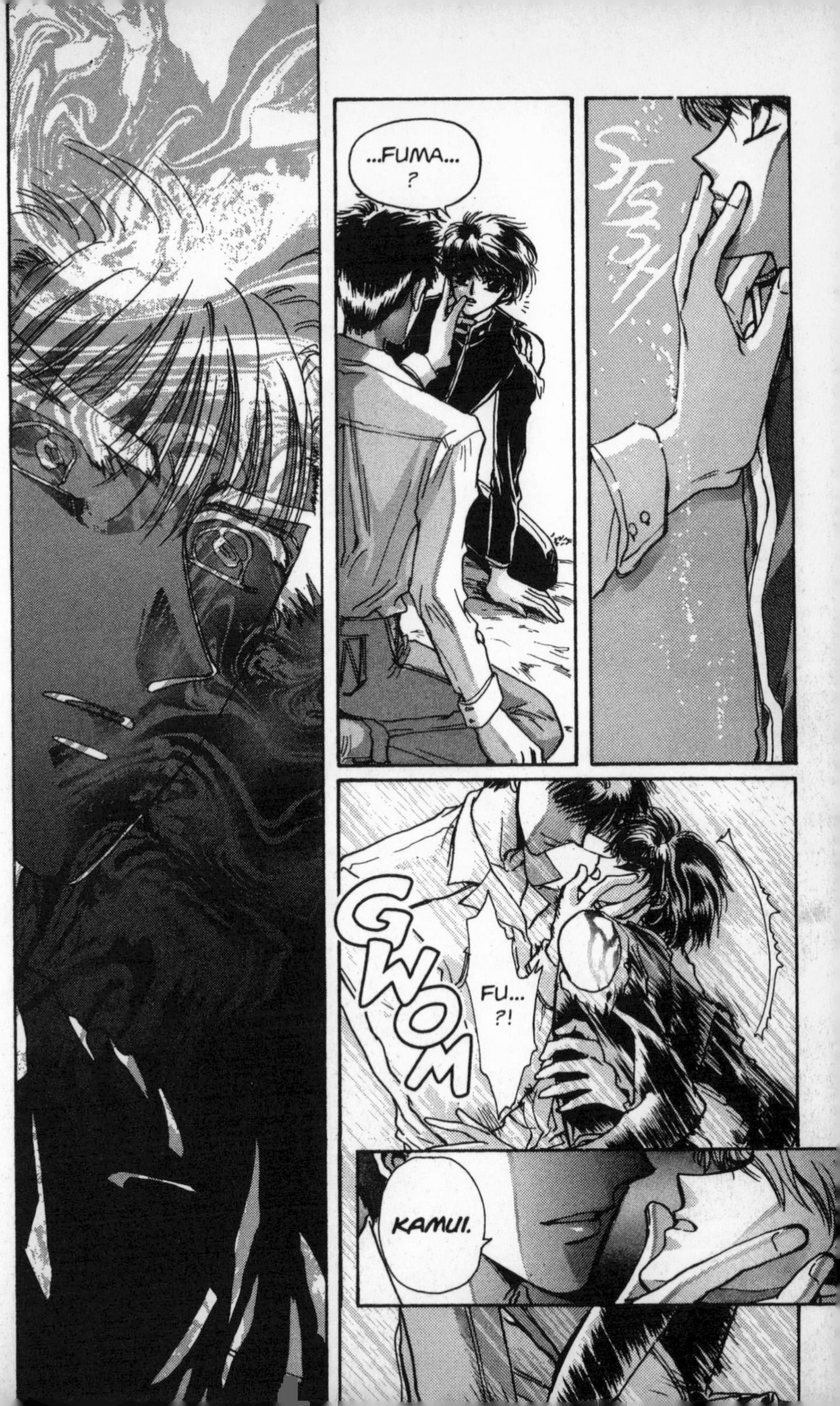
...FUMA...
?
STSCH
GWOM
FU...
?!
KAMUI.

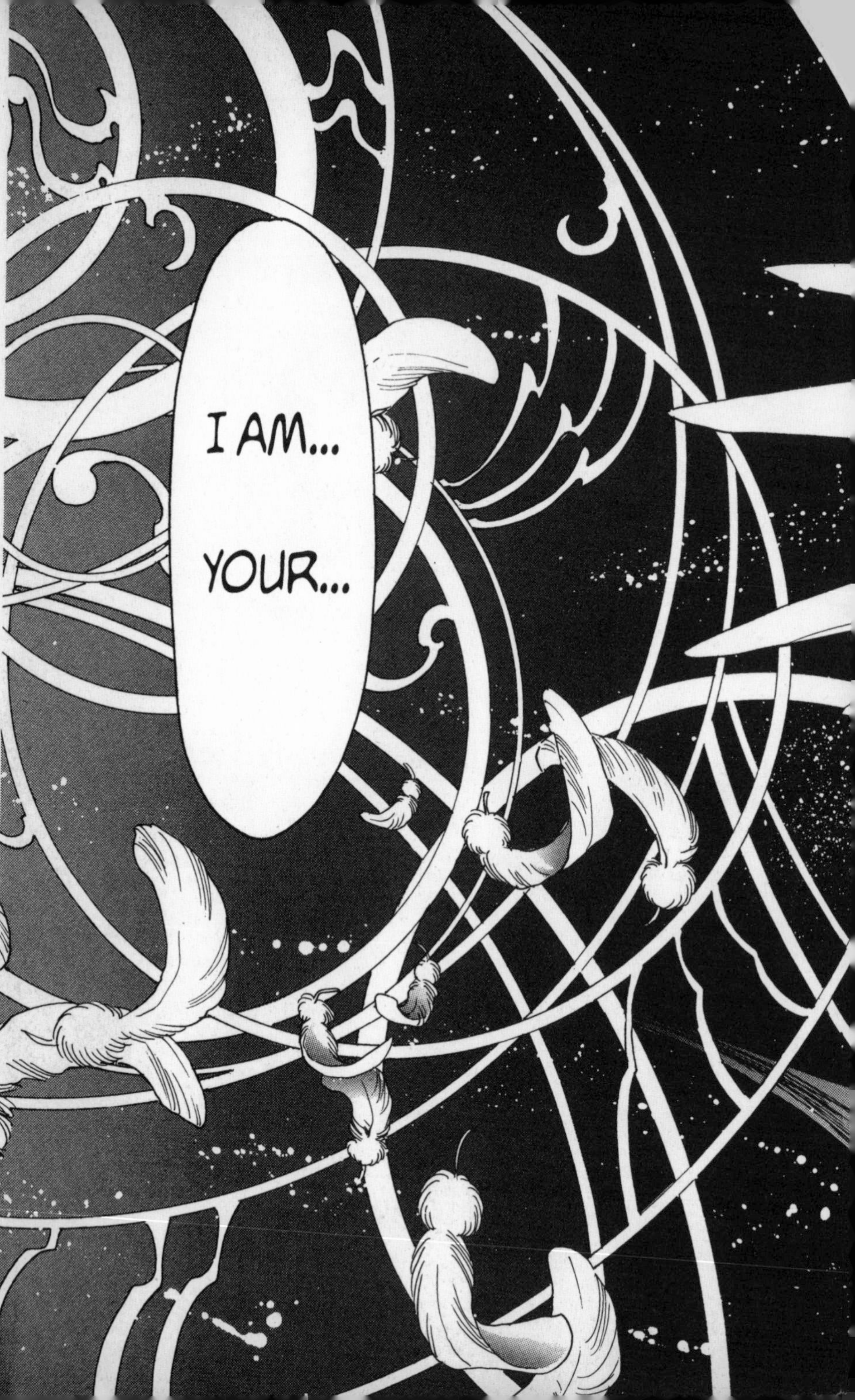
I AM...
YOUR...

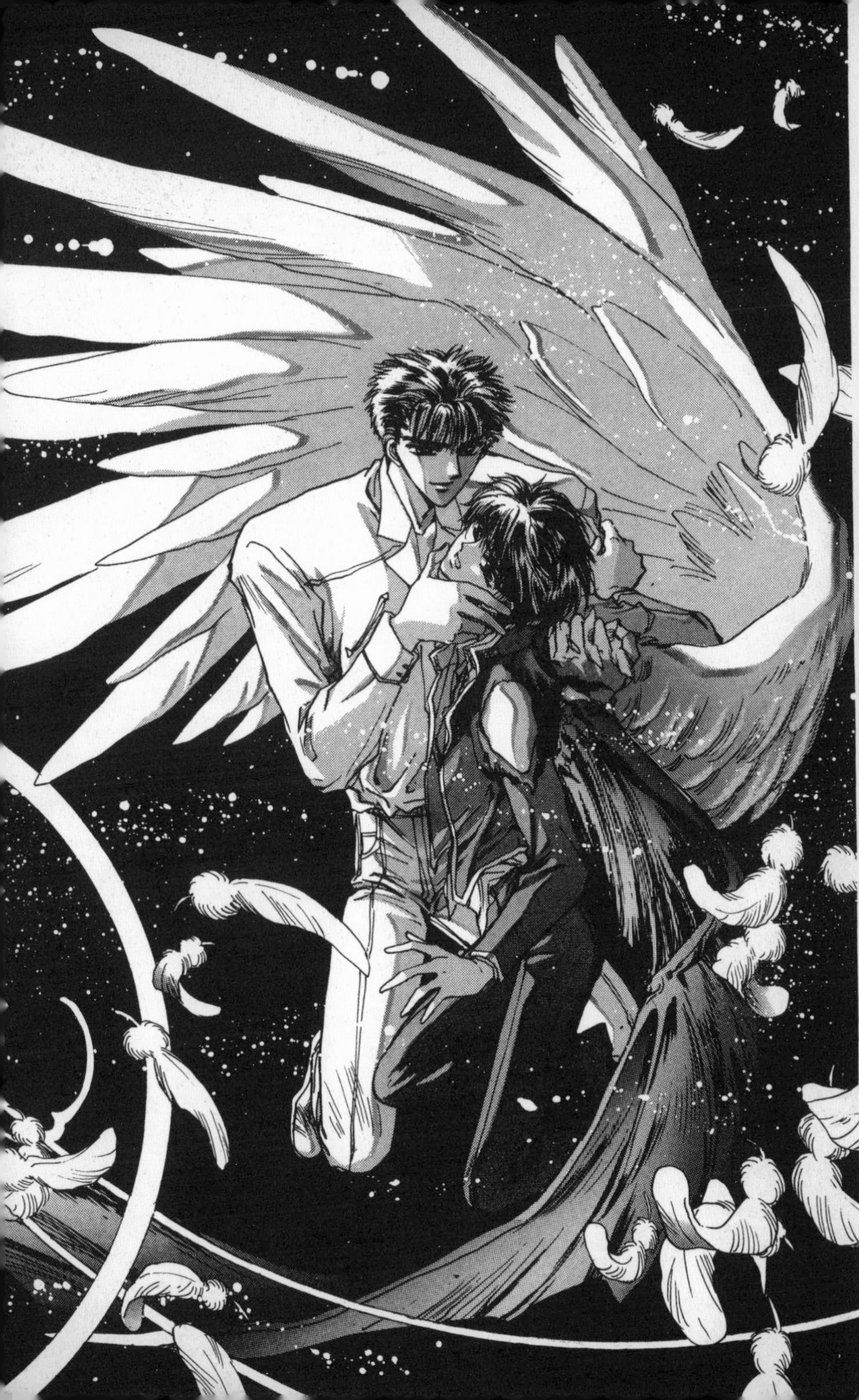

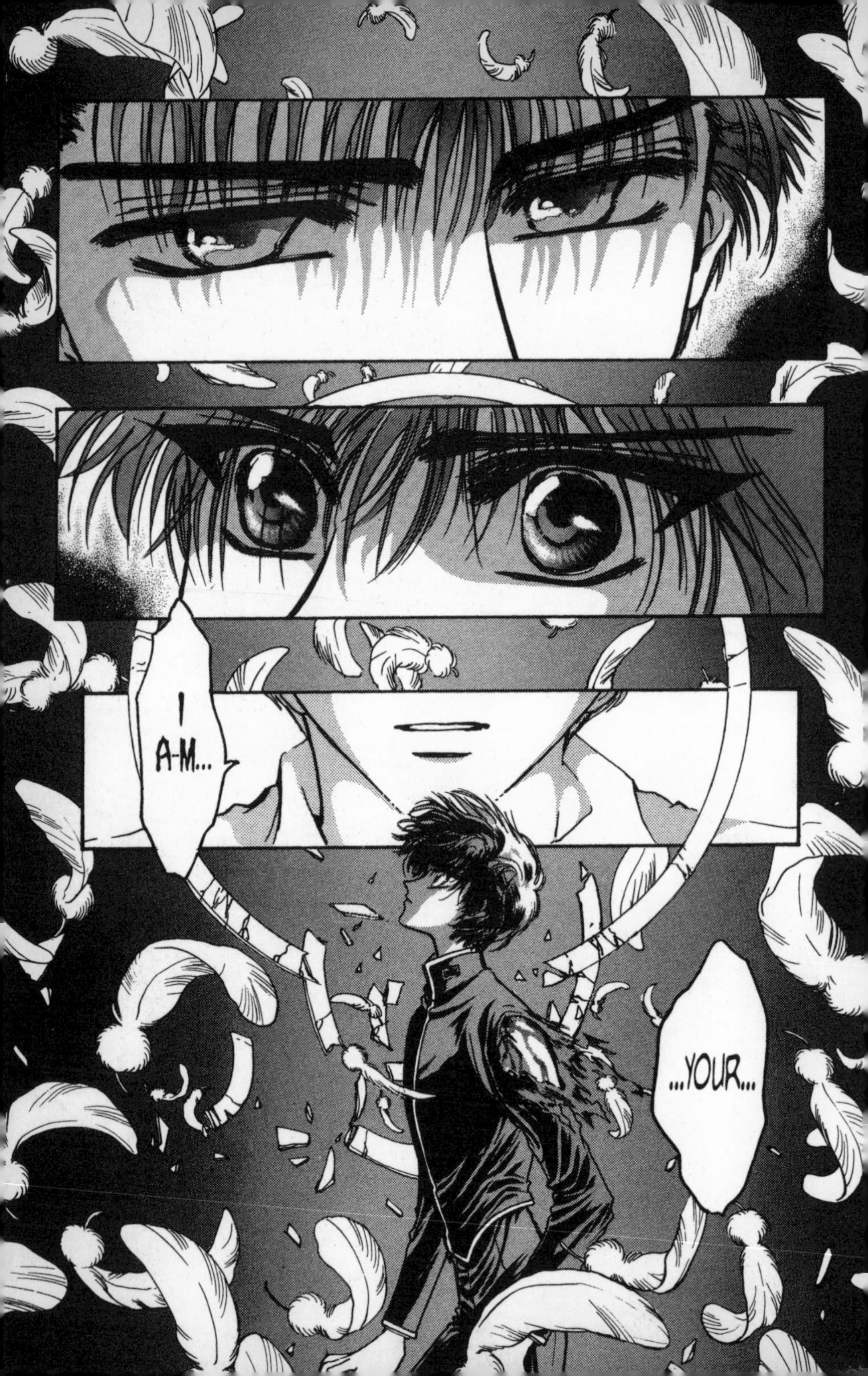
I A-M...
...YOUR...

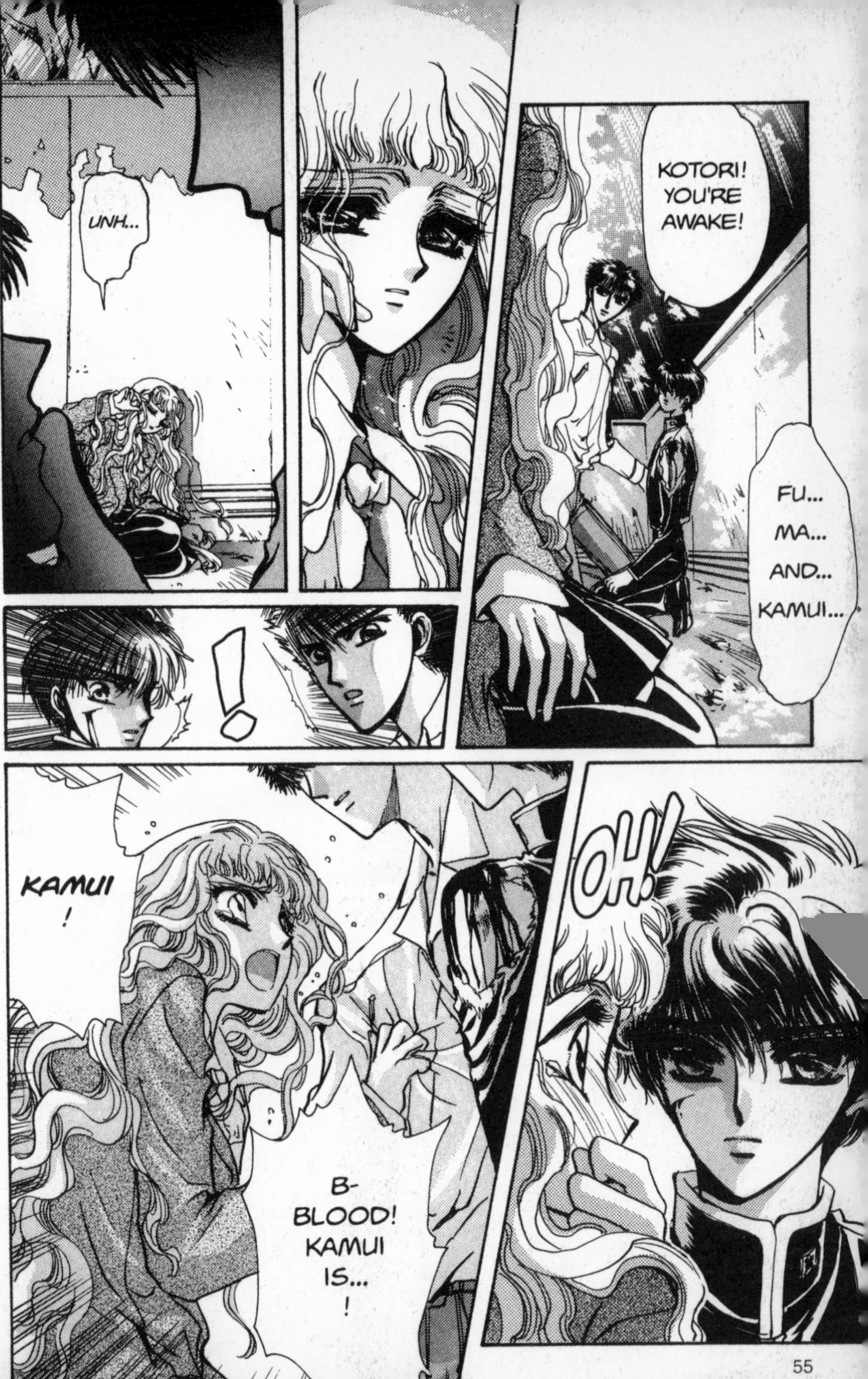
UNH...
!
KOTORI! YOU'RE AWAKE!
FU... MA... AND... KAMUI...
KAMUI !
B- BLOOD! KAMUI IS... !
OH!

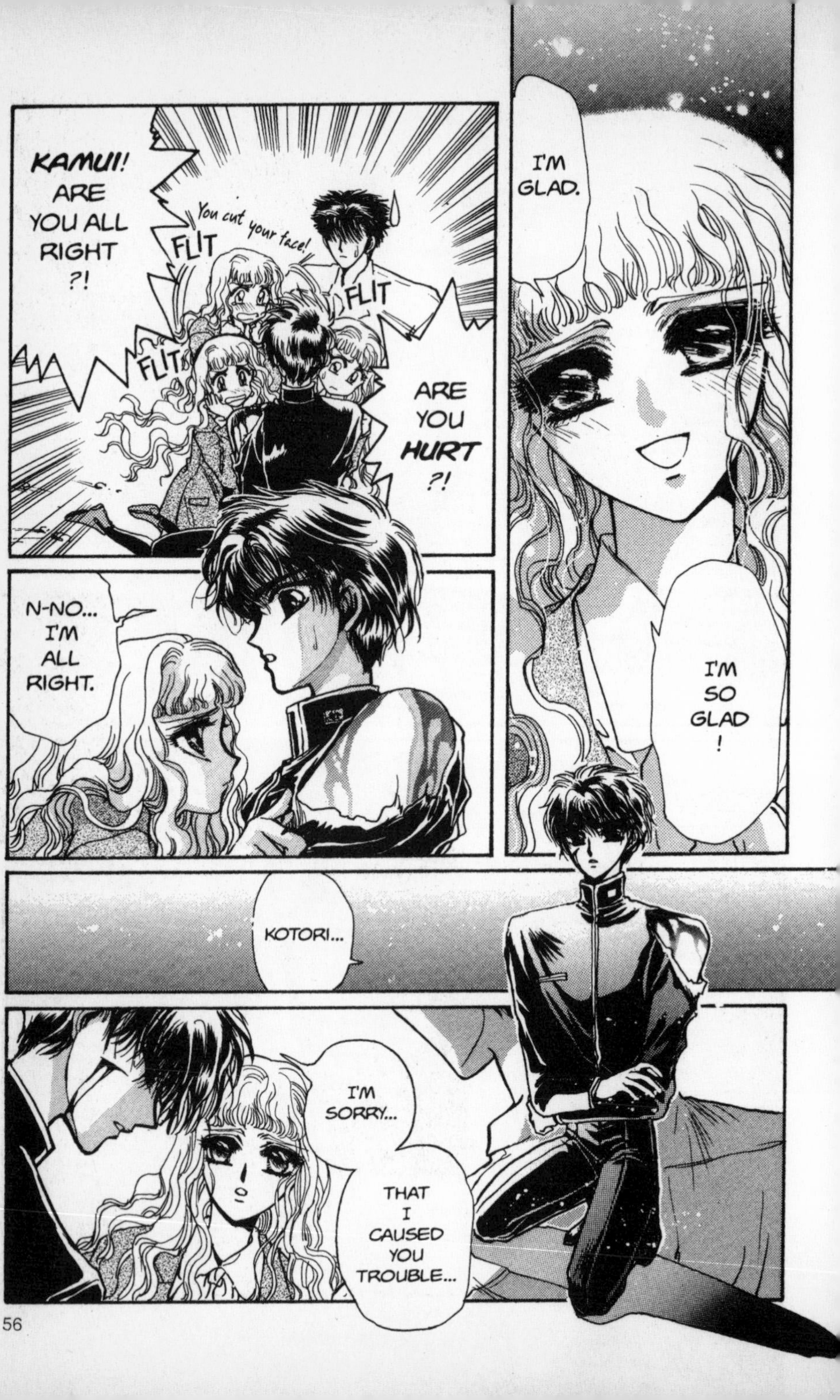
KAMUI! ARE YOU ALL RIGHT ?!
You cut your face!
FLIT
FLIT
FLIT
ARE YOU HURT ?!
N-NO... I'M ALL RIGHT.
I'M GLAD.
I'M SO GLAD !
KOTORI...
I'M SORRY...
THAT I CAUSED YOU TROUBLE...

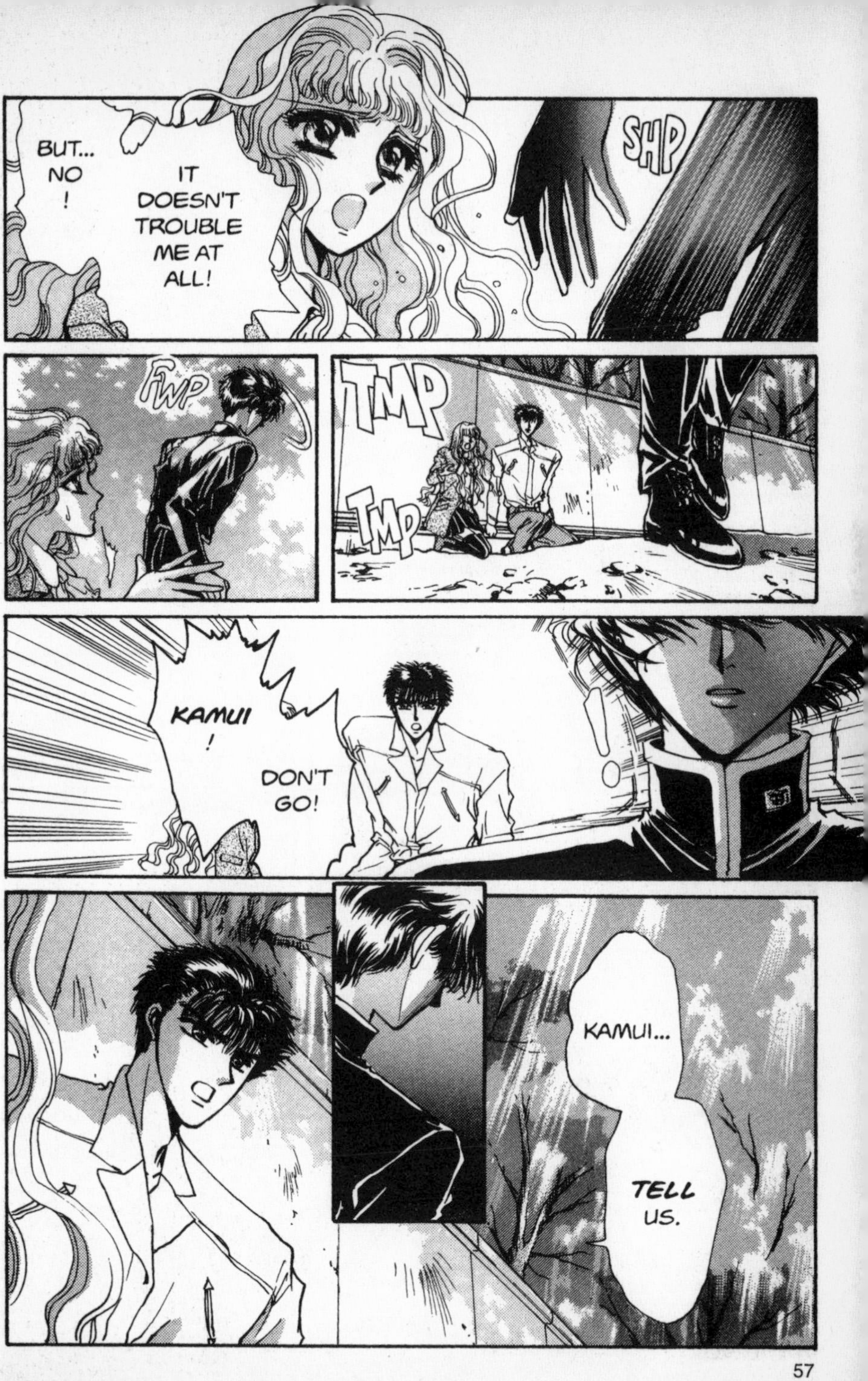
BUT... NO !
IT DOESN'T TROUBLE ME AT ALL!
SHP
FWP
TMP
TMP
KAMUI !
DON'T GO!
KAMUI...
TELL US.

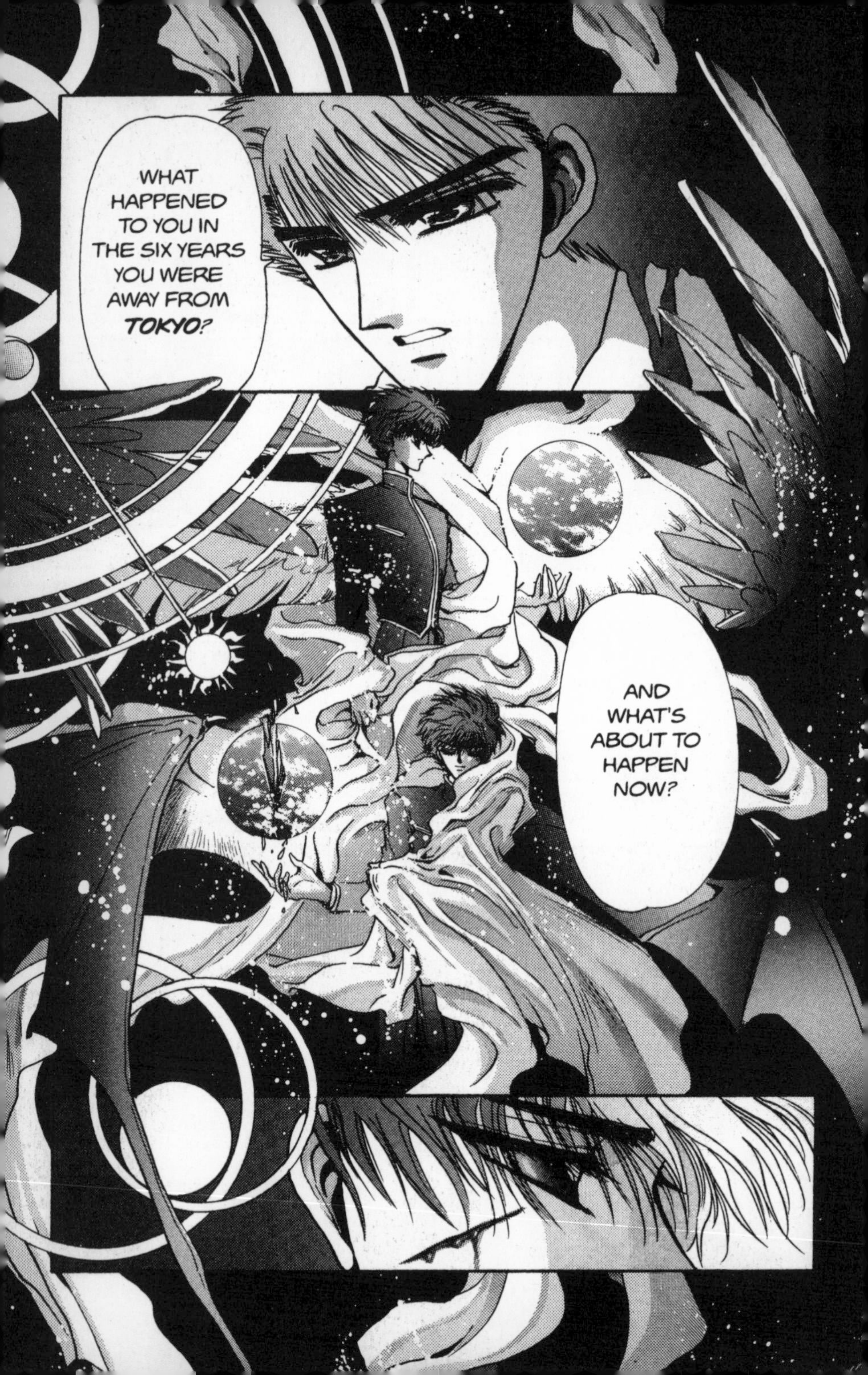
WHAT HAPPENED TO YOU IN THE SIX YEARS YOU WERE AWAY FROM TOKYO?
AND WHAT'S ABOUT TO HAPPEN NOW?

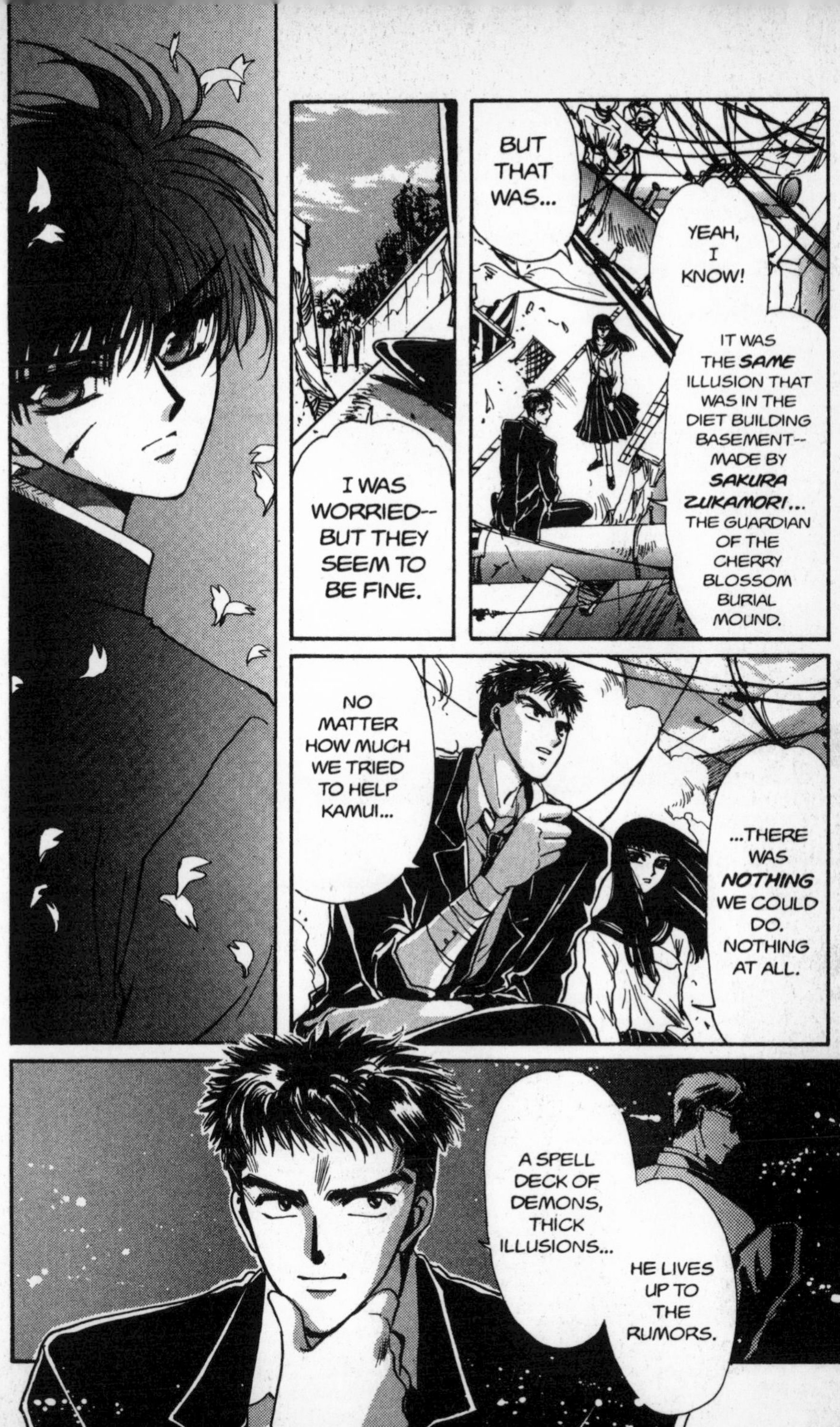
I WAS WORRIED--BUT THEY SEEM TO BE FINE.
BUT THAT WAS...
YEAH, I KNOW!
IT WAS THE SAME ILLUSION THAT WAS IN THE DIET BUILDING BASEMENT--MADE BY SAKURA ZUKAMORI... THE GUARDIAN OF THE CHERRY BLOSSOM BURIAL MOUND.
NO MATTER HOW MUCH WE TRIED TO HELP KAMUI...
...THERE WAS NOTHING WE COULD DO. NOTHING AT ALL.
A SPELL DECK OF DEMONS, THICK ILLUSIONS...
HE LIVES UP TO THE RUMORS.

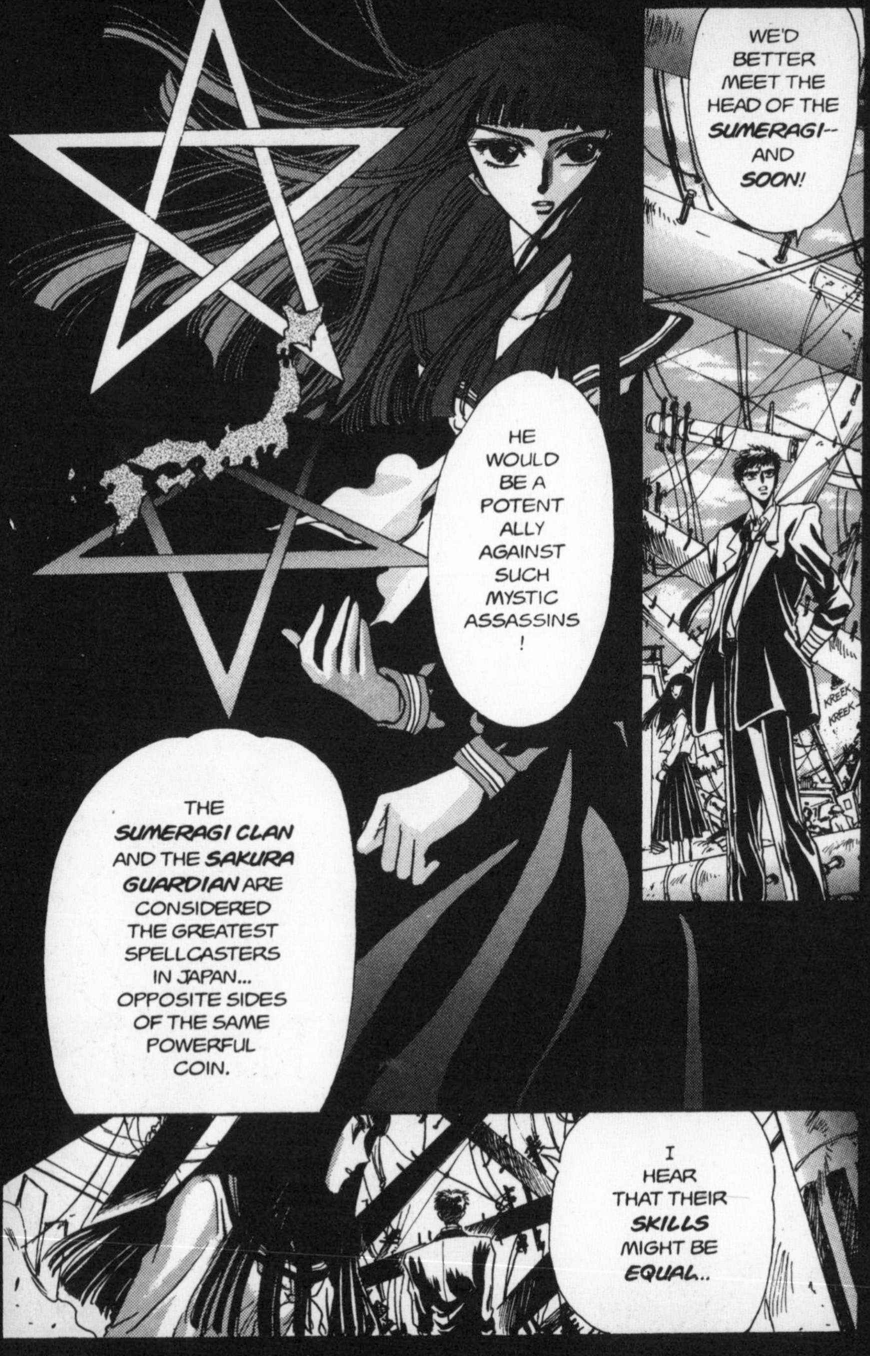
HE WOULD BE A POTENT ALLY AGAINST SUCH MYSTIC ASSASSINS!
THE SUMERAGI CLAN AND THE SAKURA GUARDIAN ARE CONSIDERED THE GREATEST SPELLCASTERS IN JAPAN... OPPOSITE SIDES OF THE SAME POWERFUL COIN.
WE'D BETTER MEET THE HEAD OF THE SUMERAGI-- AND SOON!
KREEK
KREEK
I HEAR THAT THEIR SKILLS MIGHT BE EQUAL...

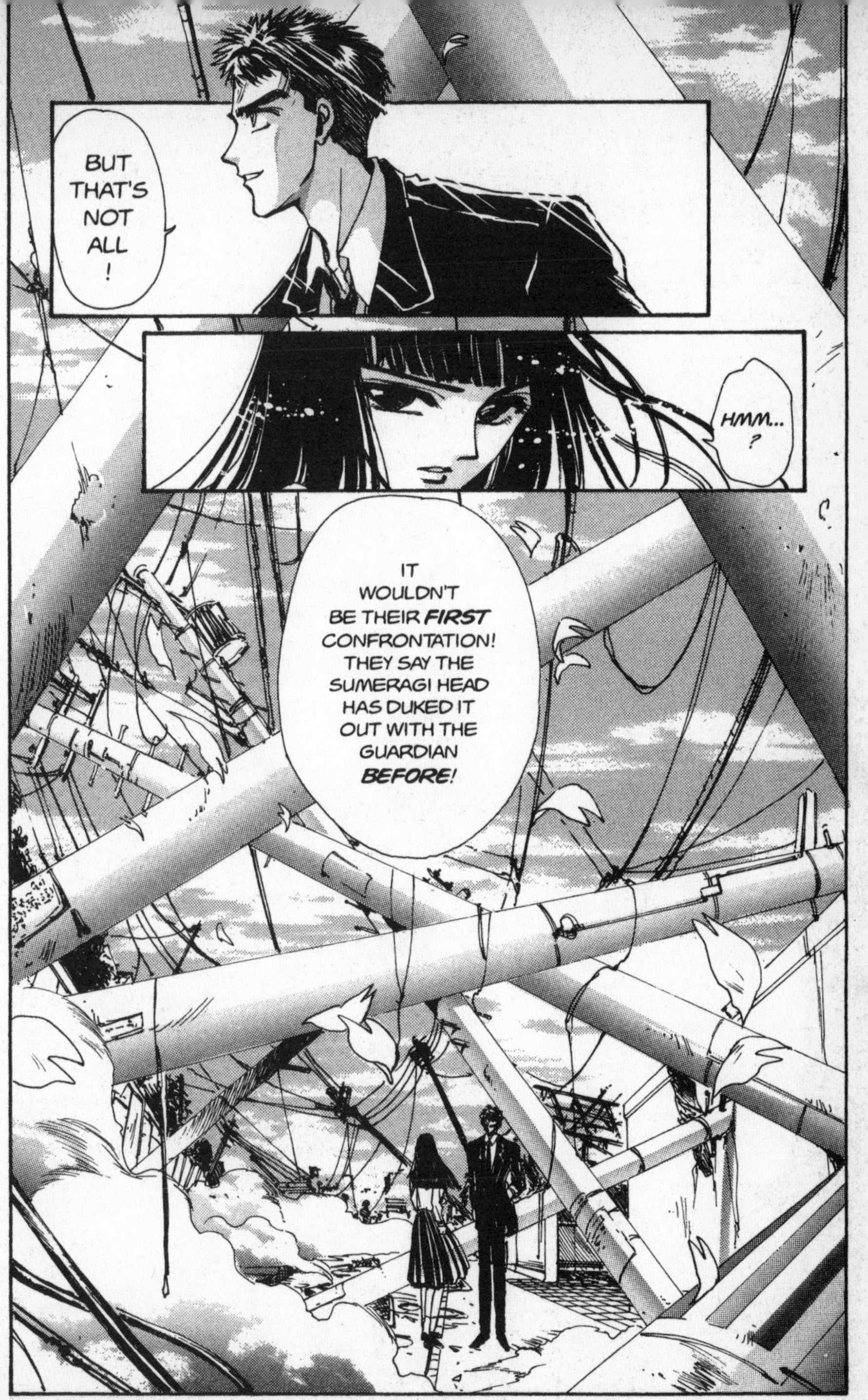
BUT THAT'S NOT ALL!
HMM...?
IT WOULDN'T BE THEIR *FIRST* CONFRONTATION! THEY SAY THE SUMERAGI HEAD HAS DUKED IT OUT WITH THE GUARDIAN *BEFORE*!

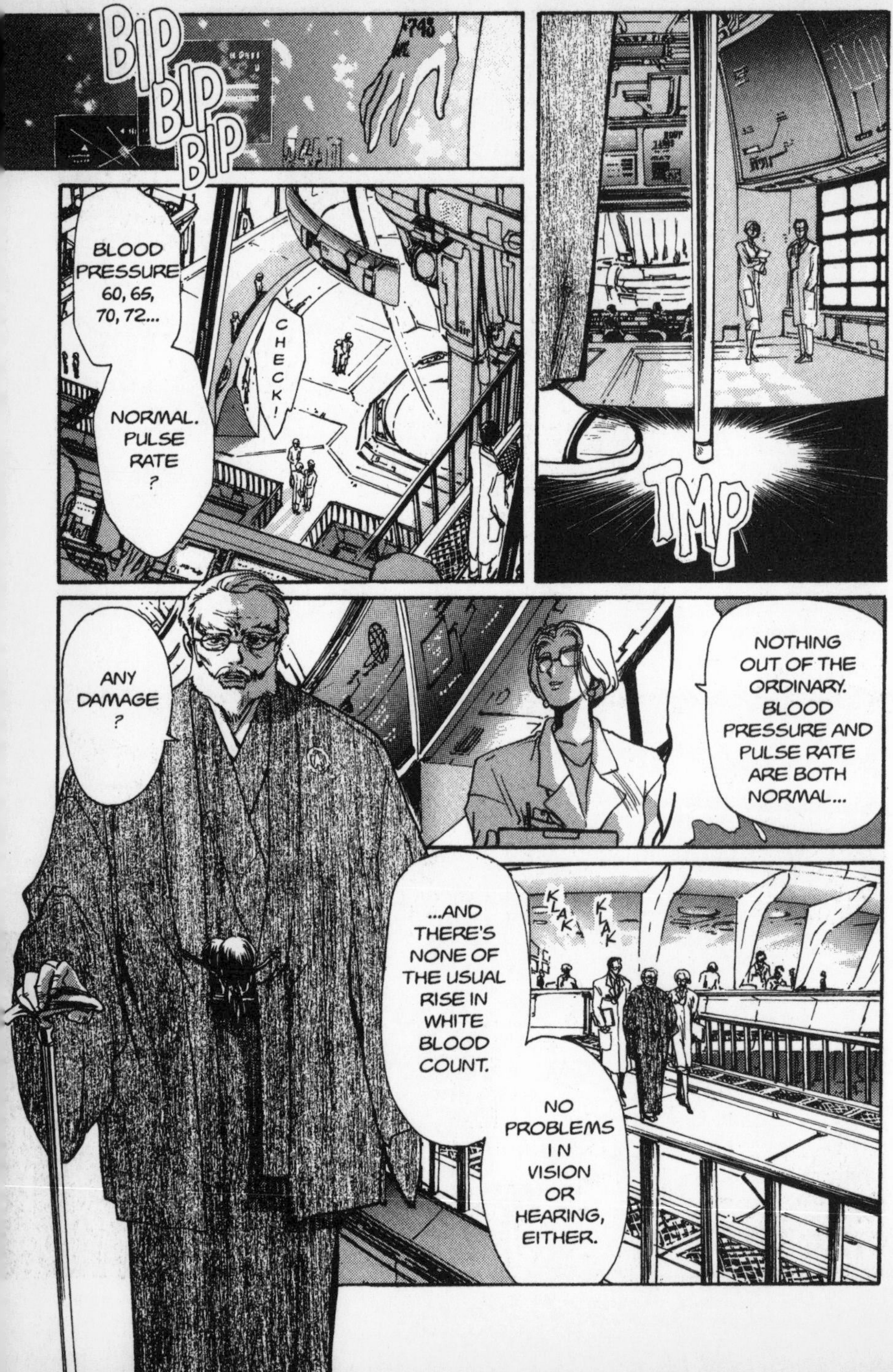
BIP BIP BIP
BLOOD PRESSURE 60, 65, 70, 72...
CHECK!
NORMAL. PULSE RATE ?
TMP
ANY DAMAGE ?
NOTHING OUT OF THE ORDINARY. BLOOD PRESSURE AND PULSE RATE ARE BOTH NORMAL...
KLAK
KLAK
...AND THERE'S NONE OF THE USUAL RISE IN WHITE BLOOD COUNT.
NO PROBLEMS IN VISION OR HEARING, EITHER.

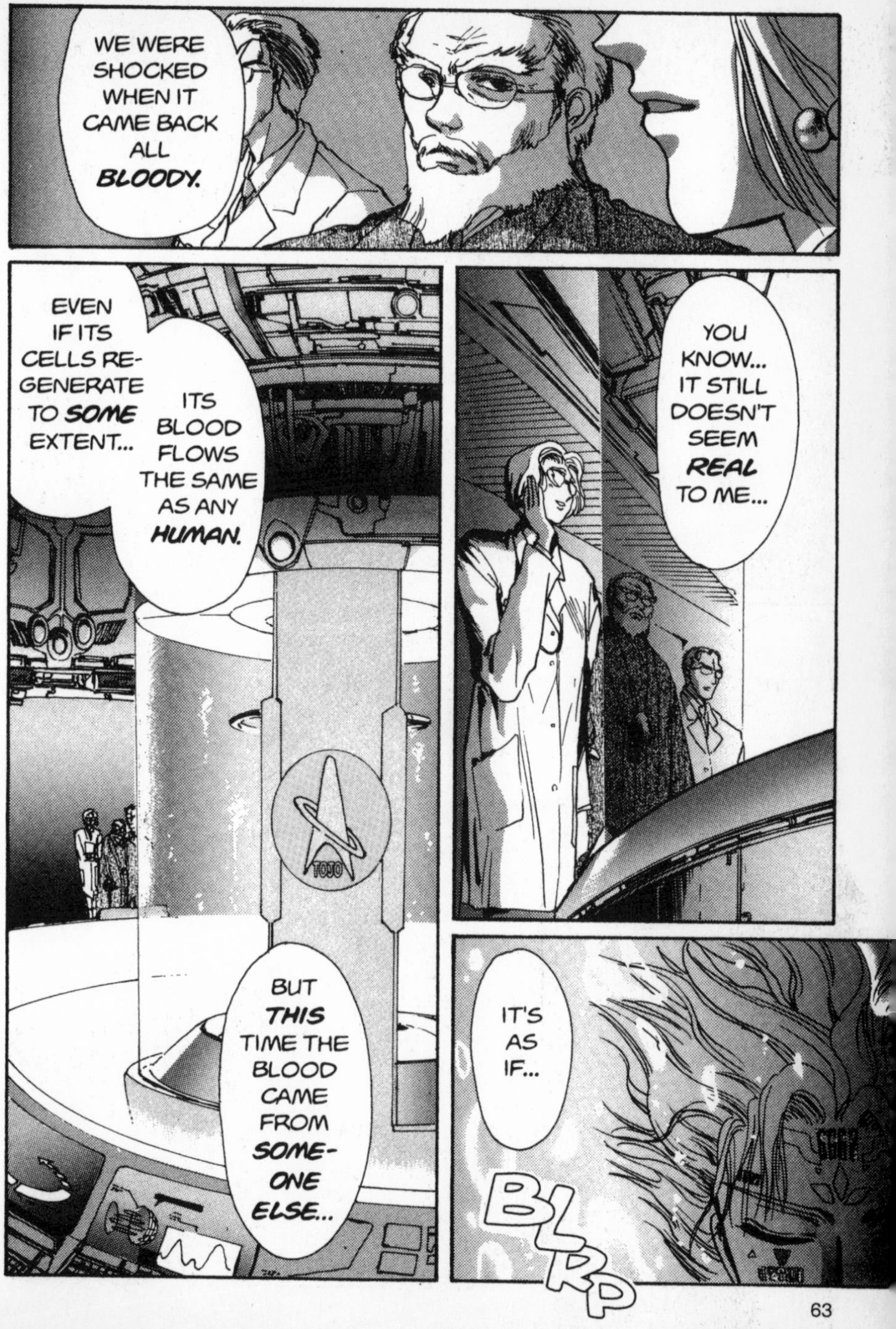
WE WERE SHOCKED WHEN IT CAME BACK ALL **BLOODY.**
EVEN IF ITS CELLS RE-GENERATE TO **SOME** EXTENT...
ITS BLOOD FLOWS THE SAME AS ANY **HUMAN.**
TOJO
BUT **THIS** TIME THE BLOOD CAME FROM **SOME-ONE ELSE...**
YOU KNOW... IT STILL DOESN'T SEEM **REAL** TO ME...
IT'S AS IF...
BLRP

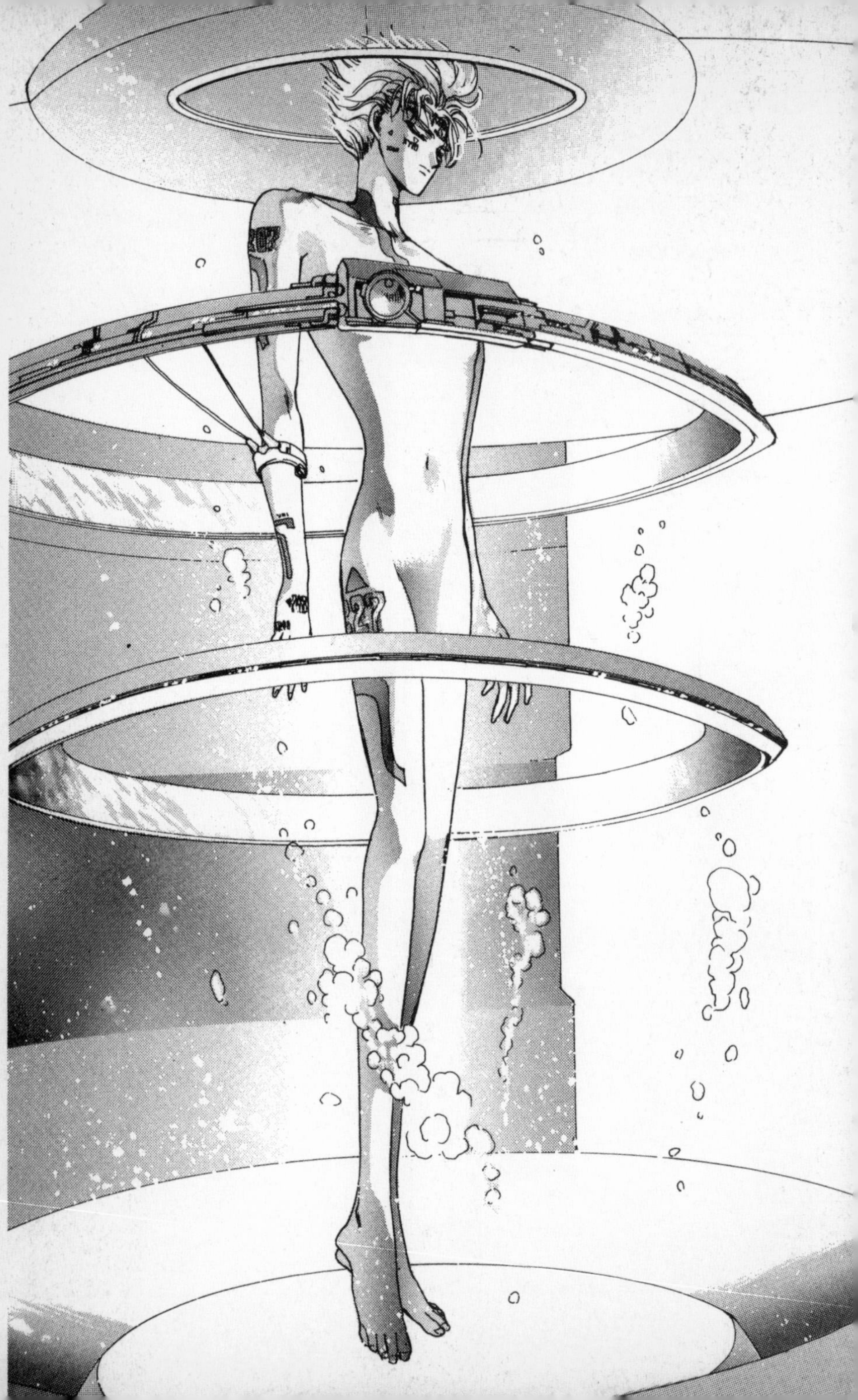

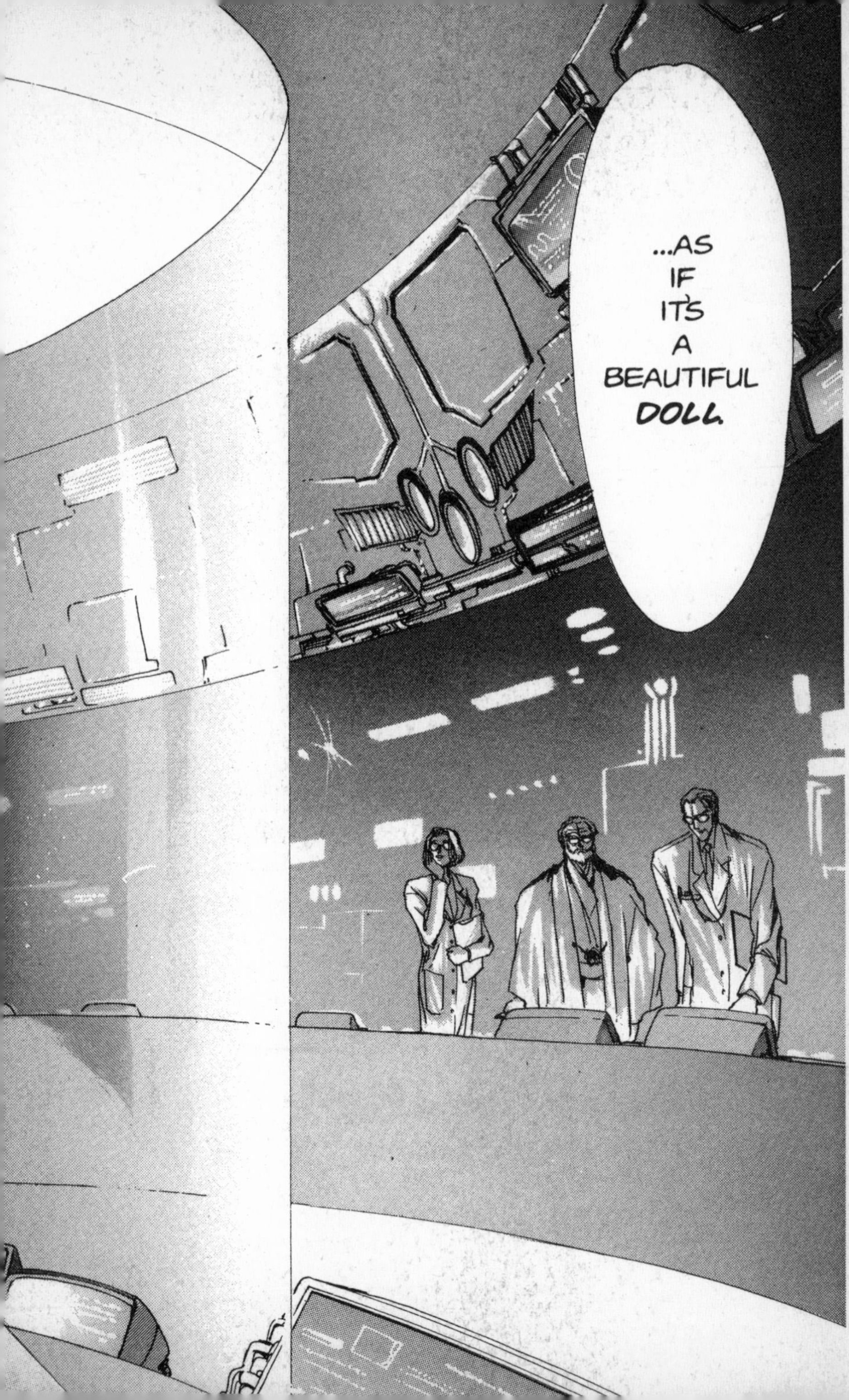
...AS IF IT'S A BEAUTIFUL DOLL.

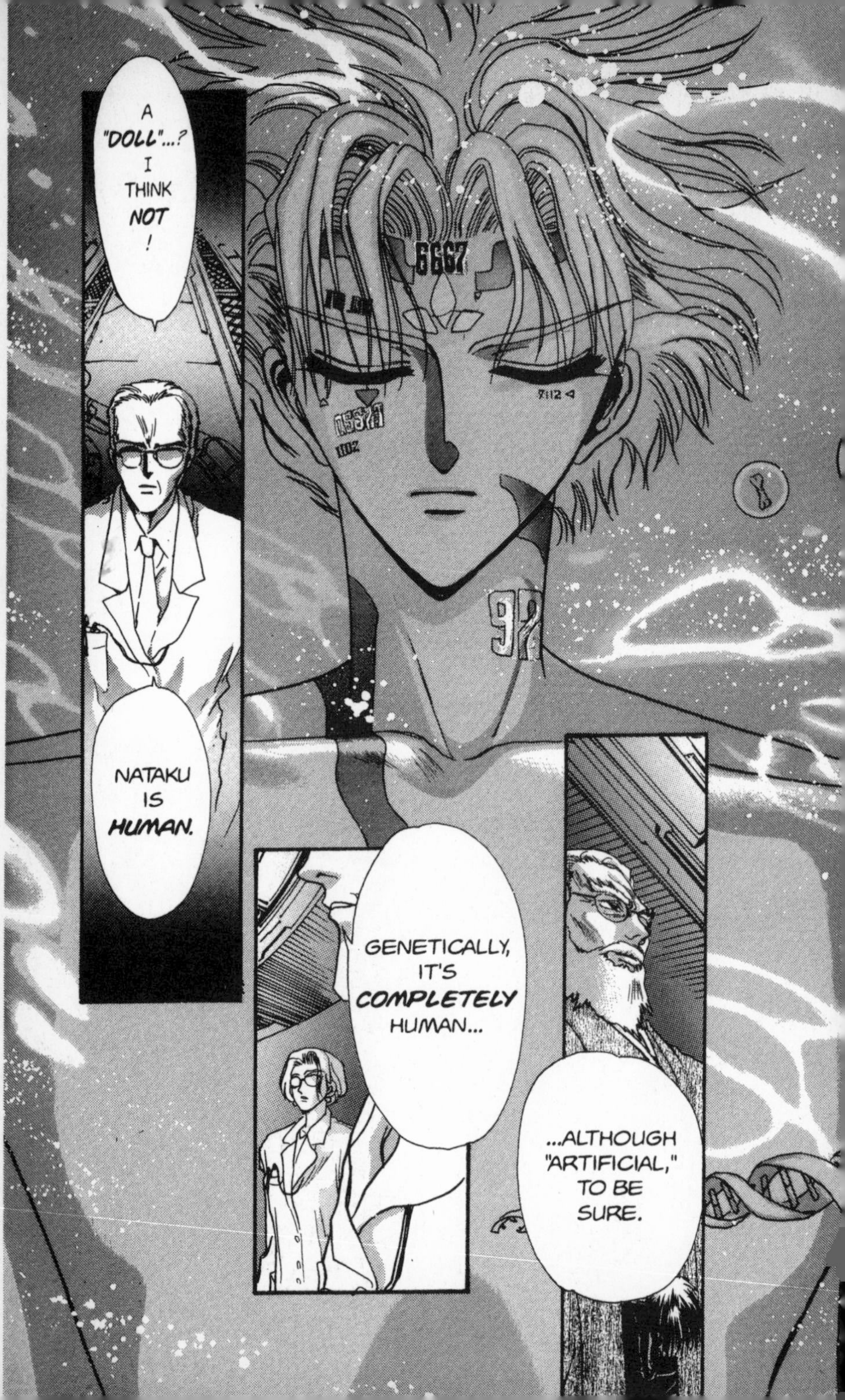
A "DOLL"...? I THINK NOT!
NATAKU IS HUMAN.
GENETICALLY, IT'S COMPLETELY HUMAN...
...ALTHOUGH "ARTIFICIAL," TO BE SURE.

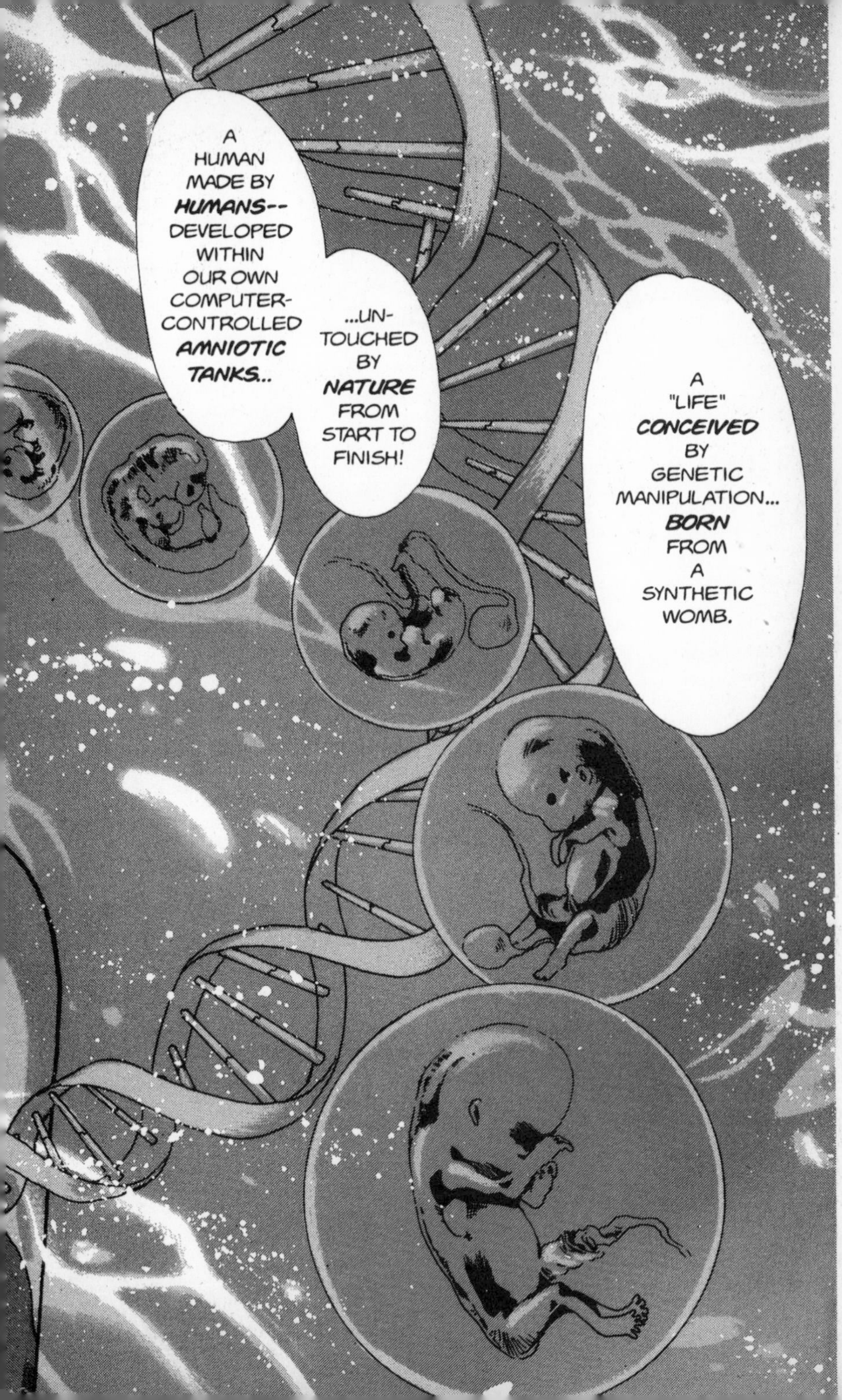
A HUMAN MADE BY **HUMANS--** DEVELOPED WITHIN OUR OWN COMPUTER-CONTROLLED **AMNIOTIC TANKS...**
...UN-TOUCHED BY **NATURE** FROM START TO FINISH!
A "LIFE" **CONCEIVED** BY GENETIC MANIPULATION... **BORN** FROM A SYNTHETIC WOMB.

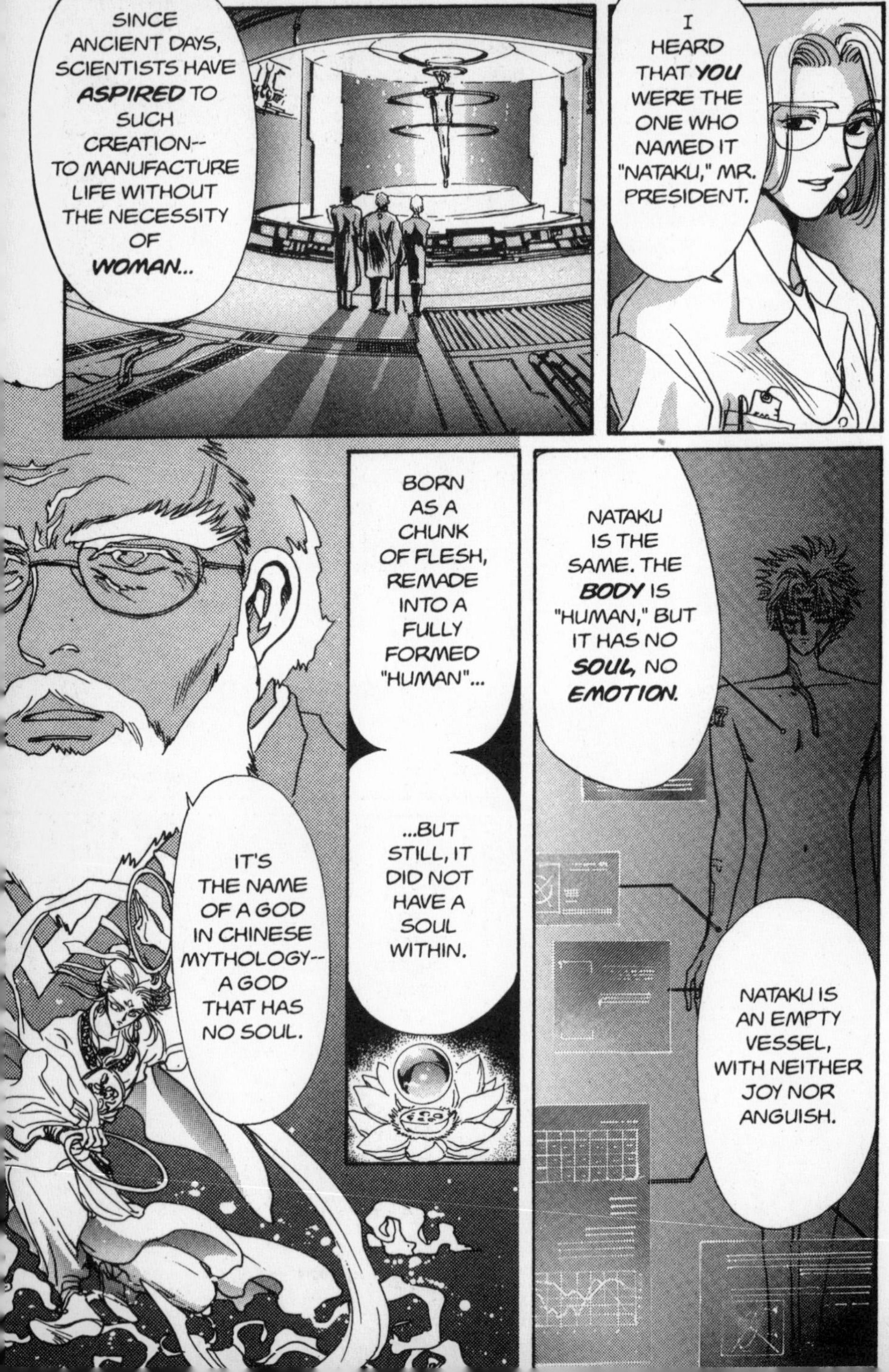
SINCE ANCIENT DAYS, SCIENTISTS HAVE ASPIRED TO SUCH CREATION-- TO MANUFACTURE LIFE WITHOUT THE NECESSITY OF WOMAN...
I HEARD THAT YOU WERE THE ONE WHO NAMED IT "NATAKU," MR. PRESIDENT.
IT'S THE NAME OF A GOD IN CHINESE MYTHOLOGY-- A GOD THAT HAS NO SOUL.
BORN AS A CHUNK OF FLESH, REMADE INTO A FULLY FORMED "HUMAN"...
...BUT STILL, IT DID NOT HAVE A SOUL WITHIN.
NATAKU IS THE SAME. THE BODY IS "HUMAN," BUT IT HAS NO SOUL, NO EMOTION.
NATAKU IS AN EMPTY VESSEL, WITH NEITHER JOY NOR ANGUISH.

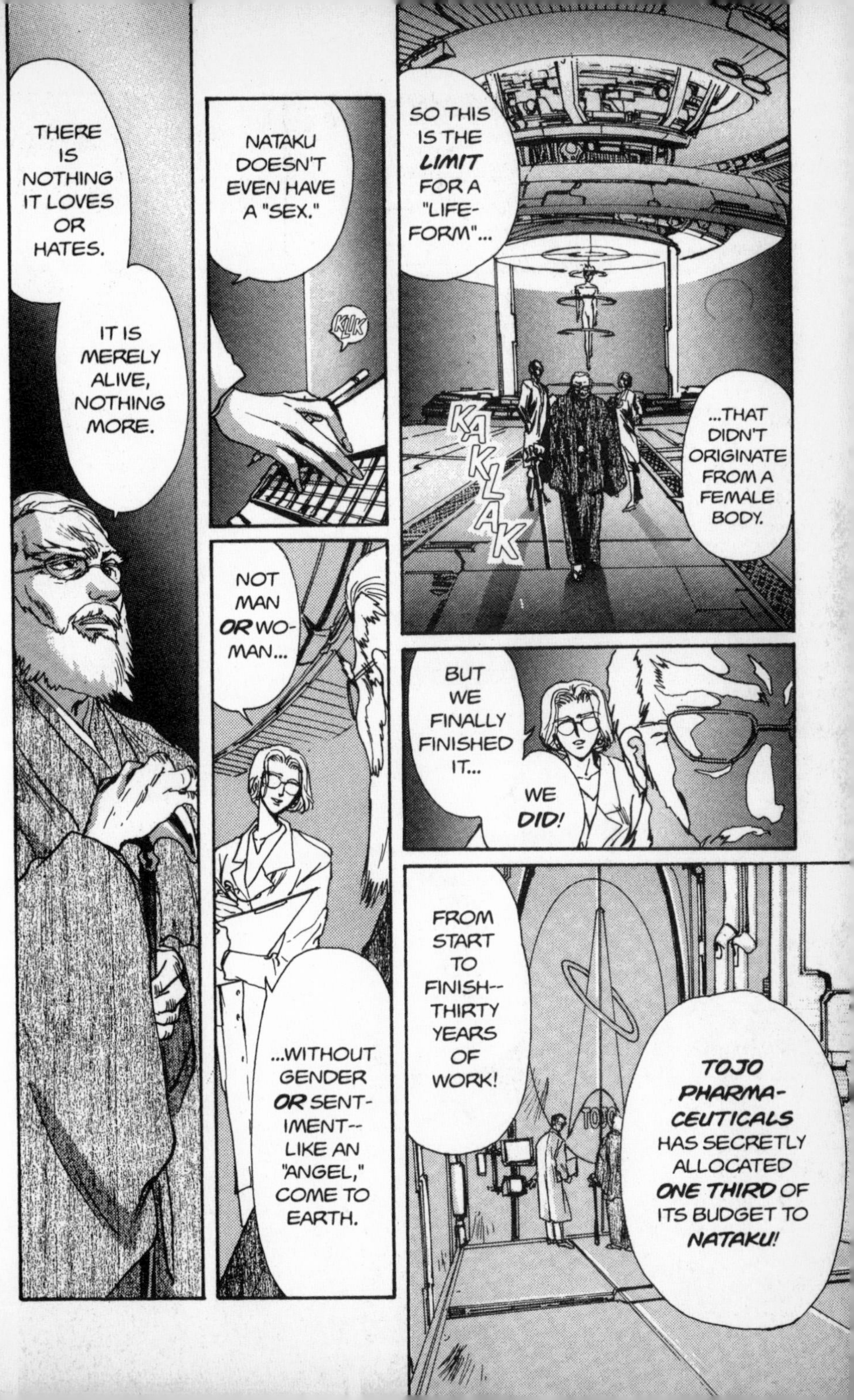
THERE IS NOTHING IT LOVES OR HATES.
IT IS MERELY ALIVE, NOTHING MORE.
NATAKU DOESN'T EVEN HAVE A "SEX."
KLIK
NOT MAN *OR* WOMAN...
...WITHOUT GENDER *OR* SENTIMENT--LIKE AN "ANGEL," COME TO EARTH.
SO THIS IS THE *LIMIT* FOR A "LIFE-FORM"...
KAKLAK
...THAT DIDN'T ORIGINATE FROM A FEMALE BODY.
BUT WE FINALLY FINISHED IT...
WE *DID*!
FROM START TO FINISH--THIRTY YEARS OF WORK!
TOJO PHARMACEUTICALS HAS SECRETLY ALLOCATED *ONE THIRD* OF ITS BUDGET TO *NATAKU*!

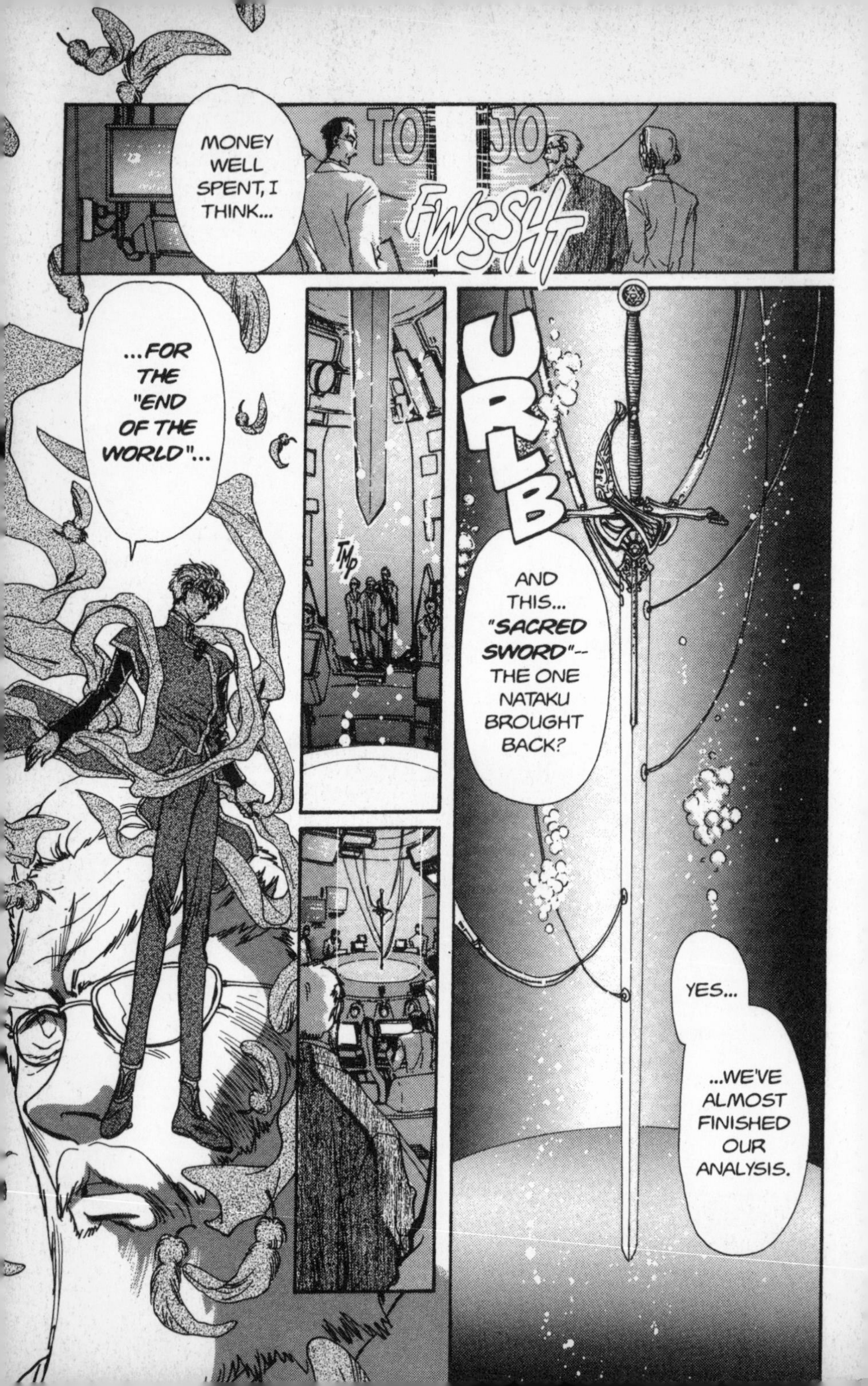
MONEY WELL SPENT, I THINK...
TO JO
FWSSHT
...FOR THE "END OF THE WORLD"...
TMP
URLB
AND THIS... "SACRED SWORD"-- THE ONE NATAKU BROUGHT BACK?
YES...
...WE'VE ALMOST FINISHED OUR ANALYSIS.

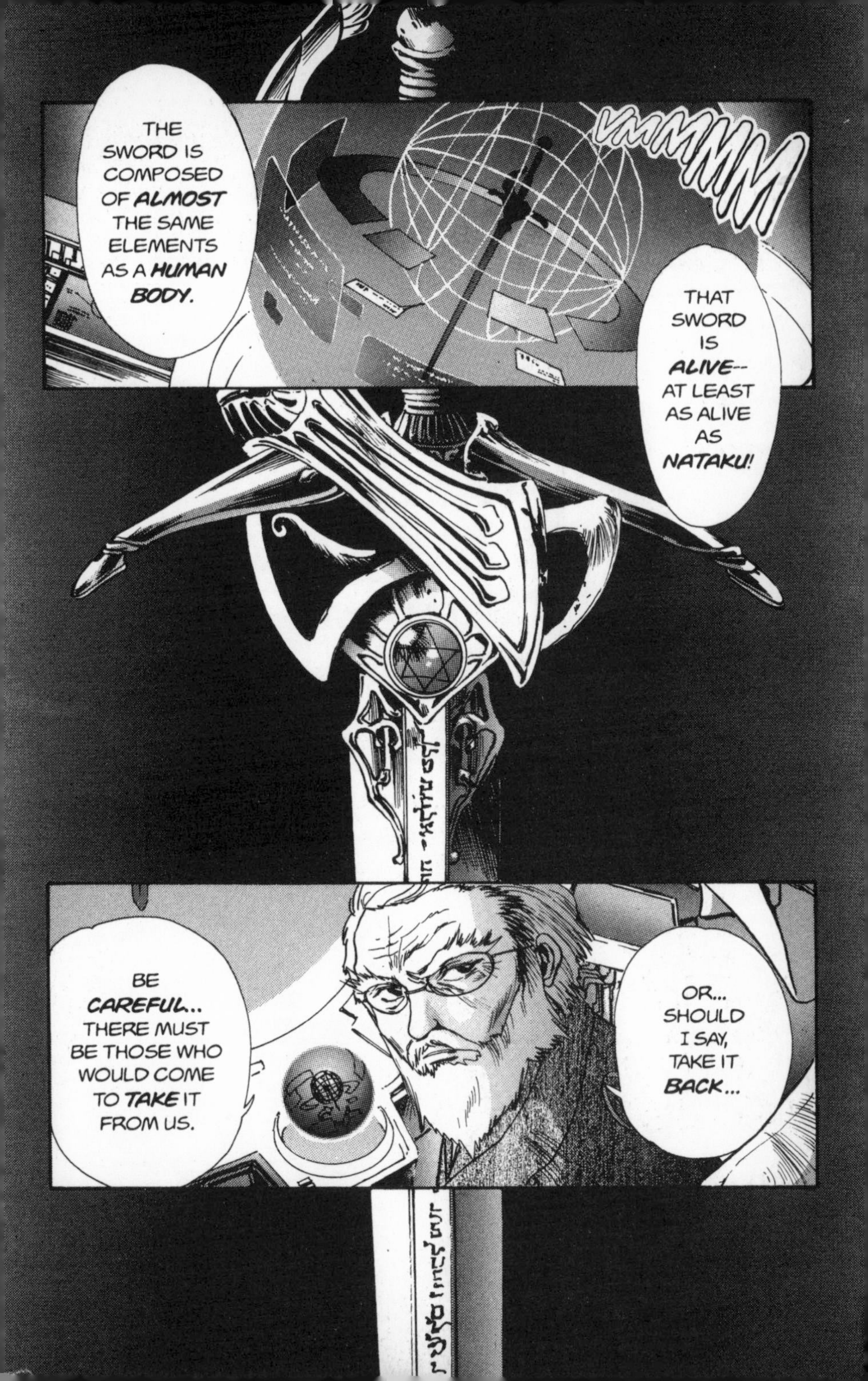
THE SWORD IS COMPOSED OF ALMOST THE SAME ELEMENTS AS A HUMAN BODY.
VMMMM
THAT SWORD IS ALIVE-- AT LEAST AS ALIVE AS NATAKU!
BE CAREFUL... THERE MUST BE THOSE WHO WOULD COME TO TAKE IT FROM US.
OR... SHOULD I SAY, TAKE IT BACK...

NO NEED TO WORRY. WHO WOULD **DREAM** THIS LAB EXISTS?

THERE'S **NONE** WHO COULD IMAGINE...

...THAT BENEATH **SUNSHINE 60** IS THE MOST SOPHISTICATED TECHNOLOGY ON THE PLANET!

THAT'S **RIGHT.**

NO.

THERE IS.

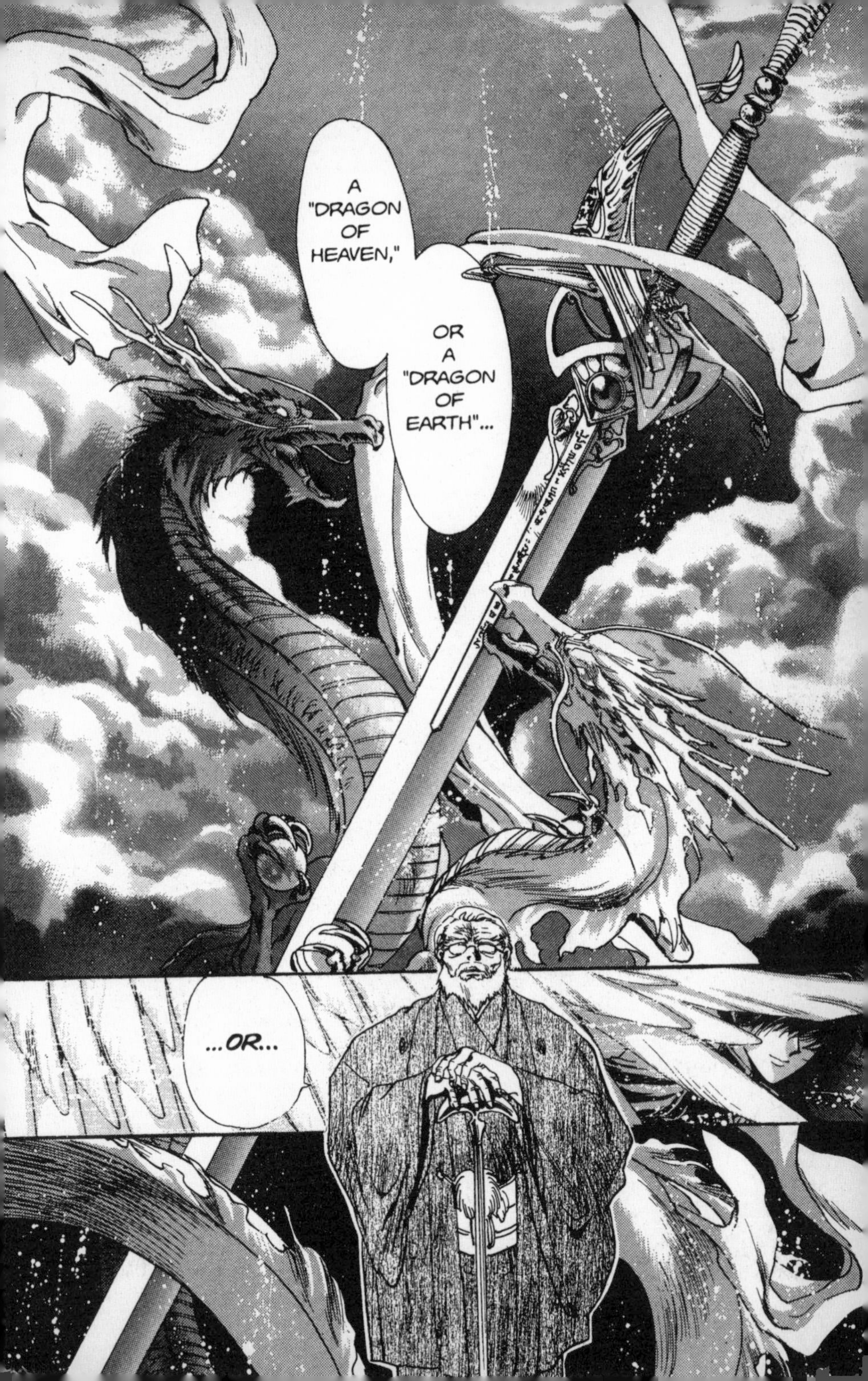
A "DRAGON OF HEAVEN,"
OR A "DRAGON OF EARTH"...
...OR...

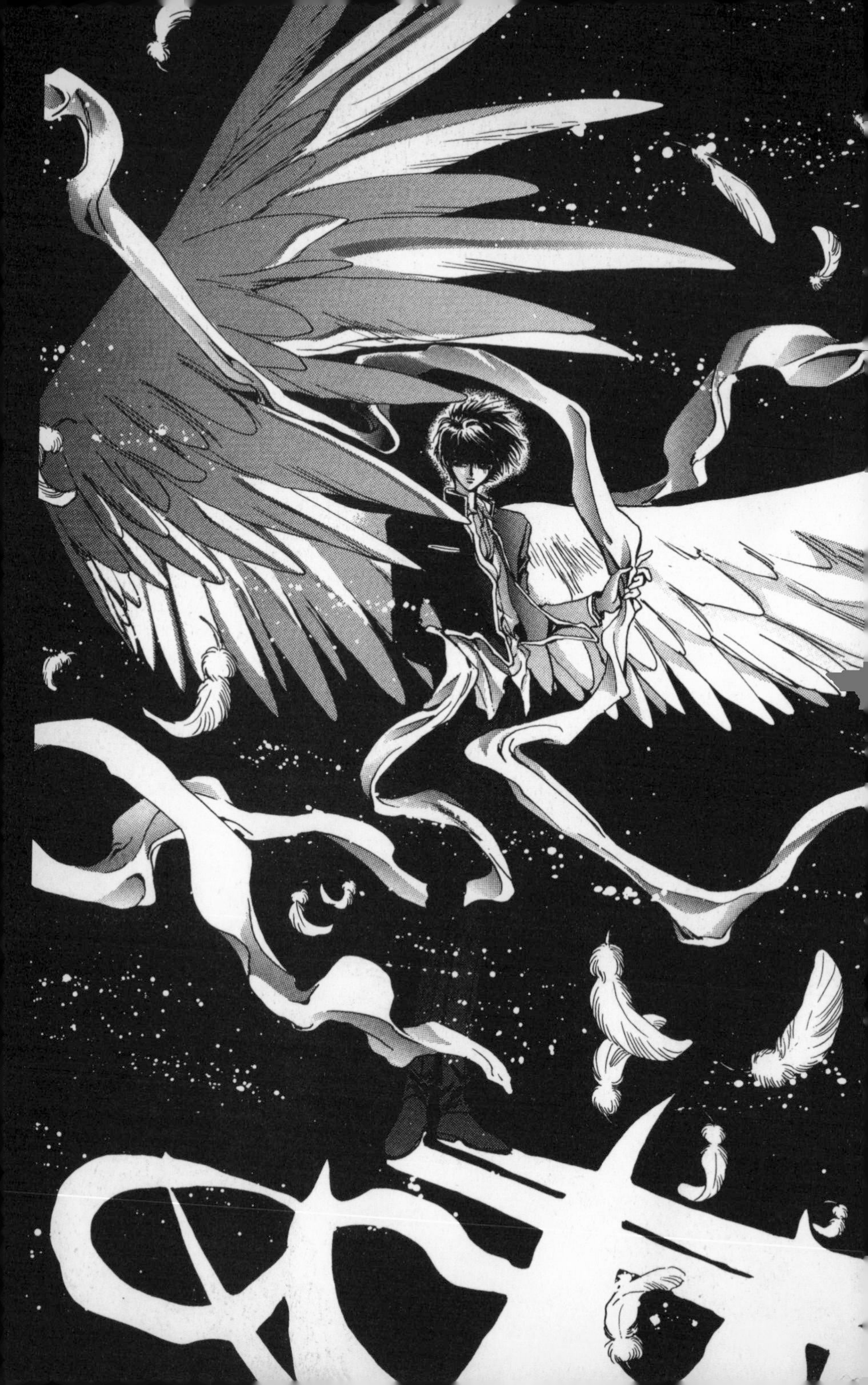

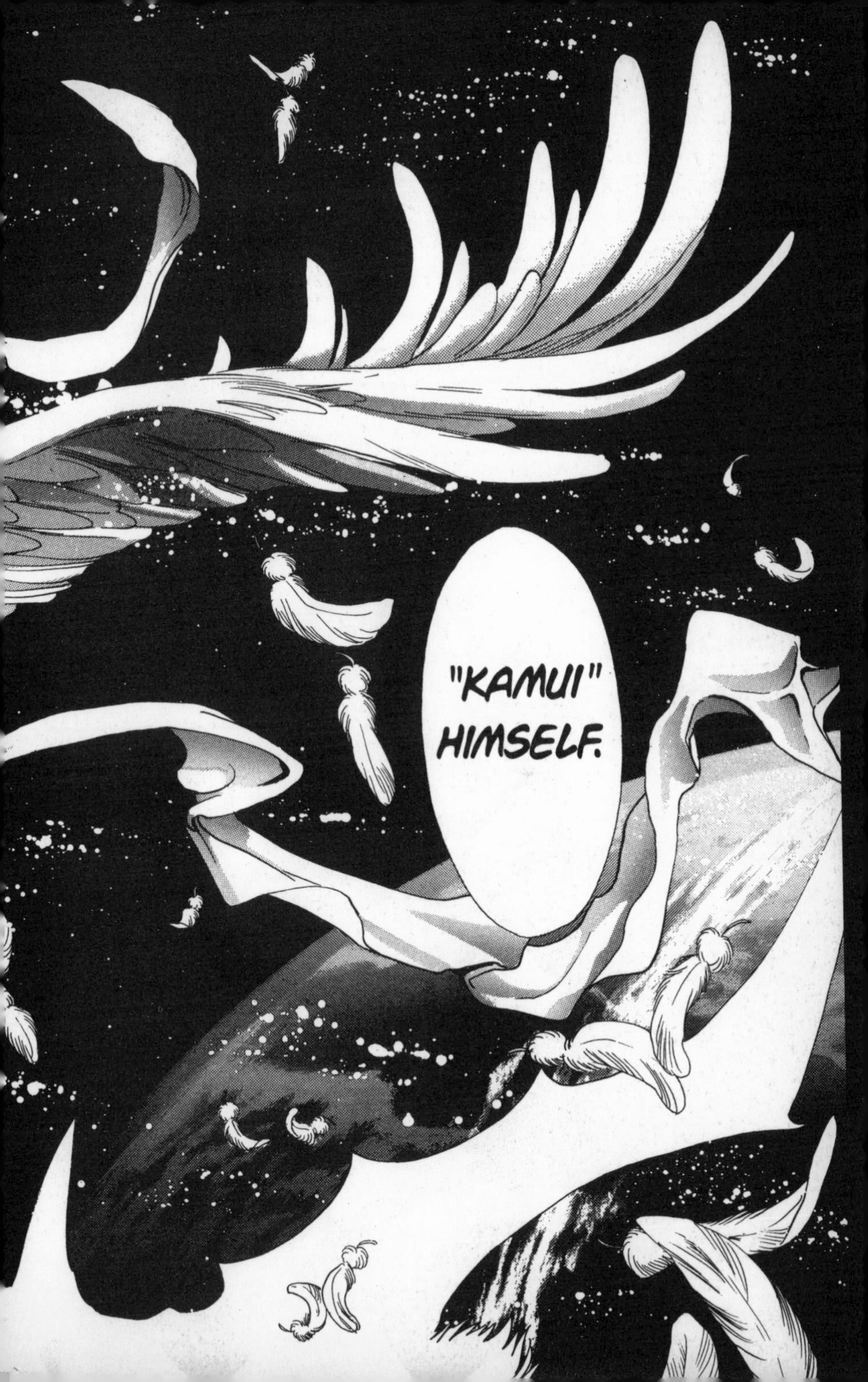
"KAMUI" HIMSELF.

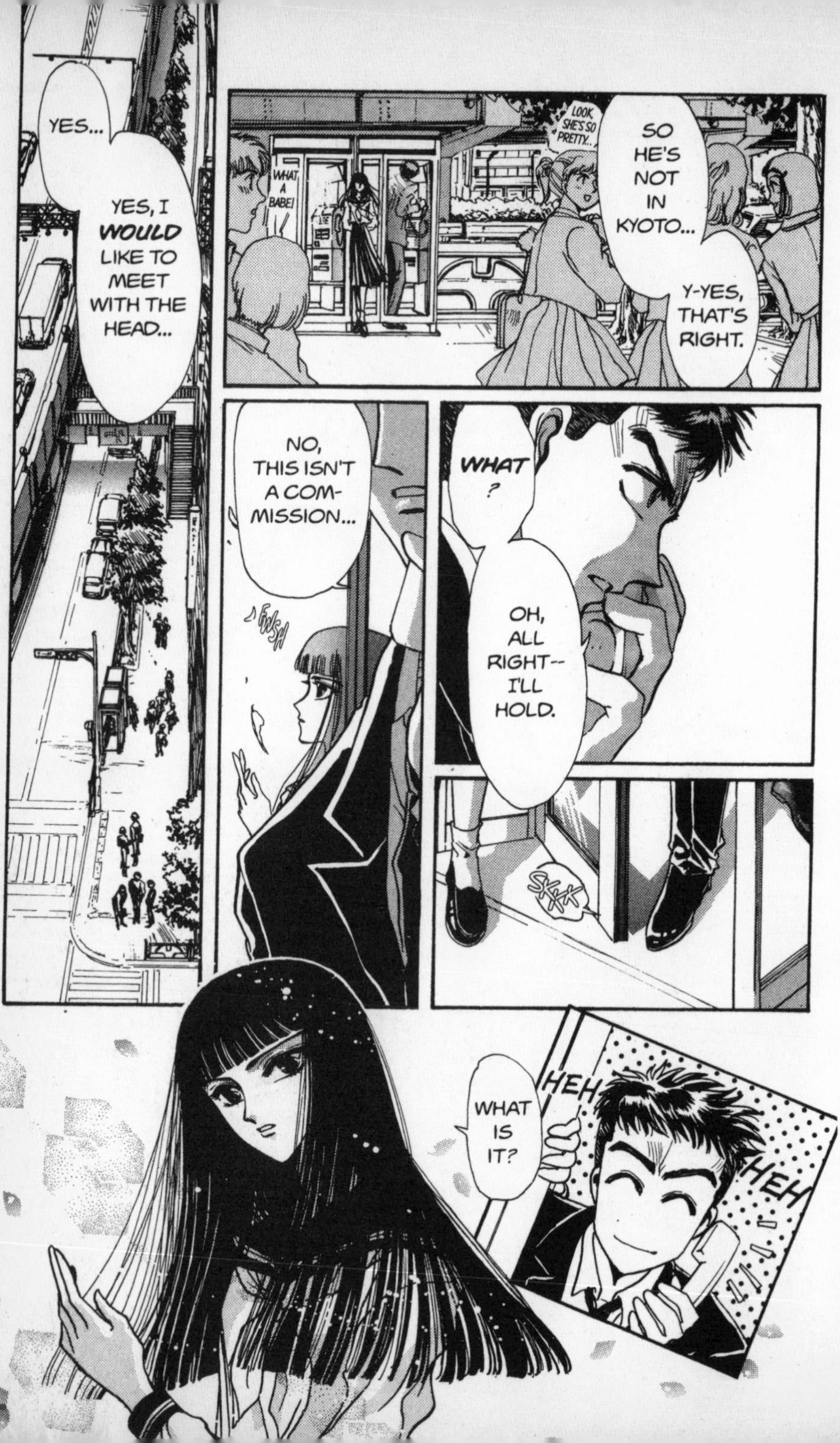
YES...
YES, I **WOULD** LIKE TO MEET WITH THE HEAD...
WHAT A BABE!
LOOK, SHE'S SO PRETTY...
SO HE'S NOT IN KYOTO...
Y-YES, THAT'S RIGHT.
NO, THIS ISN'T A COM-MISSION...
FWSH
WHAT?
OH, ALL RIGHT-- I'LL HOLD.
SKYK
WHAT IS IT?
HEH
HEH

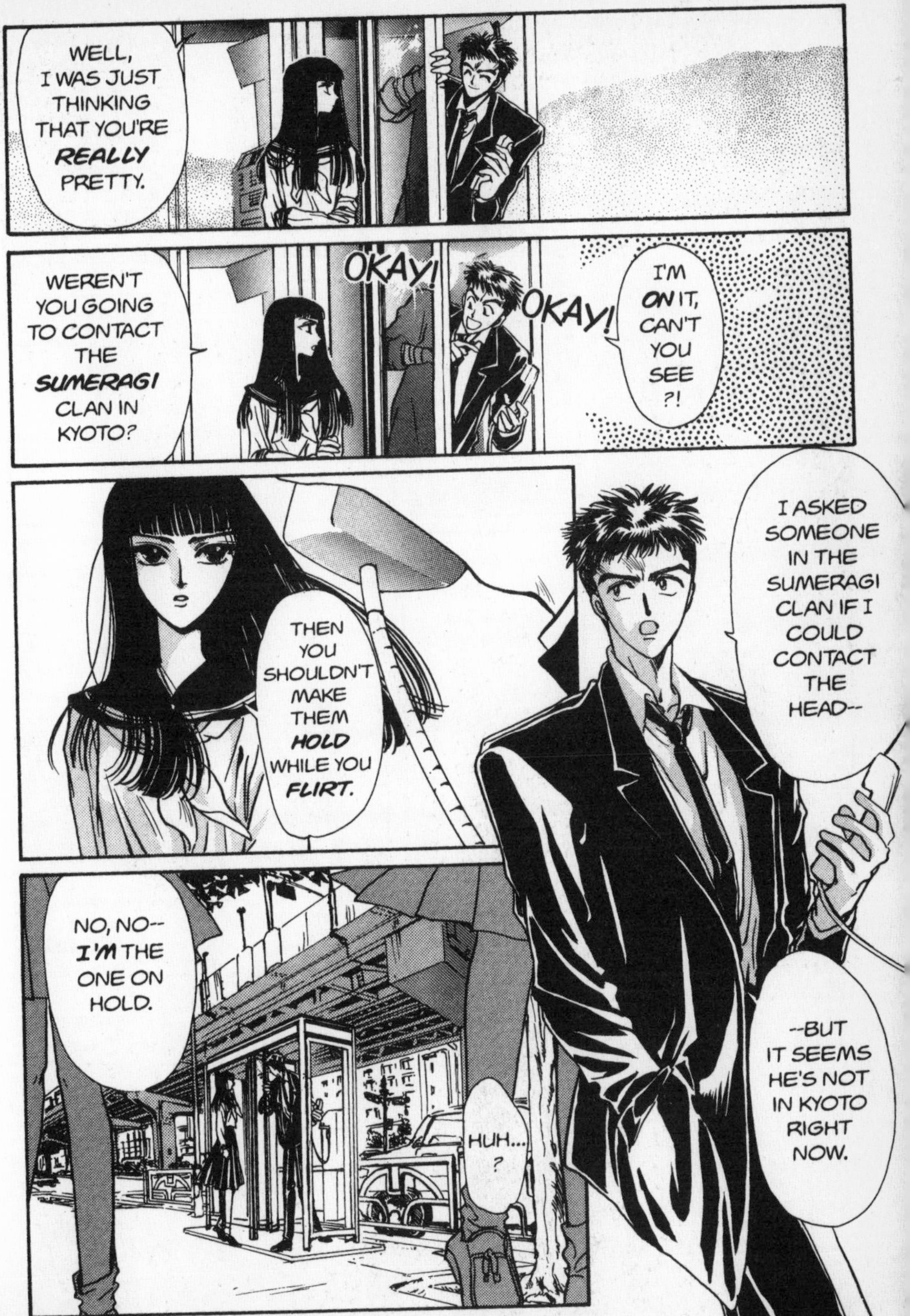
WELL, I WAS JUST THINKING THAT YOU'RE REALLY PRETTY.
WEREN'T YOU GOING TO CONTACT THE SUMERAGI CLAN IN KYOTO?
OKAY!
OKAY!
I'M ON IT, CAN'T YOU SEE?!
THEN YOU SHOULDN'T MAKE THEM HOLD WHILE YOU FLIRT.
NO, NO-- I'M THE ONE ON HOLD.
HUH...?
I ASKED SOMEONE IN THE SUMERAGI CLAN IF I COULD CONTACT THE HEAD--
--BUT IT SEEMS HE'S NOT IN KYOTO RIGHT NOW.

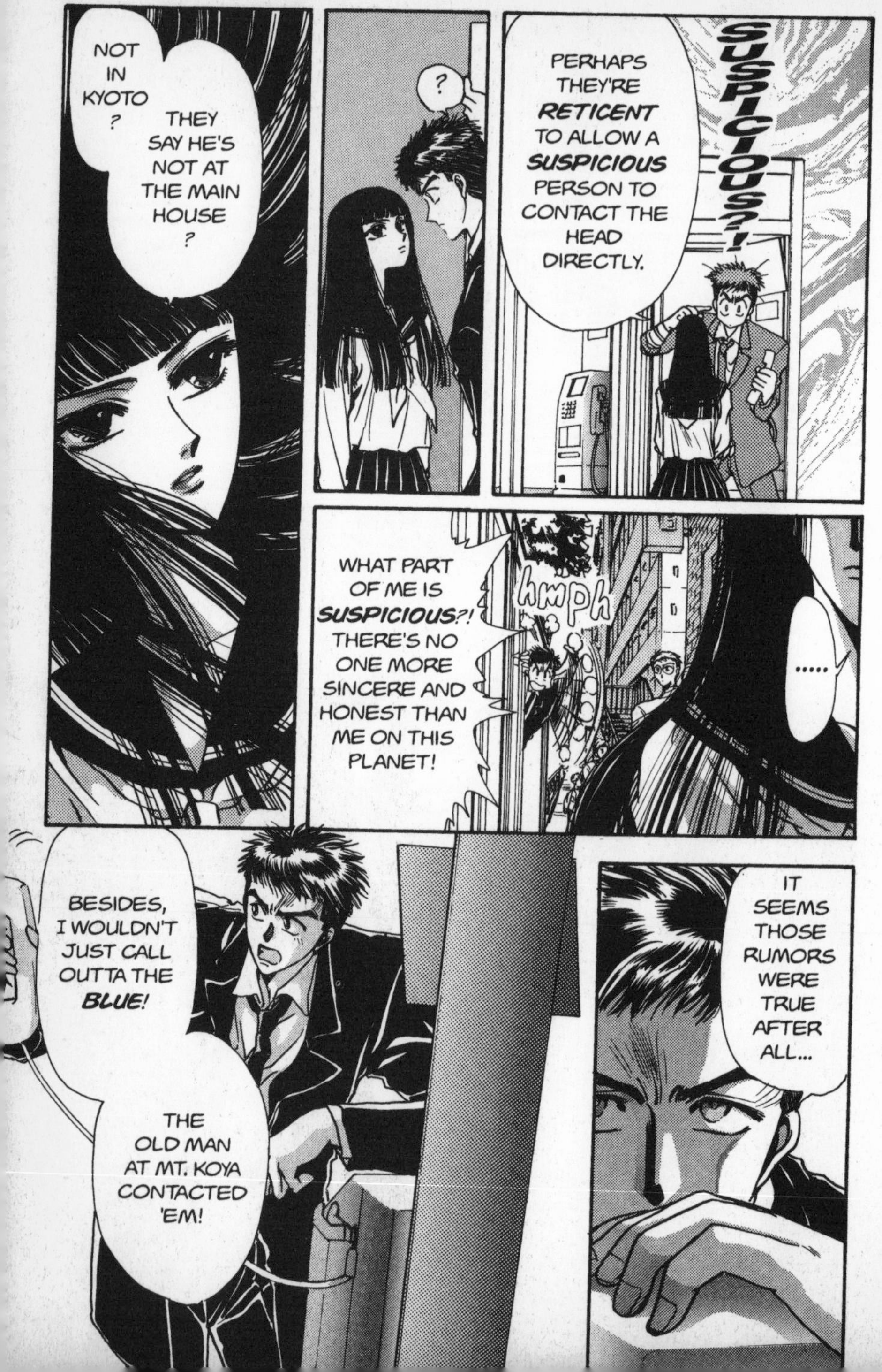
NOT IN KYOTO?
THEY SAY HE'S NOT AT THE MAIN HOUSE?
?
PERHAPS THEY'RE **RETICENT** TO ALLOW A **SUSPICIOUS** PERSON TO CONTACT THE HEAD DIRECTLY.
SUSPICIOUS?!
WHAT PART OF ME IS **SUSPICIOUS**?! THERE'S NO ONE MORE SINCERE AND HONEST THAN ME ON THIS PLANET!
hmph
.....
BESIDES, I WOULDN'T JUST CALL OUTTA THE **BLUE**!
THE OLD MAN AT MT. KOYA CONTACTED 'EM!
IT SEEMS THOSE RUMORS WERE TRUE AFTER ALL...

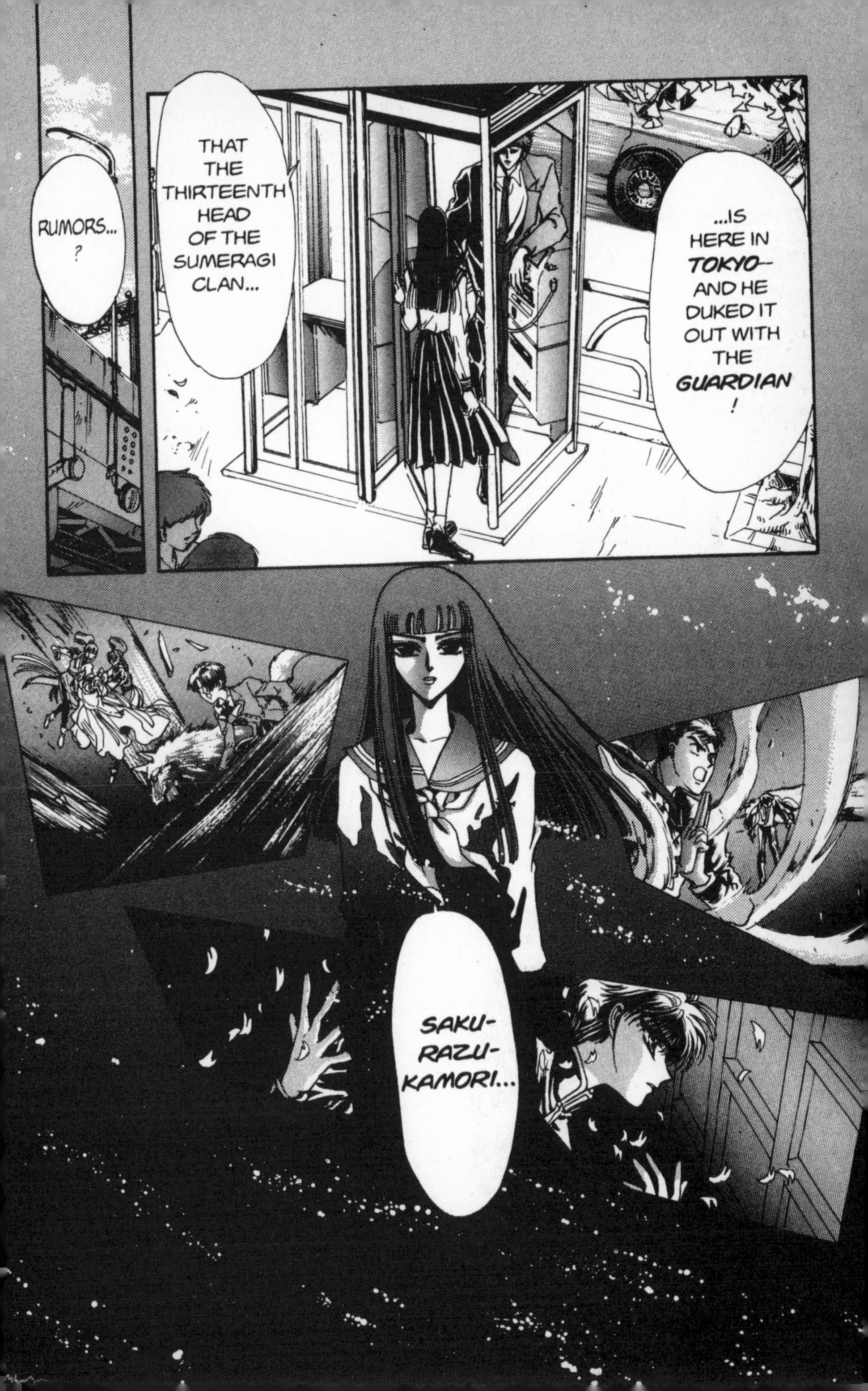
RUMORS... ?
THAT THE THIRTEENTH HEAD OF THE SUMERAGI CLAN...
...IS HERE IN TOKYO- AND HE DUKED IT OUT WITH THE GUARDIAN!
SAKU-RAZU-KAMORI...

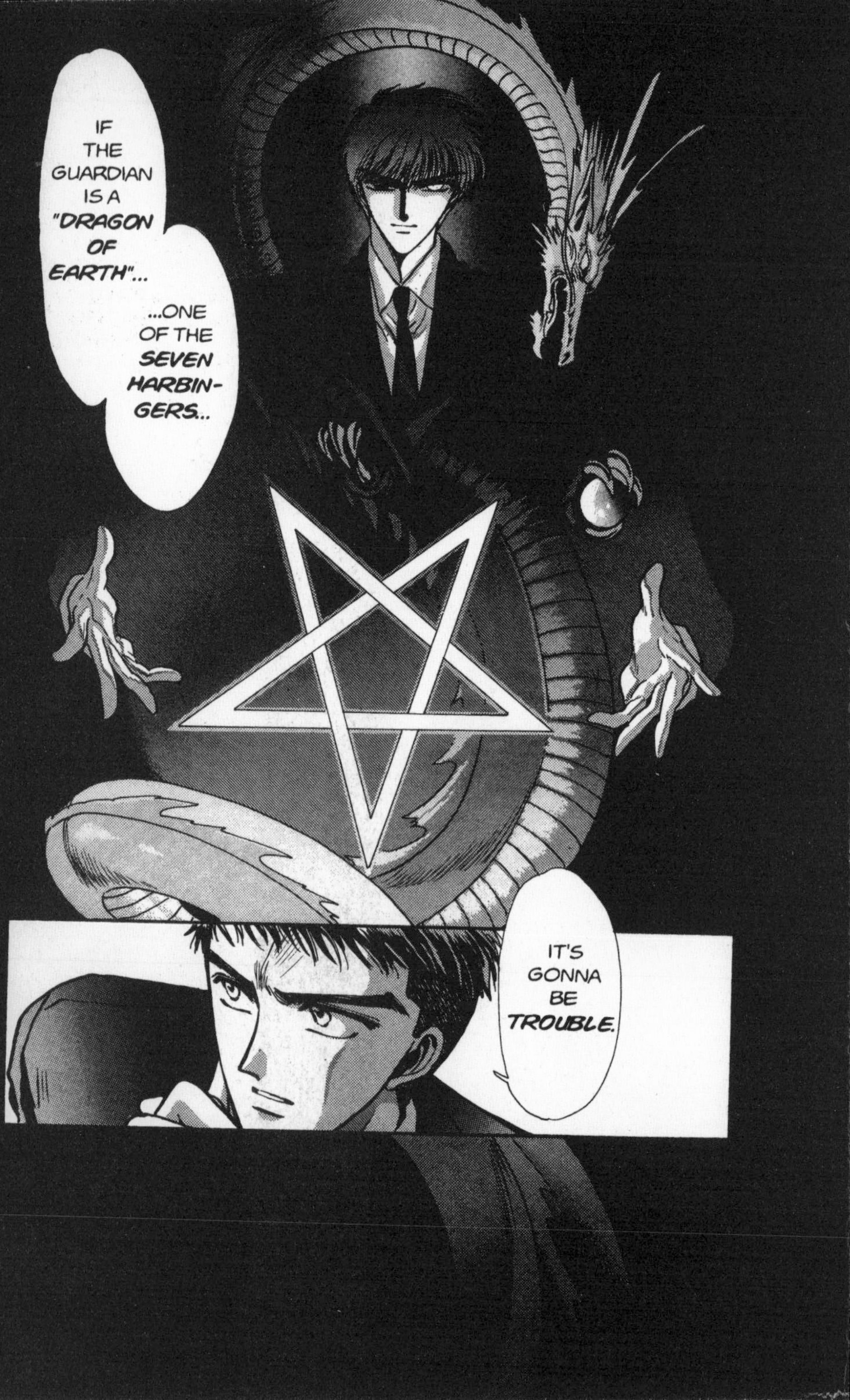

IF THE GUARDIAN IS A "*DRAGON OF EARTH*"...
...ONE OF THE *SEVEN HARBIN-GERS*...
IT'S GONNA BE *TROUBLE*.

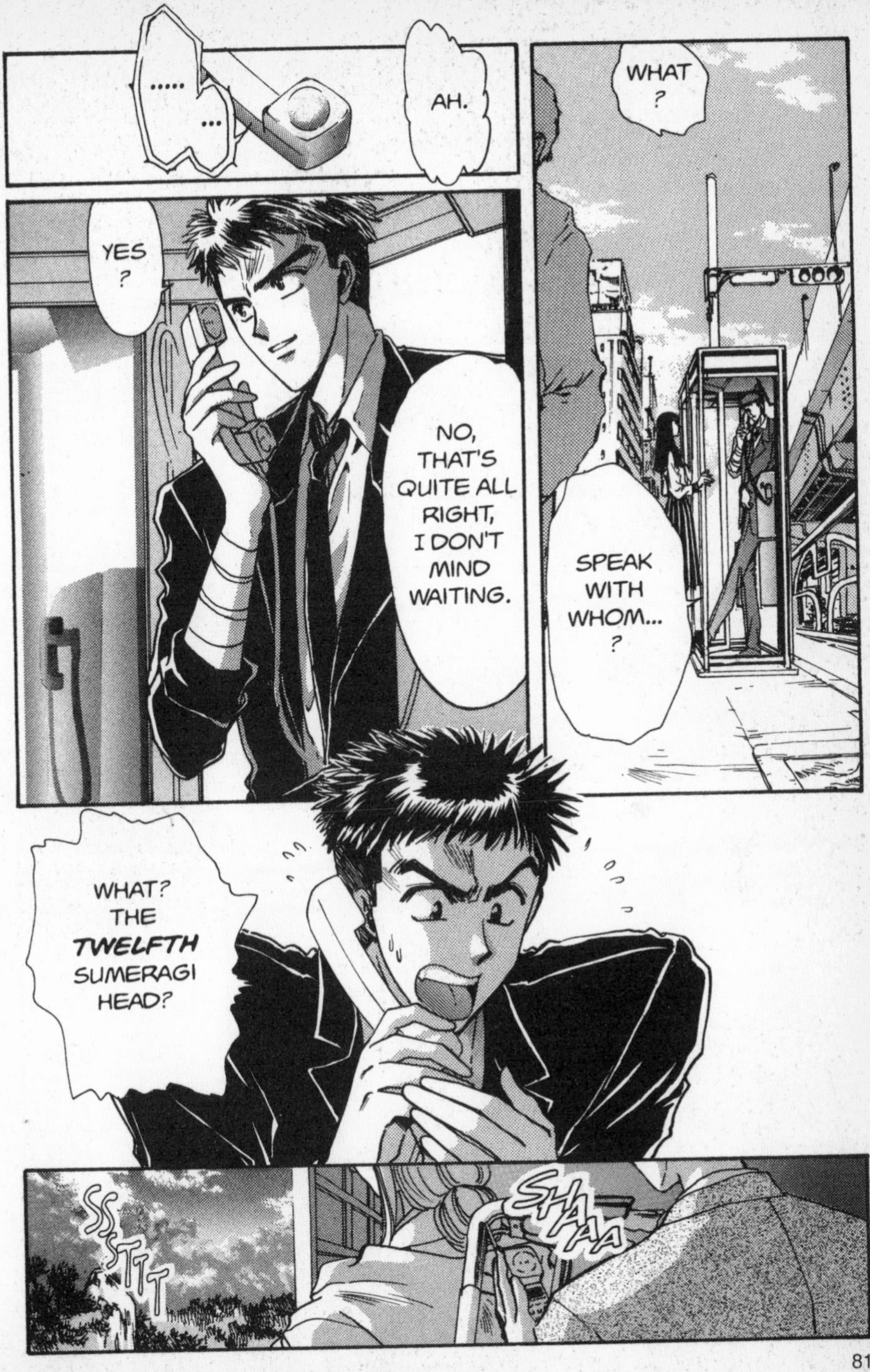
......
...
AH.
YES ?
NO, THAT'S QUITE ALL RIGHT, I DON'T MIND WAITING.
WHAT ?
SPEAK WITH WHOM... ?
WHAT? THE TWELFTH SUMERAGI HEAD?
SSSTTT
SHAAAA

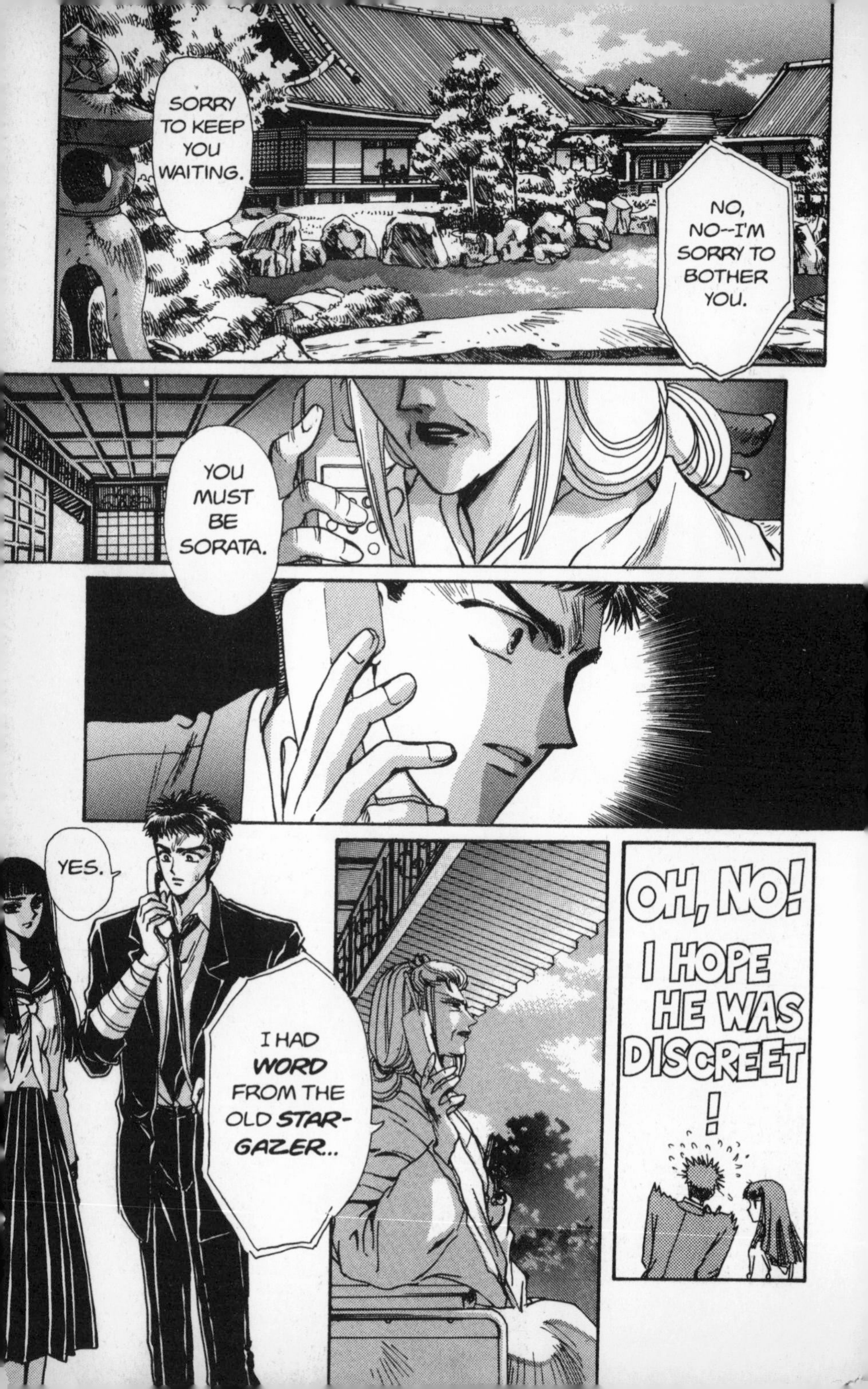
SORRY TO KEEP YOU WAITING.
NO, NO--I'M SORRY TO BOTHER YOU.
YOU MUST BE SORATA.
YES.
I HAD WORD FROM THE OLD STAR-GAZER...
OH, NO! I HOPE HE WAS DISCREET!

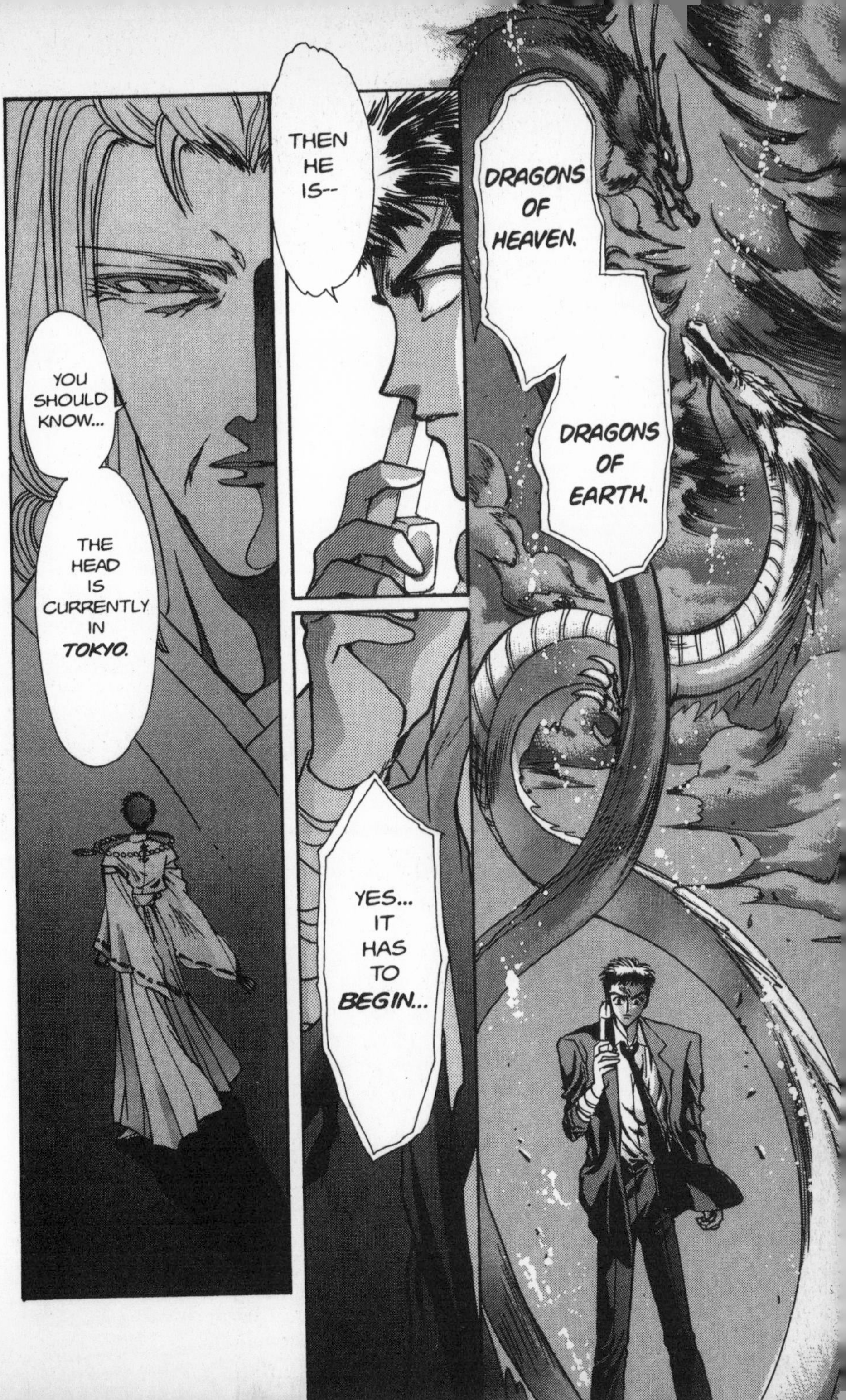
YOU SHOULD KNOW...
THE HEAD IS CURRENTLY IN TOKYO.
THEN HE IS--
YES... IT HAS TO BEGIN...
DRAGONS OF HEAVEN.
DRAGONS OF EARTH.

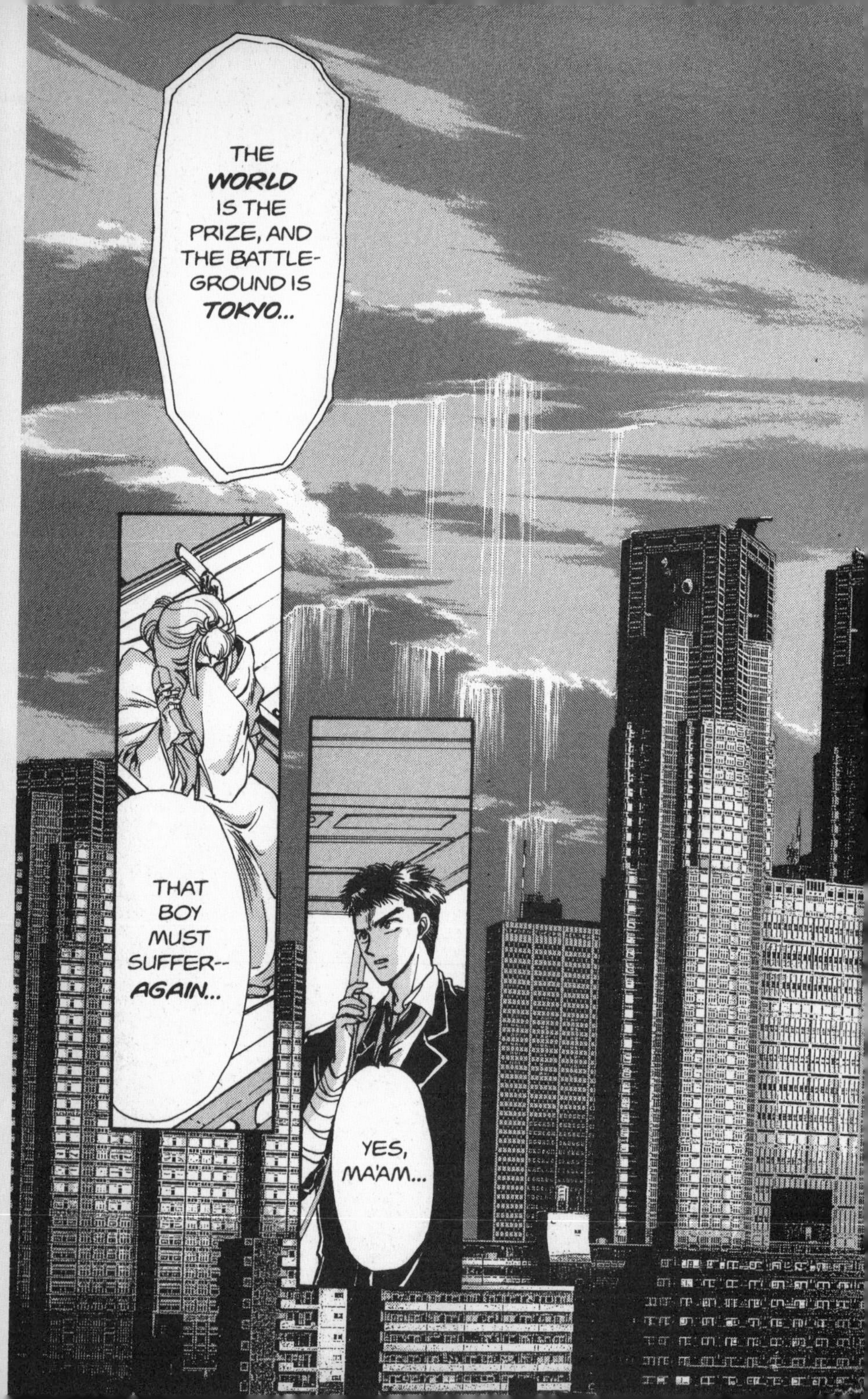
THE WORLD IS THE PRIZE, AND THE BATTLE-GROUND IS TOKYO...
YES, MA'AM...
THAT BOY MUST SUFFER-- AGAIN...

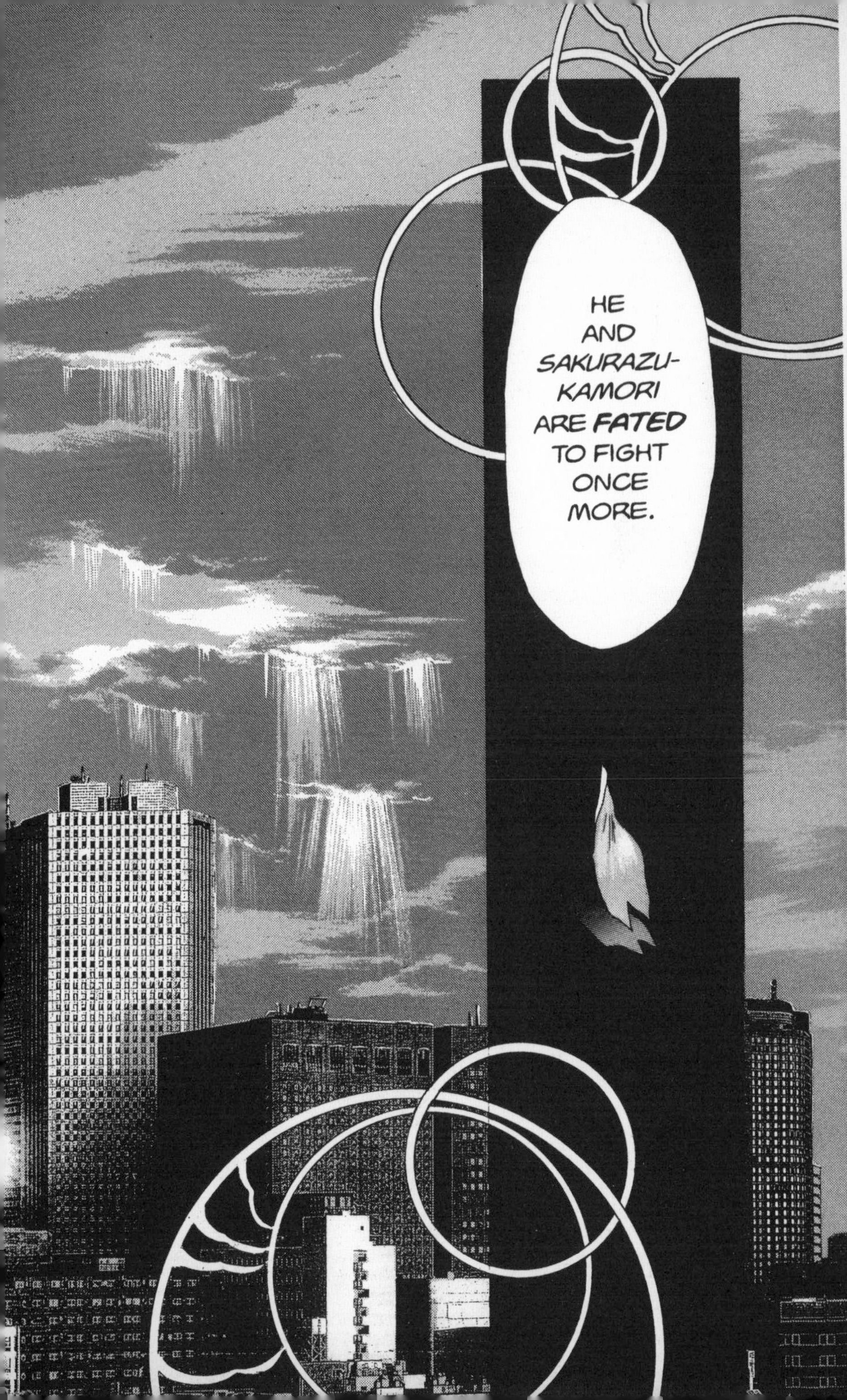
HE AND SAKURAZU-KAMORI ARE **FATED** TO FIGHT ONCE MORE.

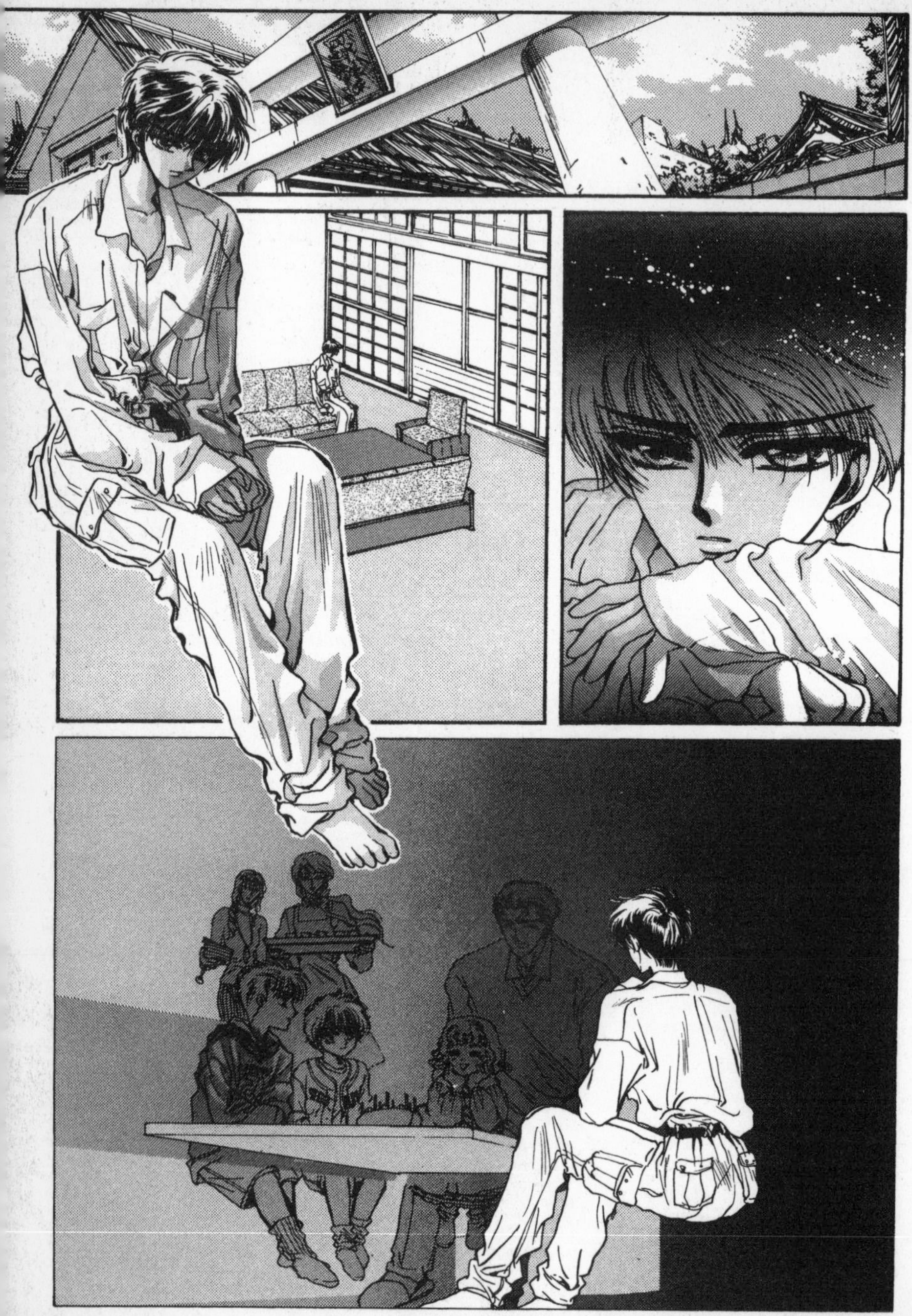

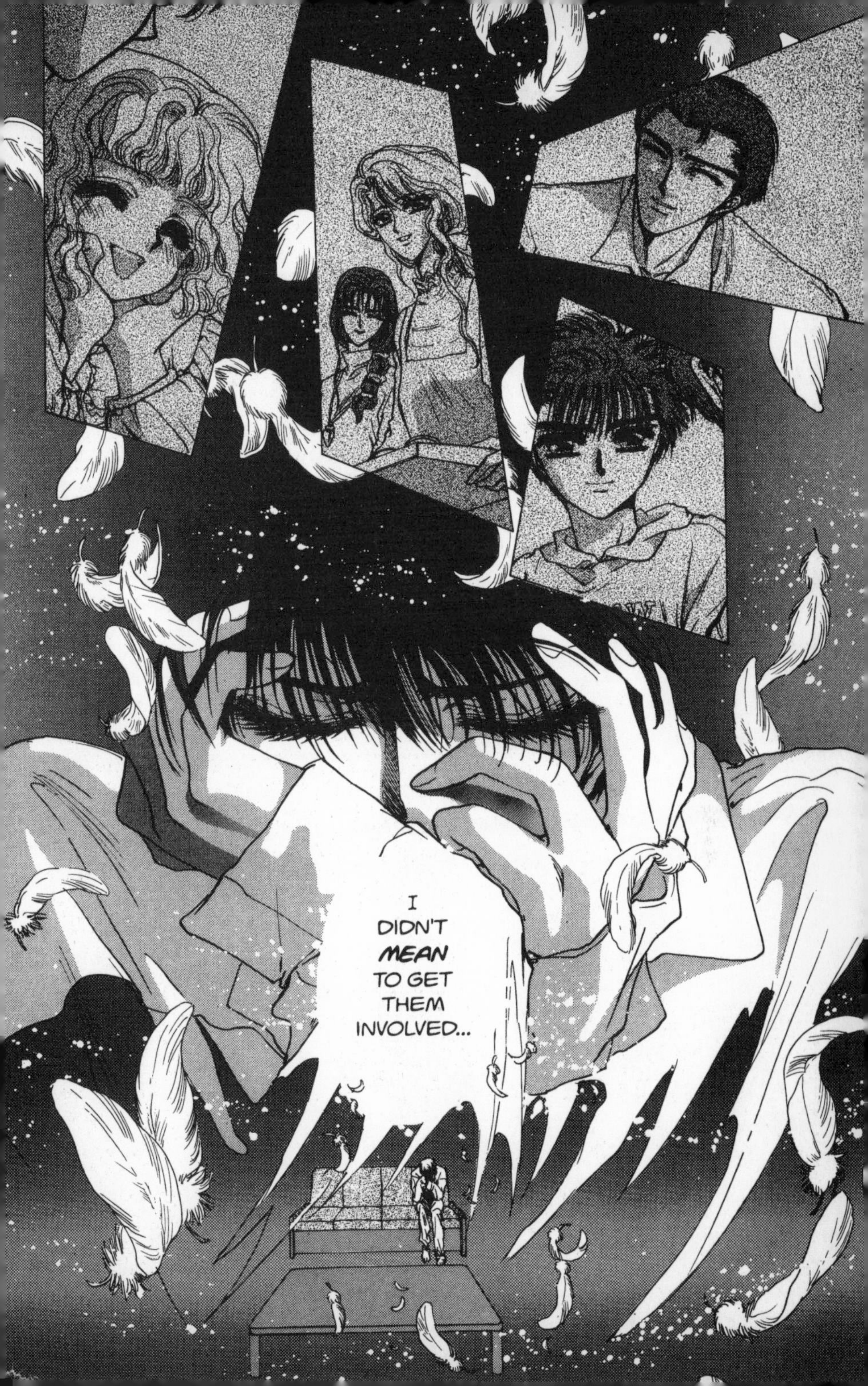
I DIDN'T *MEAN* TO GET THEM INVOLVED...

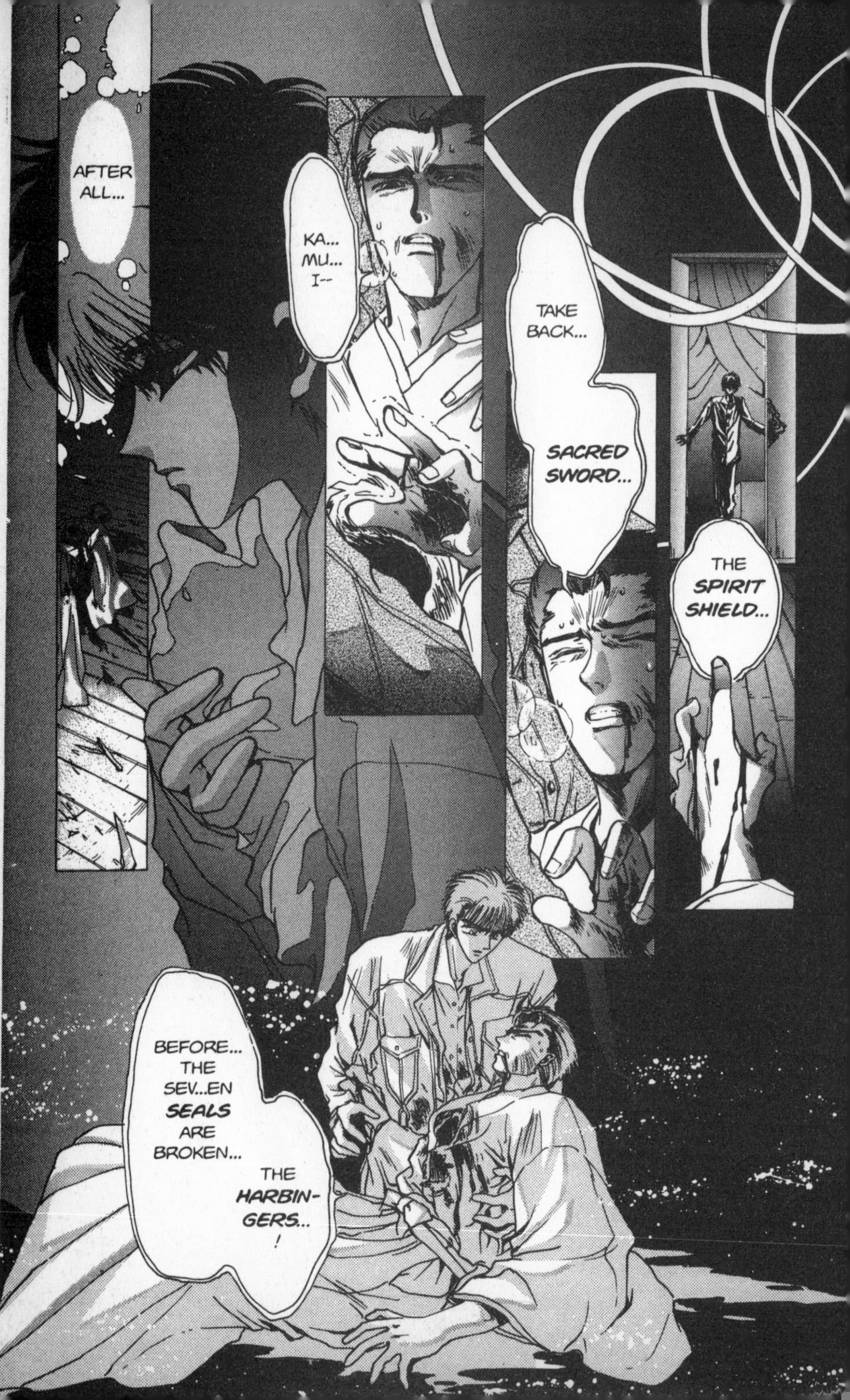
AFTER ALL...
KA... MU... I--
TAKE BACK... SACRED SWORD...
THE SPIRIT SHIELD...
BEFORE... THE SEV...EN SEALS ARE BROKEN... THE HARBIN-GERS... !

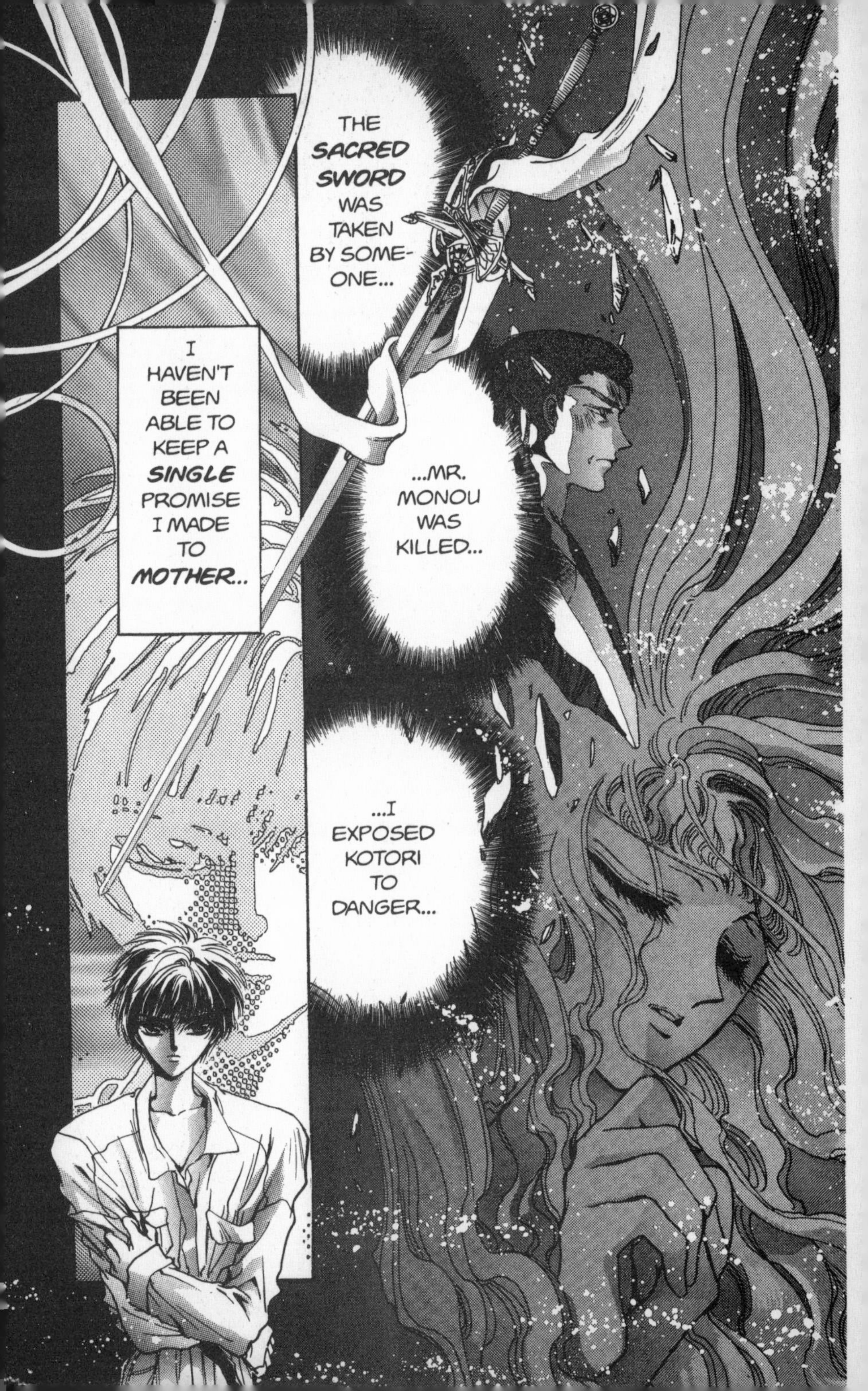
THE SACRED SWORD WAS TAKEN BY SOME-ONE...
I HAVEN'T BEEN ABLE TO KEEP A SINGLE PROMISE I MADE TO MOTHER...
...MR. MONOU WAS KILLED...
...I EXPOSED KOTORI TO DANGER...

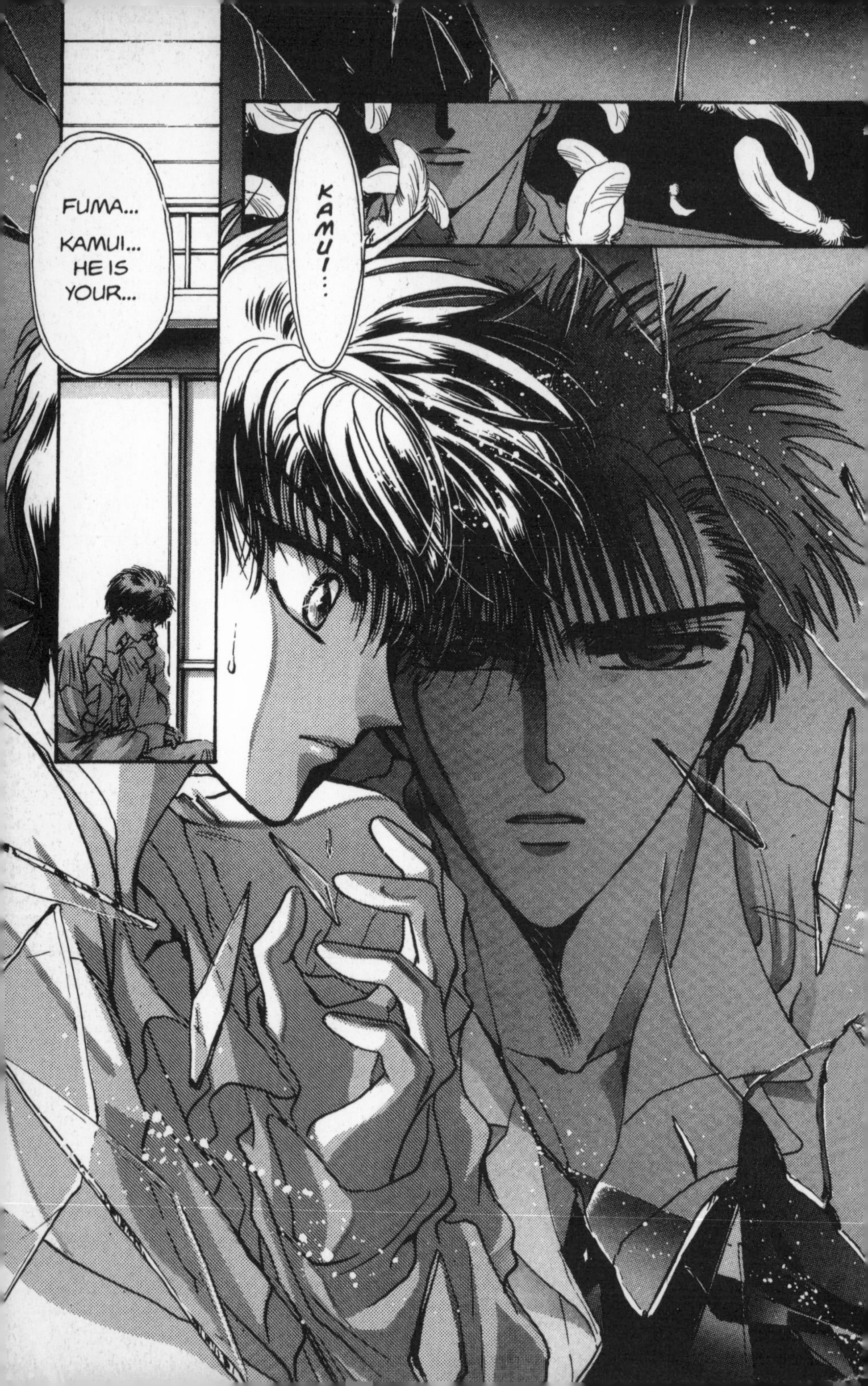
FUMA... KAMUI... HE IS YOUR...
KAMUI...

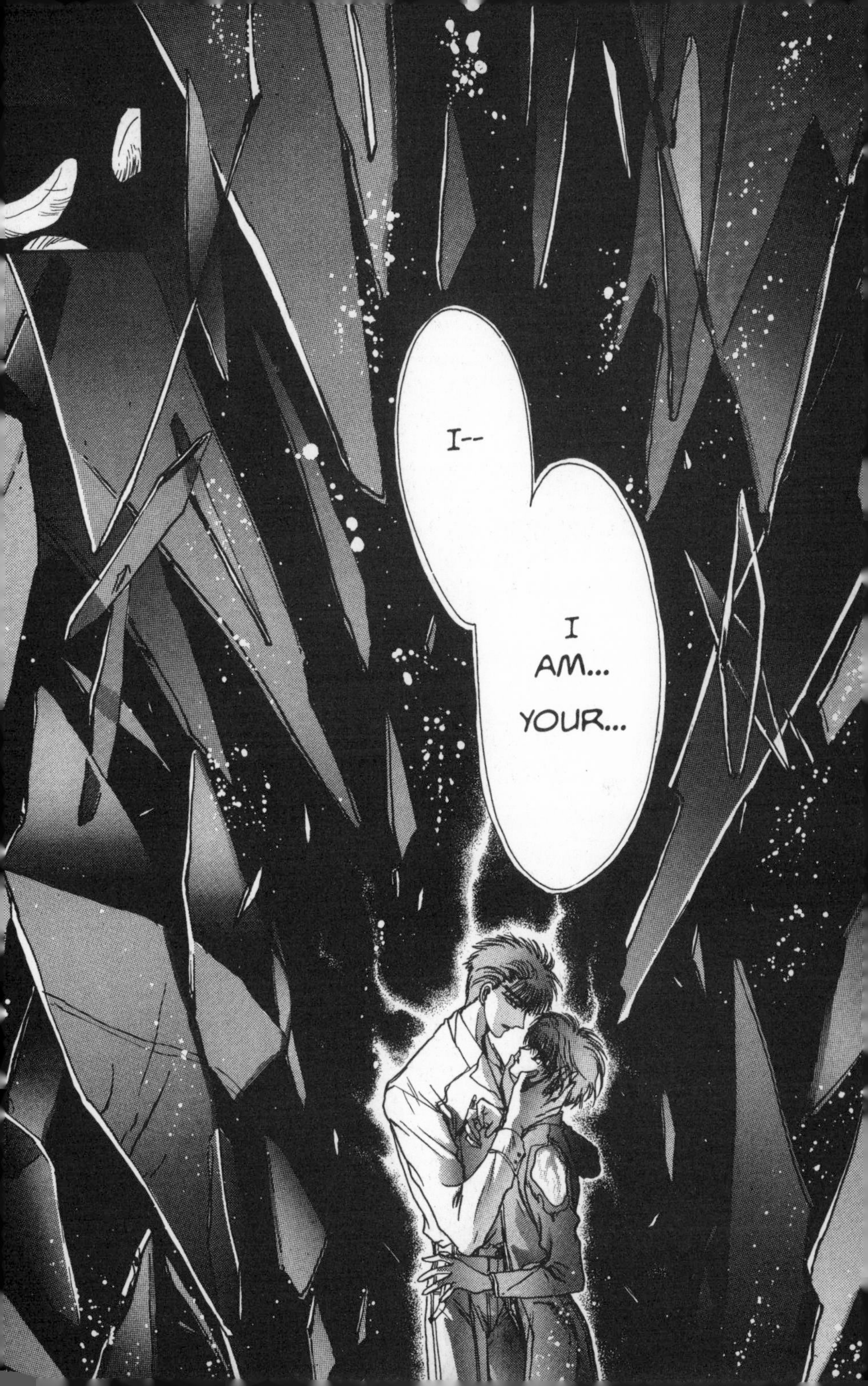
I--
I AM... YOUR...

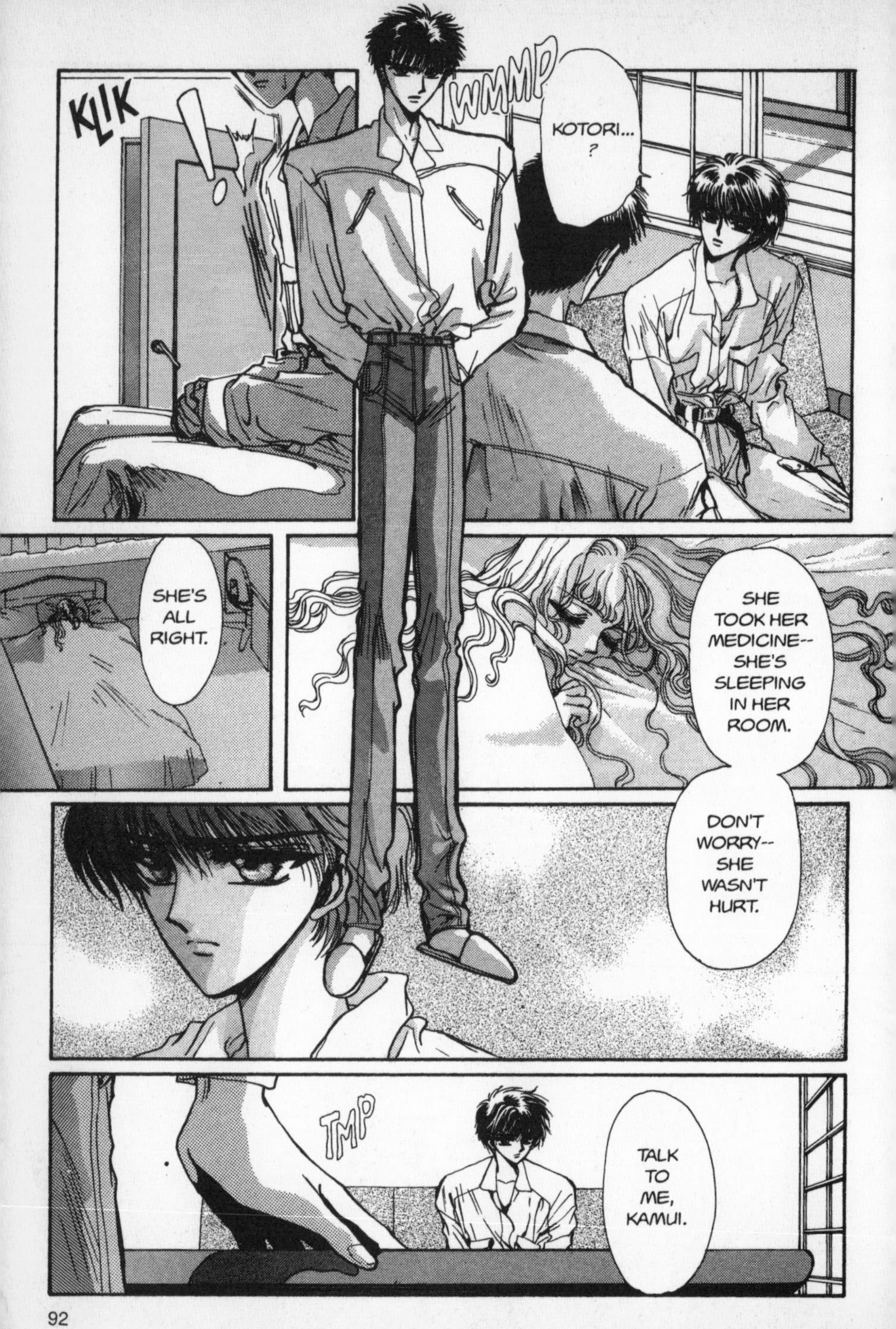
KLIK
WMMP
KOTORI... ?
SHE'S ALL RIGHT.
SHE TOOK HER MEDICINE-- SHE'S SLEEPING IN HER ROOM.
DON'T WORRY-- SHE WASN'T HURT.
TMP
TALK TO ME, KAMUI.

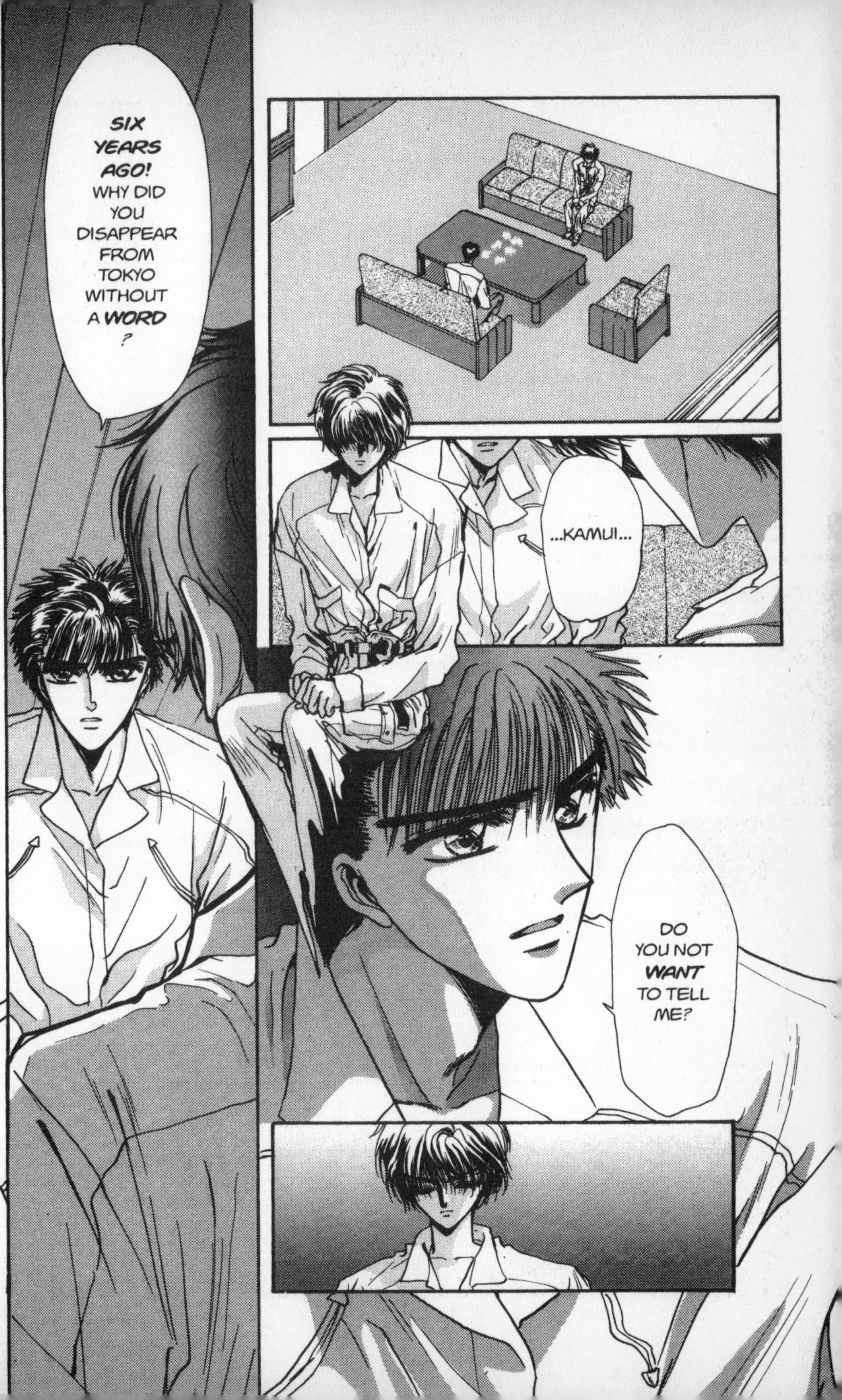
SIX YEARS AGO! WHY DID YOU DISAPPEAR FROM TOKYO WITHOUT A WORD ?
...KAMUI...
DO YOU NOT WANT TO TELL ME?

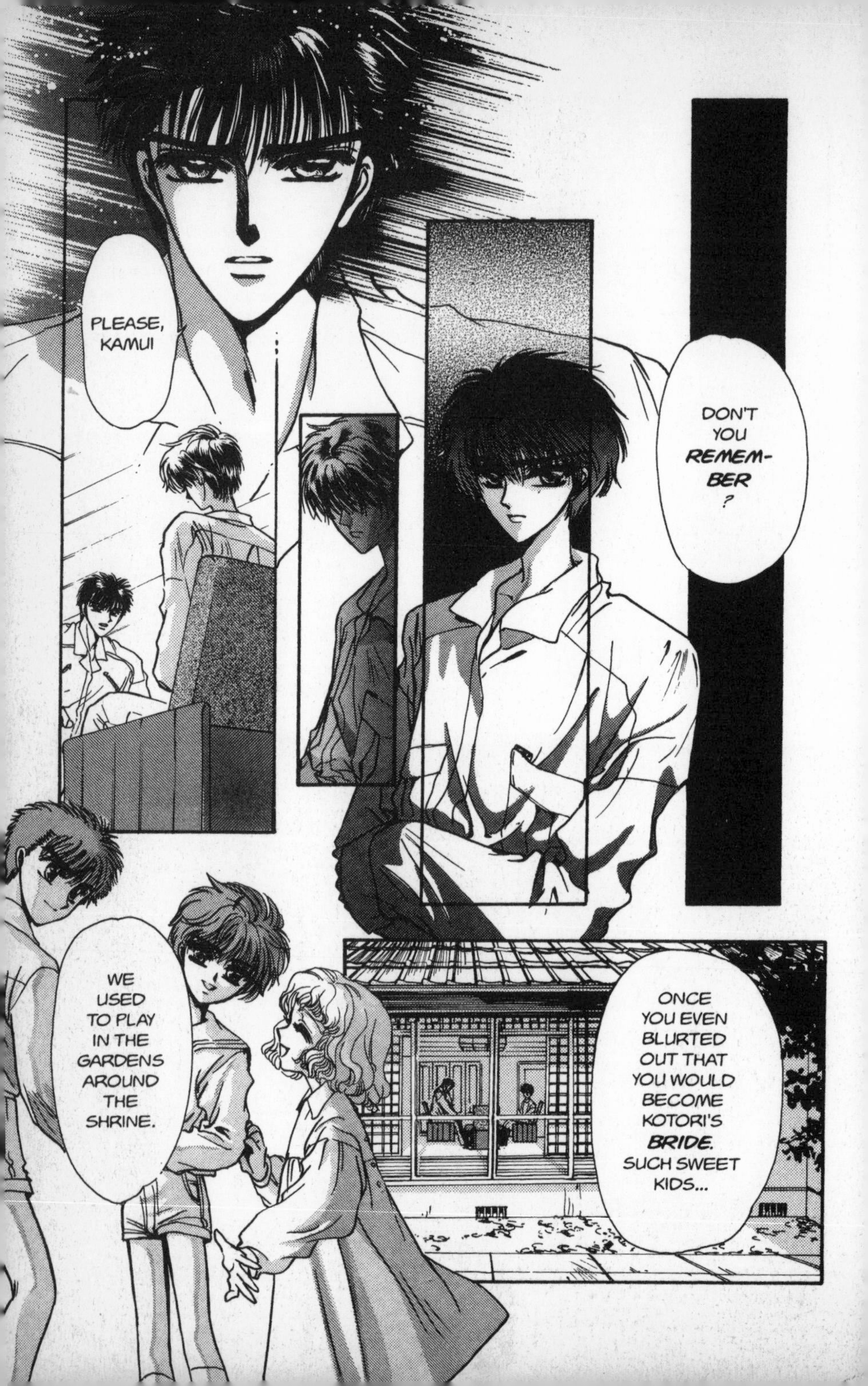
PLEASE, KAMUI
DON'T YOU REMEMBER?
WE USED TO PLAY IN THE GARDENS AROUND THE SHRINE.
ONCE YOU EVEN BLURTED OUT THAT YOU WOULD BECOME KOTORI'S BRIDE. SUCH SWEET KIDS...

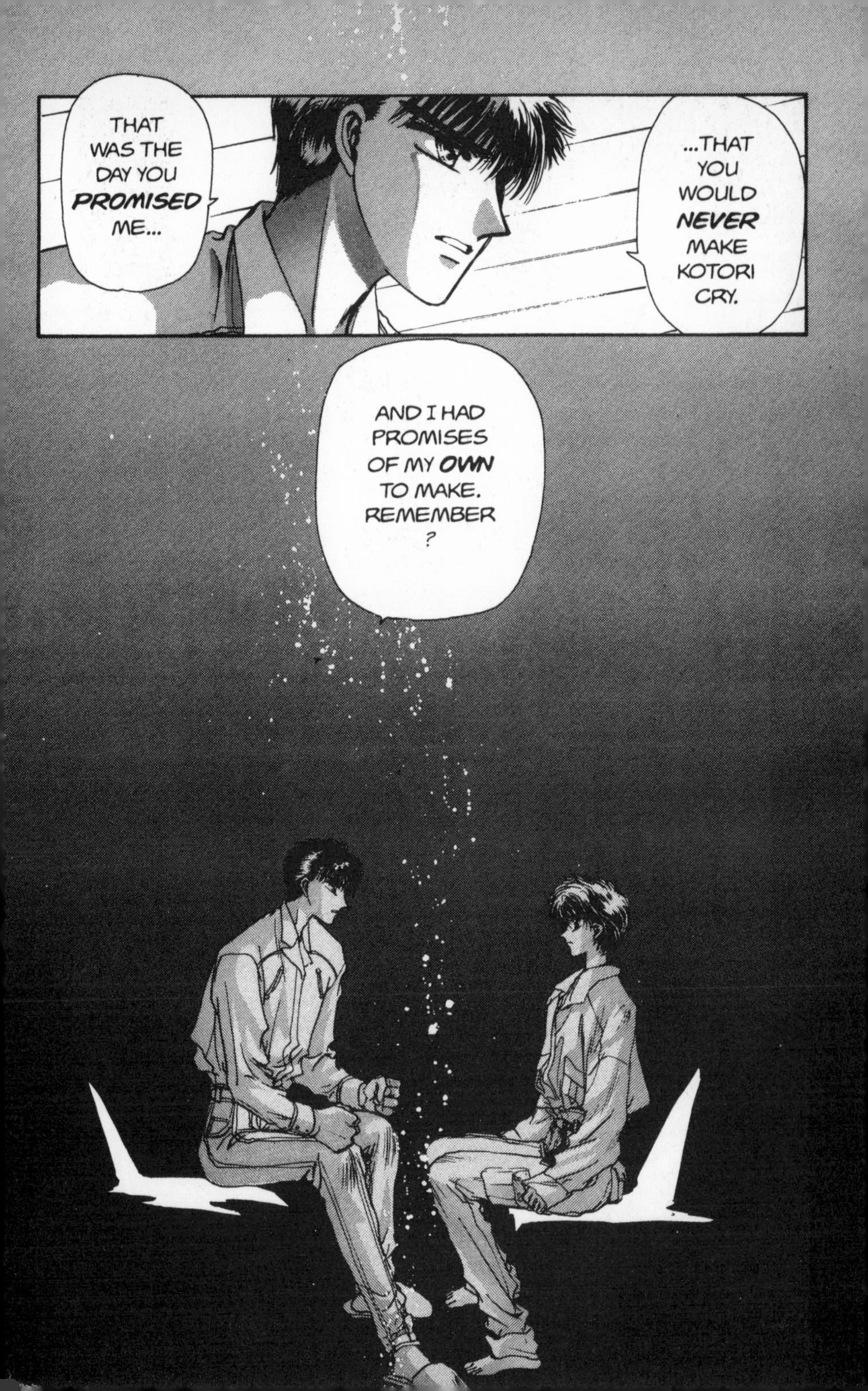
THAT WAS THE DAY YOU **PROMISED** ME...
...THAT YOU WOULD **NEVER** MAKE KOTORI CRY.
AND I HAD PROMISES OF MY **OWN** TO MAKE. REMEMBER ?

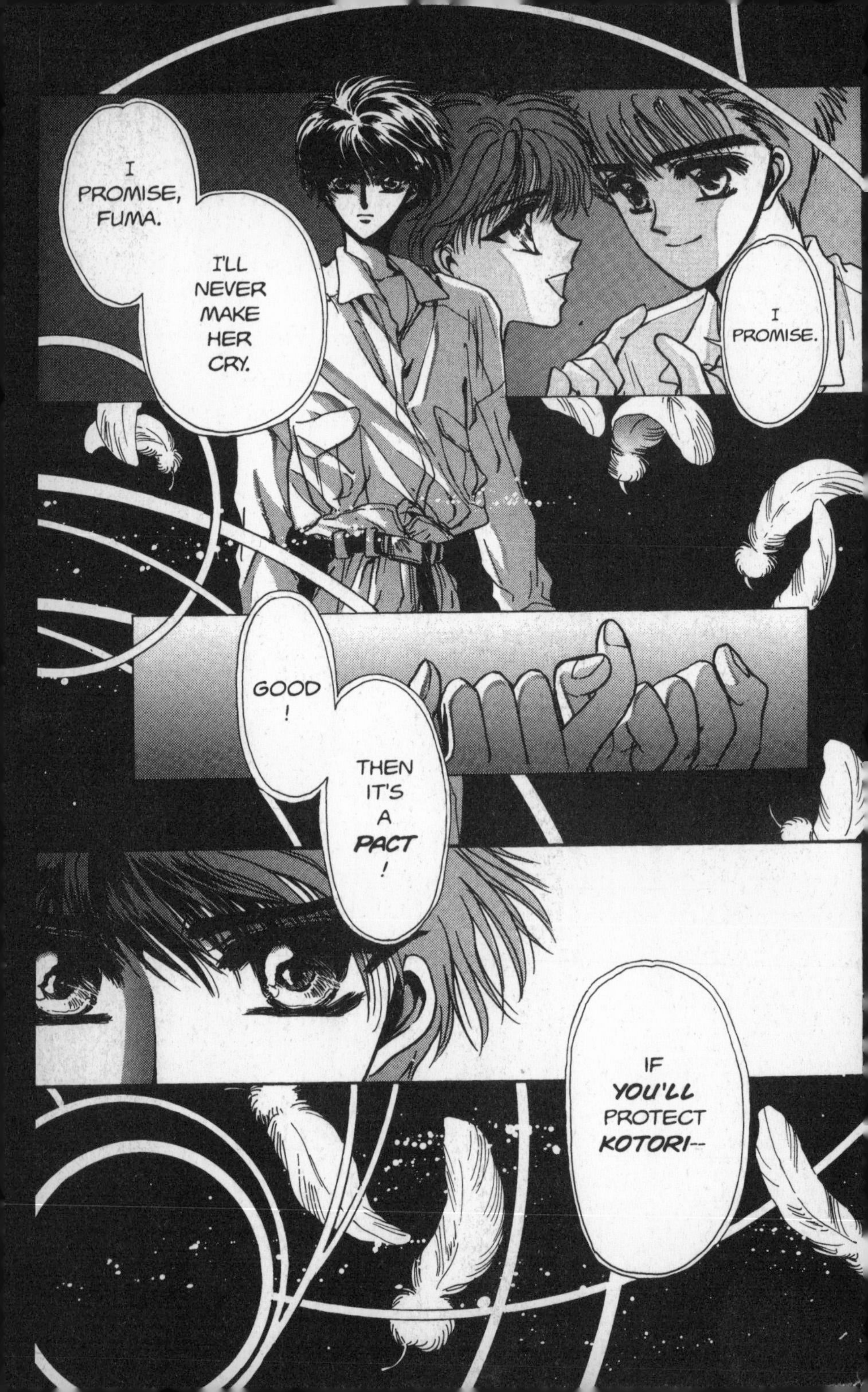
I PROMISE, FUMA.
I'LL NEVER MAKE HER CRY.
I PROMISE.
GOOD!
THEN IT'S A *PACT*!
IF *YOU'LL* PROTECT *KOTORI*--

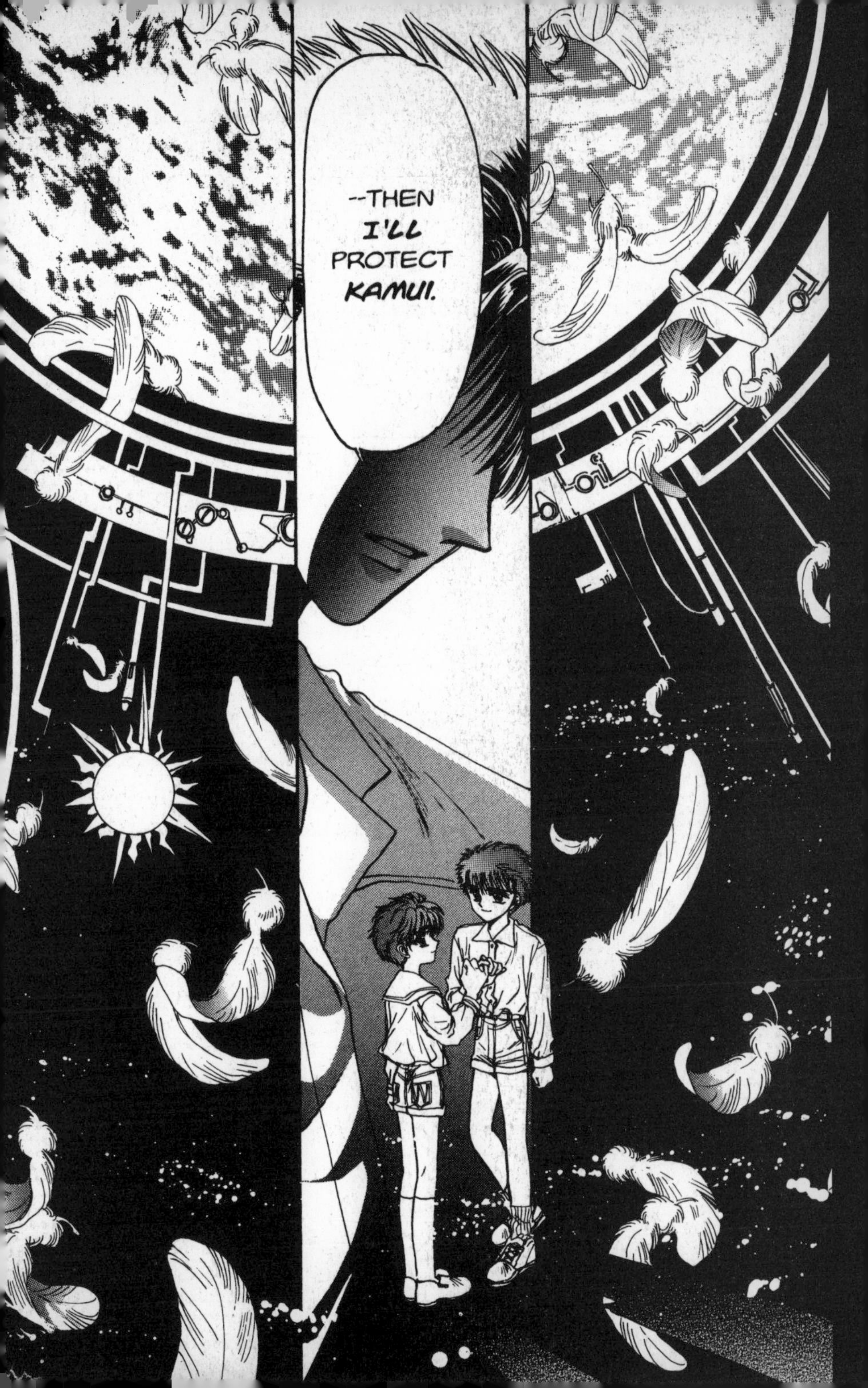
--THEN I'LL PROTECT KAMUI.

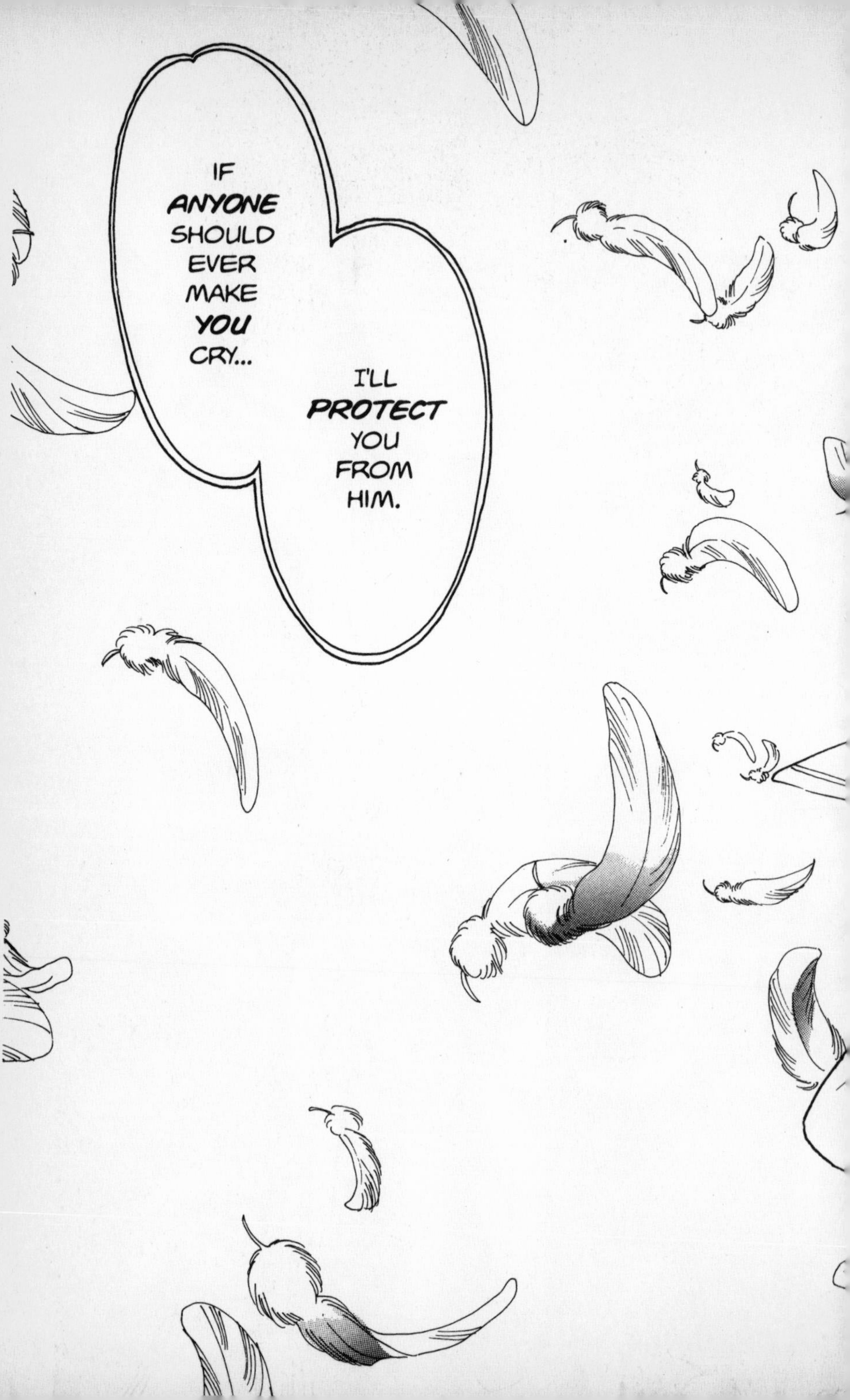
IF ANYONE SHOULD EVER MAKE YOU CRY...
I'LL PROTECT YOU FROM HIM.

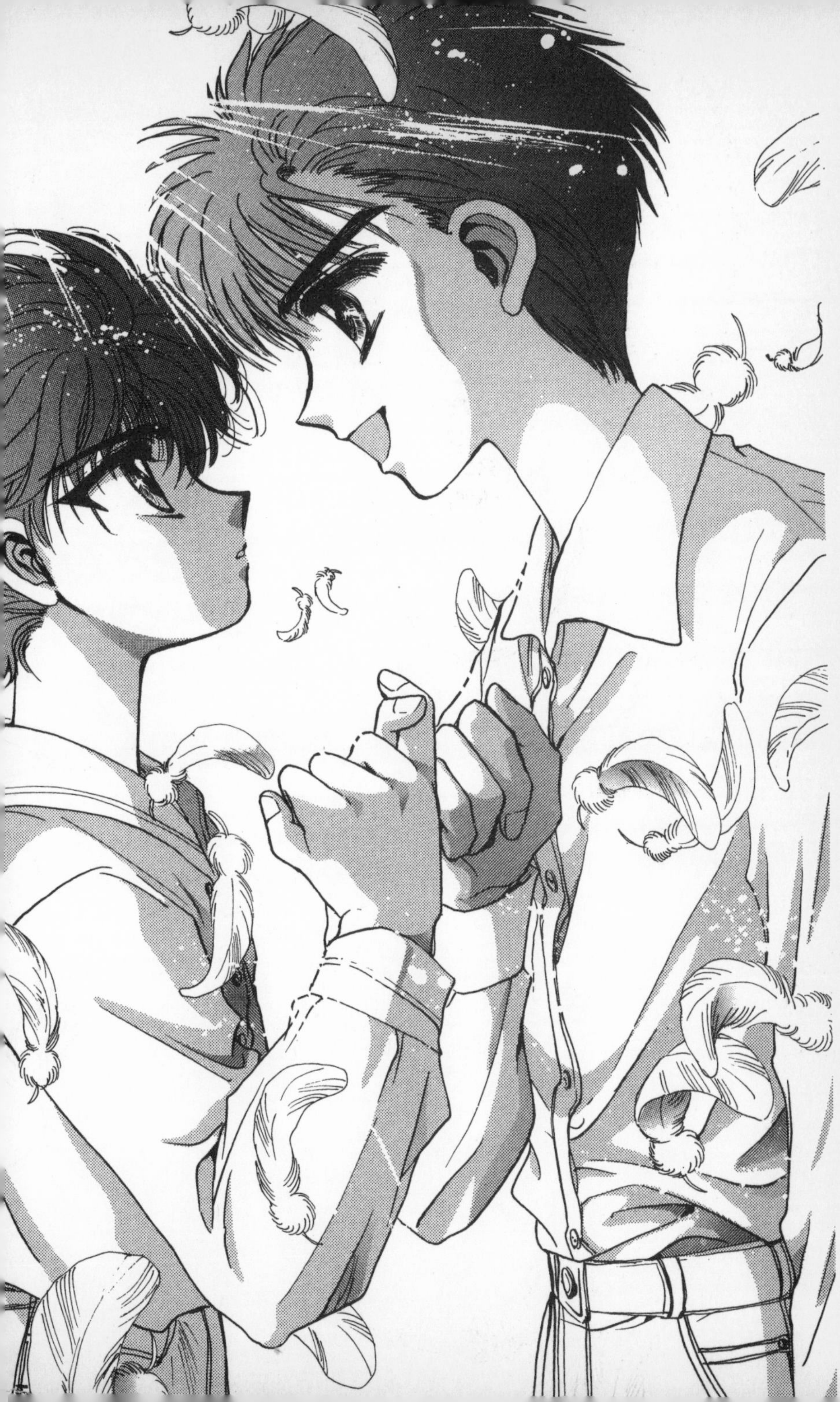

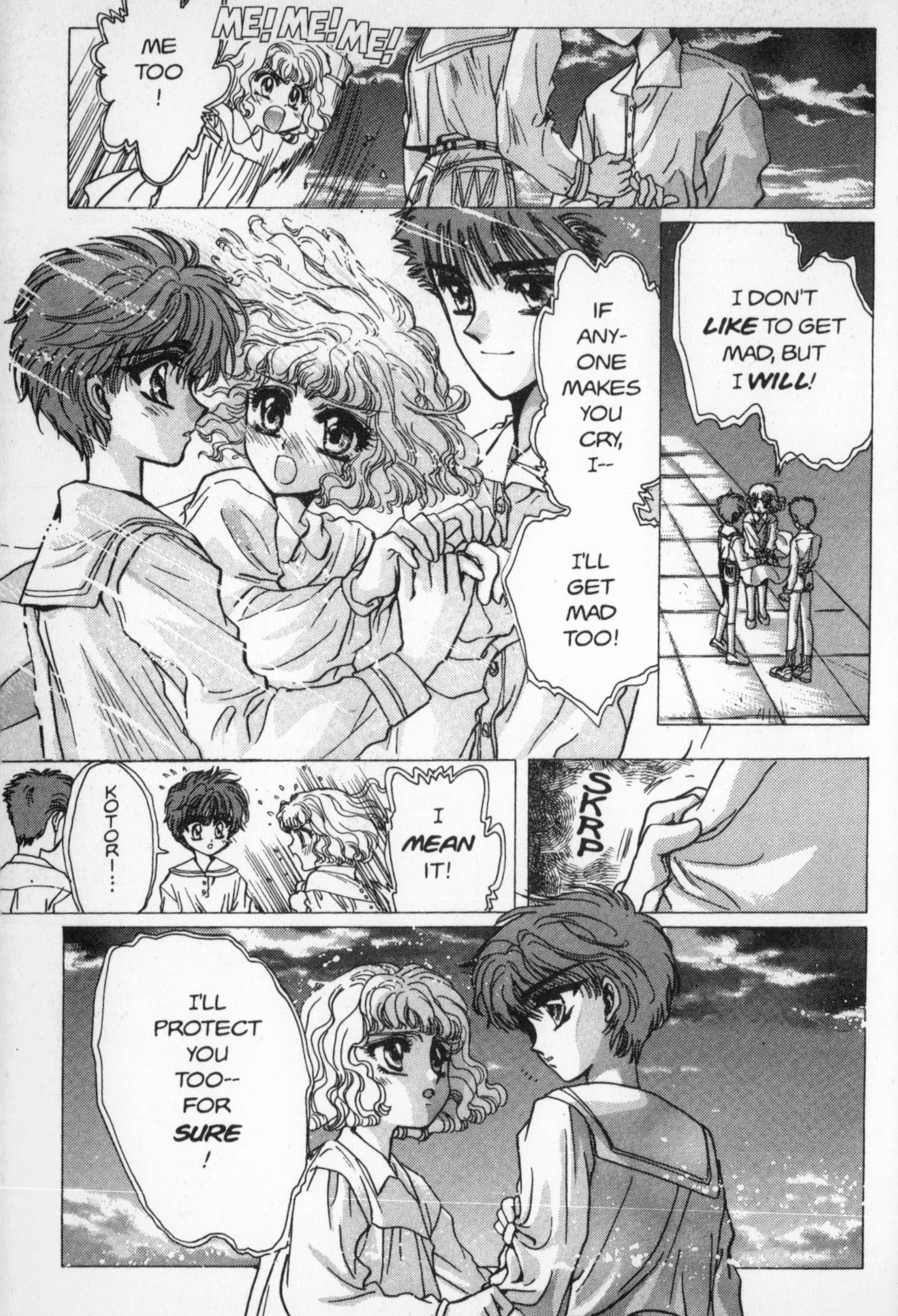
ME TOO !
ME! ME! ME!
IF ANY-ONE MAKES YOU CRY, I--
I'LL GET MAD TOO!
I DON'T LIKE TO GET MAD, BUT I WILL!
KOTORI...
I MEAN IT!
SKRP
I'LL PROTECT YOU TOO-- FOR SURE !

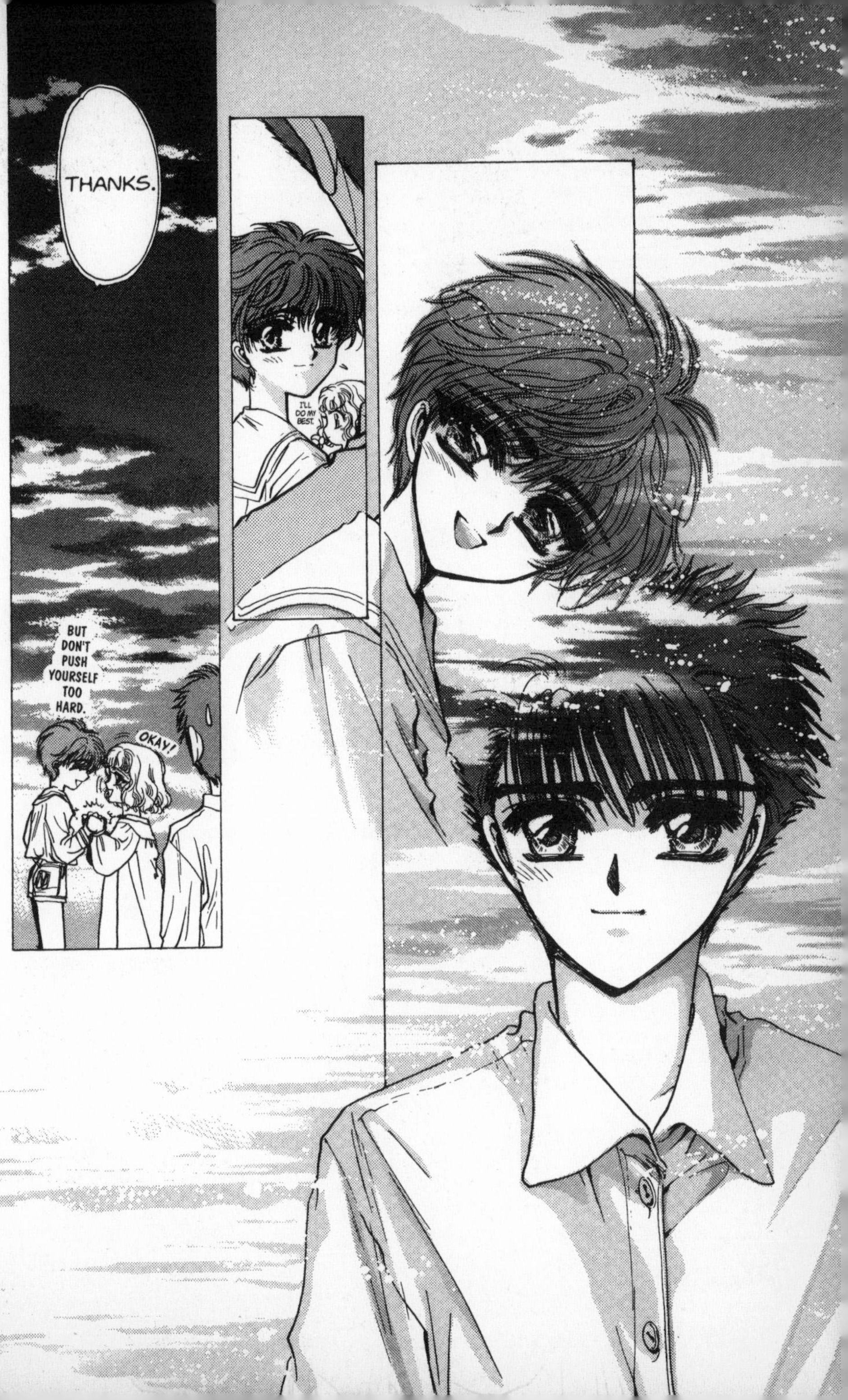
THANKS.
BUT DON'T PUSH YOURSELF TOO HARD.
OKAY!
I'LL DO MY BEST.

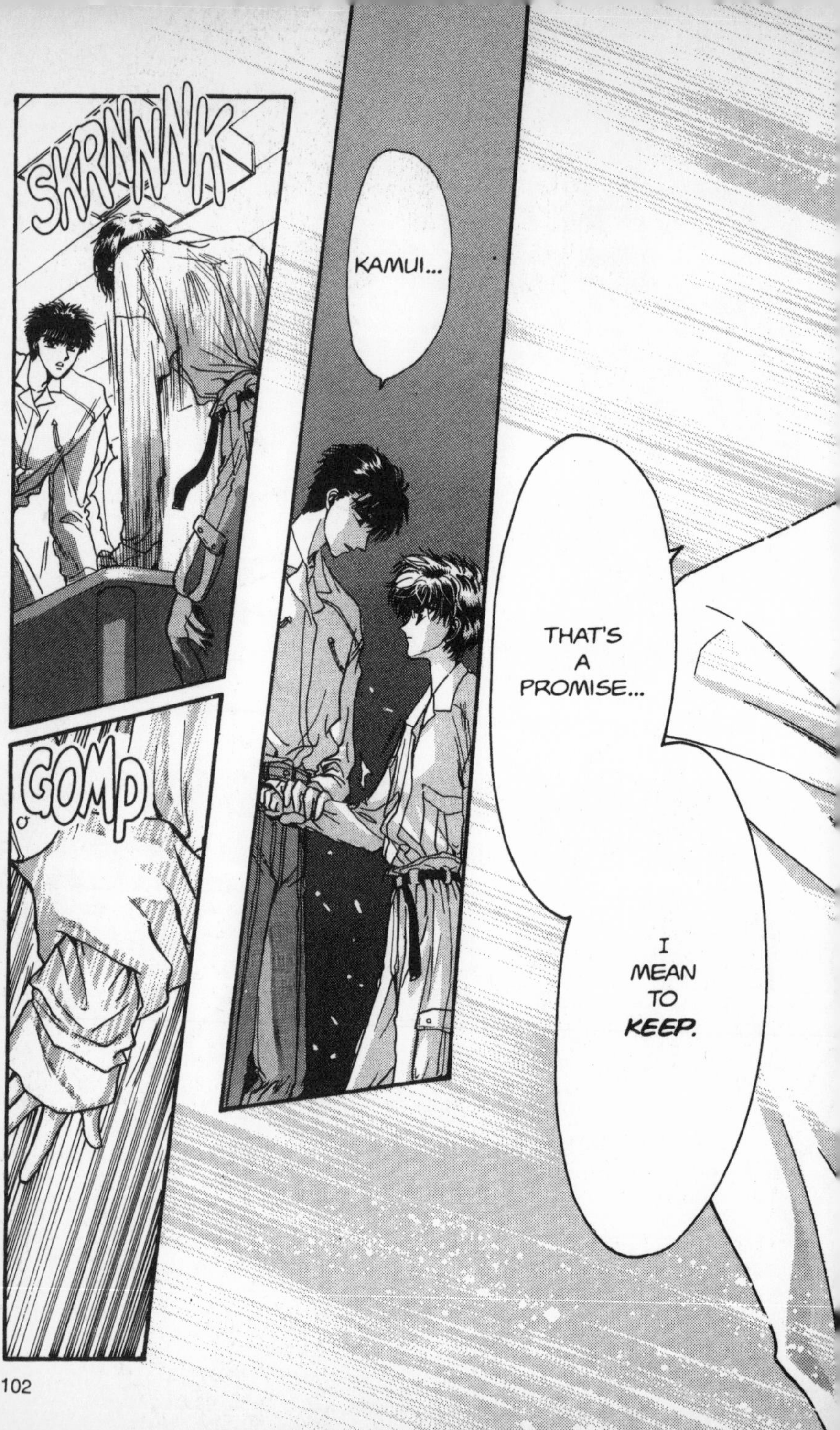
SKRNNNK
GOMP
KAMUI...
THAT'S A PROMISE...
I MEAN TO KEEP.

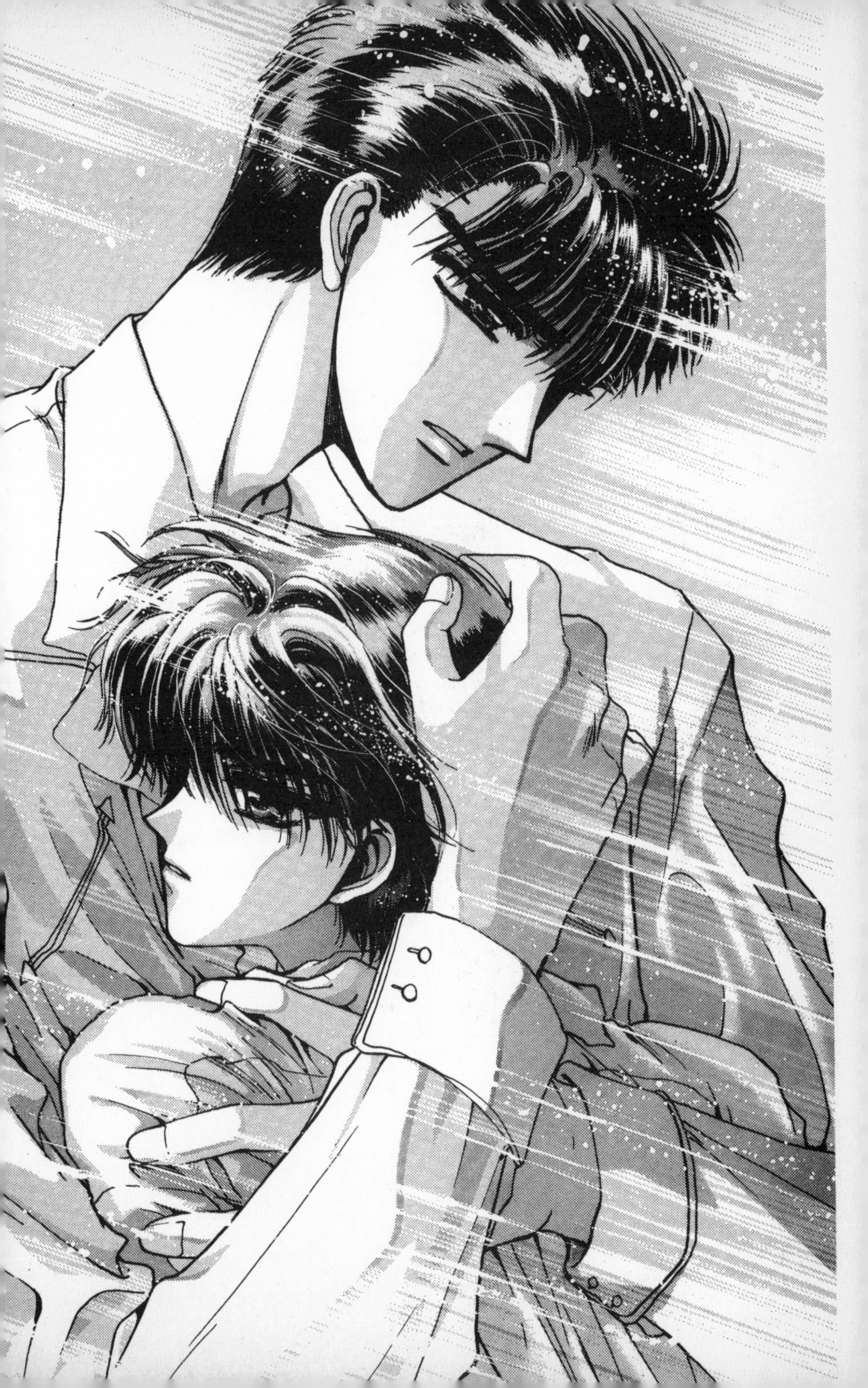

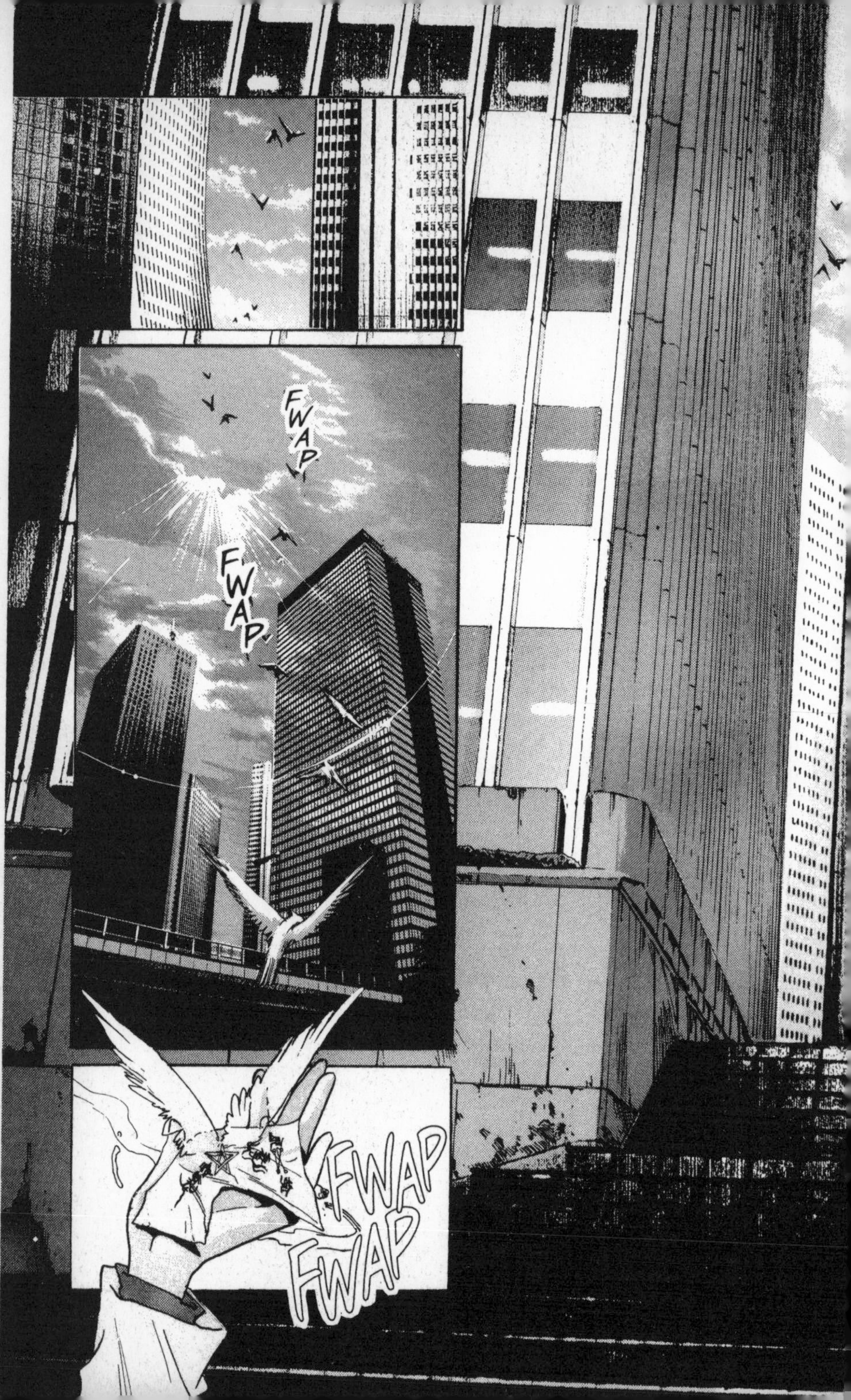
FWAP
FWAP
FWAP
FWAP

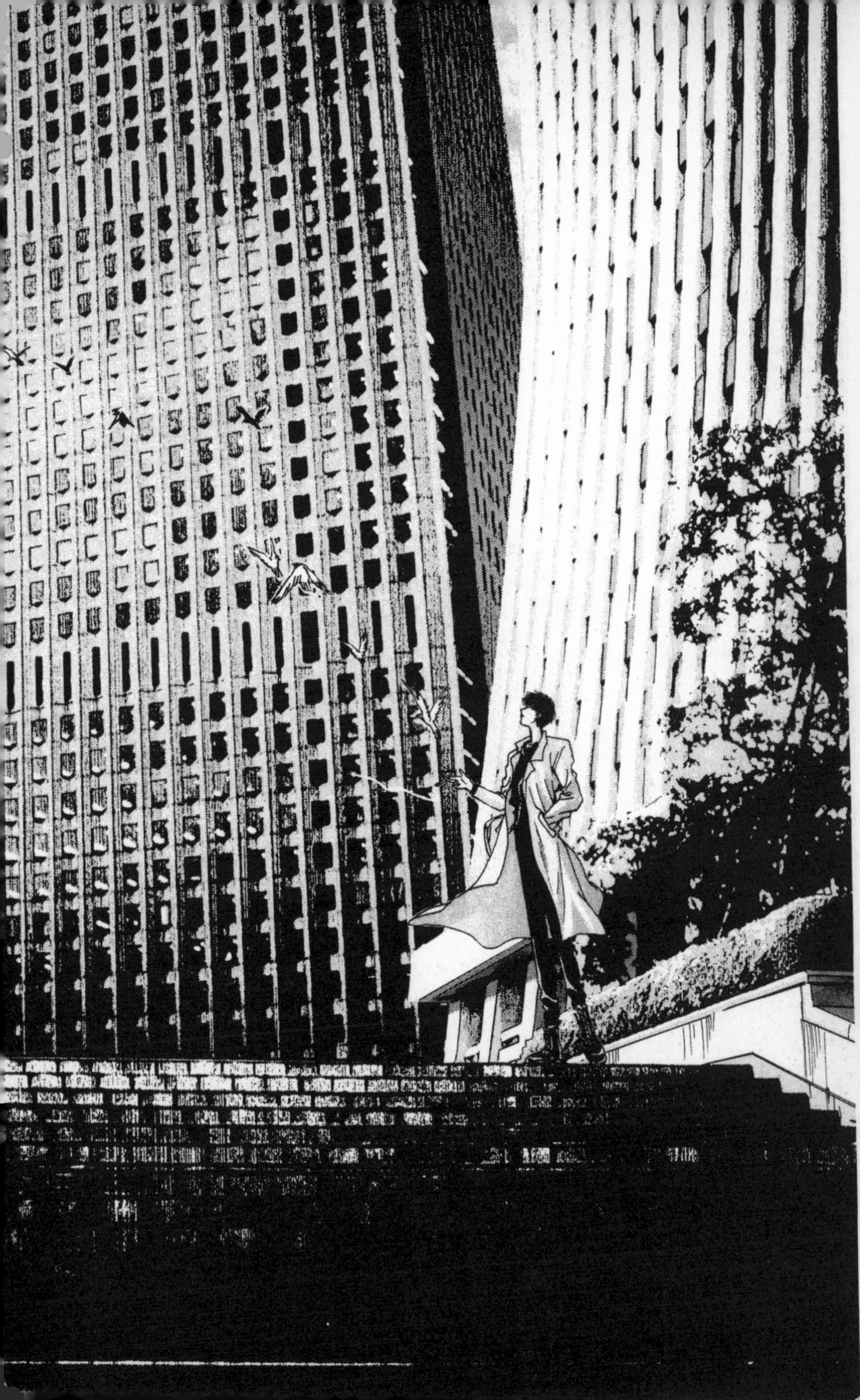

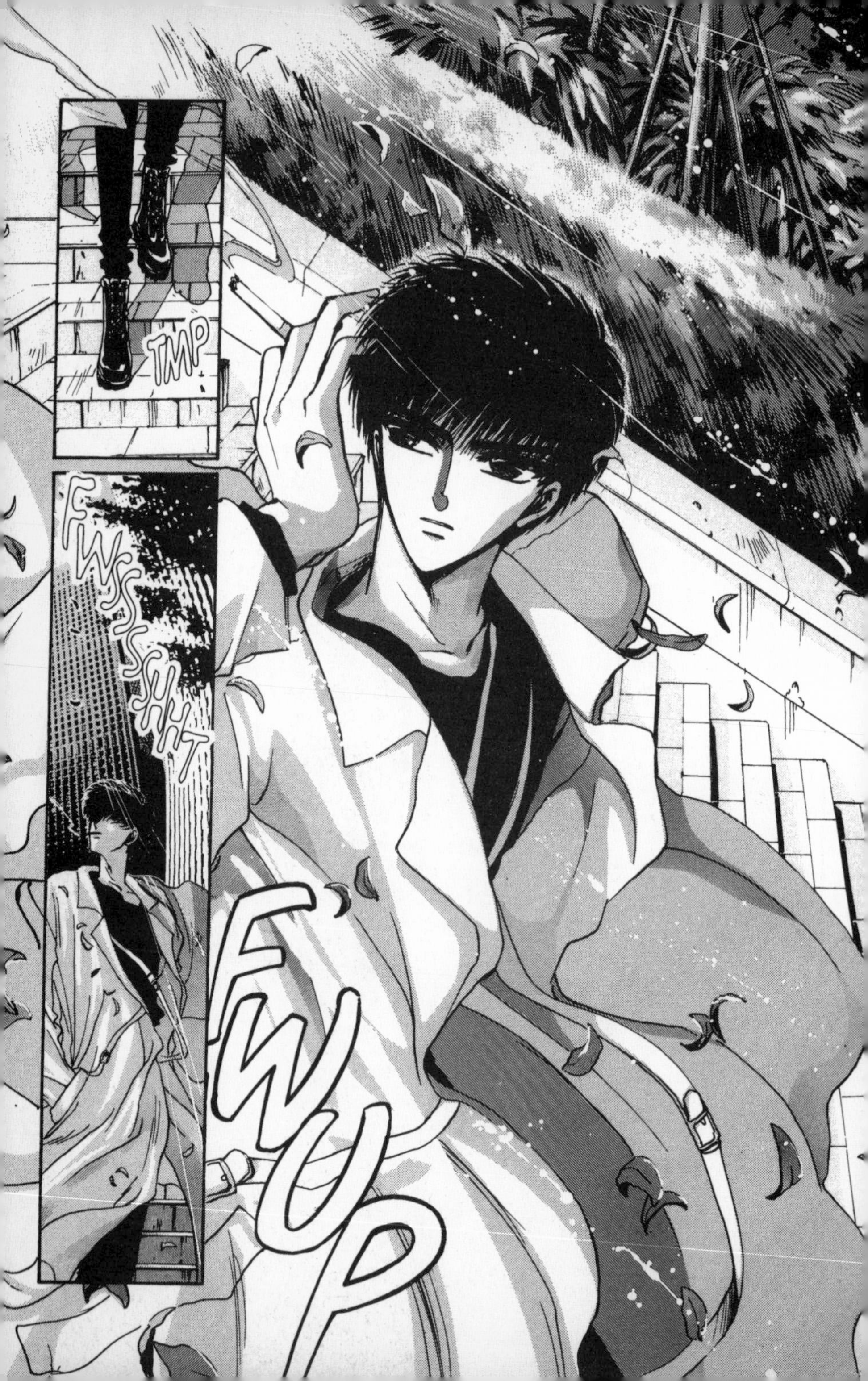
TMP
FWSSSSHHT
FWUD

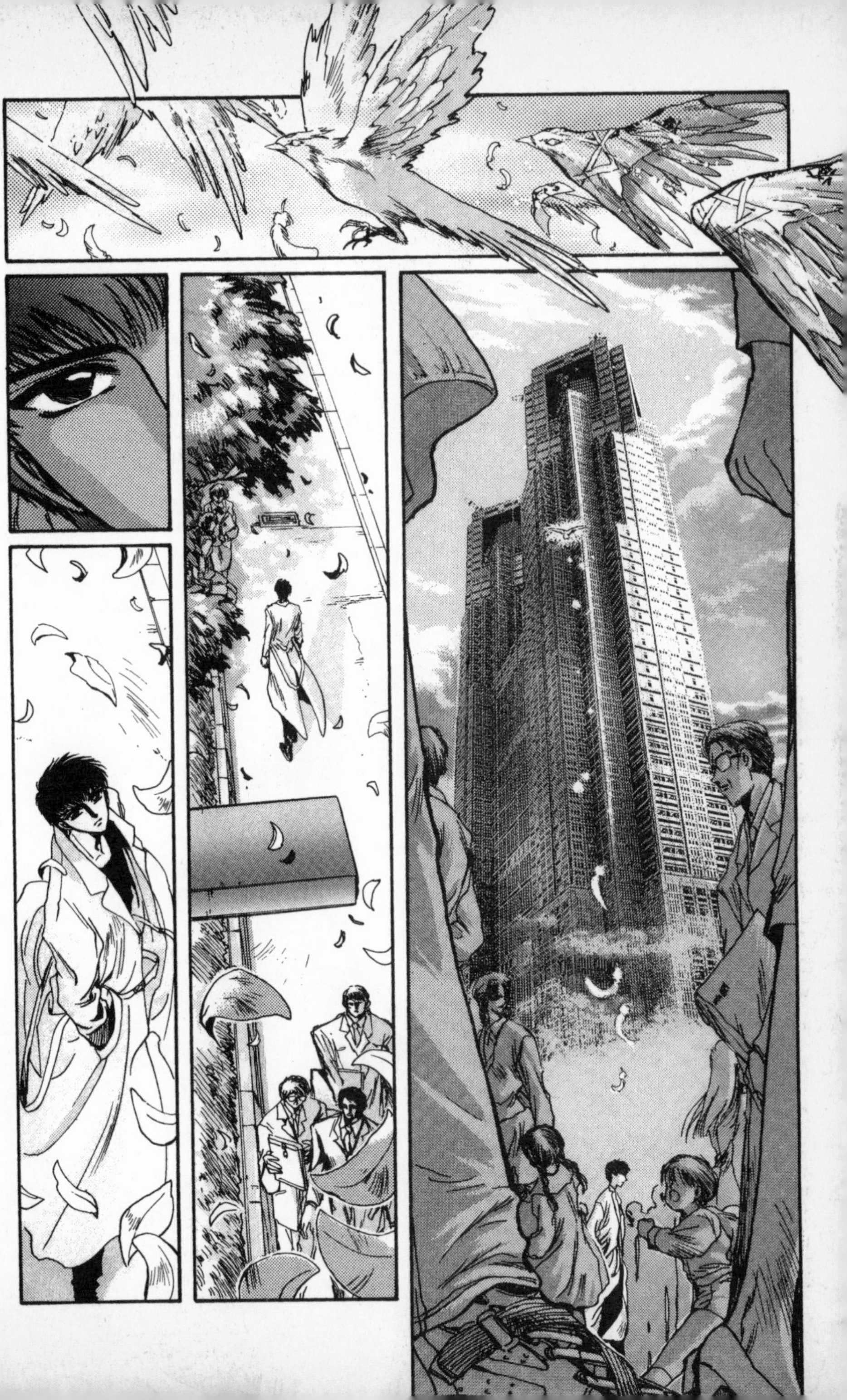

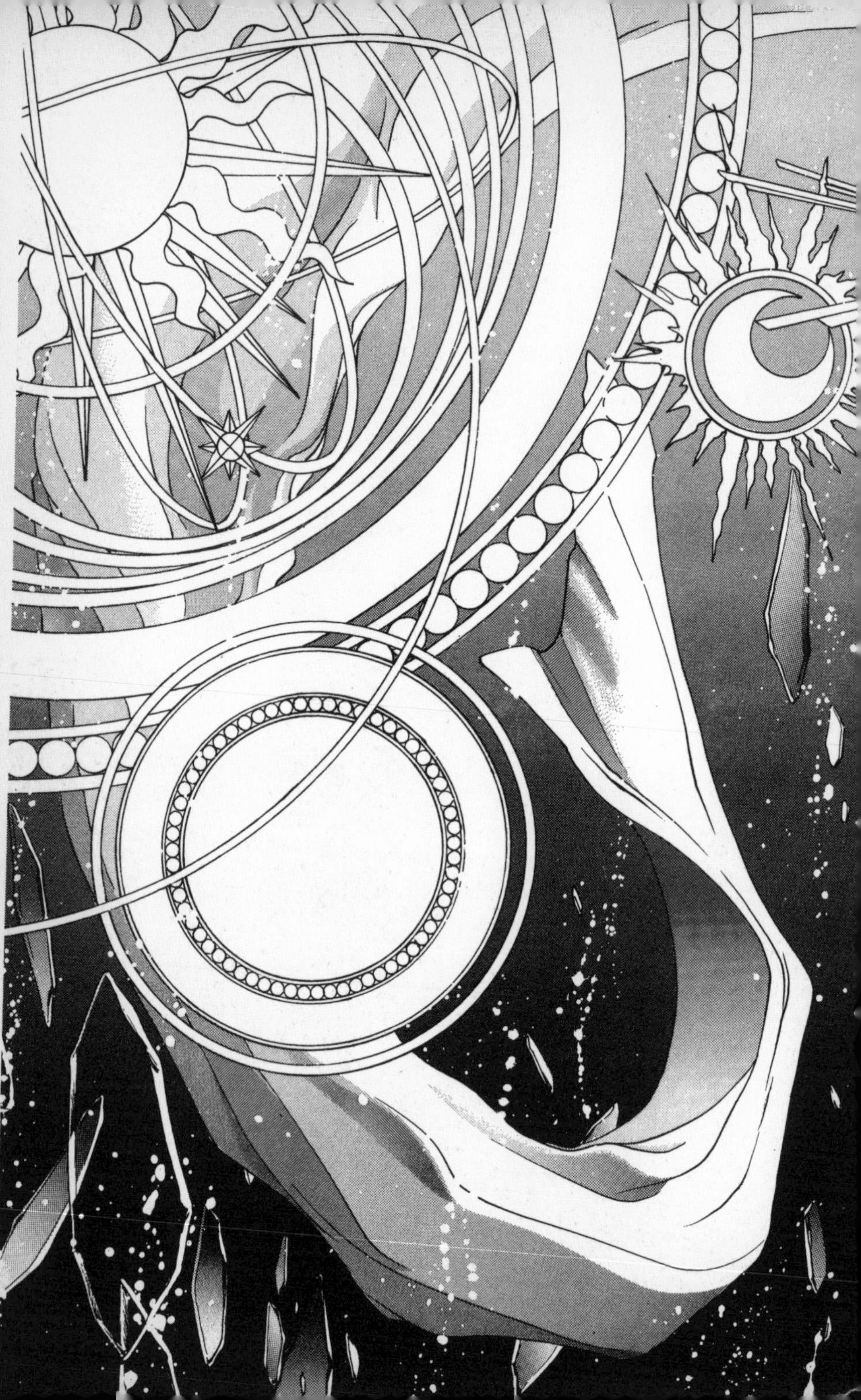

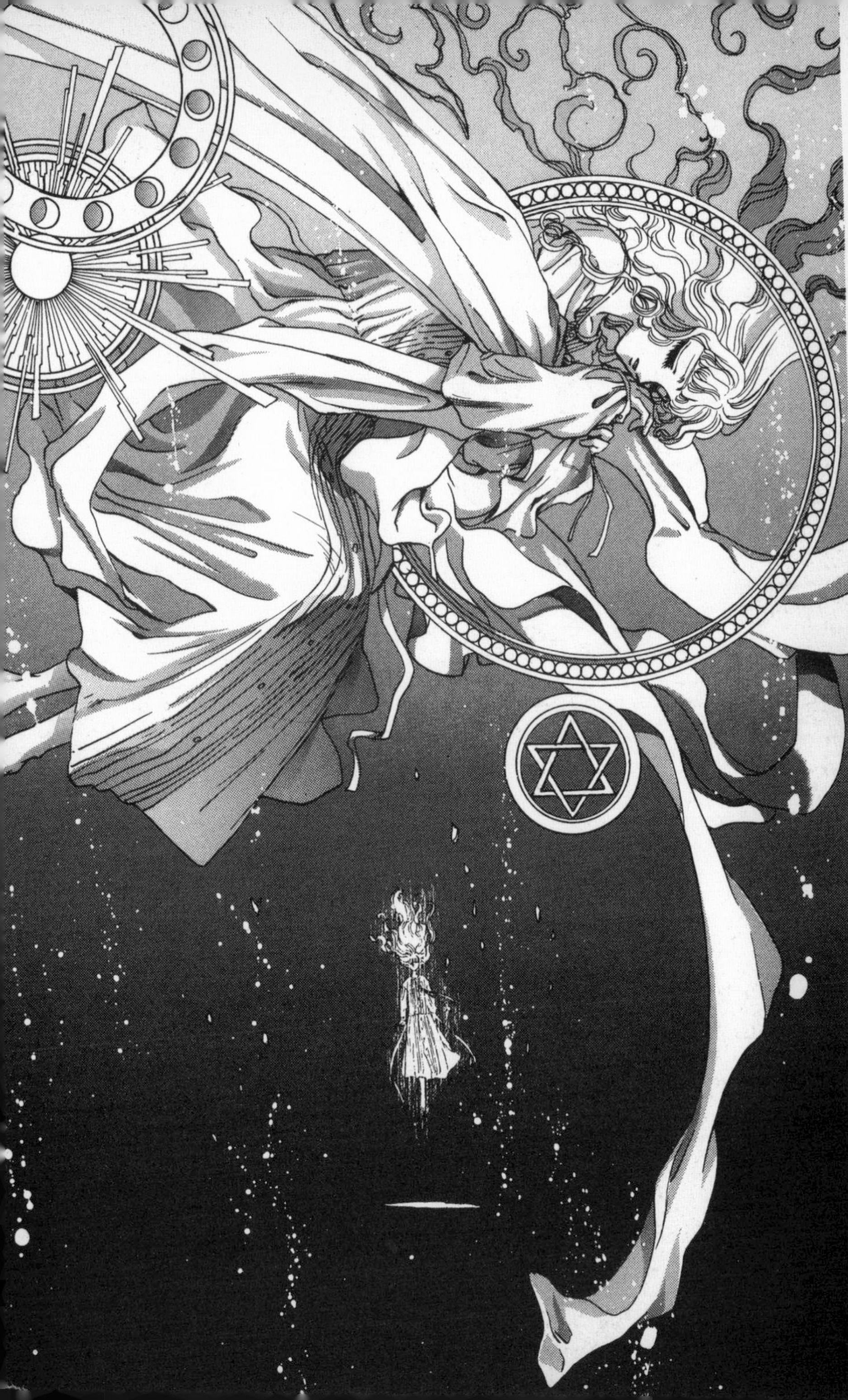

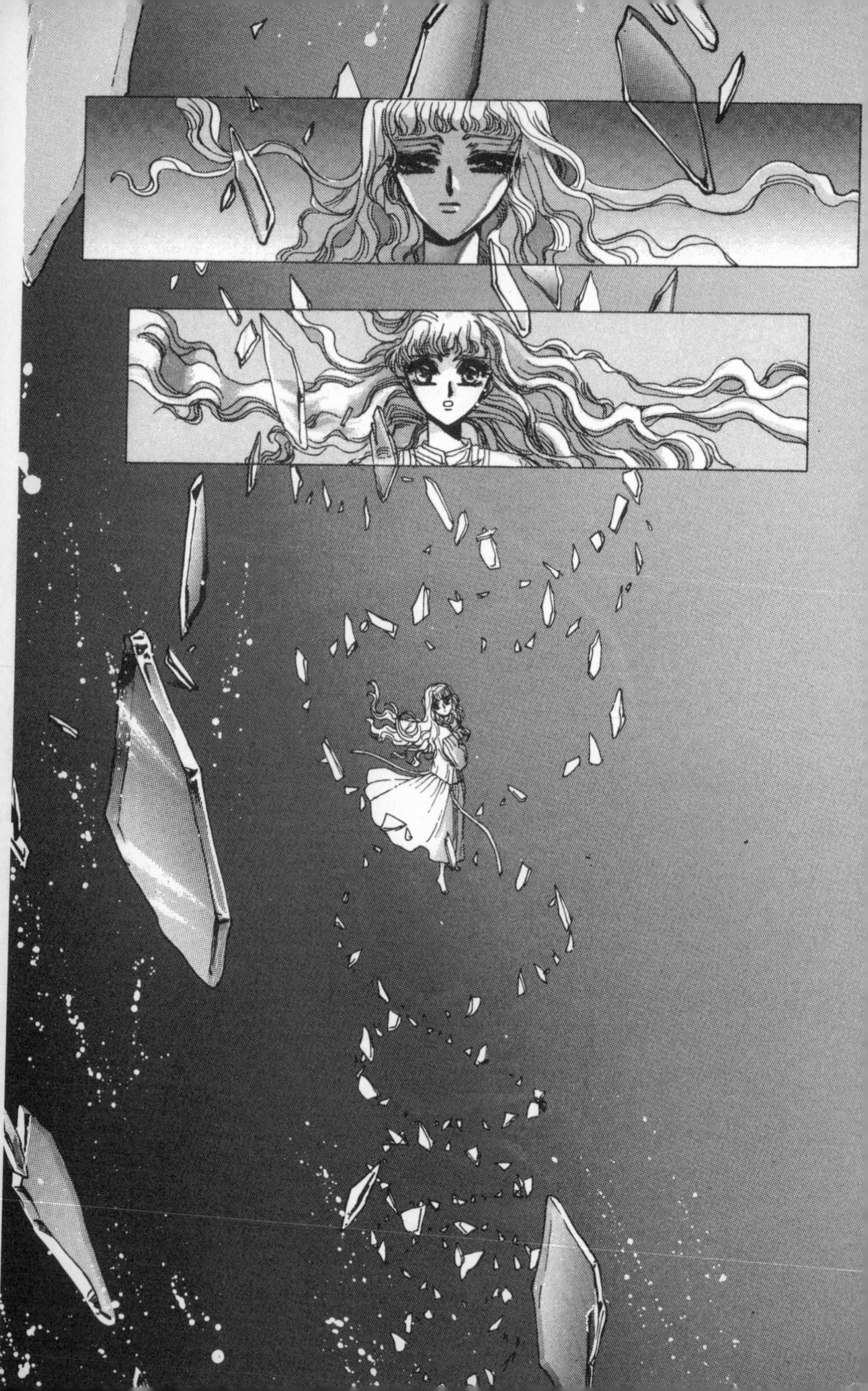

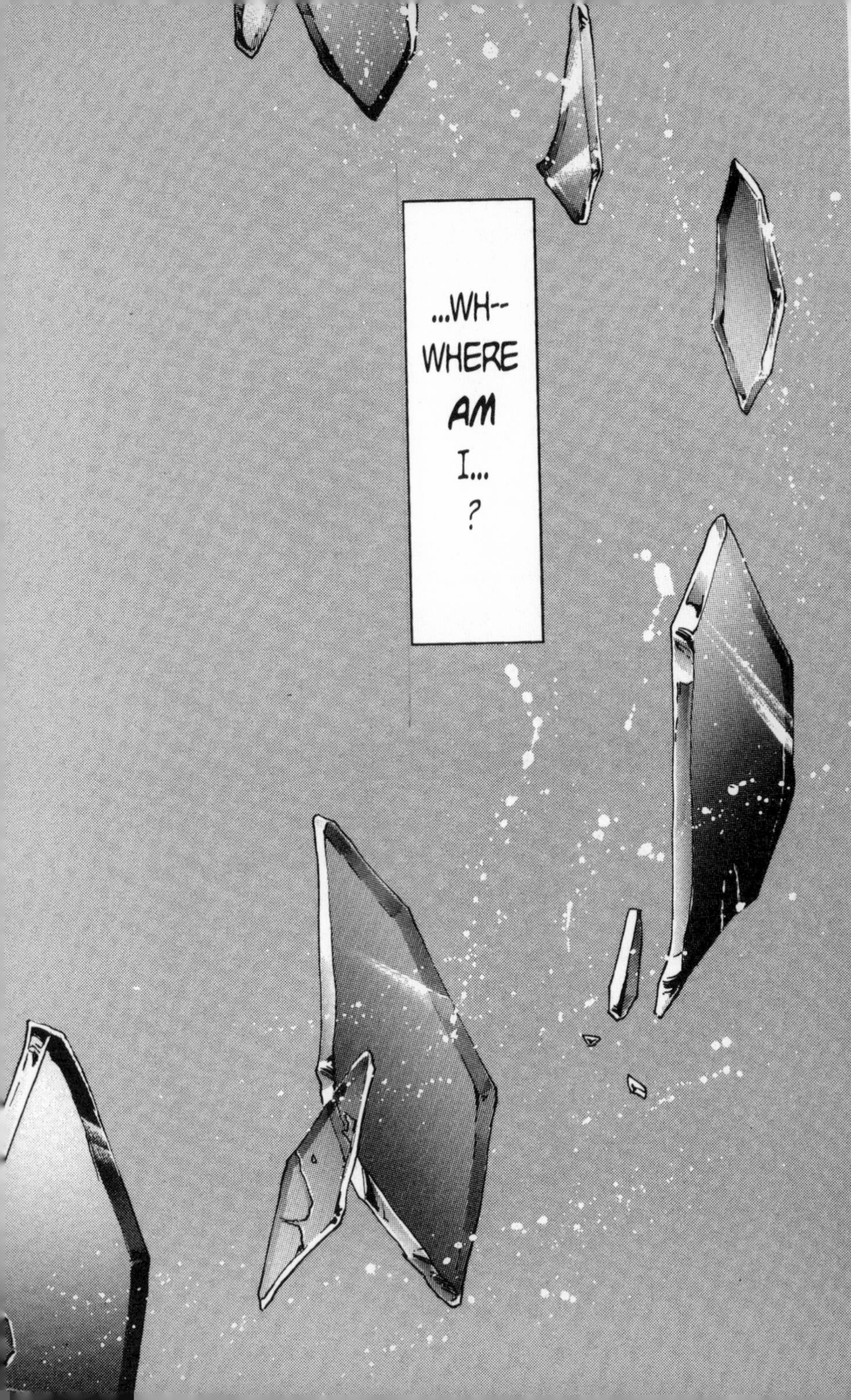
...WH--
WHERE
AM
I...
?

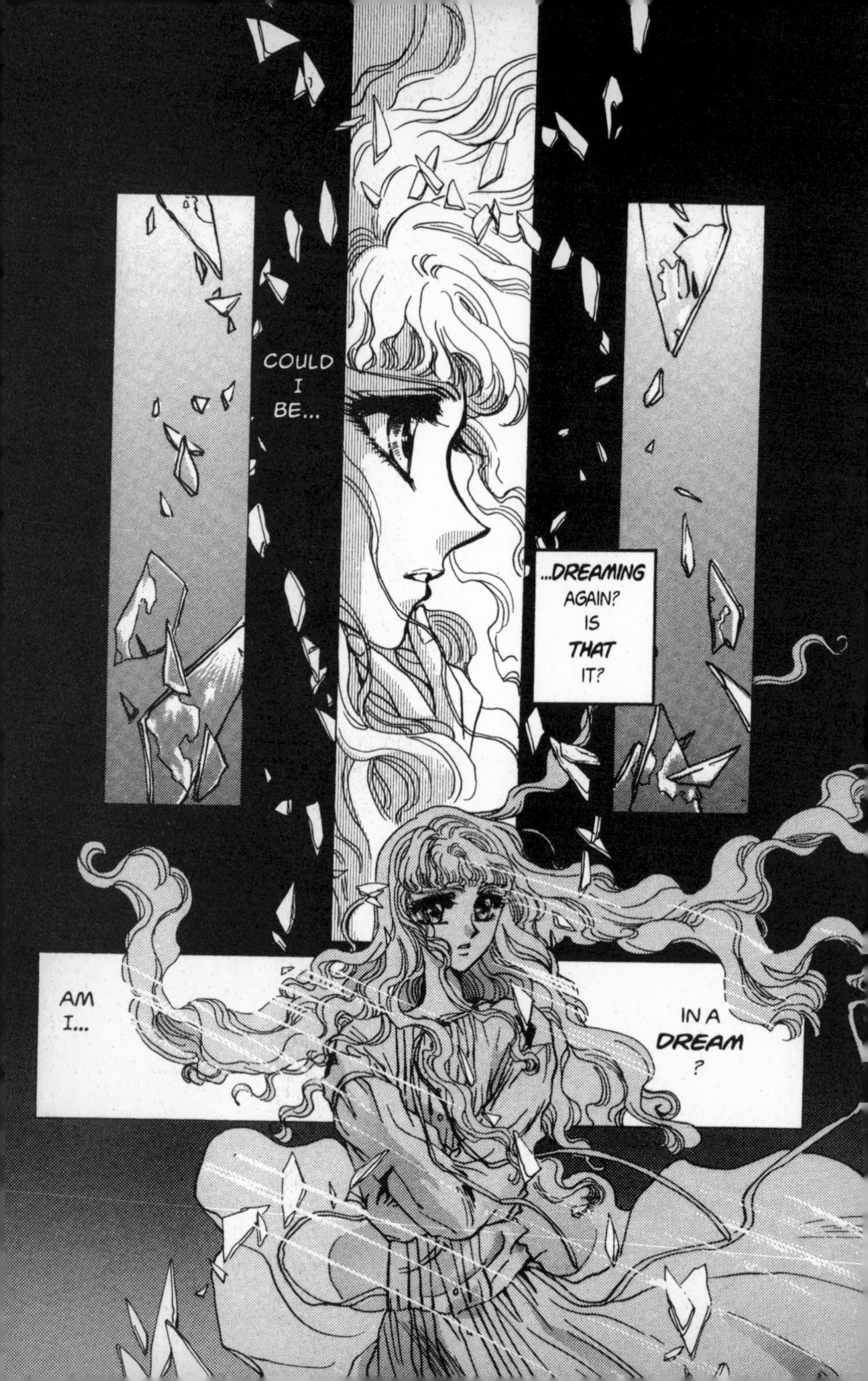
COULD I BE...
...DREAMING AGAIN? IS THAT IT?
AM I...
IN A DREAM?

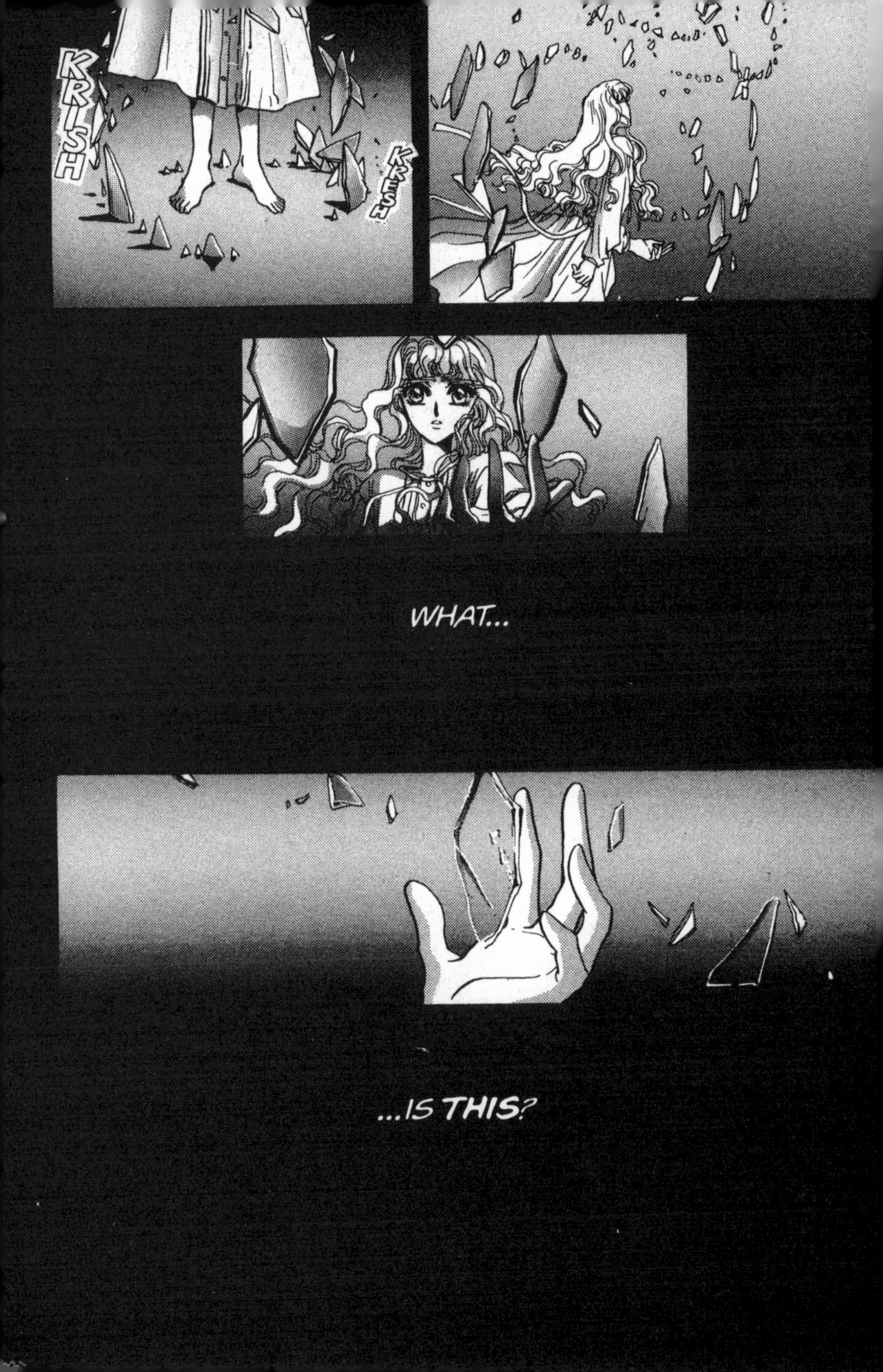
KRISH
KRESH
WHAT...
...IS THIS?

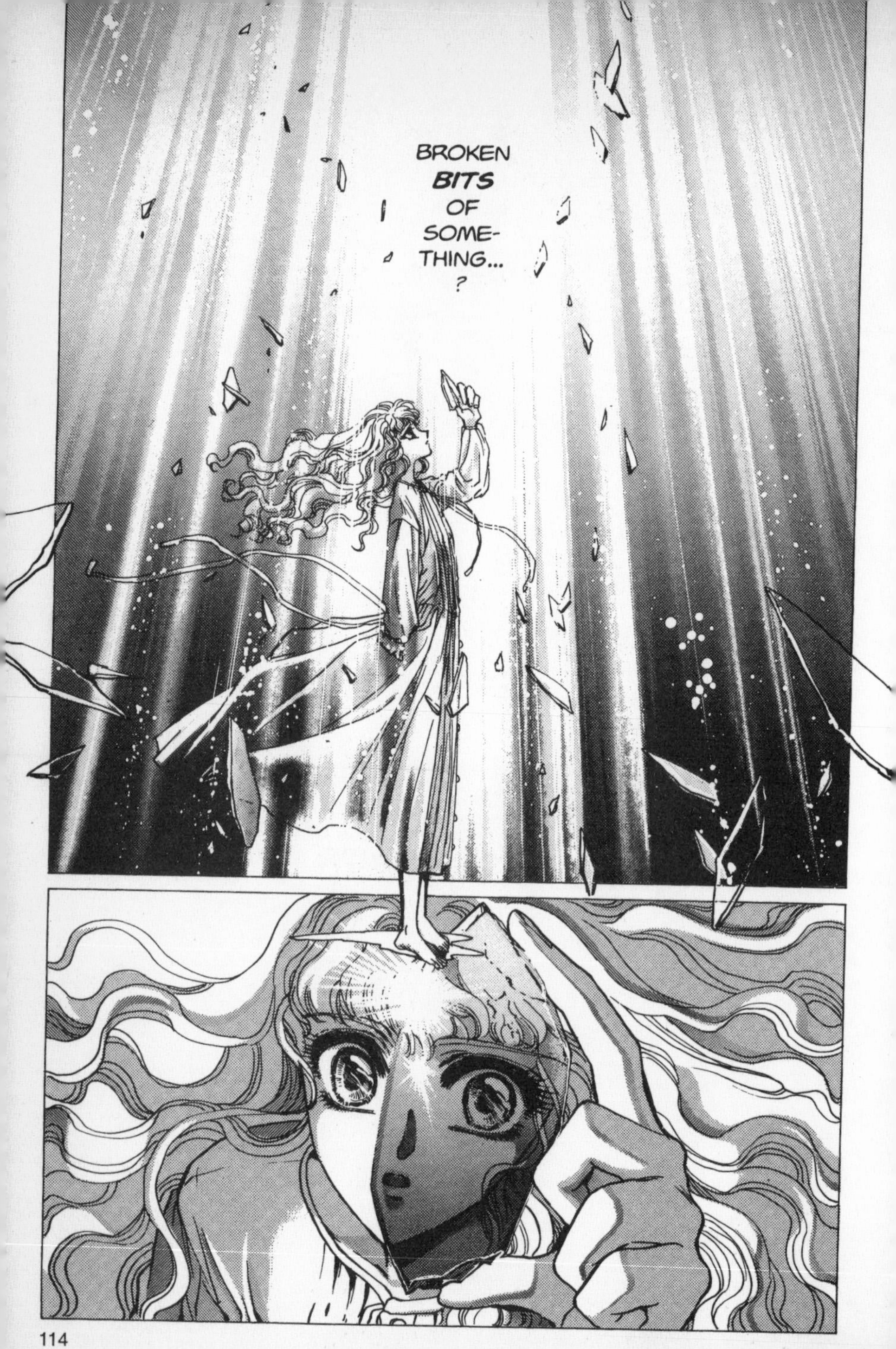
BROKEN **BITS** OF SOME-THING...
?

PIECES...

OF
THE
EARTH...
?

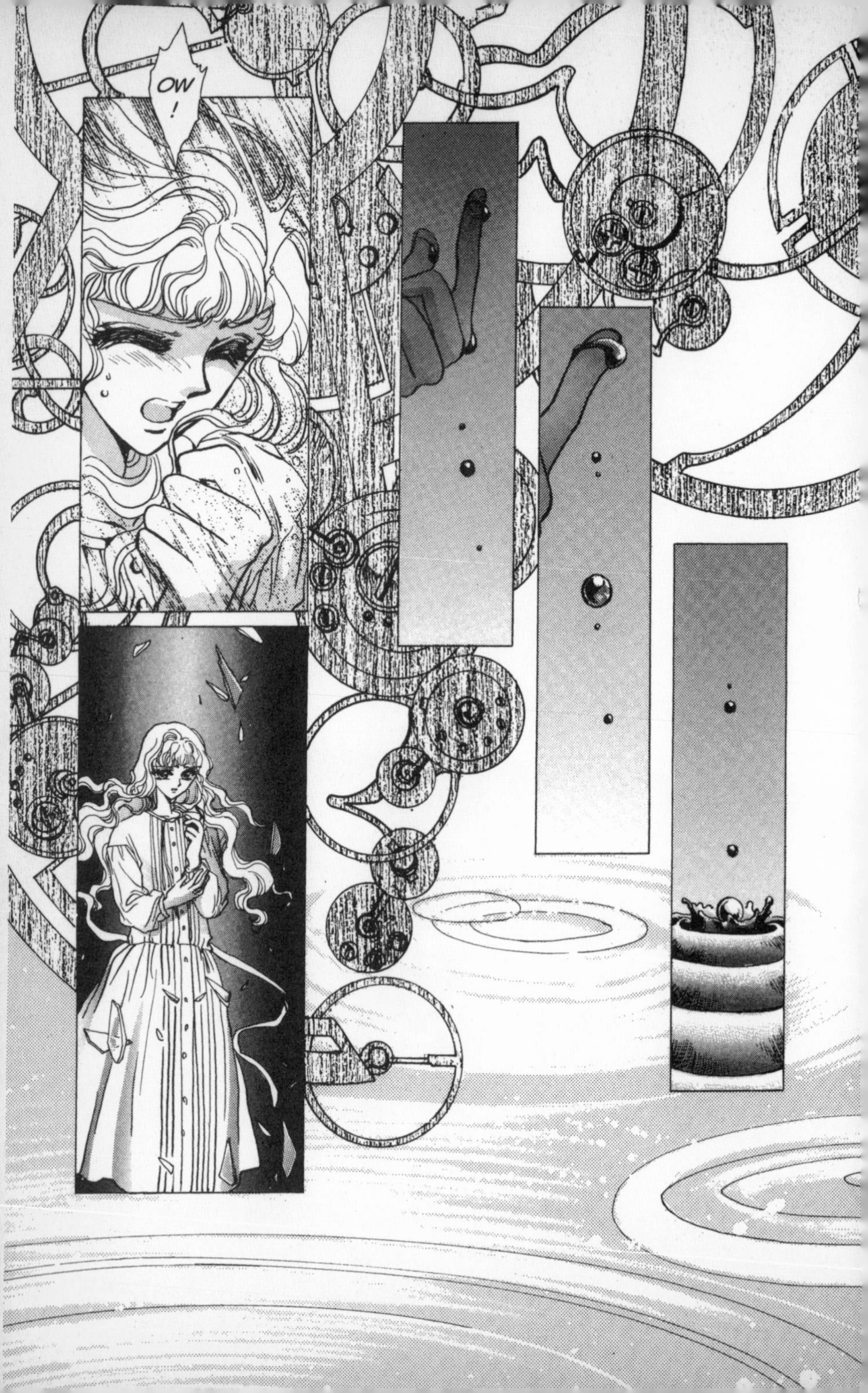
OW !

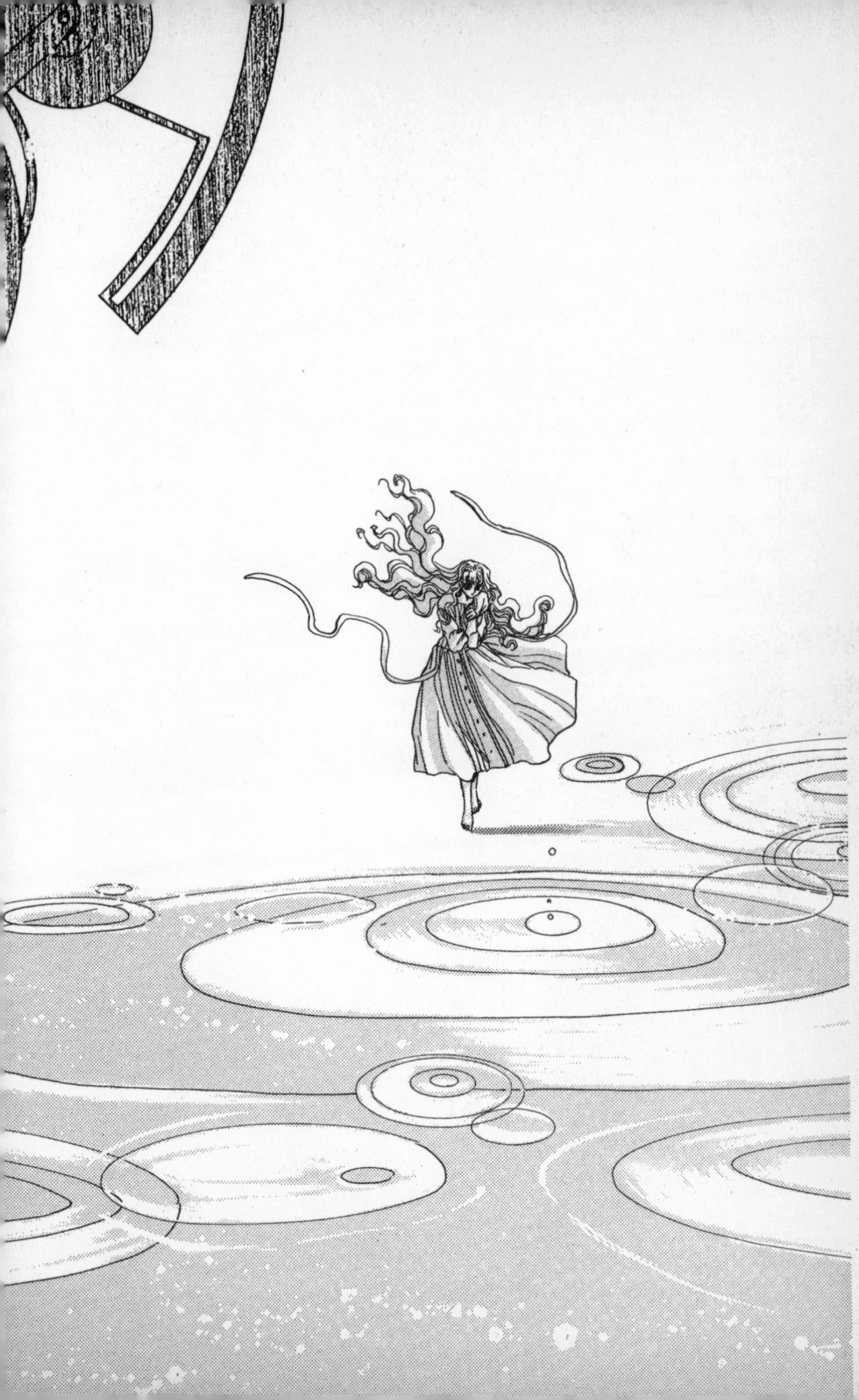

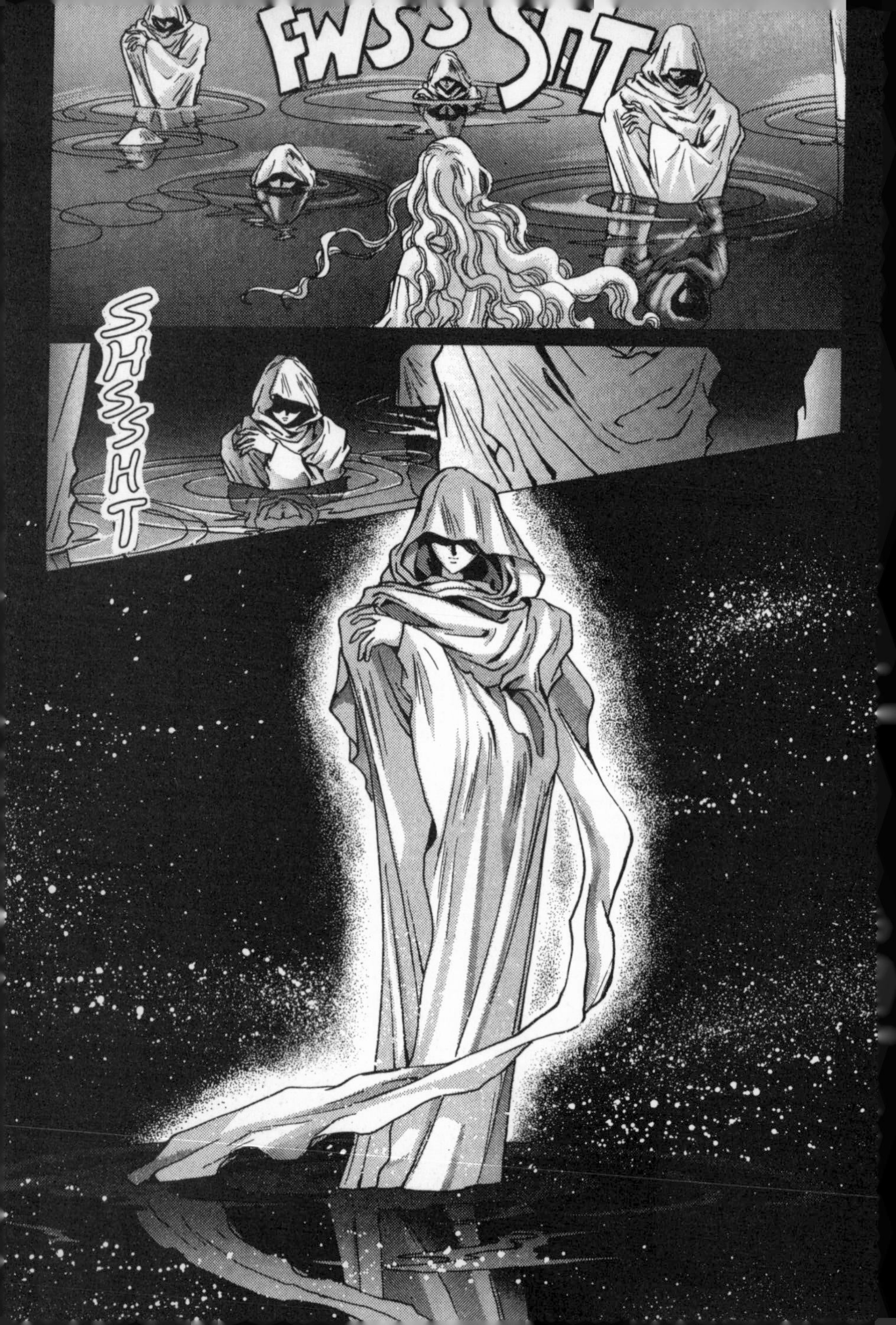
FWSSSHT
SHSSHT

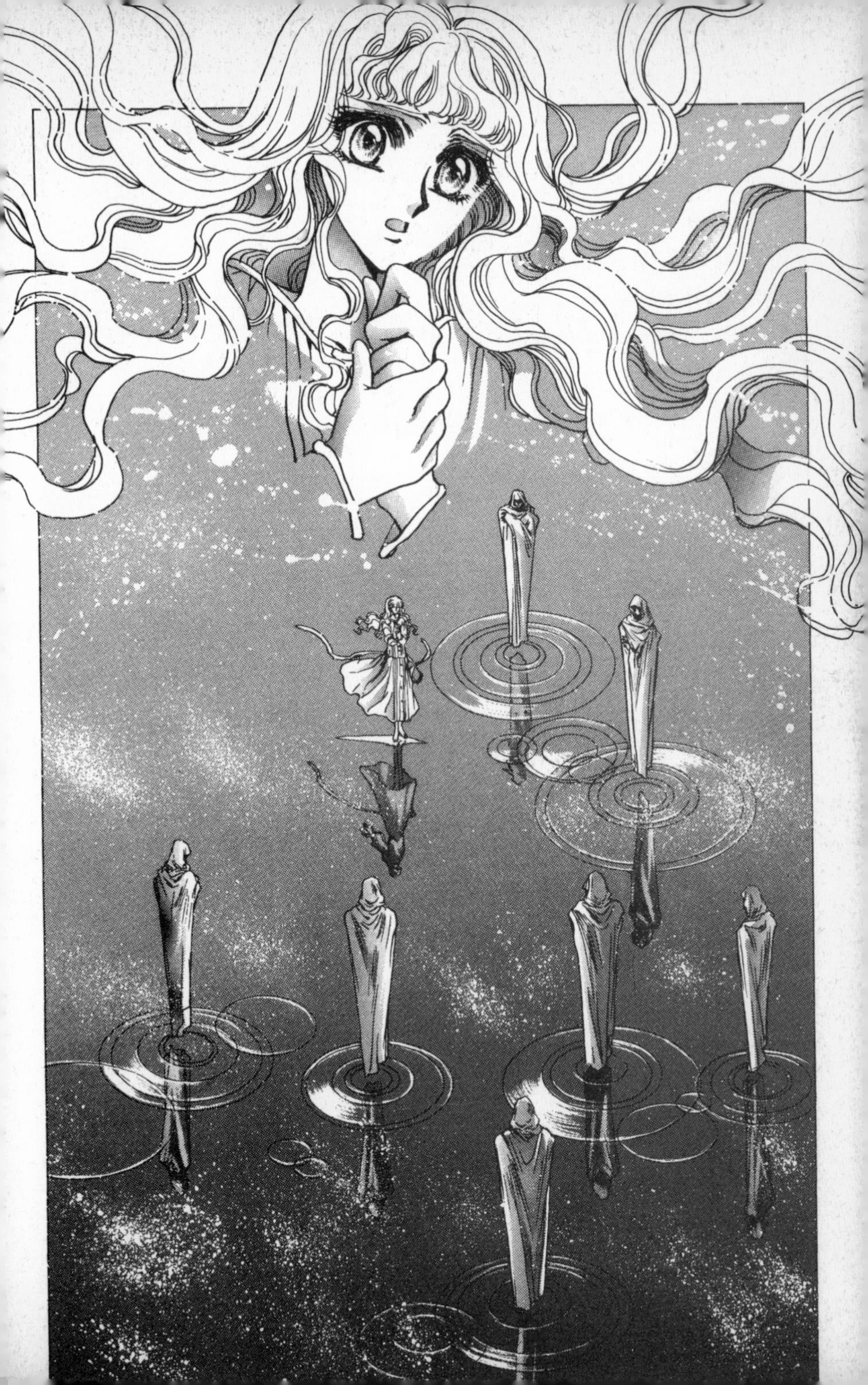

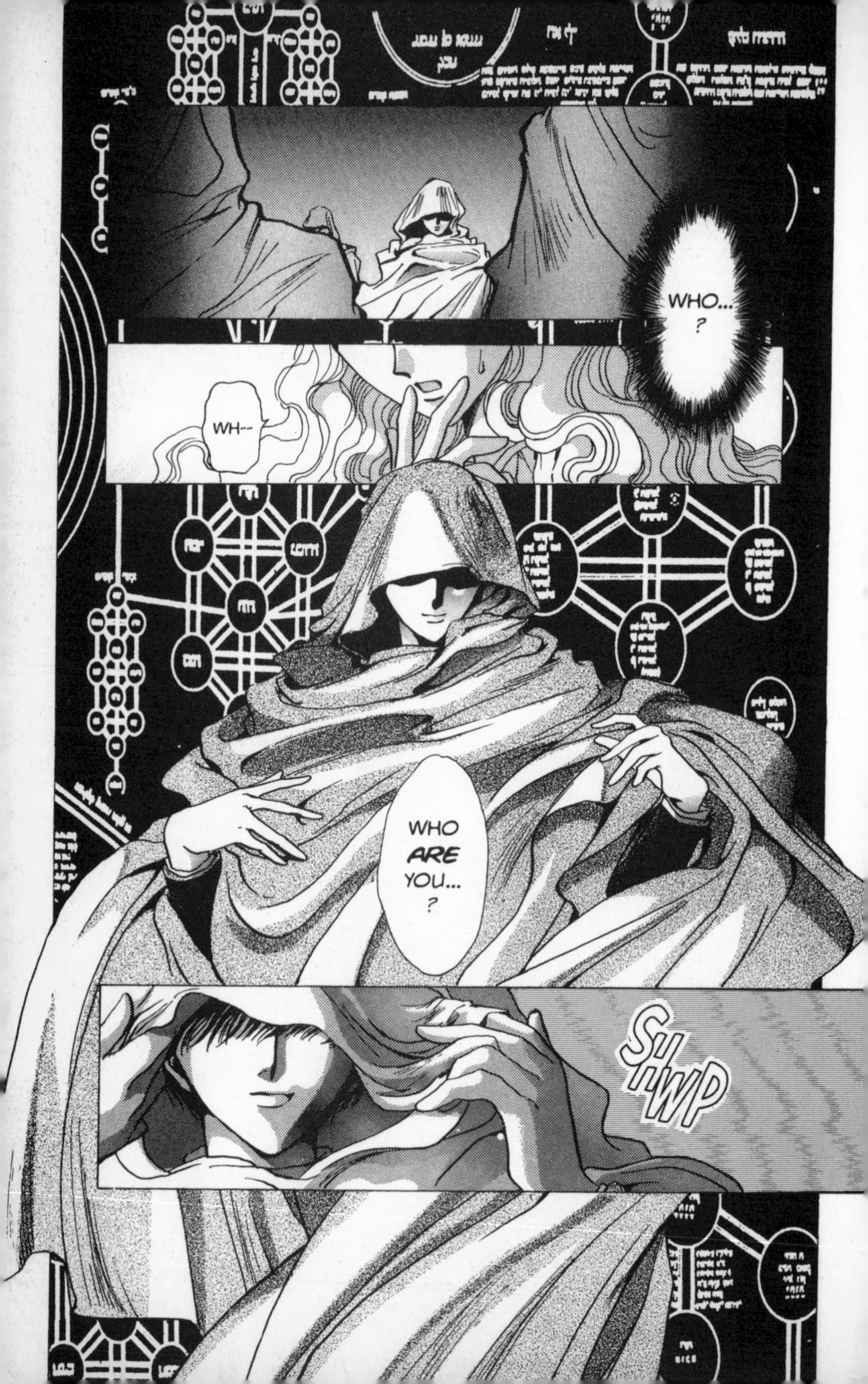
WHO... ?
WH--
WHO **ARE** YOU... ?
SHWP

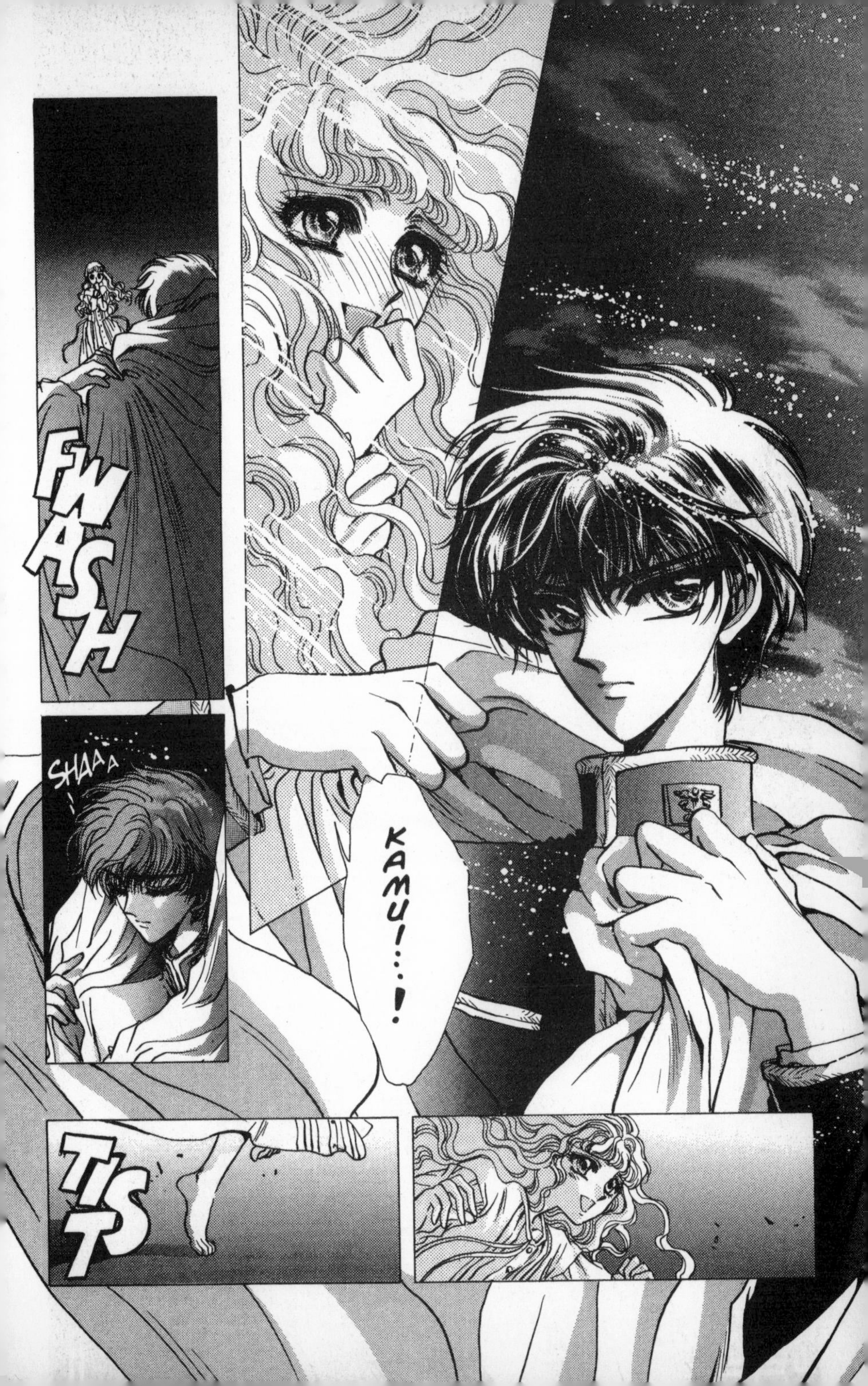
FWASH
SHAAA
KAMUI...!
TIST

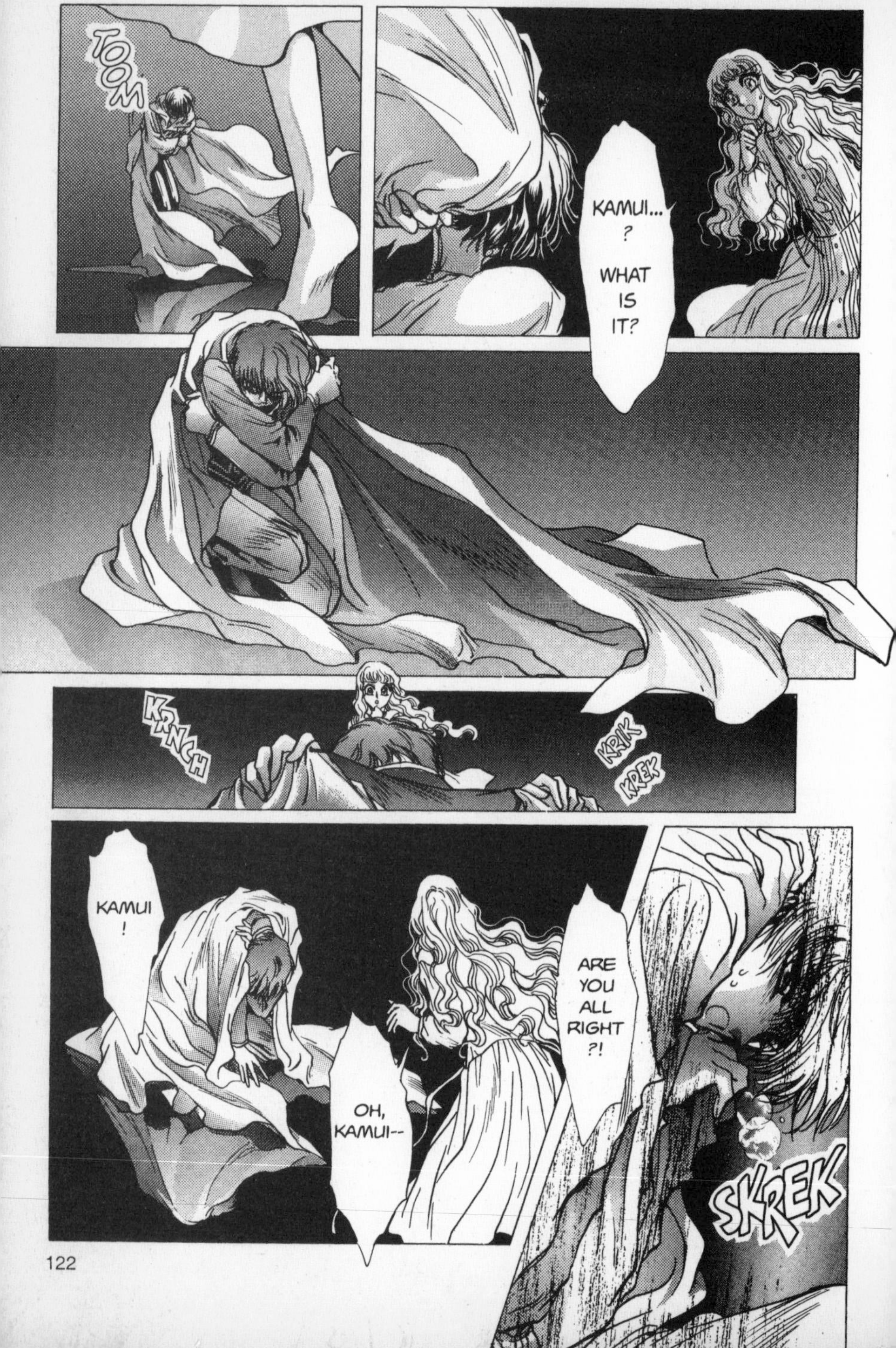
TOOM
KAMUI... ? WHAT IS IT?
KRNCH
KRIK
KREK
KAMUI!
OH, KAMUI--
ARE YOU ALL RIGHT?!
SKREK

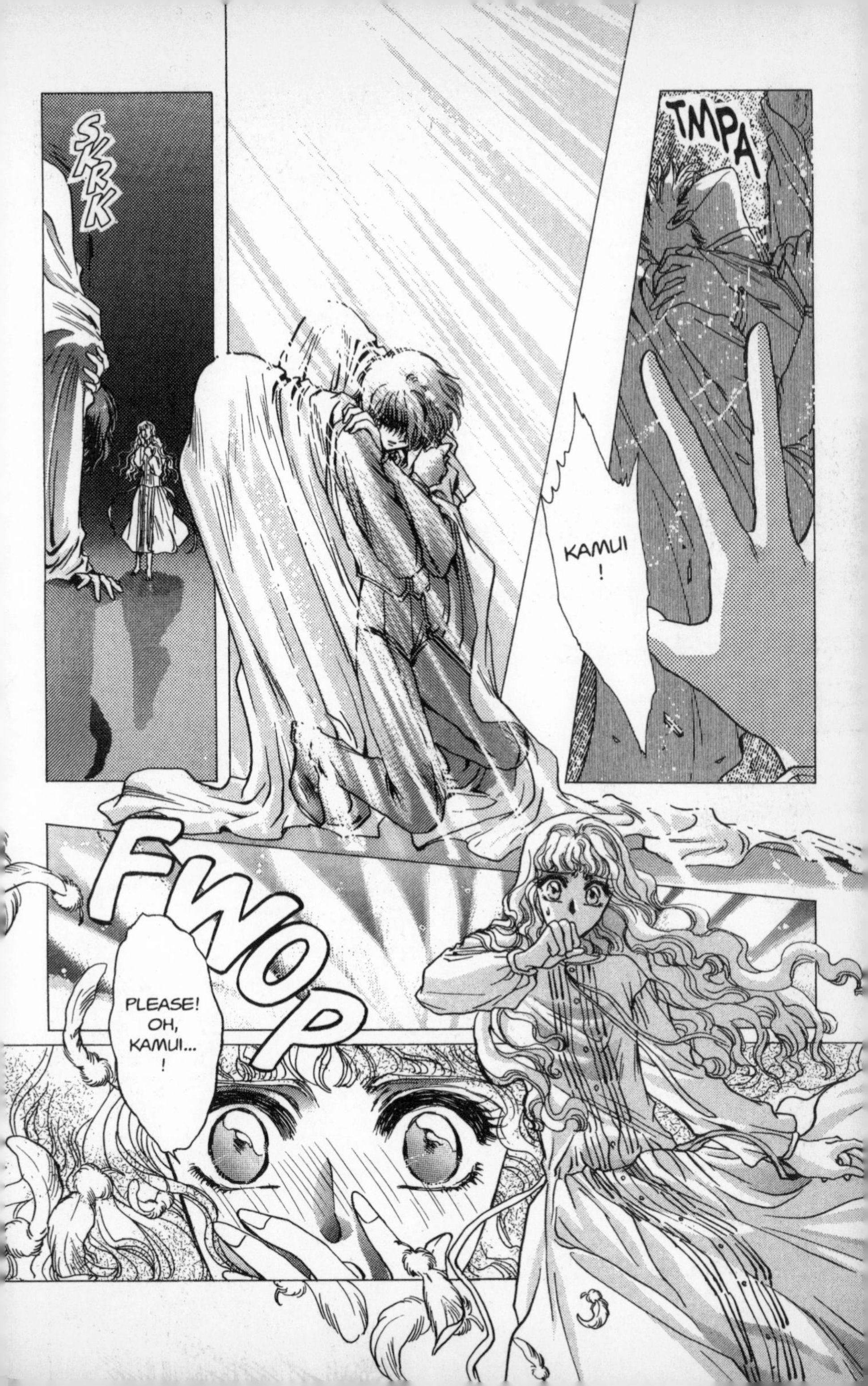
SKRK
TMPA
KAMUI !
FWOP
PLEASE! OH, KAMUI... !

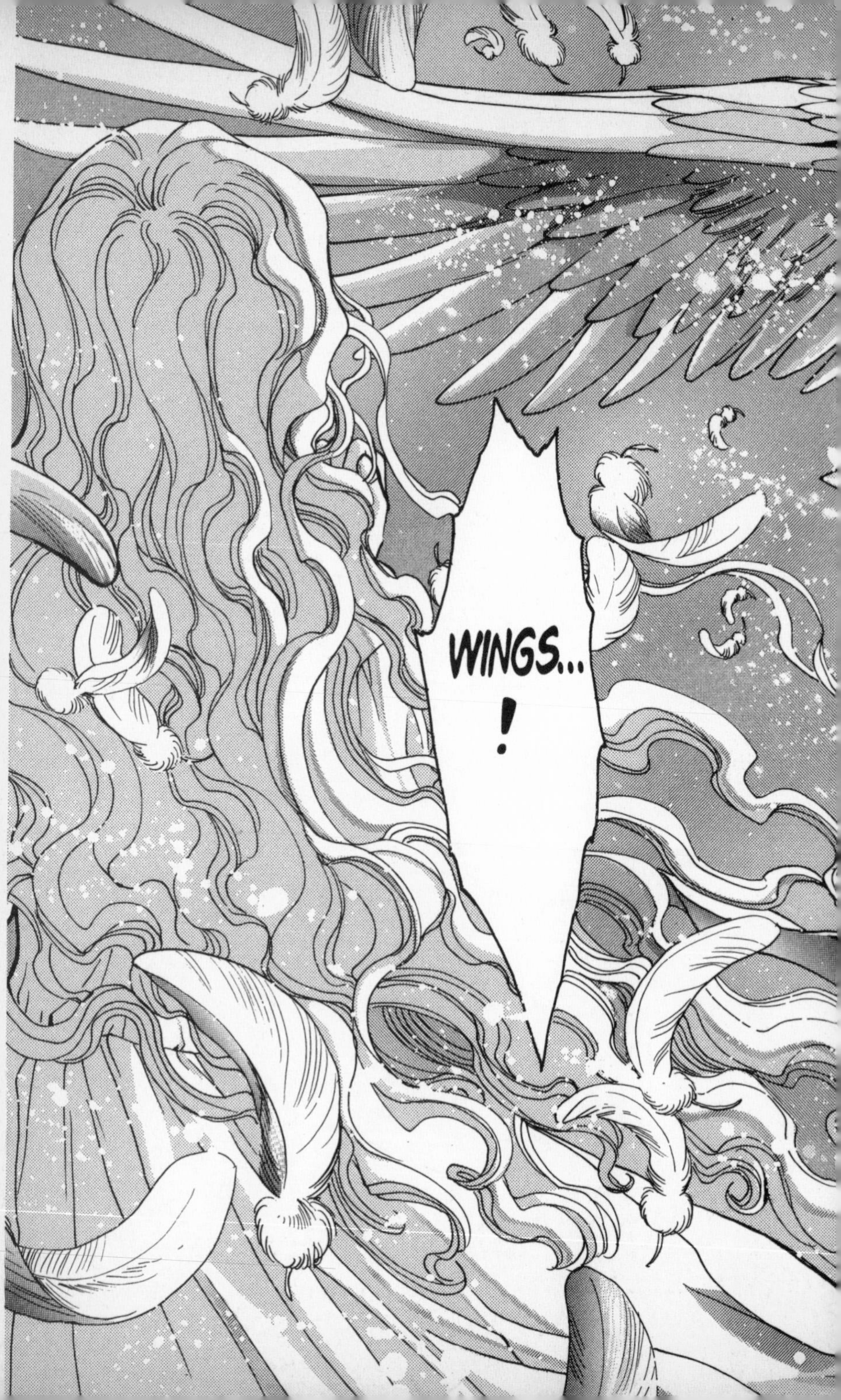
WINGS... !

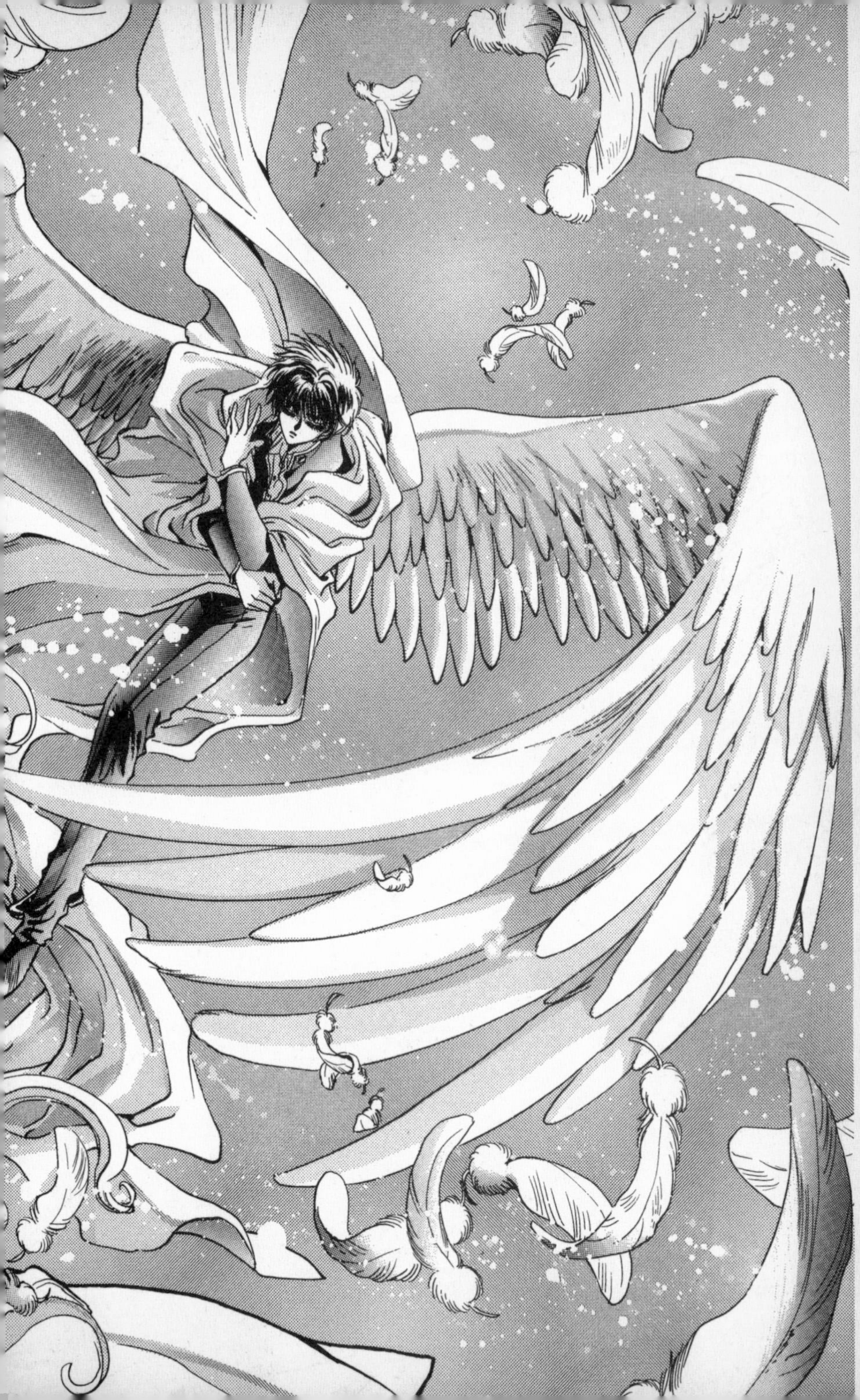

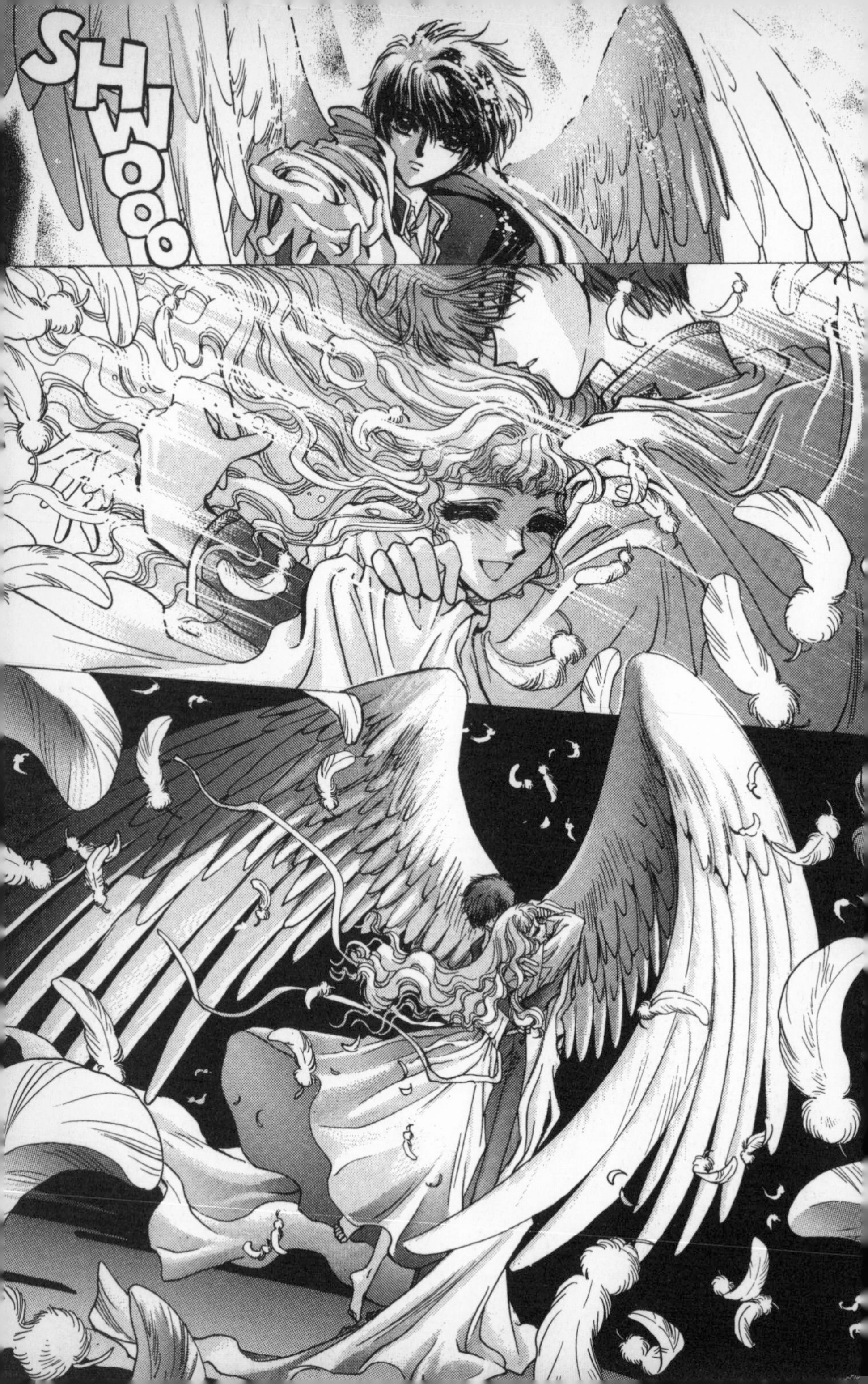
SHWOOO

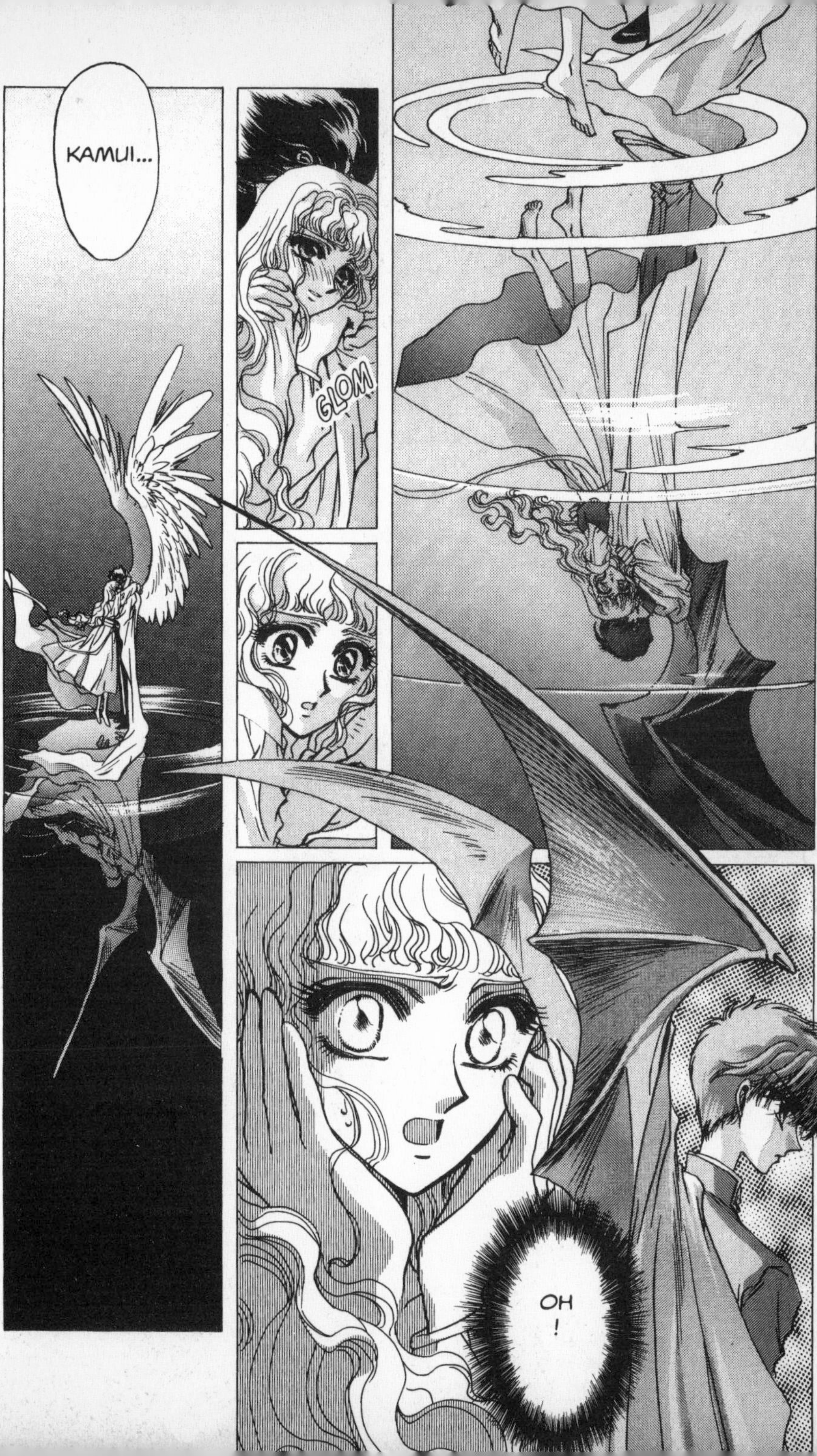
KAMUI...
GLOM
OH!

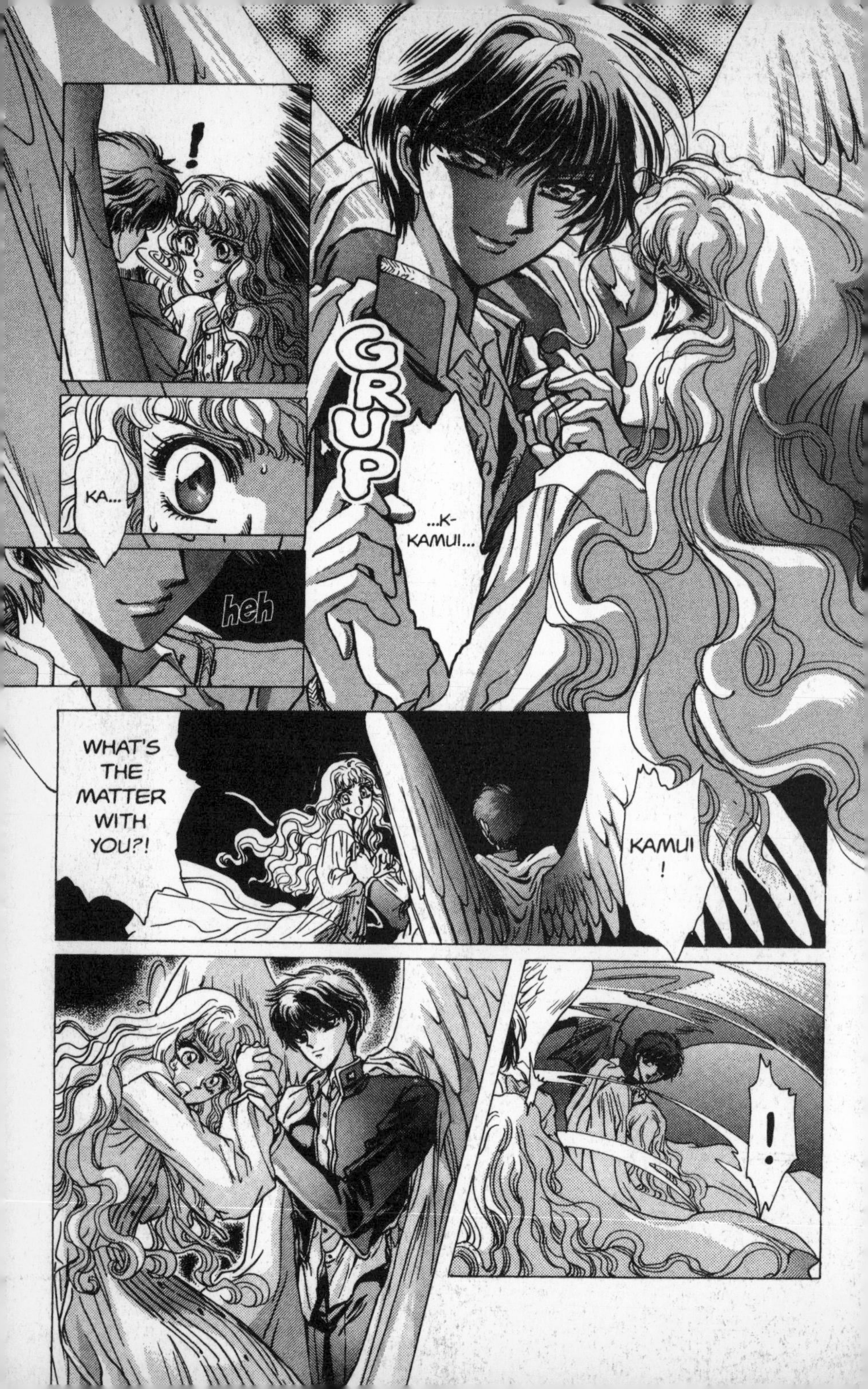
!
KA...
heh
GRUP
...K- KAMUI...
WHAT'S THE MATTER WITH YOU?!
KAMUI!
!

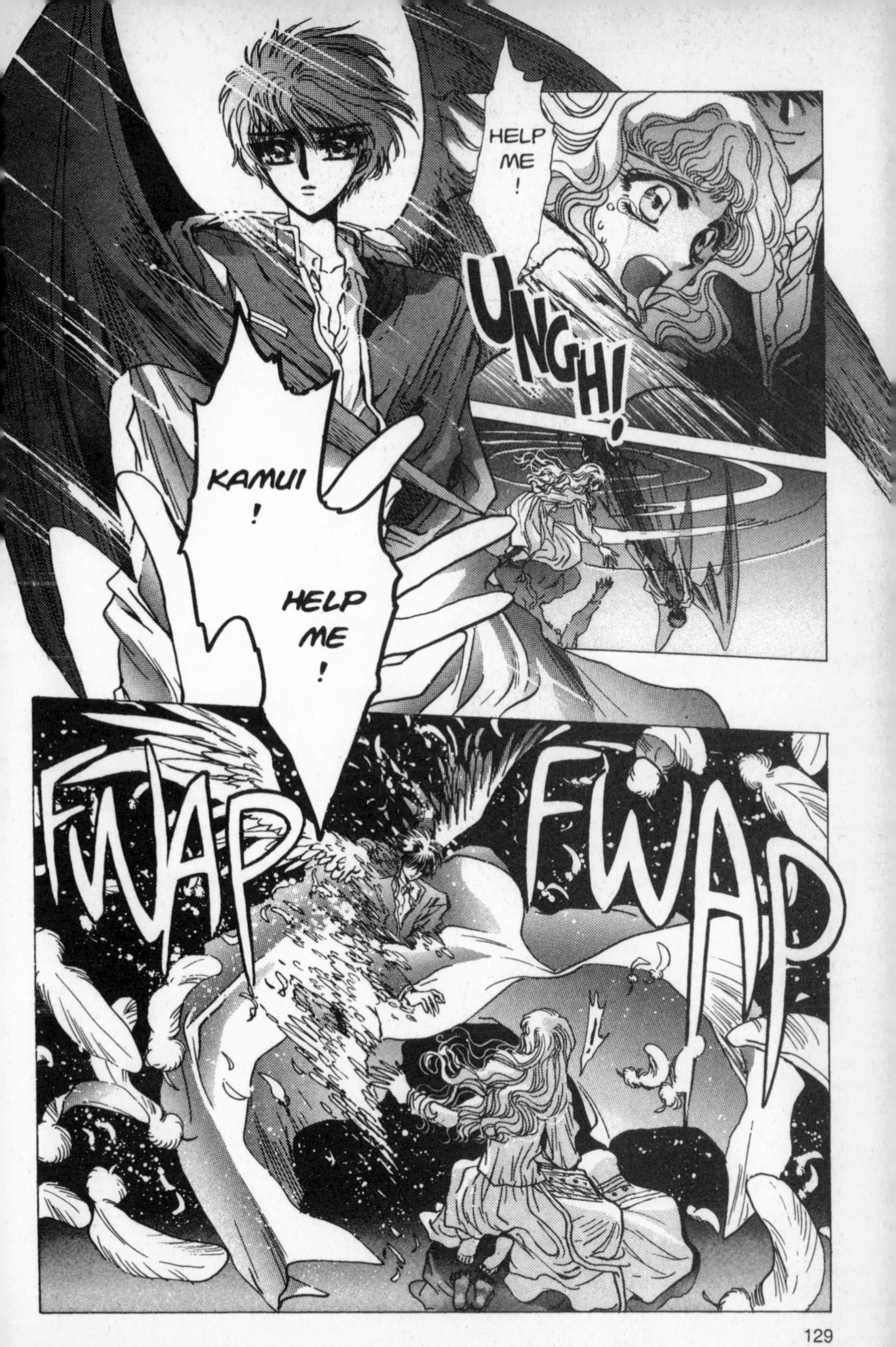
KAMUI! HELP ME!
HELP ME!
UNGH!
FWAP
FWAP

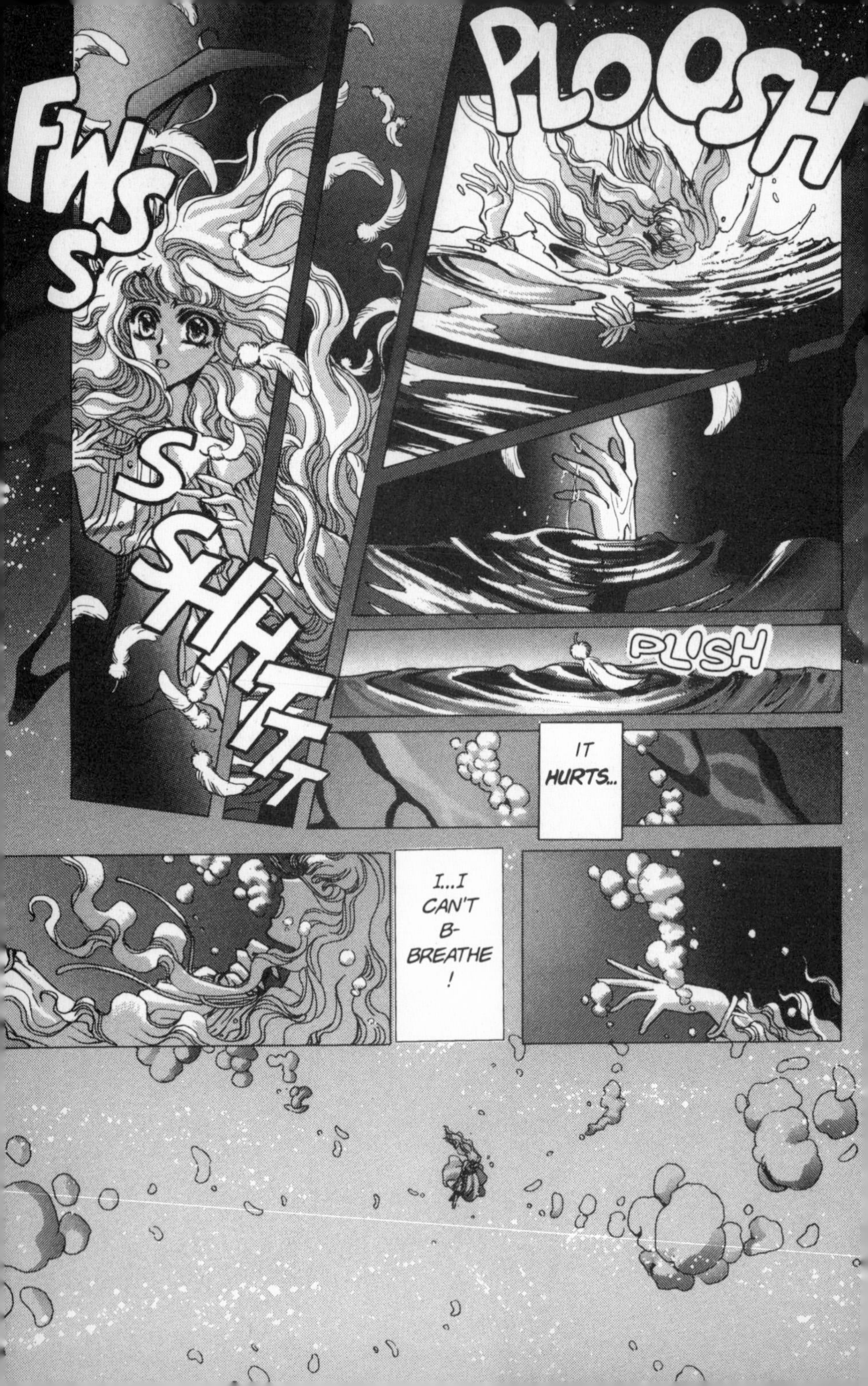
FWSSS
SSHHTTT
PLOOSH
PLISH
IT HURTS...
I...I CAN'T B-BREATHE!

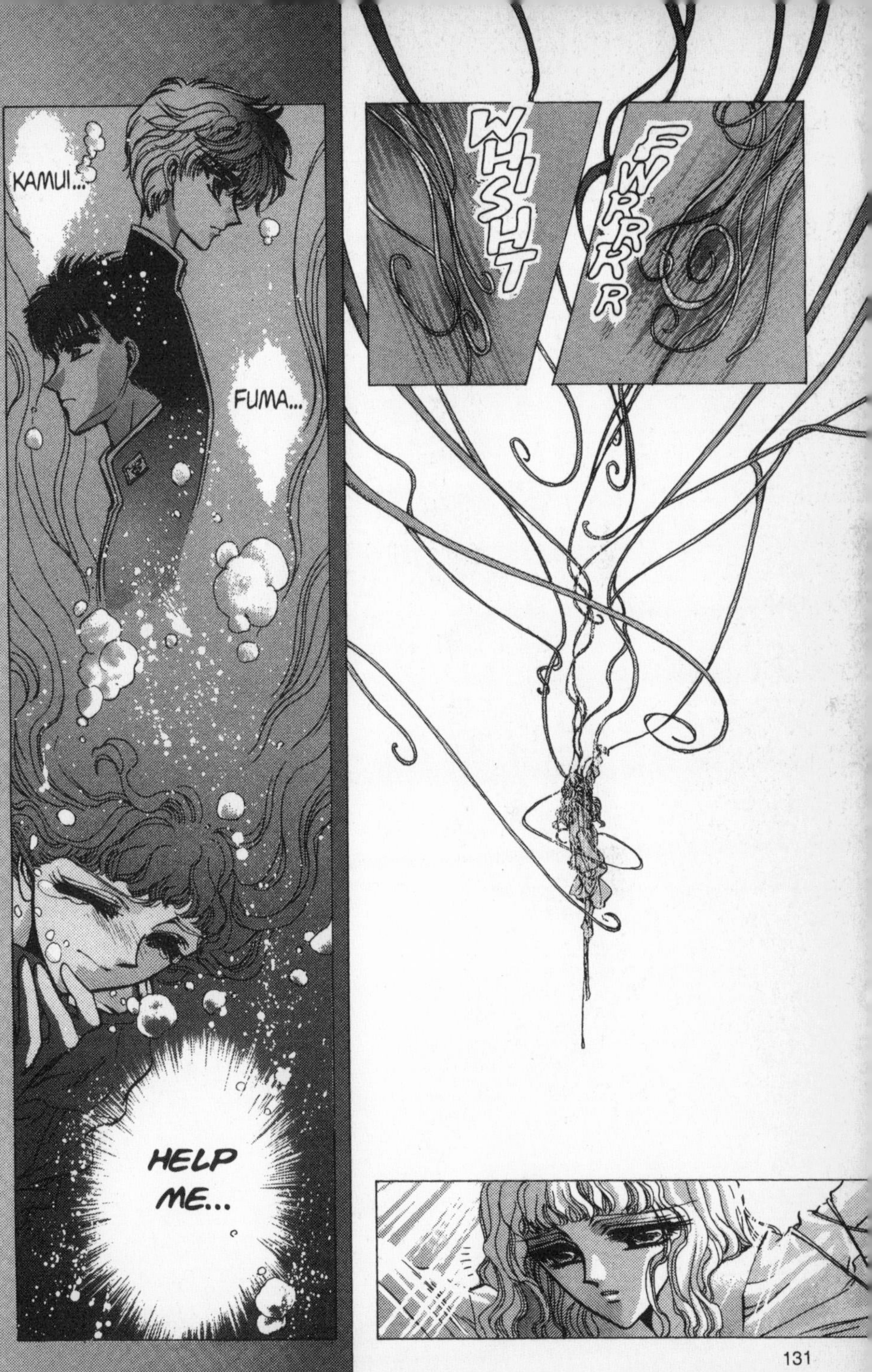
KAMUI...
FUMA...
HELP ME...
WHISHT
FWRRRR

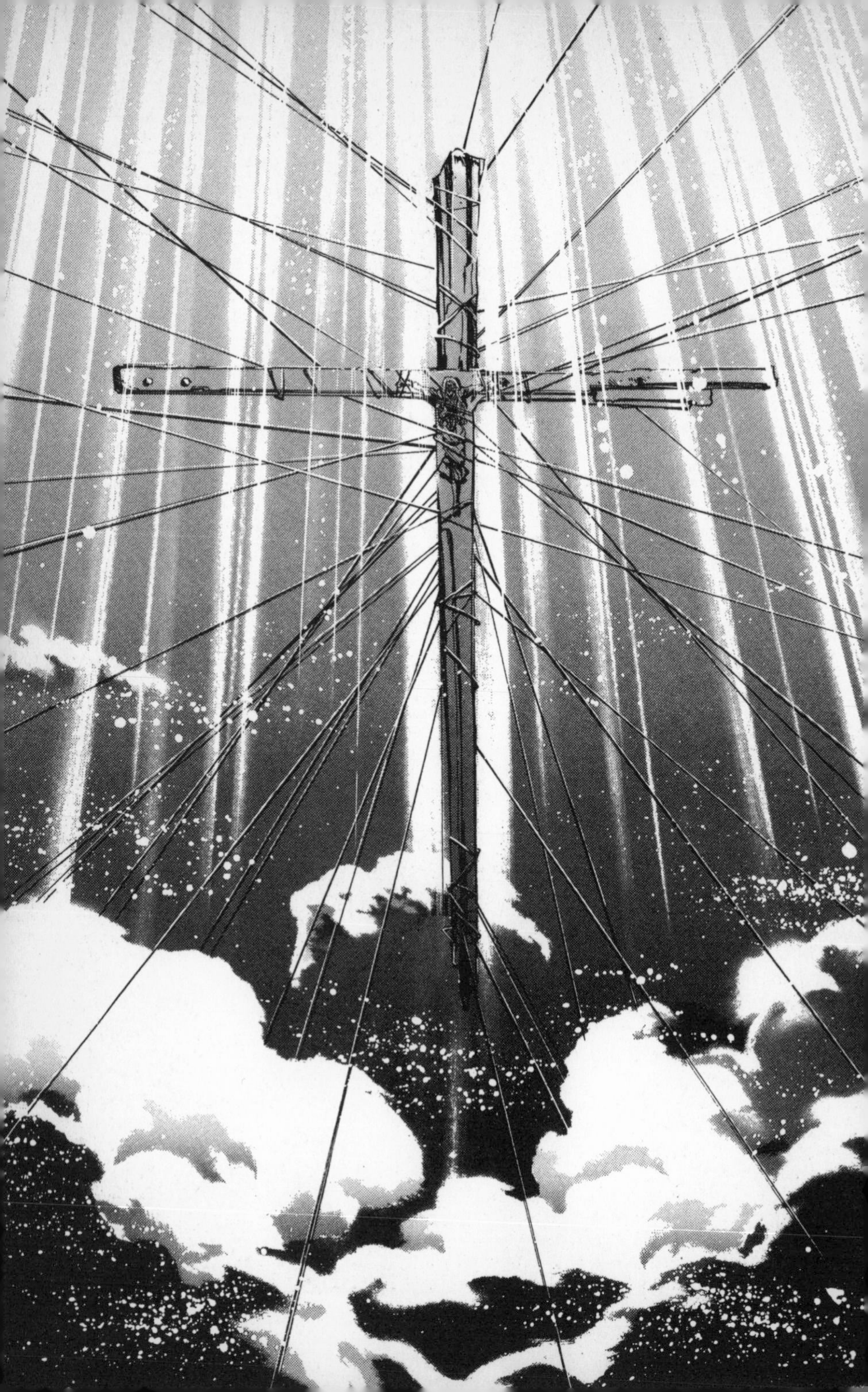

SKREEK

SKRAAA

WHOOOOO

TH-THAT'S...

...ME...
?

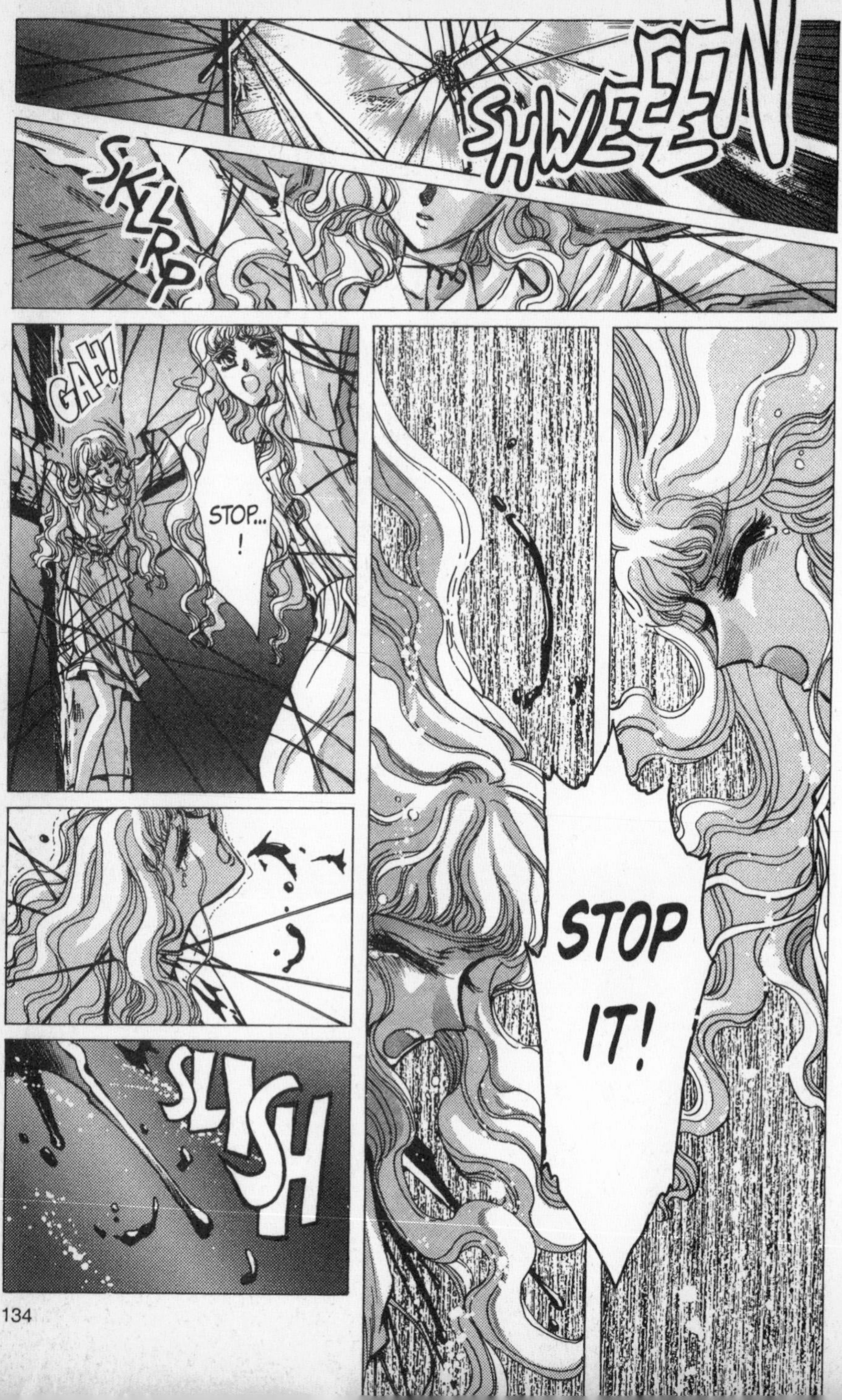
SHWEEEN
SKLRP
GAH!
STOP... !
STOP IT!
SLISH

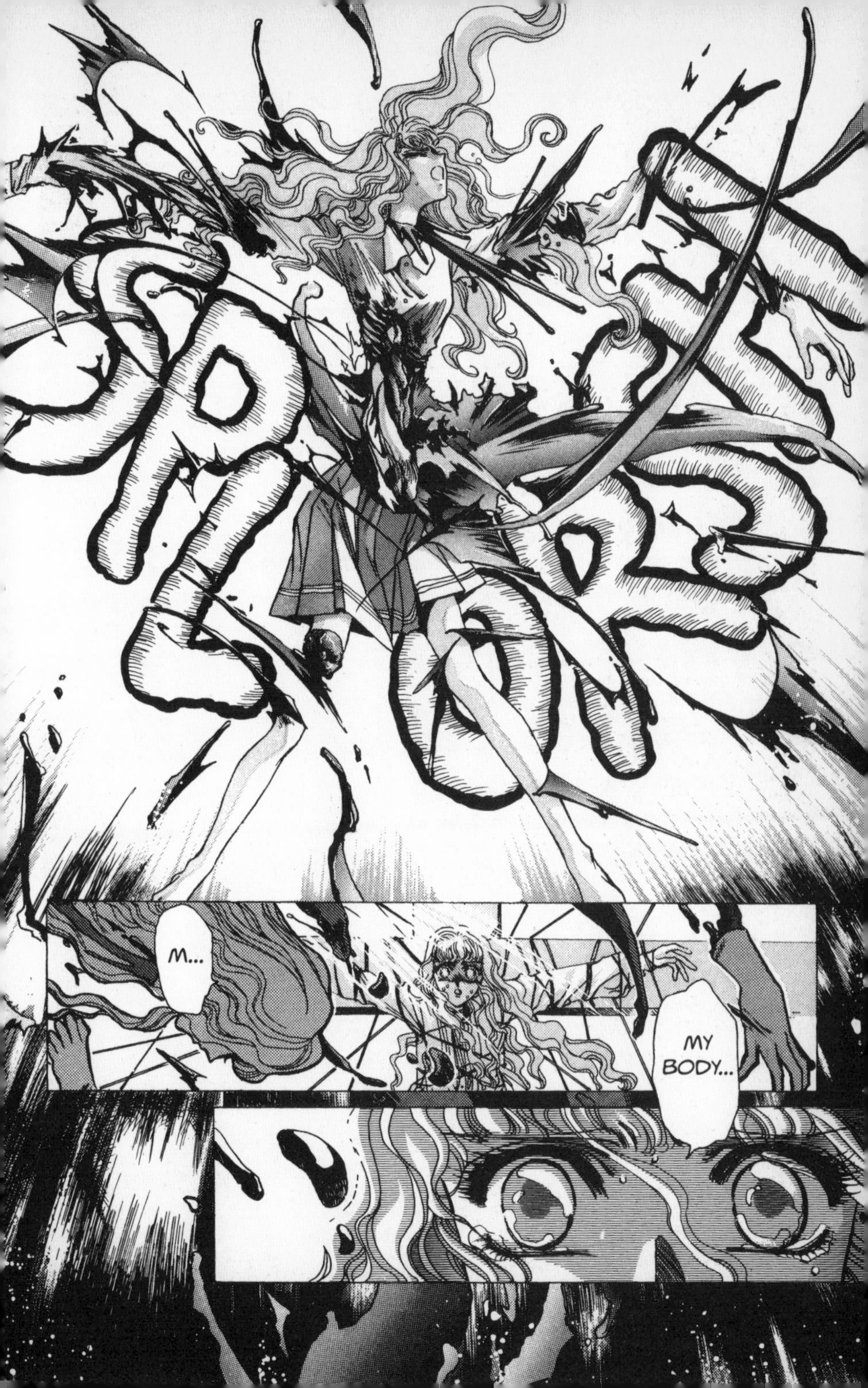
M...
MY BODY...

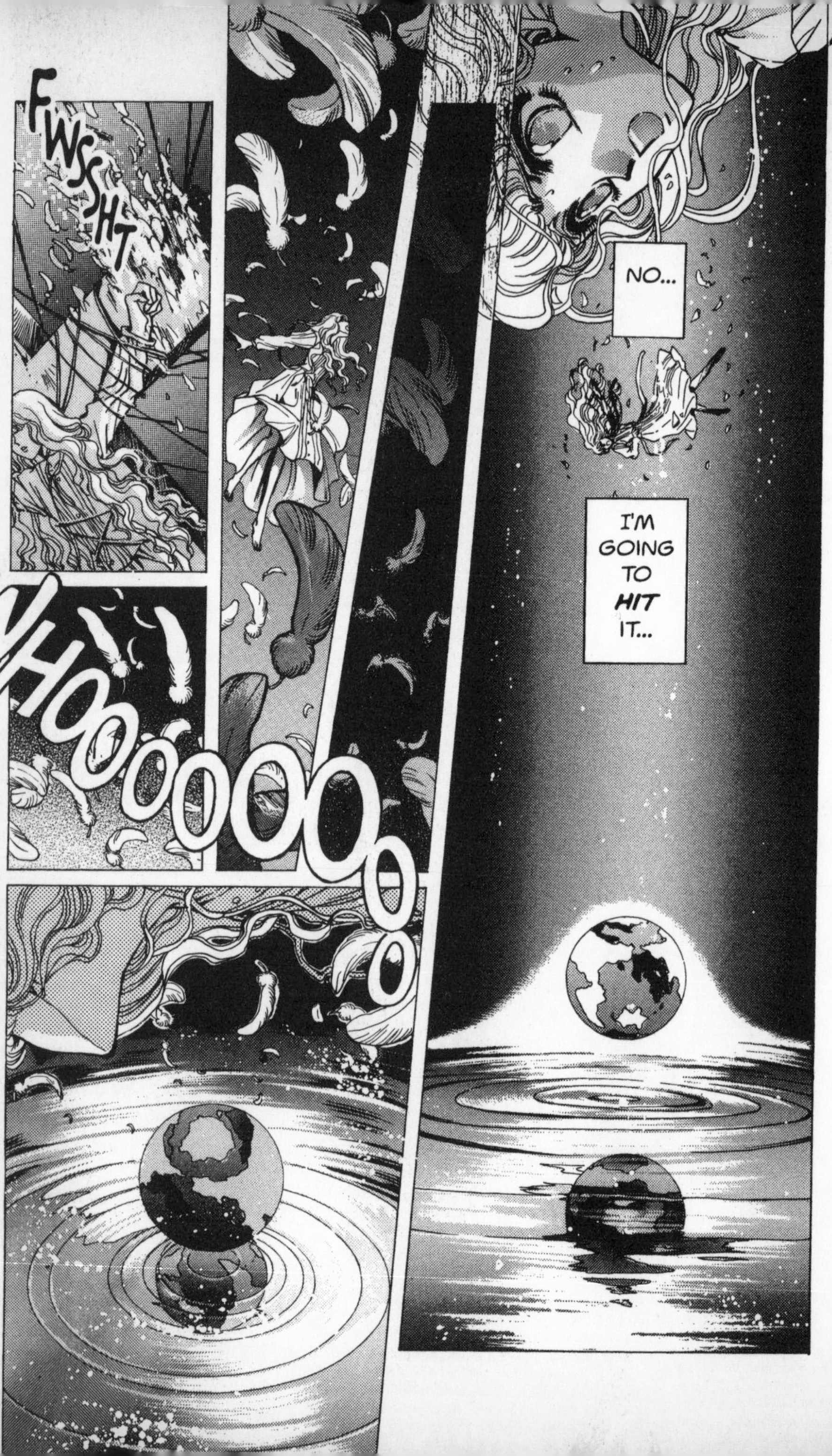
FWSSHT
WHOOOOOOOOOO
NO...
I'M GOING TO *HIT* IT...

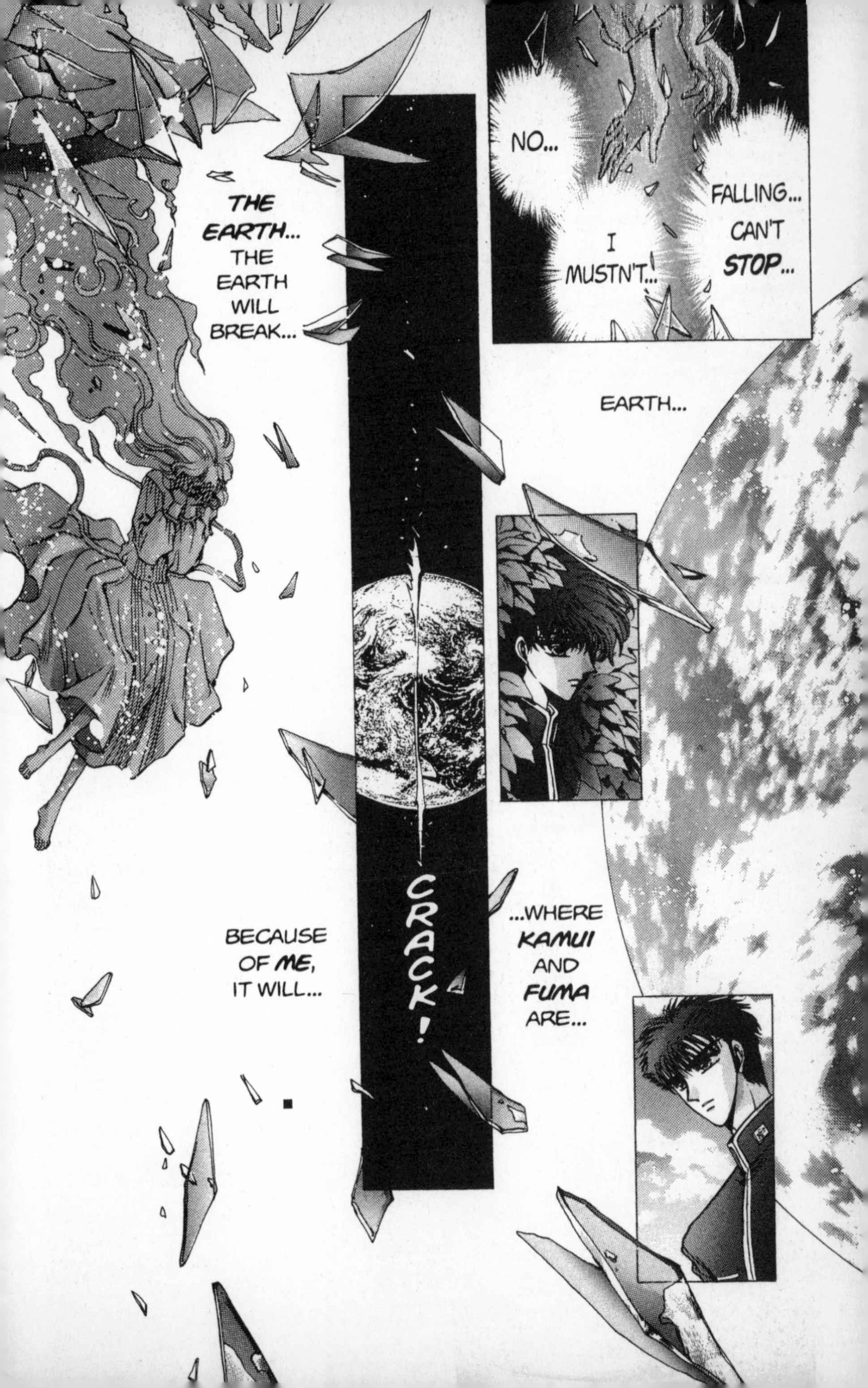
THE EARTH... THE EARTH WILL BREAK...
BECAUSE OF ME, IT WILL...
CRACK!
NO...
I MUSTN'T...
FALLING... CAN'T STOP...
EARTH...
...WHERE KAMUI AND FUMA ARE...

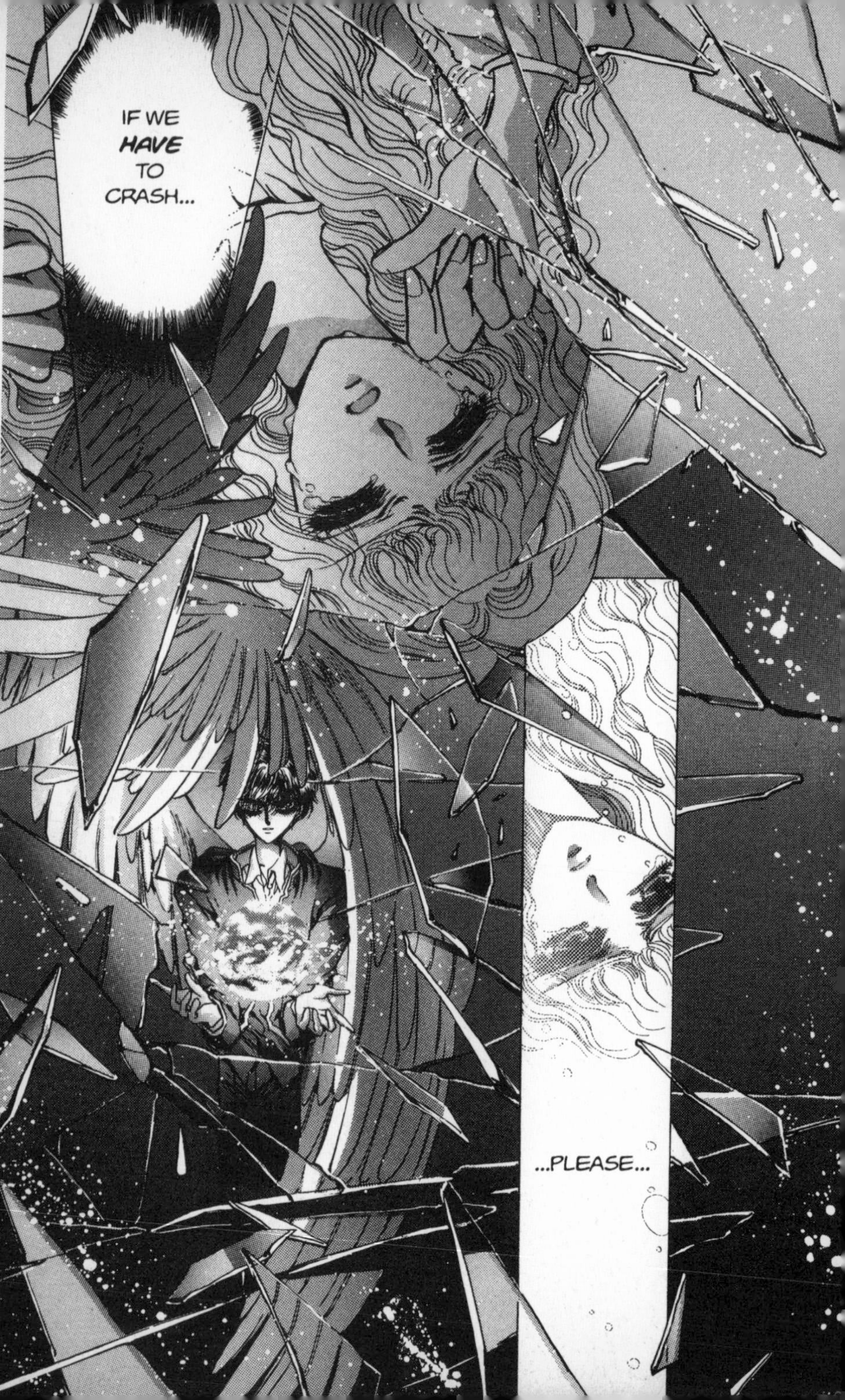
IF WE *HAVE* TO CRASH...
...PLEASE...

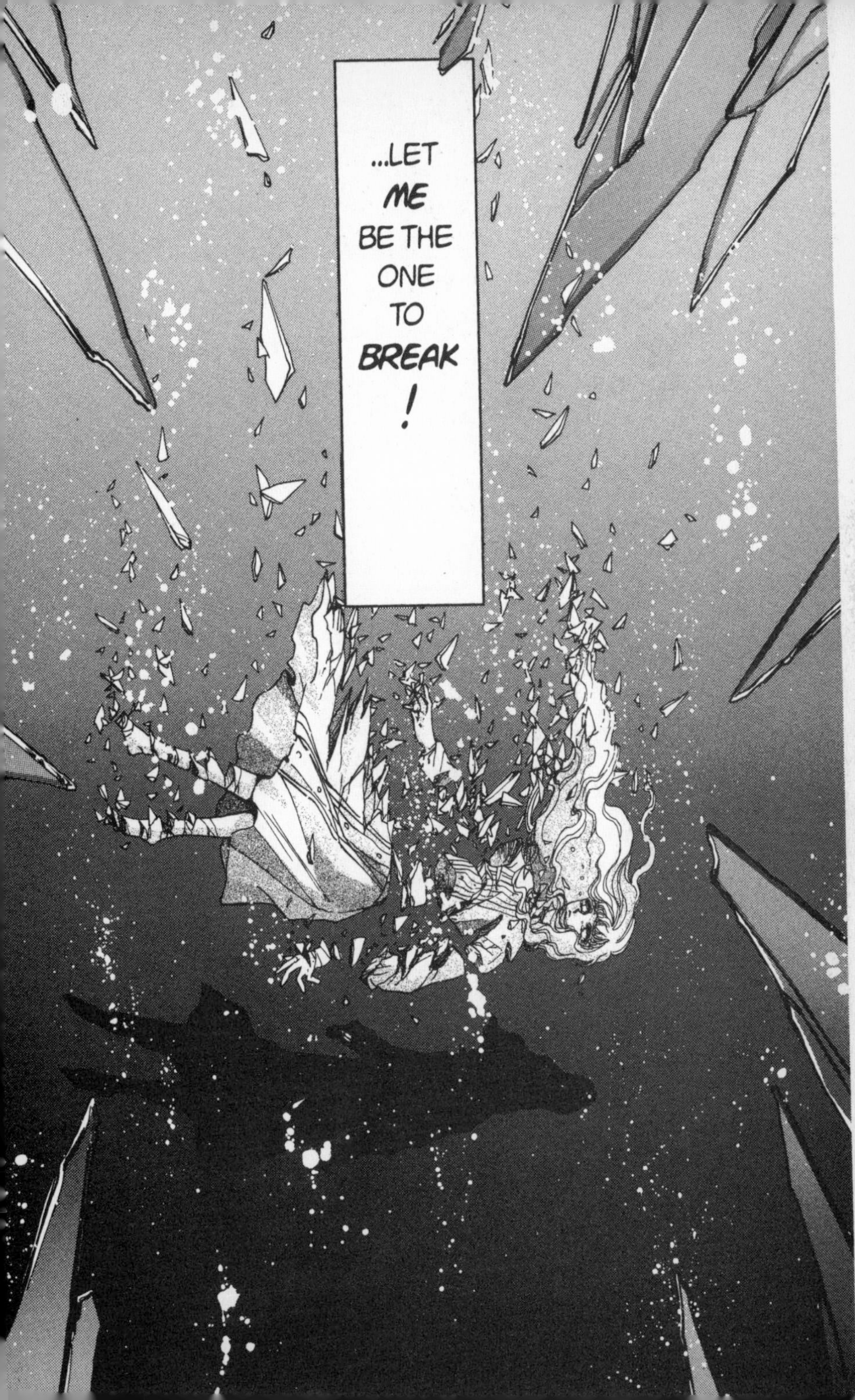
...LET ME BE THE ONE TO BREAK!

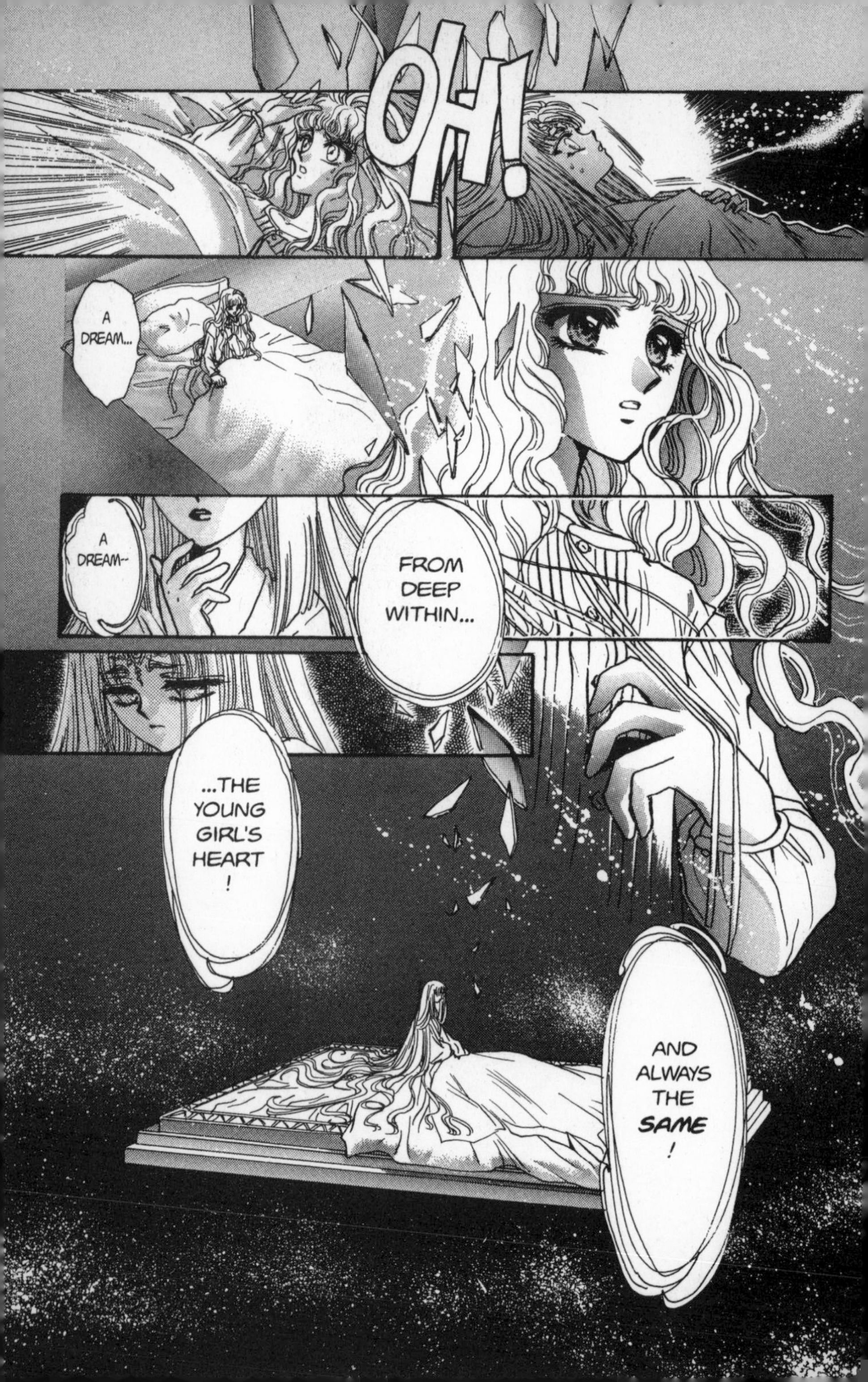
OH!
A DREAM...
A DREAM--
FROM DEEP WITHIN...
...THE YOUNG GIRL'S HEART!
AND ALWAYS THE *SAME*!

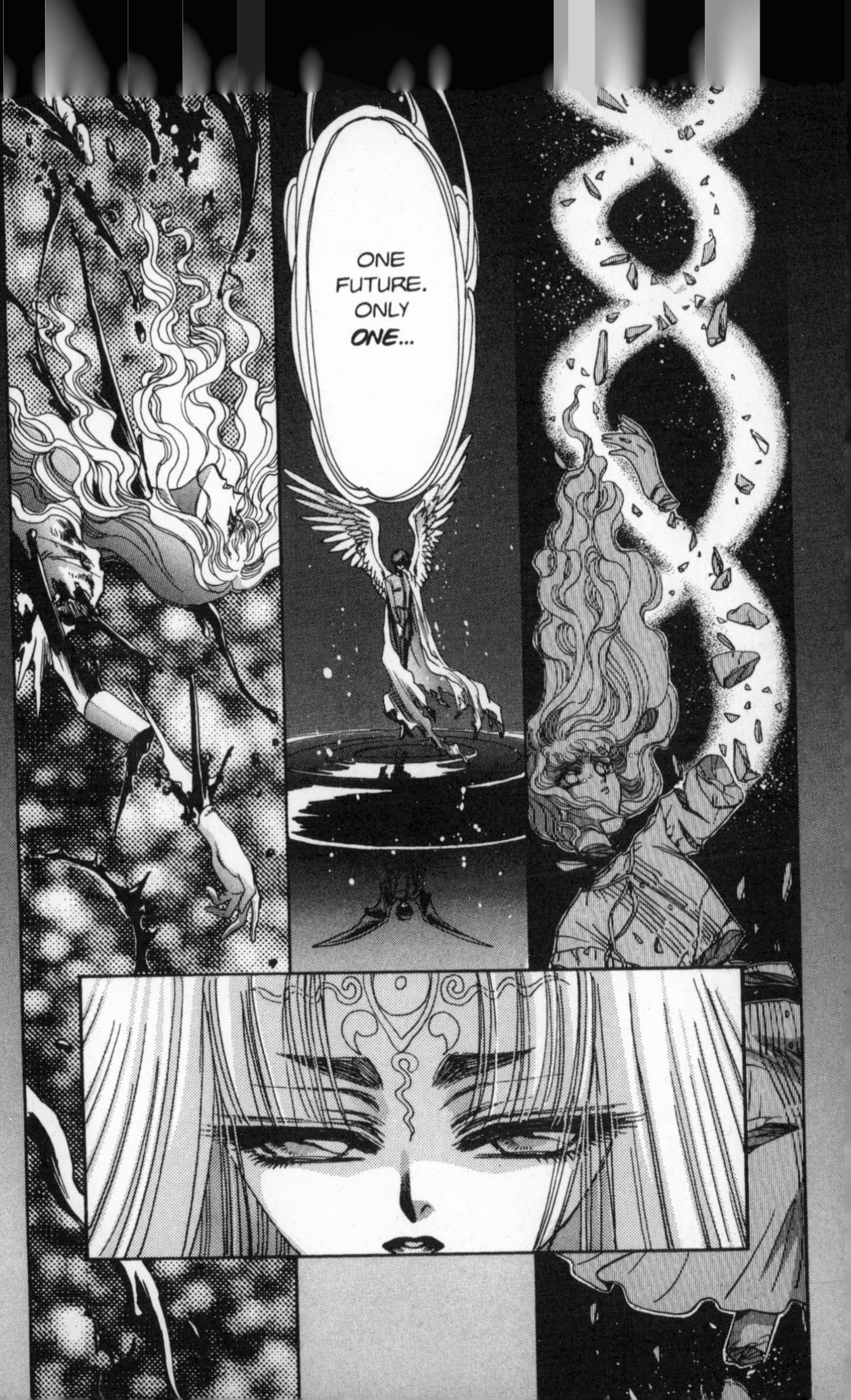
ONE FUTURE. ONLY *ONE*...

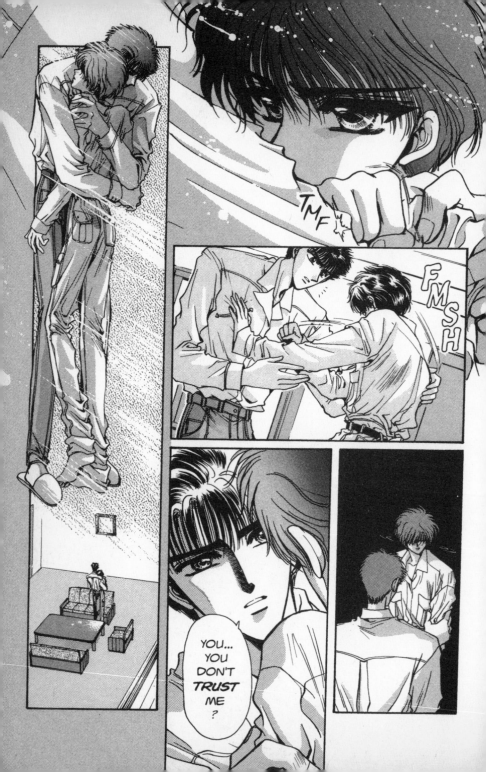

TMF

FMSH

YOU...
YOU
DON'T
TRUST
ME
?

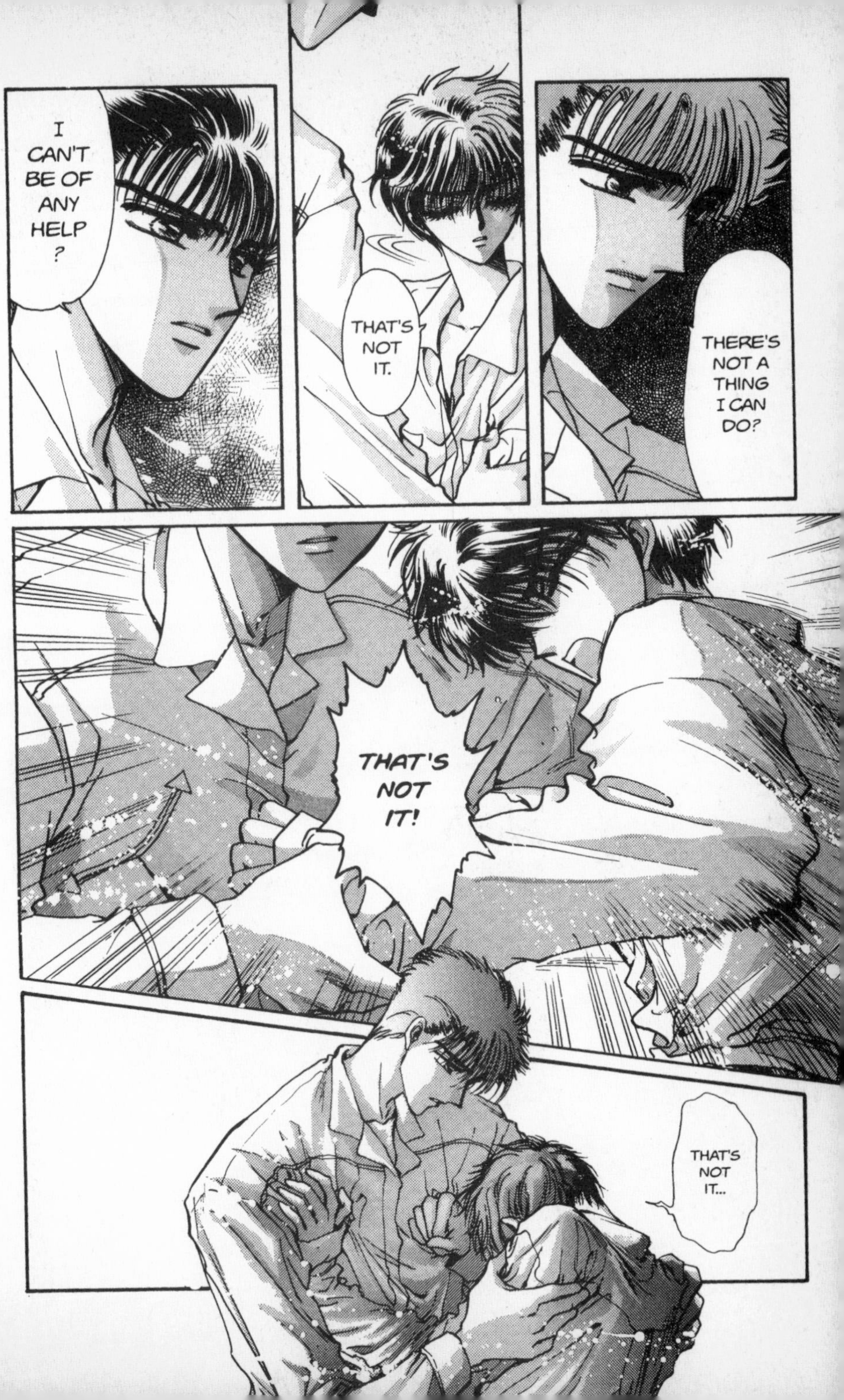
I CAN'T BE OF ANY HELP ?
THAT'S NOT IT.
THERE'S NOT A THING I CAN DO?
THAT'S NOT IT!
THAT'S NOT IT...

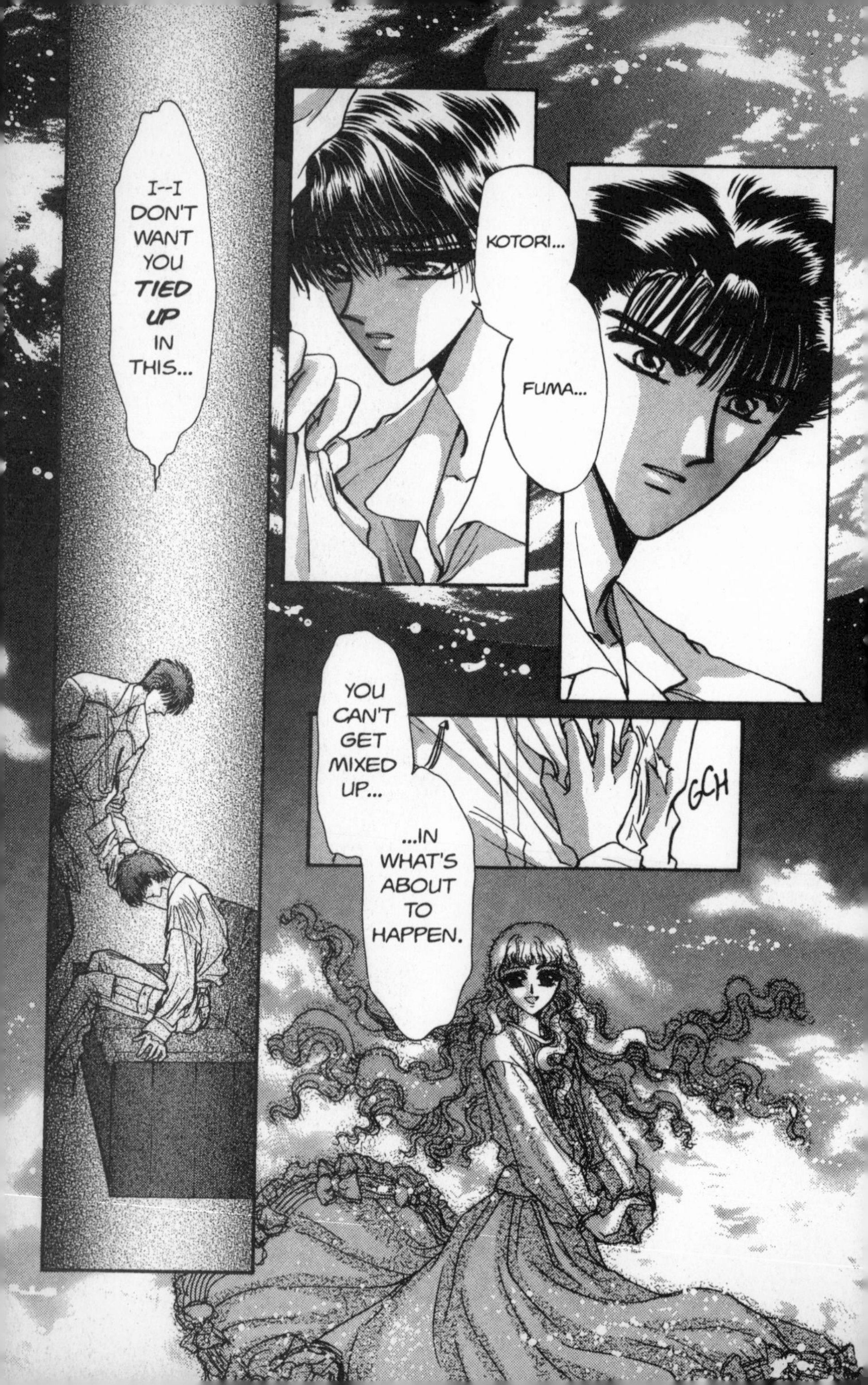
I--I DON'T WANT YOU TIED UP IN THIS...
KOTORI...
FUMA...
YOU CAN'T GET MIXED UP...
GCH
...IN WHAT'S ABOUT TO HAPPEN.

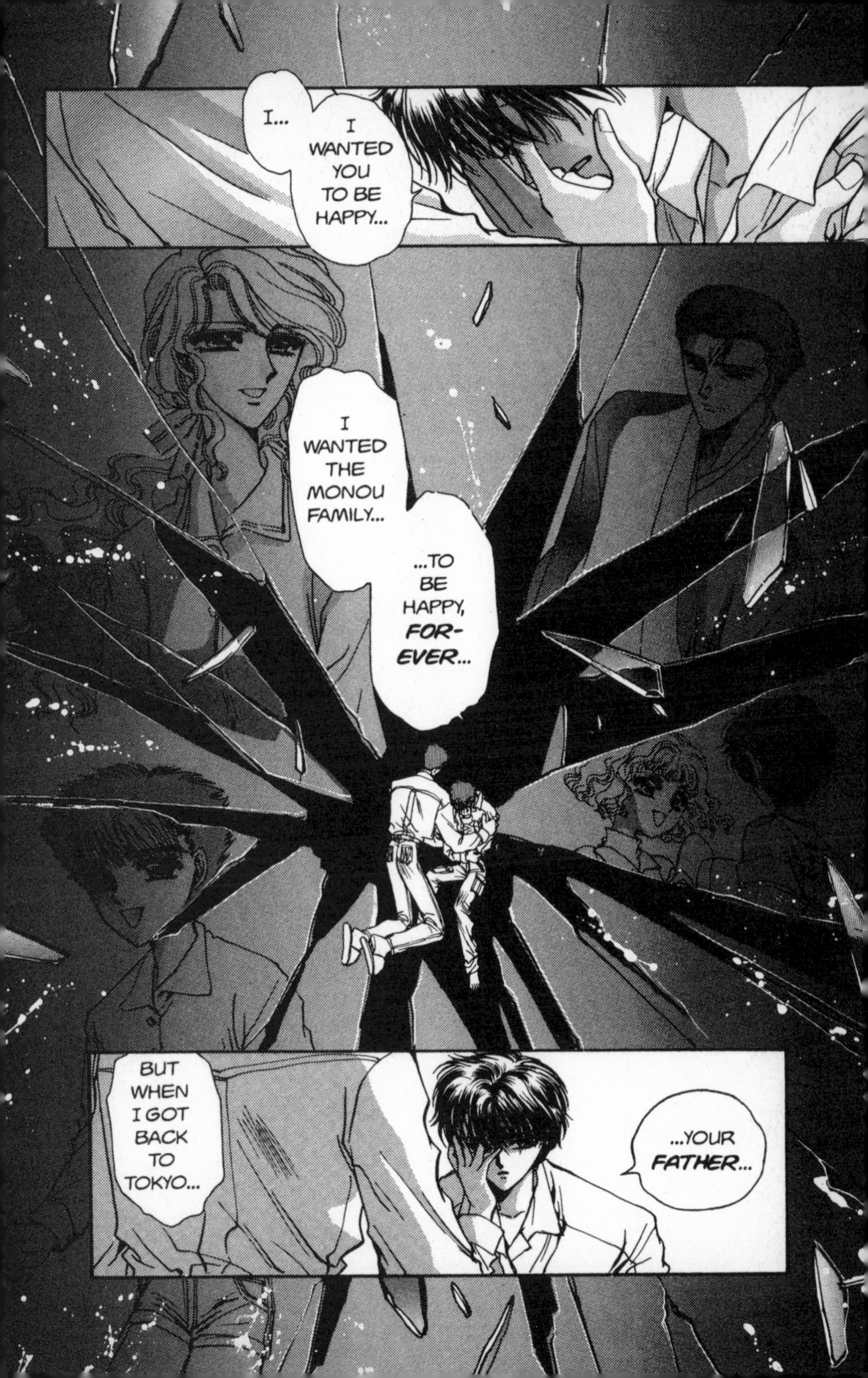

I...
I WANTED YOU TO BE HAPPY...
I WANTED THE MONOU FAMILY...
...TO BE HAPPY, FOR-EVER...
BUT WHEN I GOT BACK TO TOKYO...
...YOUR FATHER...

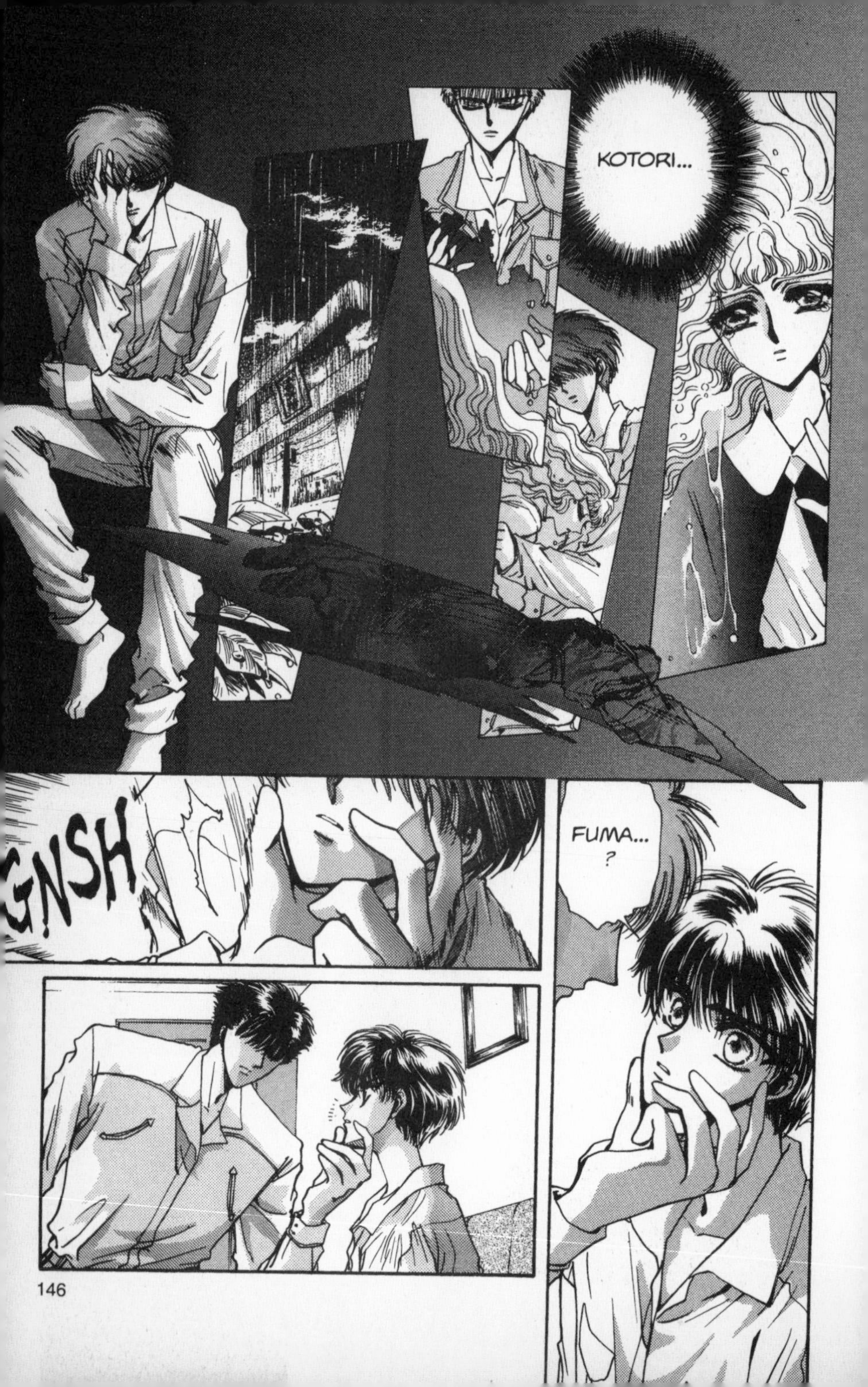
KOTORI...
GNSH
FUMA...
?

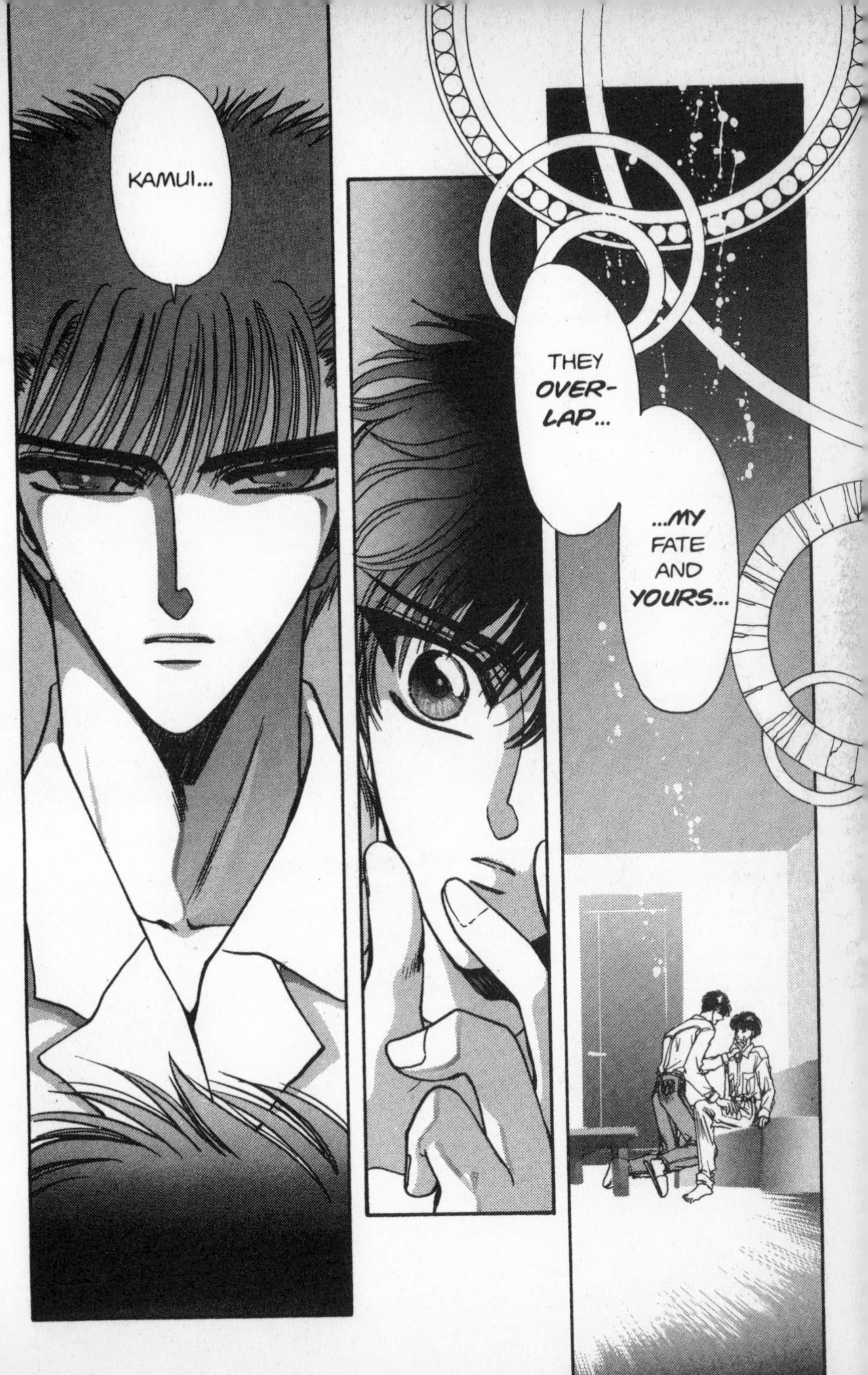
KAMUI...
THEY OVER-LAP...
...MY FATE AND YOURS...

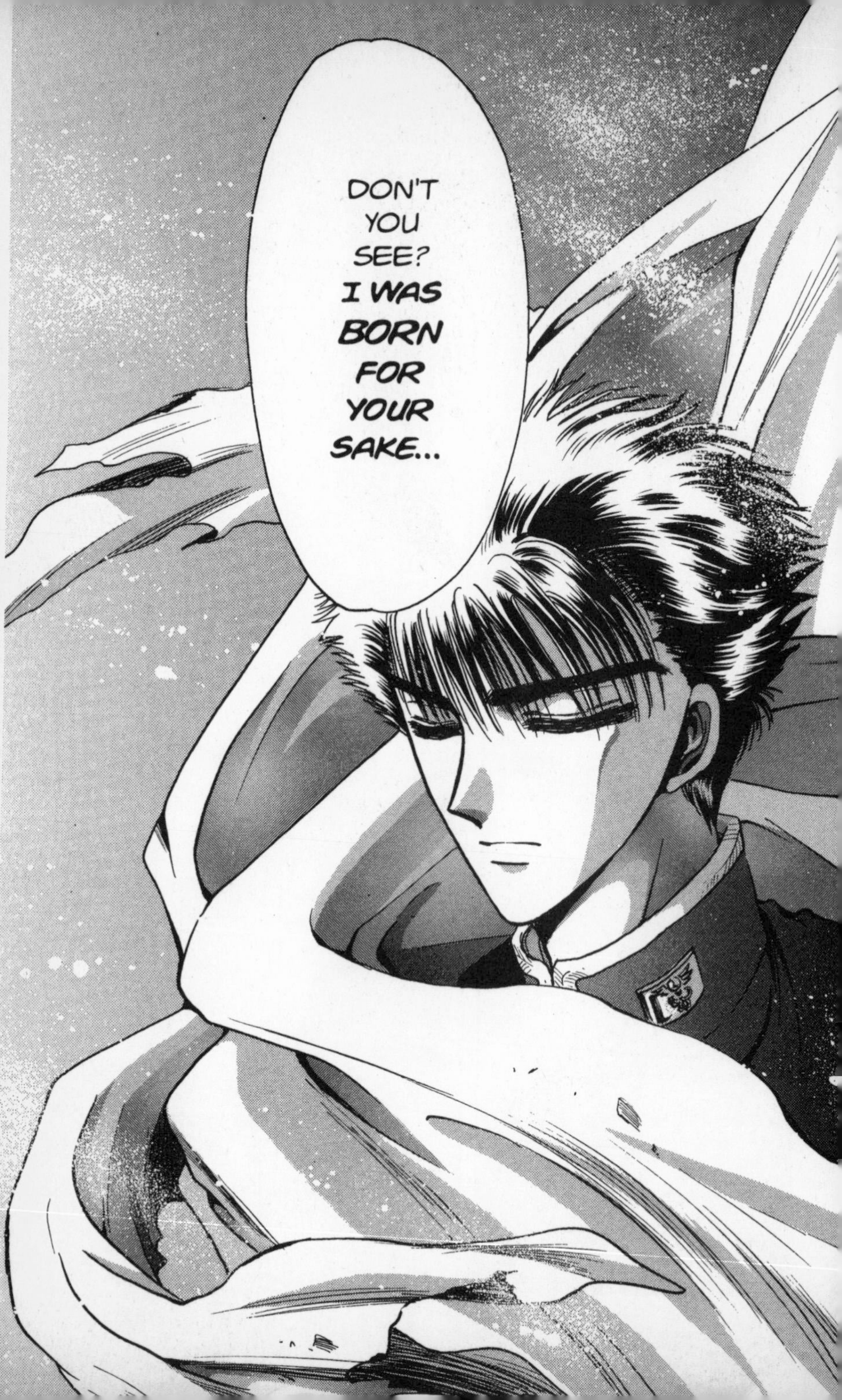
DON'T YOU SEE? I WAS BORN FOR YOUR SAKE...

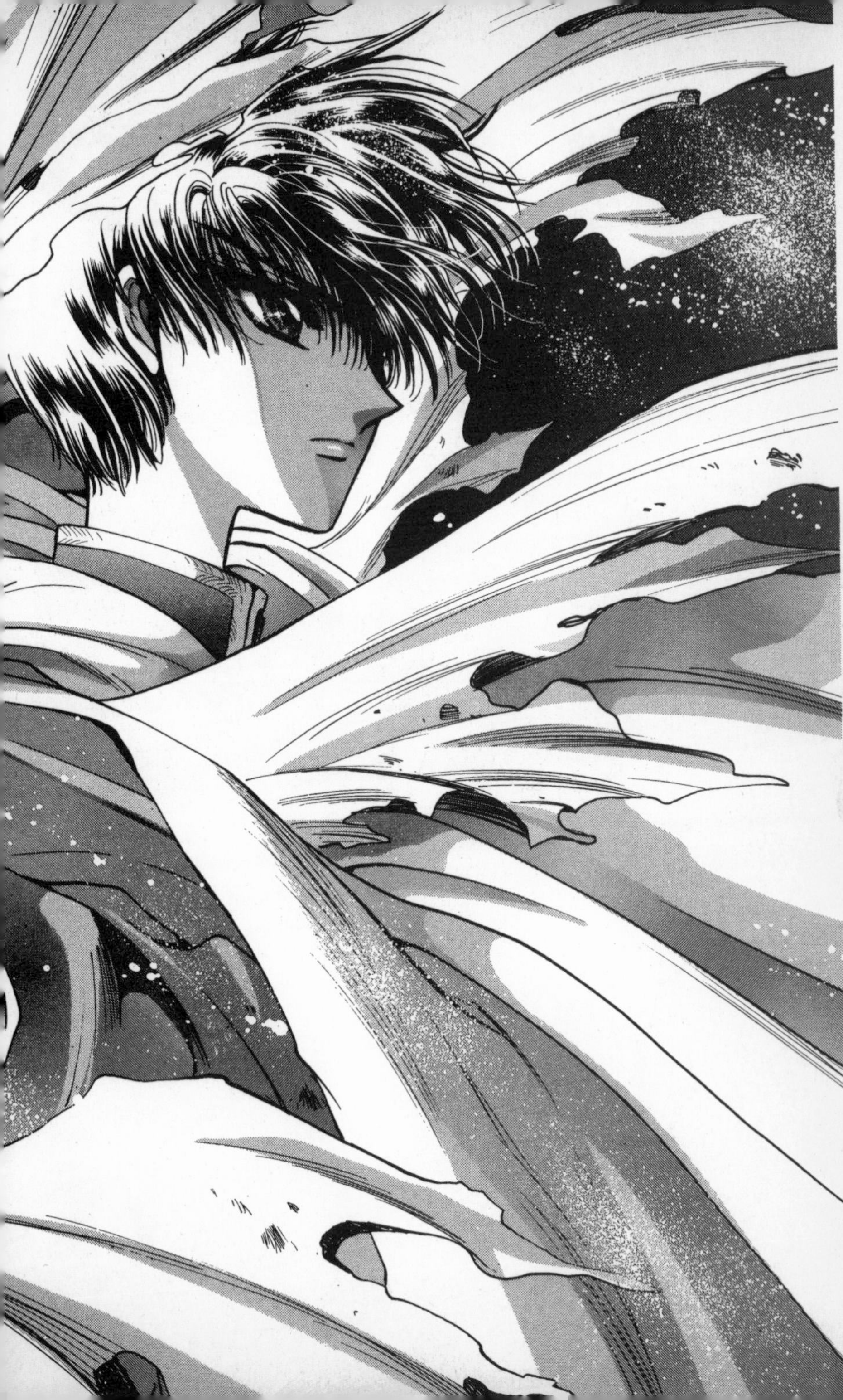

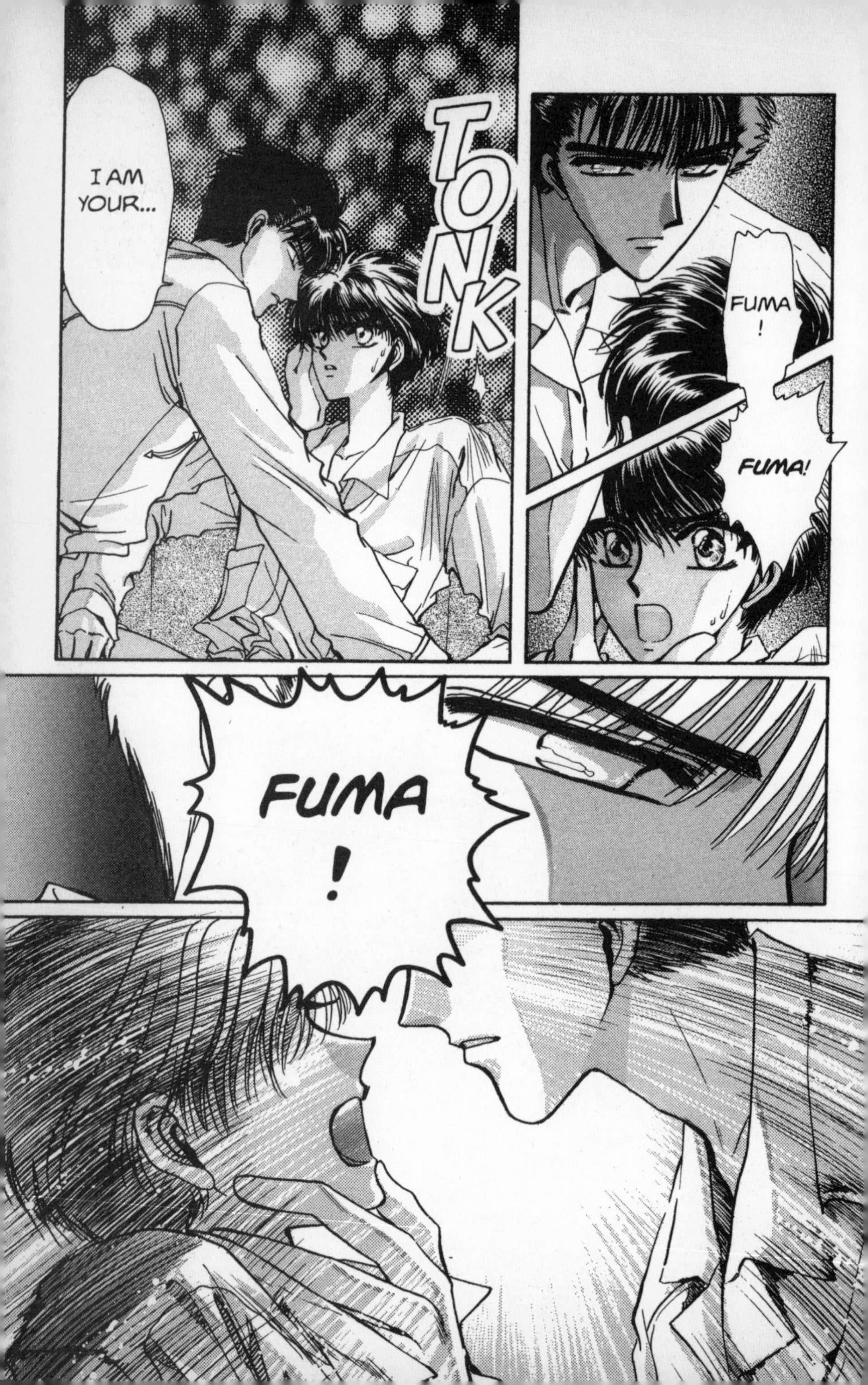
I AM YOUR...
TONK
FUMA !
FUMA!
FUMA !

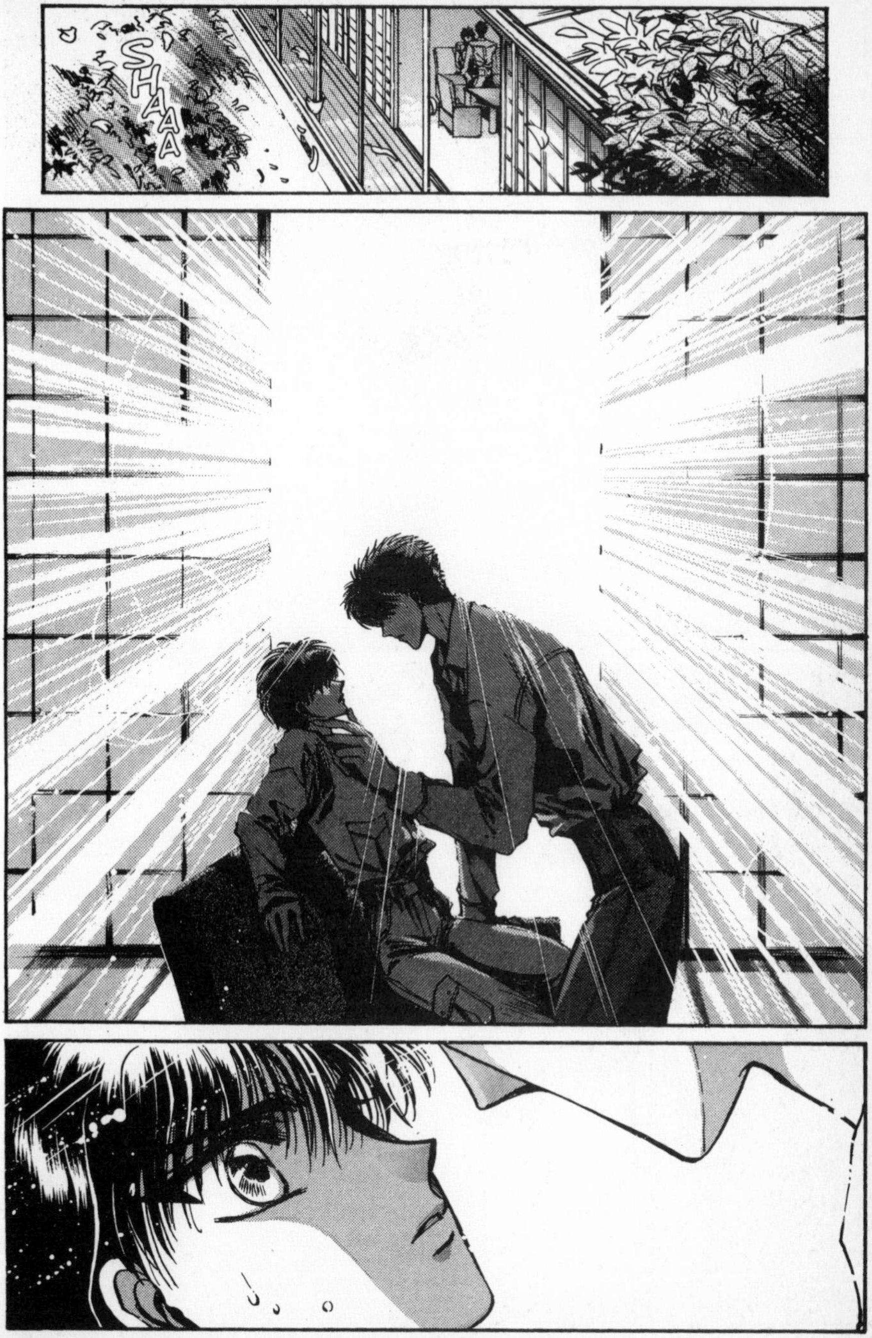
SHAAA

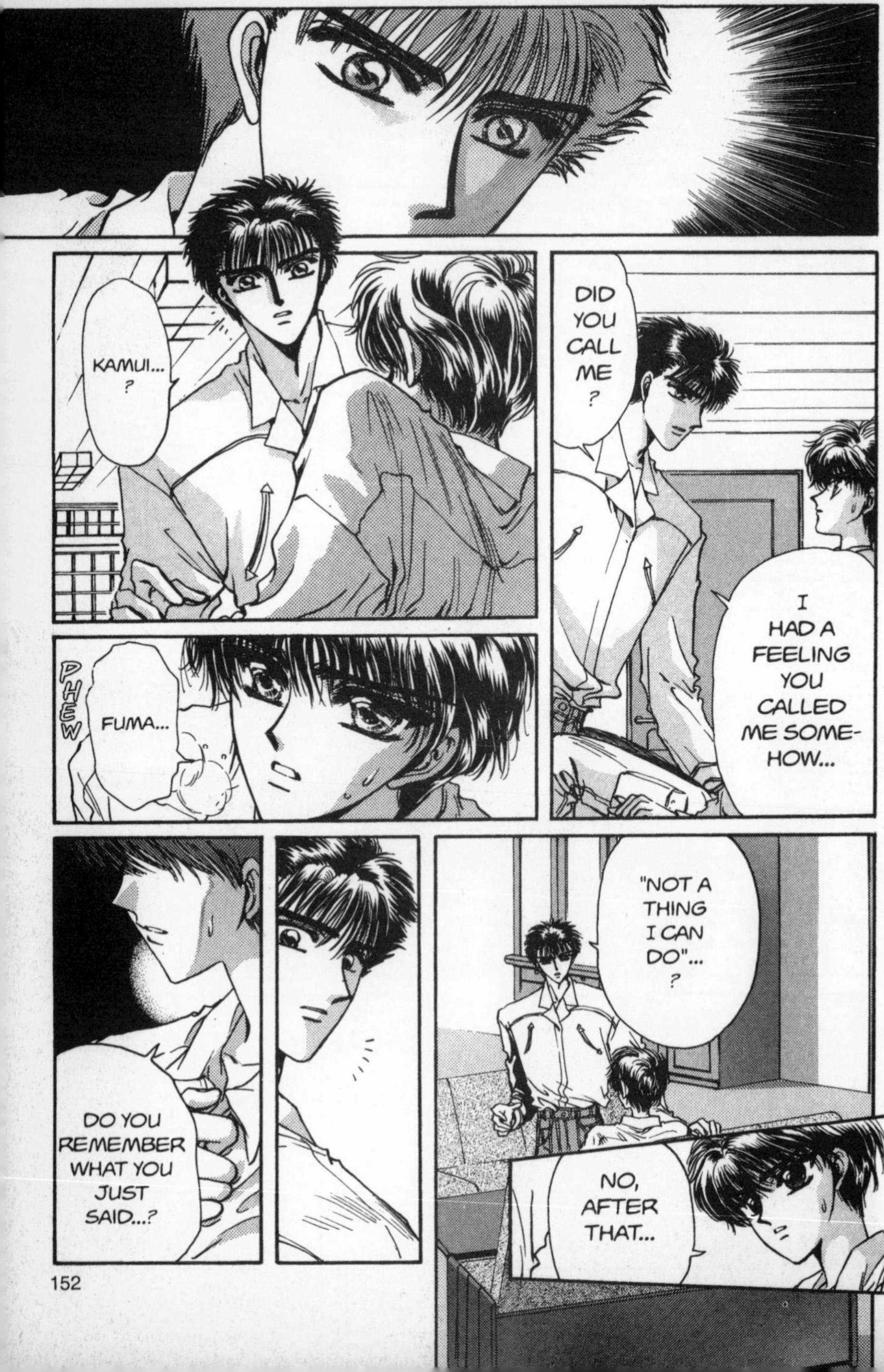
KAMUI...?
DID YOU CALL ME?
I HAD A FEELING YOU CALLED ME SOME-HOW...
PHEW
FUMA...
DO YOU REMEMBER WHAT YOU JUST SAID...?
"NOT A THING I CAN DO"...?
NO, AFTER THAT...

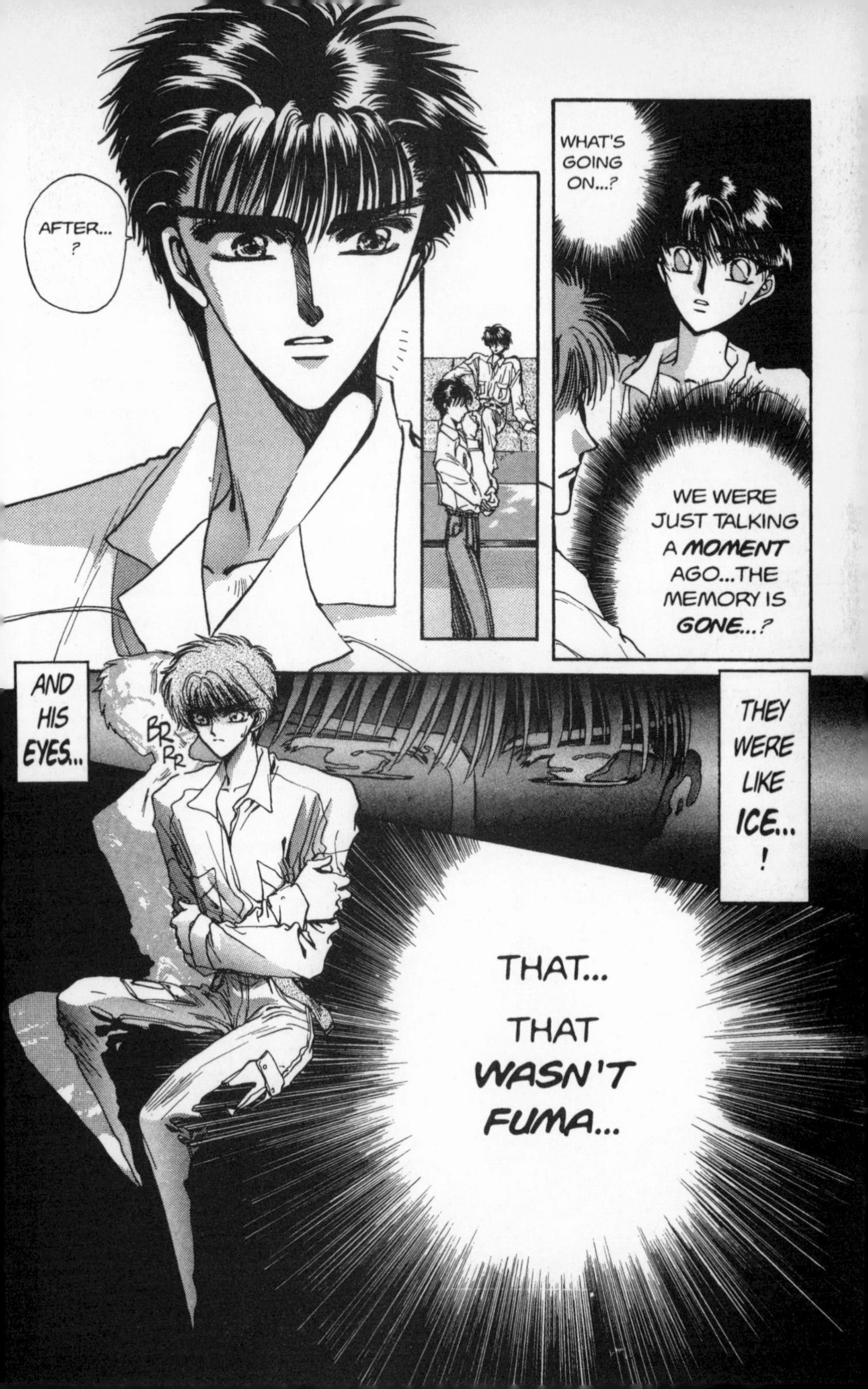
AFTER... ?
WHAT'S GOING ON...?
WE WERE JUST TALKING A MOMENT AGO...THE MEMORY IS GONE...?
AND HIS EYES...
BRRR
THEY WERE LIKE ICE... !
THAT...
THAT WASN'T FUMA...

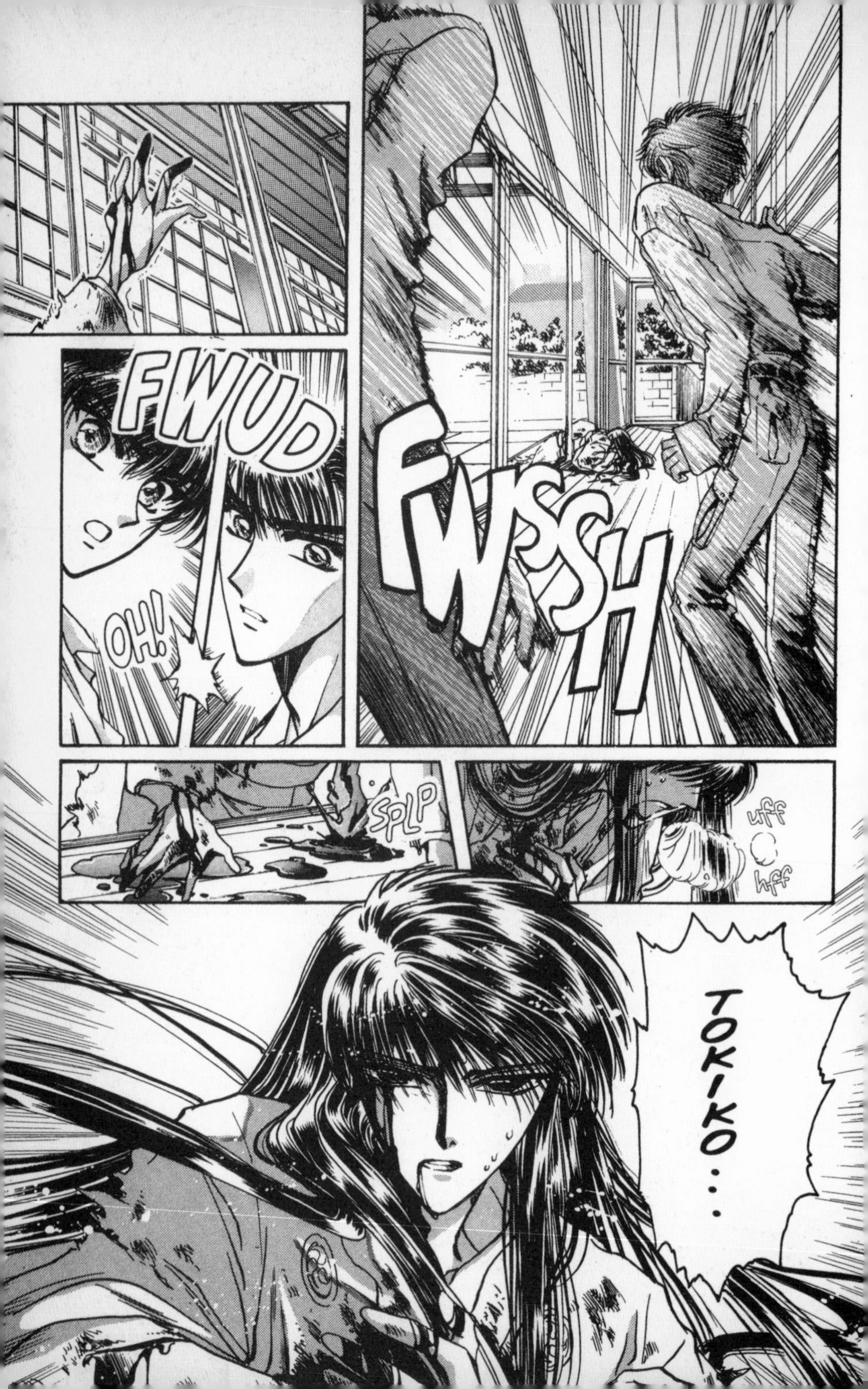
FWUD
OH!
FWSSH
SPLP
uff
hff
TOKIKO...

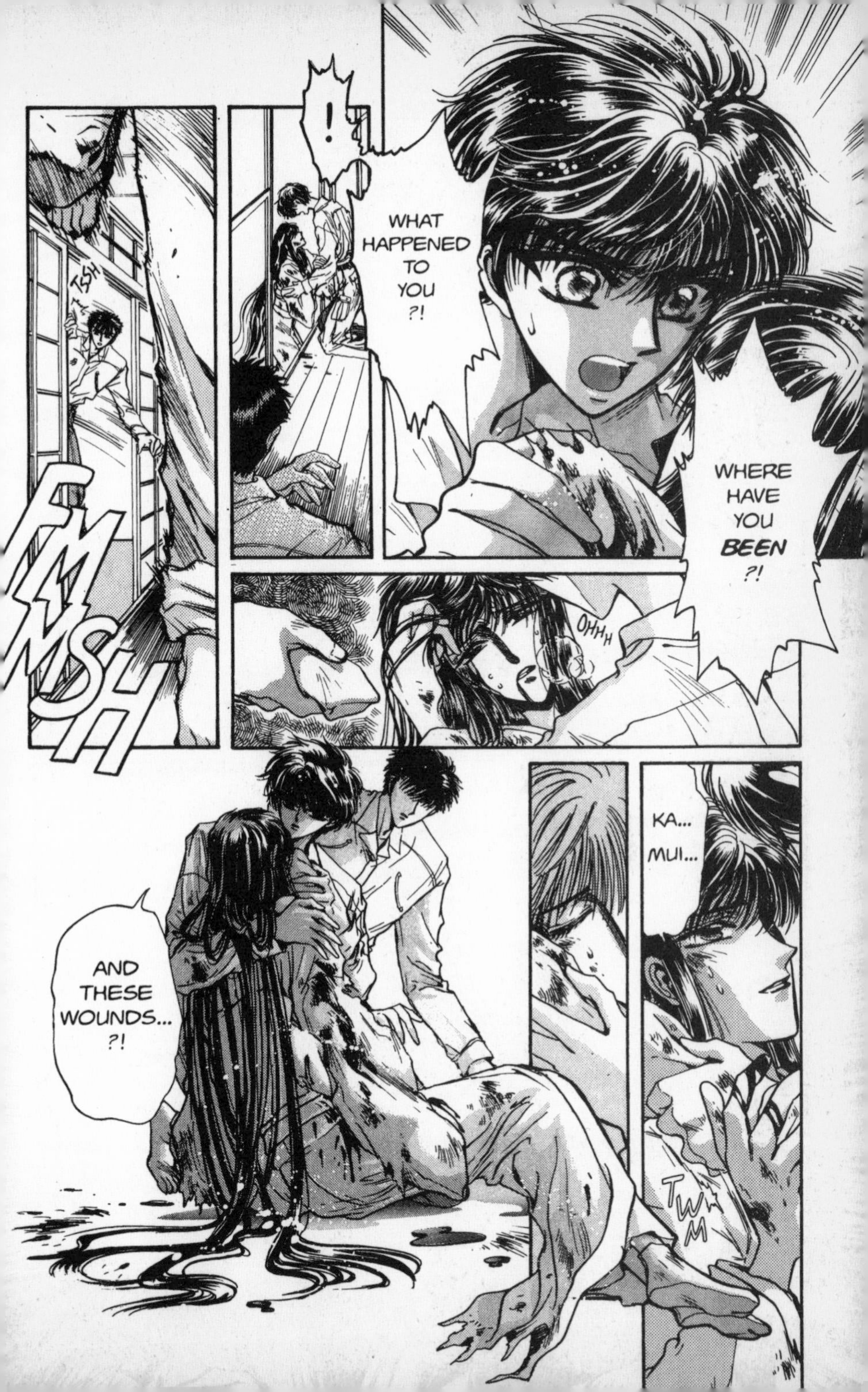
TSH
FMMSH
!
WHAT HAPPENED TO YOU ?!
WHERE HAVE YOU **BEEN** ?!
OHHH
AND THESE WOUNDS... ?!
KA... MUI...
TWM

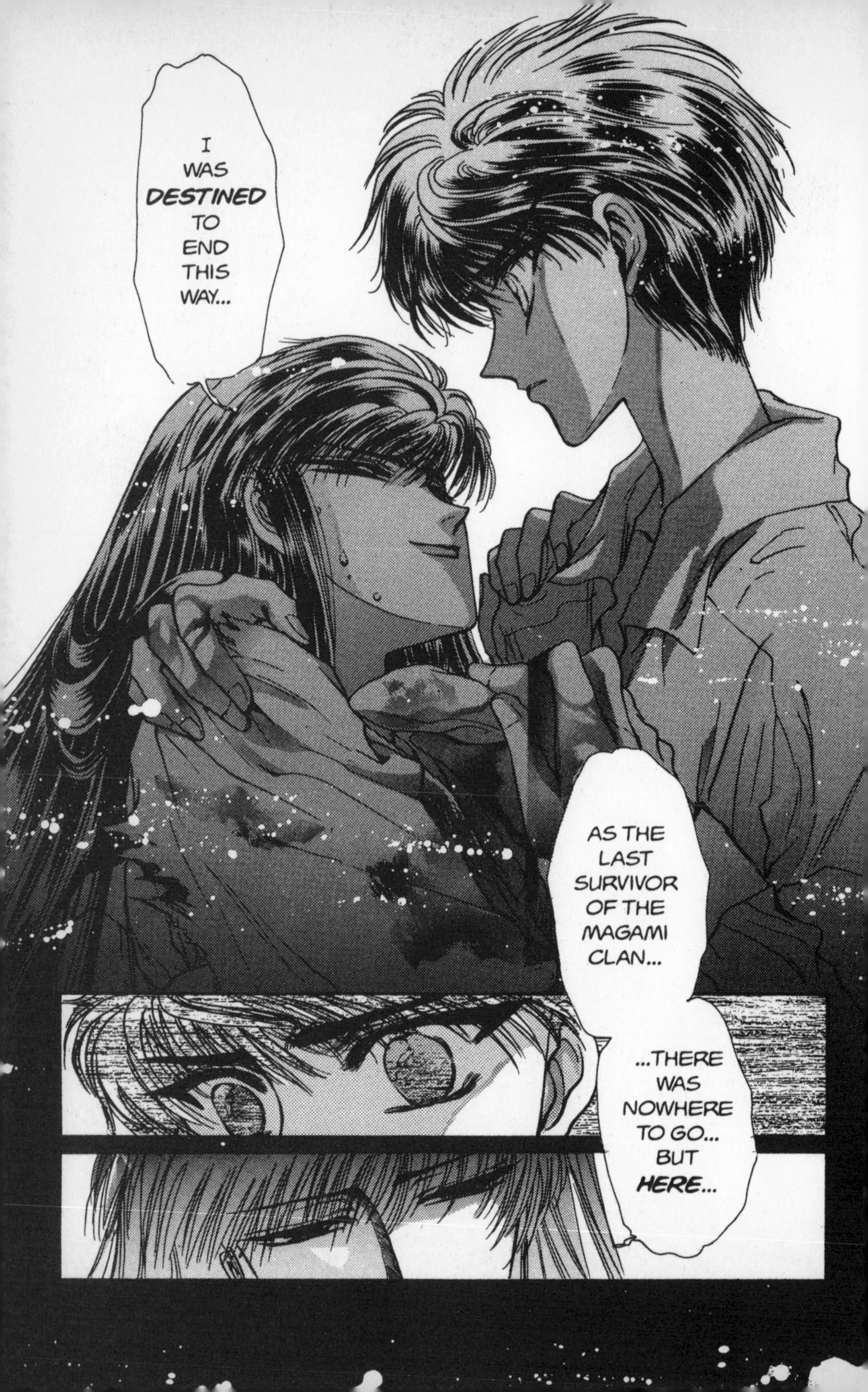
I WAS DESTINED TO END THIS WAY...
AS THE LAST SURVIVOR OF THE MAGAMI CLAN...
...THERE WAS NOWHERE TO GO... BUT HERE...

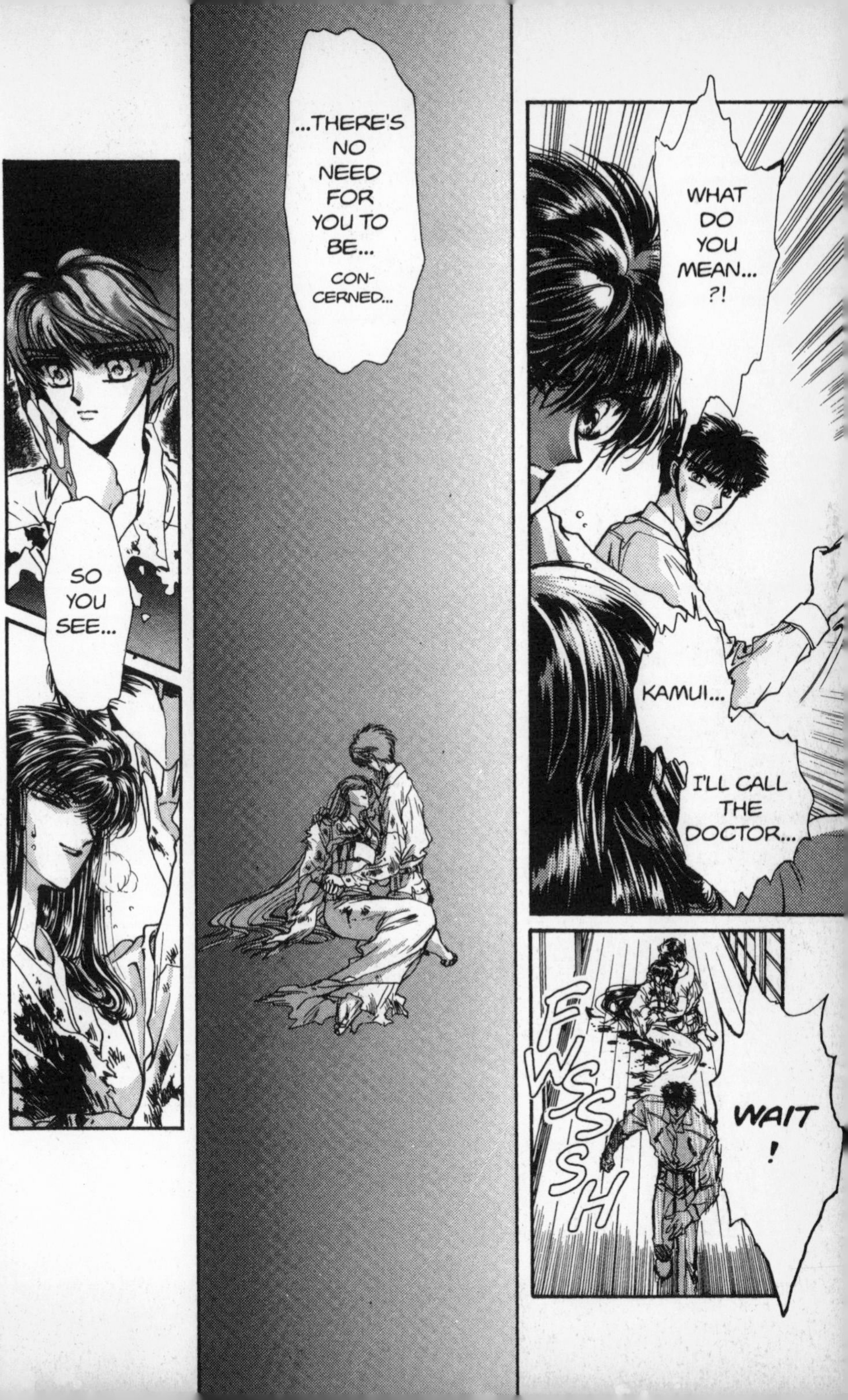
SO YOU SEE...
...THERE'S NO NEED FOR YOU TO BE... CON-CERNED...
WHAT DO YOU MEAN... ?!
KAMUI...
I'LL CALL THE DOCTOR...
FWSSH
WAIT !

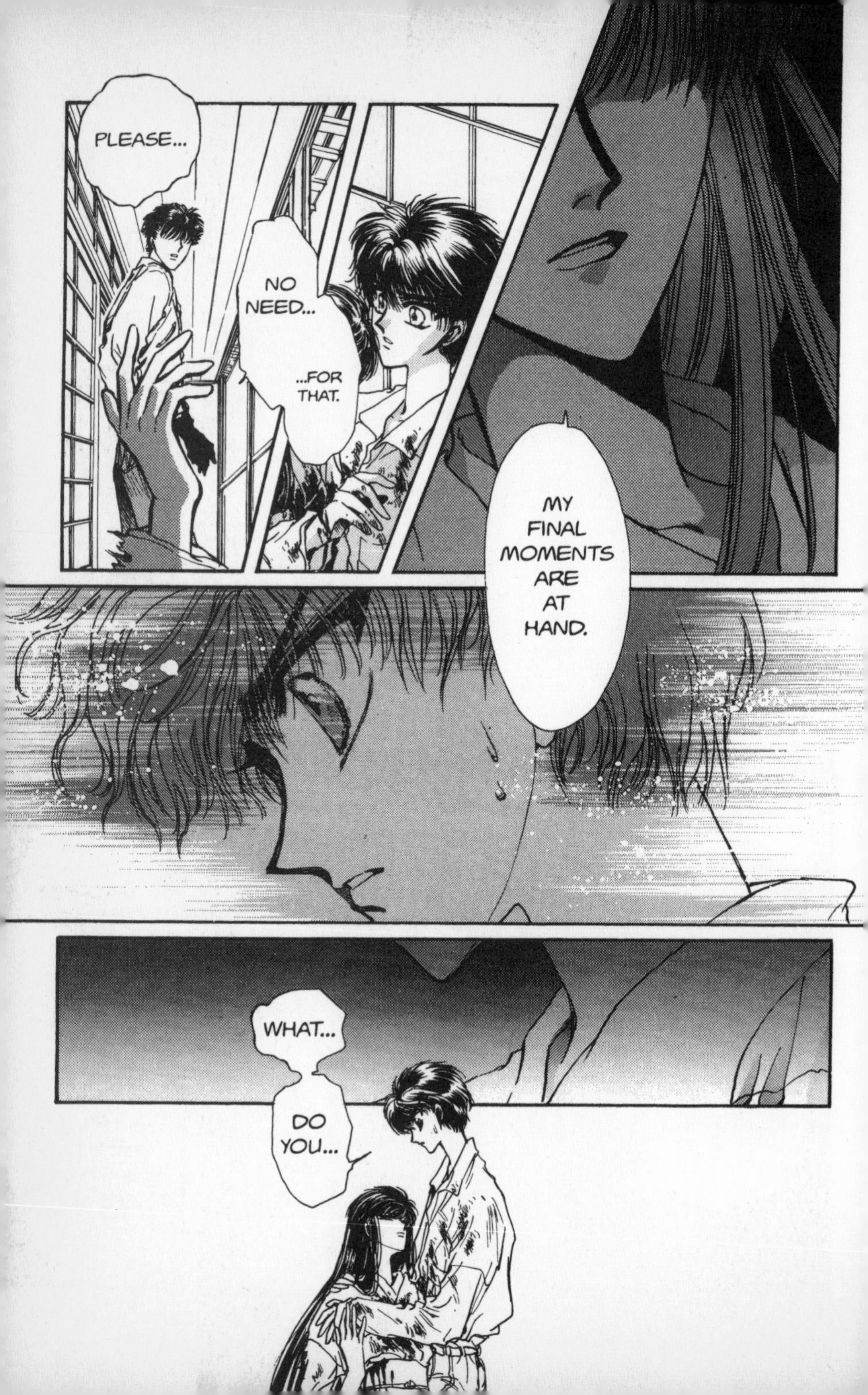
PLEASE...
NO NEED...
...FOR THAT.
MY FINAL MOMENTS ARE AT HAND.
WHAT...
DO YOU...

KAMUI... LISTEN TO ME.

THE **SACRED SWORD**... WAS **DESTINED** TO BE TAKEN.

THE **FIRST** SACRED SWORD... WAS **DESTINED** TO BE TAKEN-- WITHOUT FAIL...

--FROM A **WOMAN'S** BODY..."

FROM A...?

THE **FIRST**...?

SIX YEARS AGO...

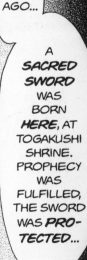

A **SACRED SWORD** WAS BORN **HERE**, AT TOGAKUSHI SHRINE. PROPHECY WAS FULFILLED, THE SWORD WAS **PRO-TECTED**...

"THE **SACRED SWORD** WILL **BE BORN** FROM THIS **TOGAKUSHI SHRINE**--

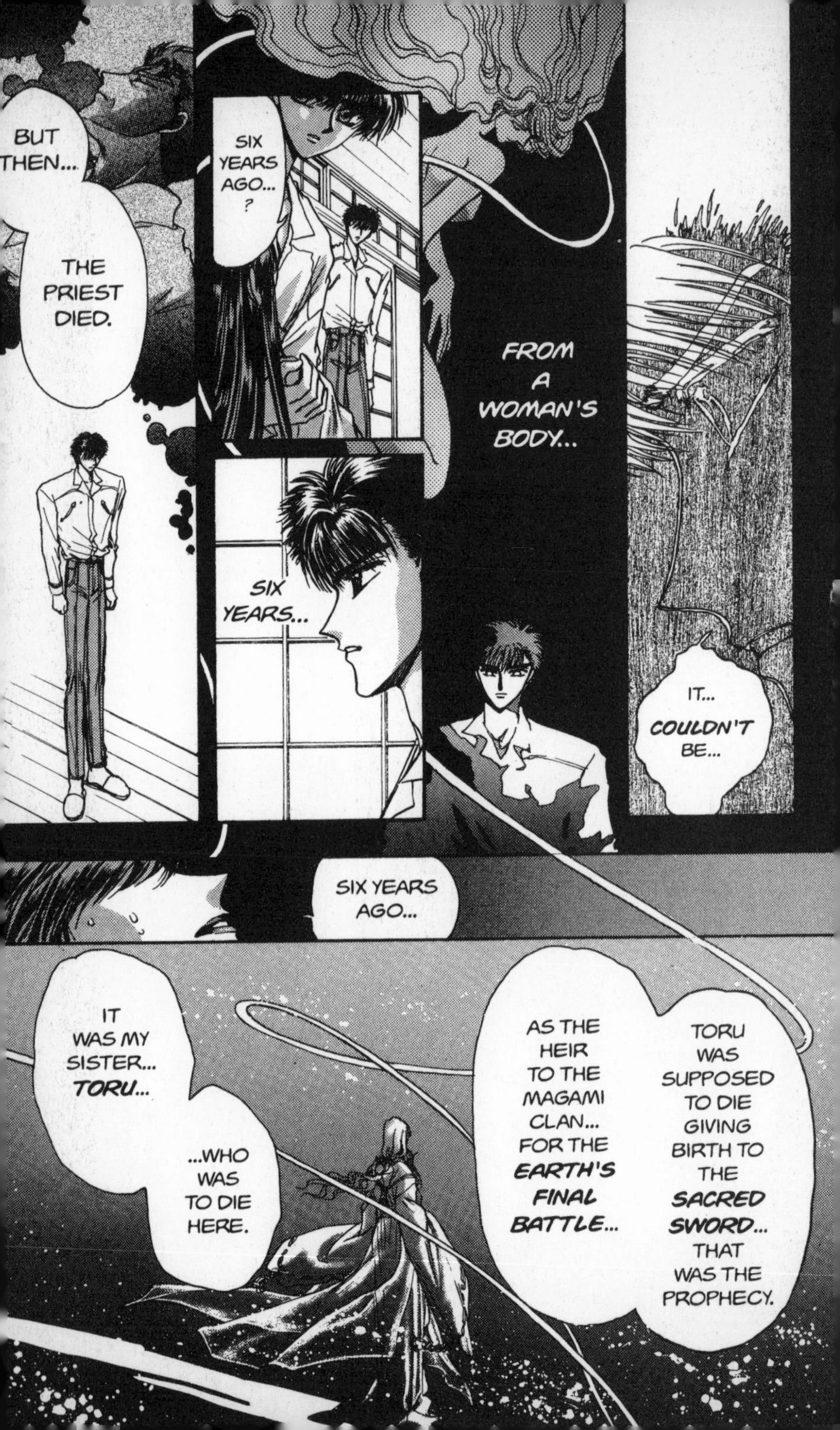
BUT THEN...
THE PRIEST DIED.
SIX YEARS AGO... ?
SIX YEARS...
FROM A WOMAN'S BODY...
IT... COULDN'T BE...
SIX YEARS AGO...
IT WAS MY SISTER... TORU...
...WHO WAS TO DIE HERE.
AS THE HEIR TO THE MAGAMI CLAN... FOR THE EARTH'S FINAL BATTLE...
TORU WAS SUPPOSED TO DIE GIVING BIRTH TO THE SACRED SWORD... THAT WAS THE PROPHECY.

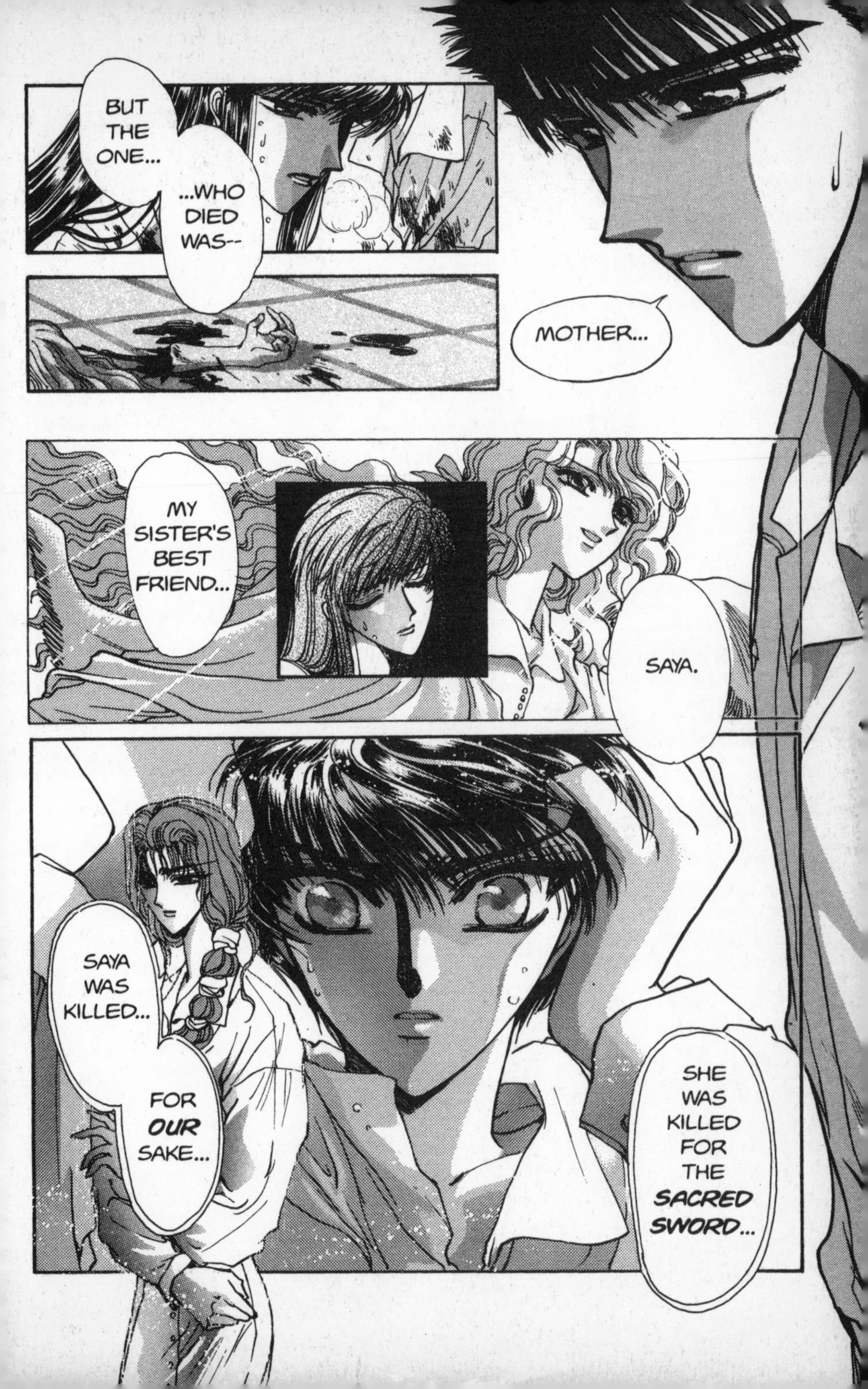
BUT THE ONE...
...WHO DIED WAS--
MOTHER...
MY SISTER'S BEST FRIEND...
SAYA.
SAYA WAS KILLED...
FOR **OUR** SAKE...
SHE WAS KILLED FOR THE ***SACRED SWORD***...

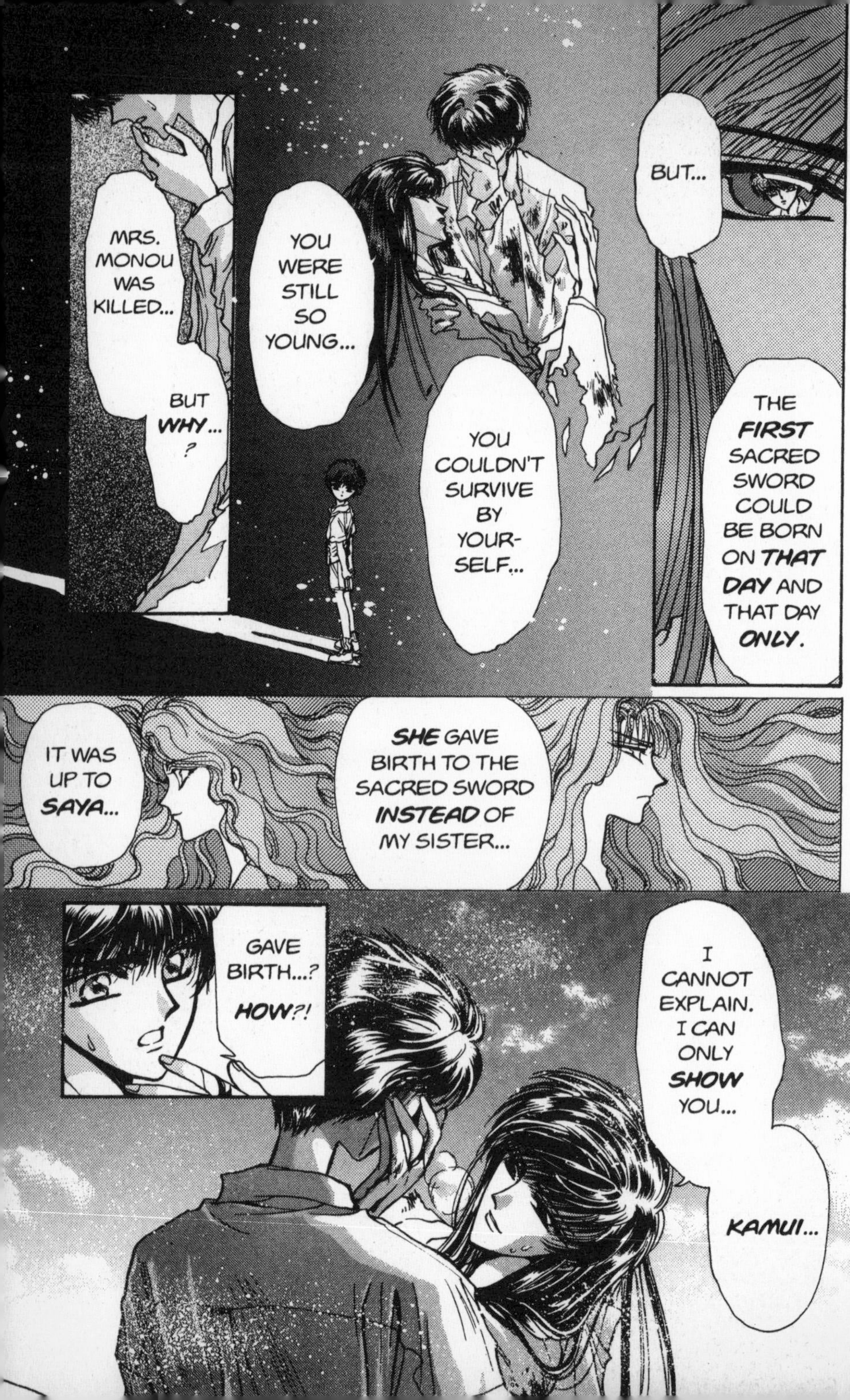
MRS. MONOU WAS KILLED...
BUT WHY... ?
YOU WERE STILL SO YOUNG...
YOU COULDN'T SURVIVE BY YOUR-SELF...
BUT...
THE FIRST SACRED SWORD COULD BE BORN ON THAT DAY AND THAT DAY ONLY.
IT WAS UP TO SAYA...
SHE GAVE BIRTH TO THE SACRED SWORD INSTEAD OF MY SISTER...
GAVE BIRTH...? HOW?!
I CANNOT EXPLAIN. I CAN ONLY SHOW YOU...
KAMUI...

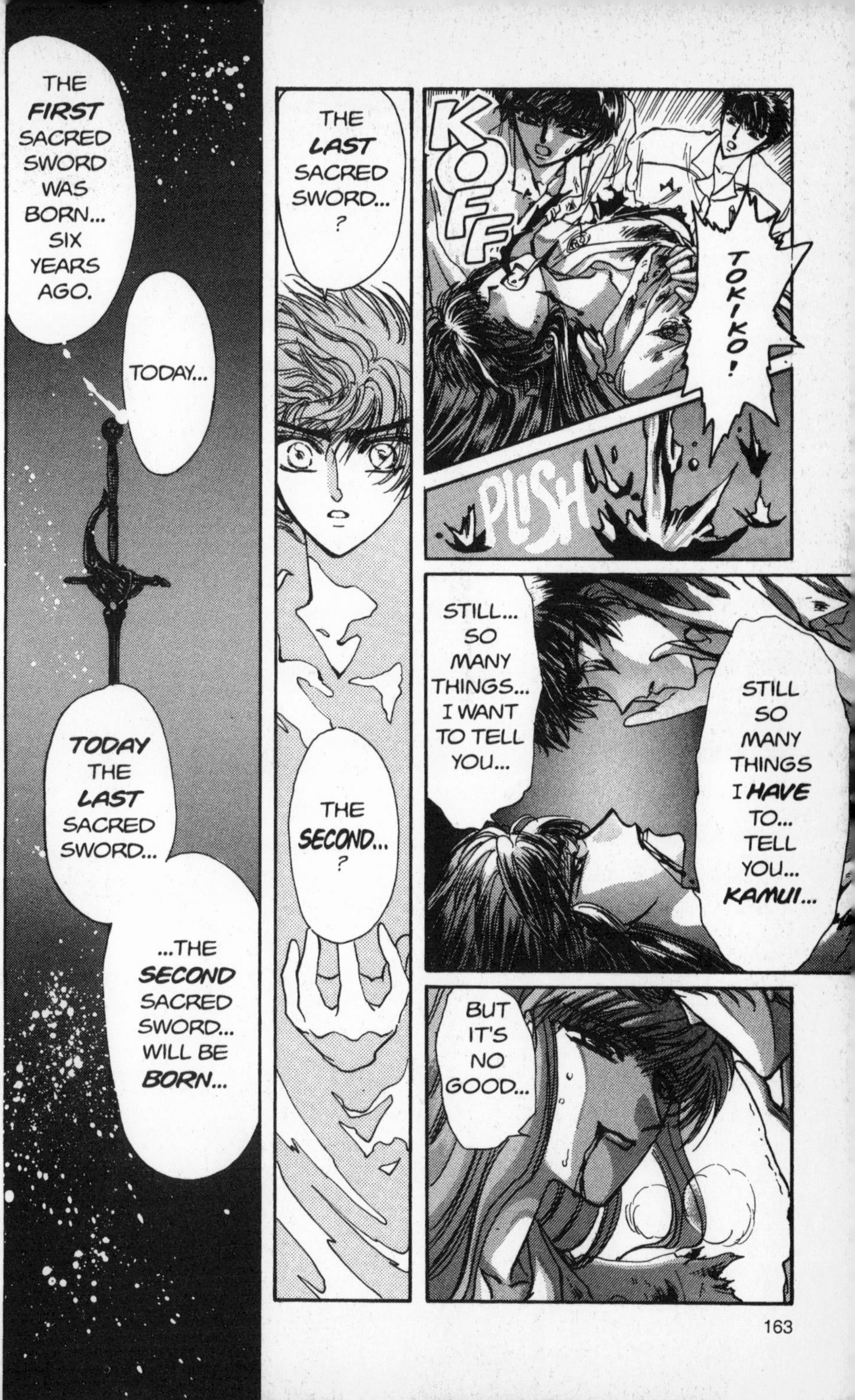
THE *FIRST* SACRED SWORD WAS BORN... SIX YEARS AGO.
TODAY...
TODAY THE *LAST* SACRED SWORD...
...THE *SECOND* SACRED SWORD... WILL BE *BORN*...
THE *LAST* SACRED SWORD... ?
THE *SECOND*... ?
KOFF
TOKIKO!
PUSH
STILL... SO MANY THINGS... I WANT TO TELL YOU...
STILL SO MANY THINGS I *HAVE* TO... TELL YOU... *KAMUI*...
BUT IT'S NO GOOD...

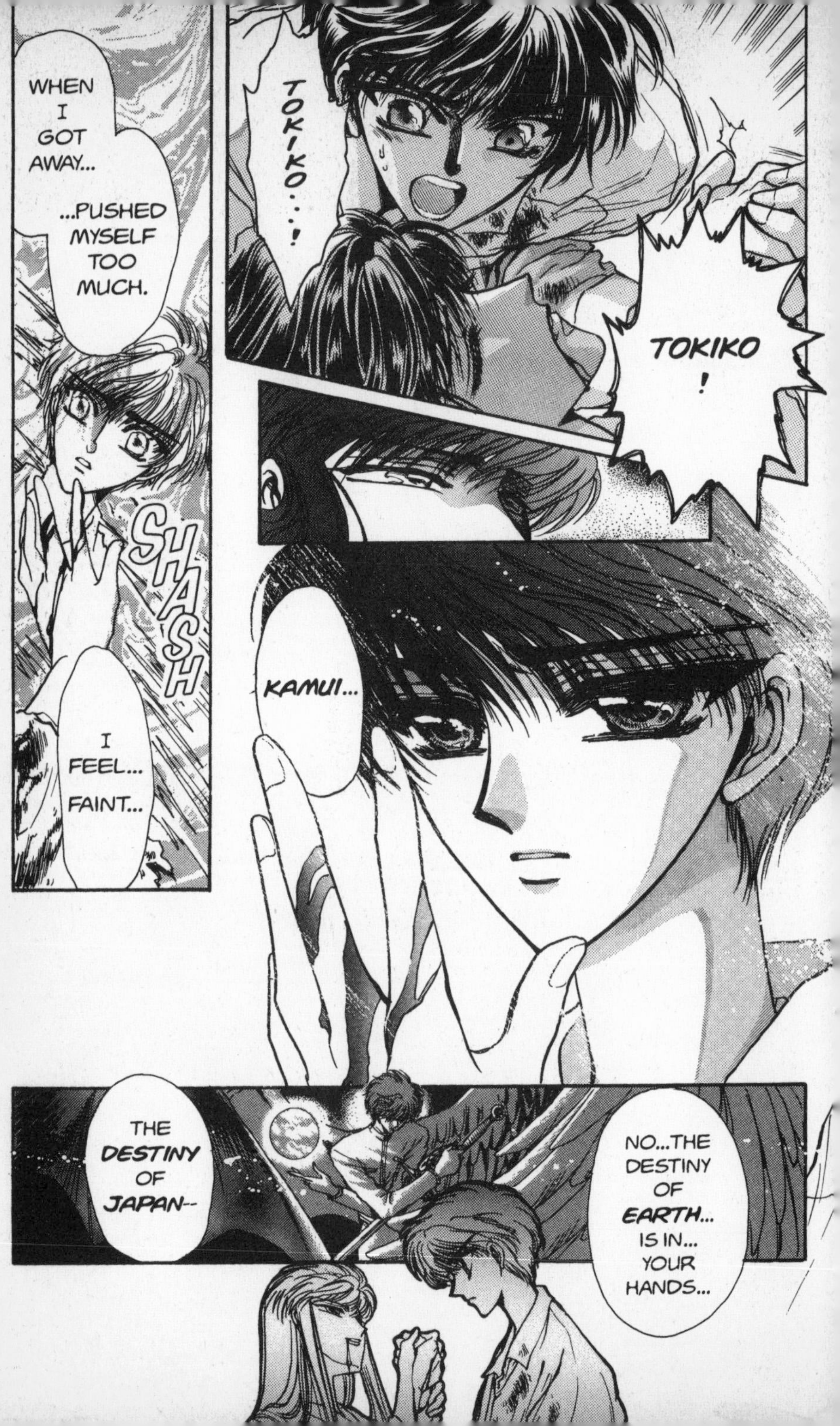

WHEN I GOT AWAY...
...PUSHED MYSELF TOO MUCH.
SHASH
I FEEL... FAINT...
TOKIKO...!
TOKIKO!
KAMUI...
THE DESTINY OF JAPAN--
NO...THE DESTINY OF EARTH... IS IN... YOUR HANDS...

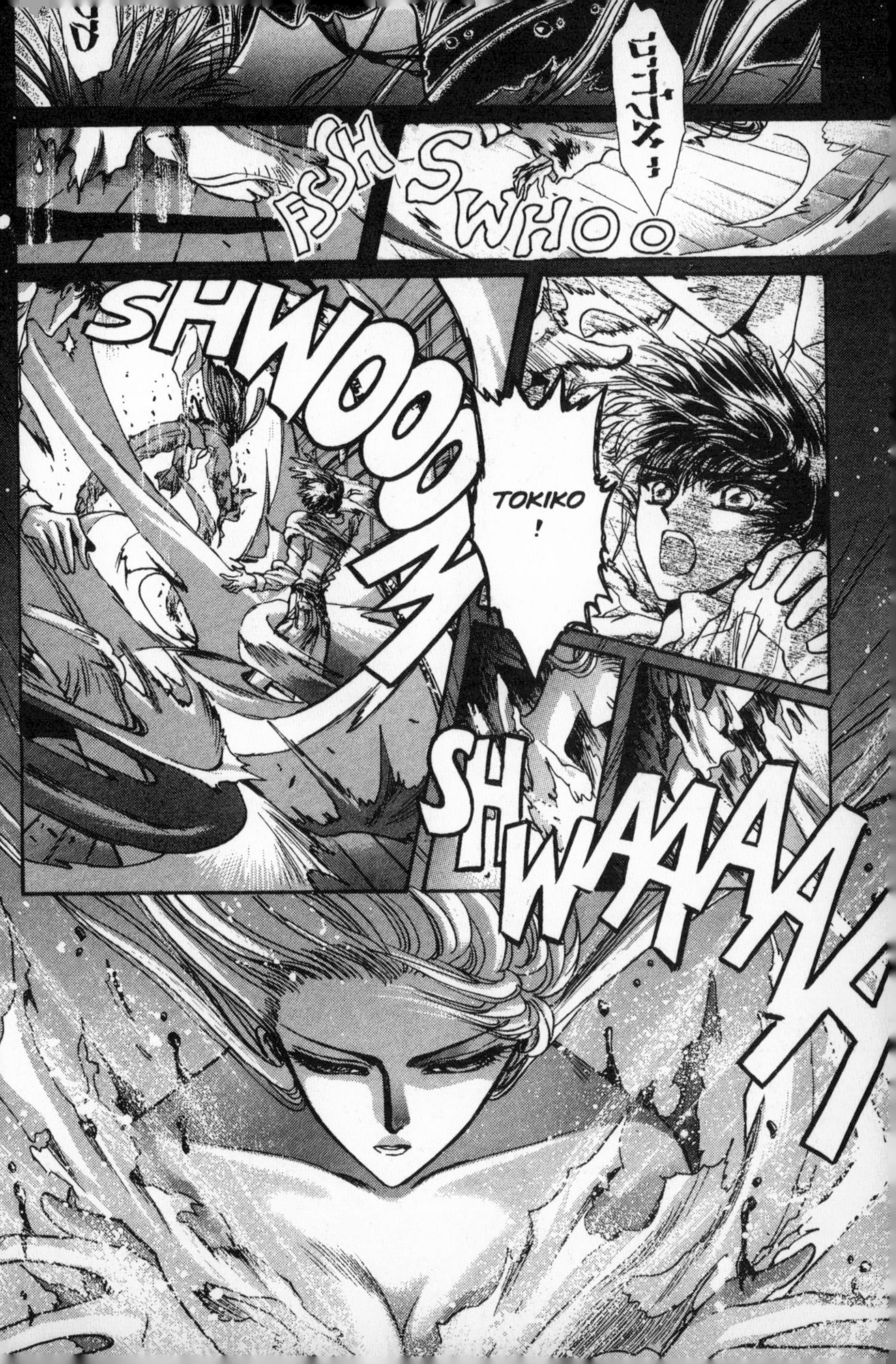
FSSH
SWHOO
SHWOOOOM
TOKIKO!
SHWAAAAK!

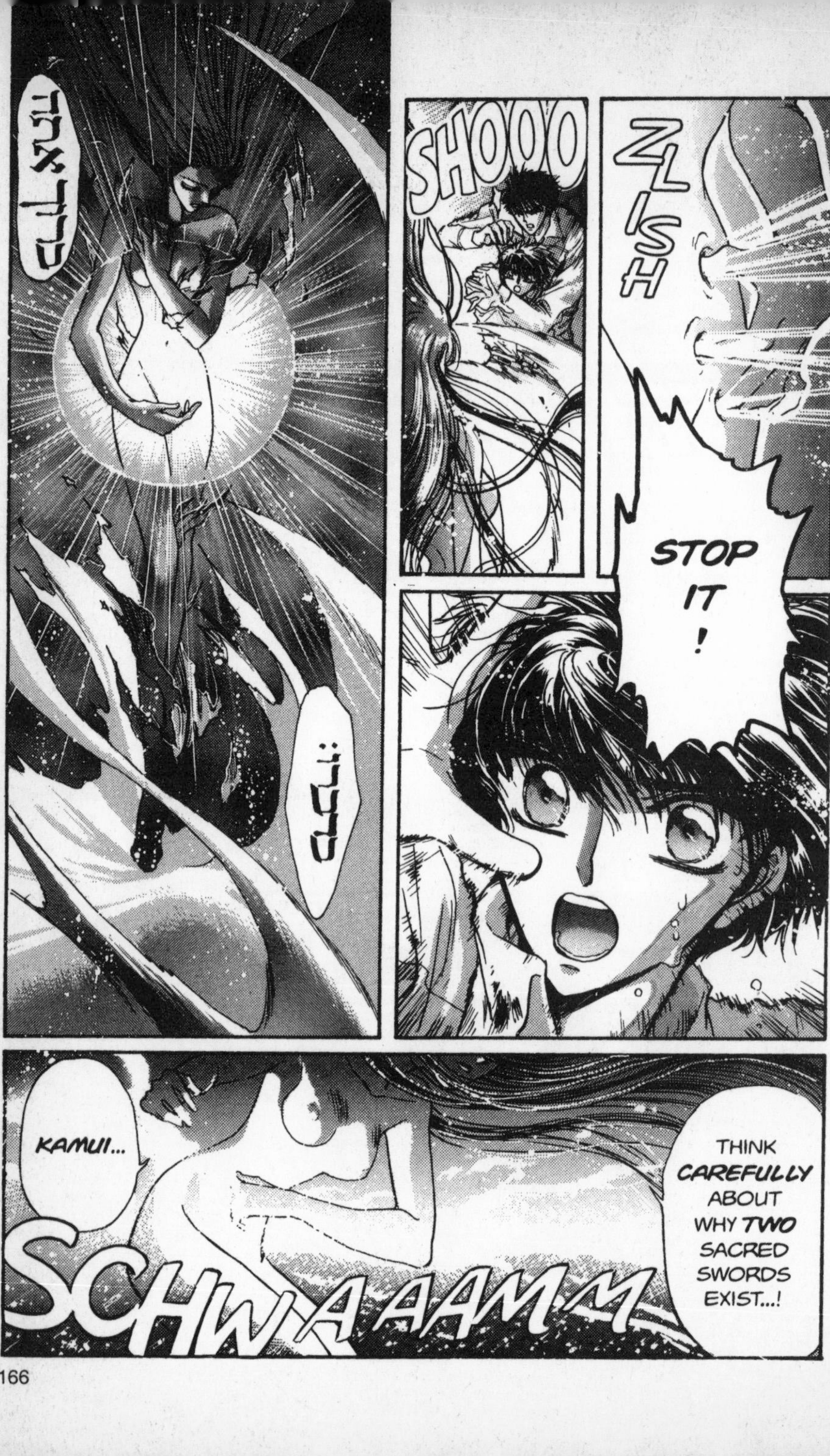
SHOOO
ZLISH
STOP IT!
KAMUI...
SCHWAAAMM
THINK CAREFULLY ABOUT WHY TWO SACRED SWORDS EXIST...!

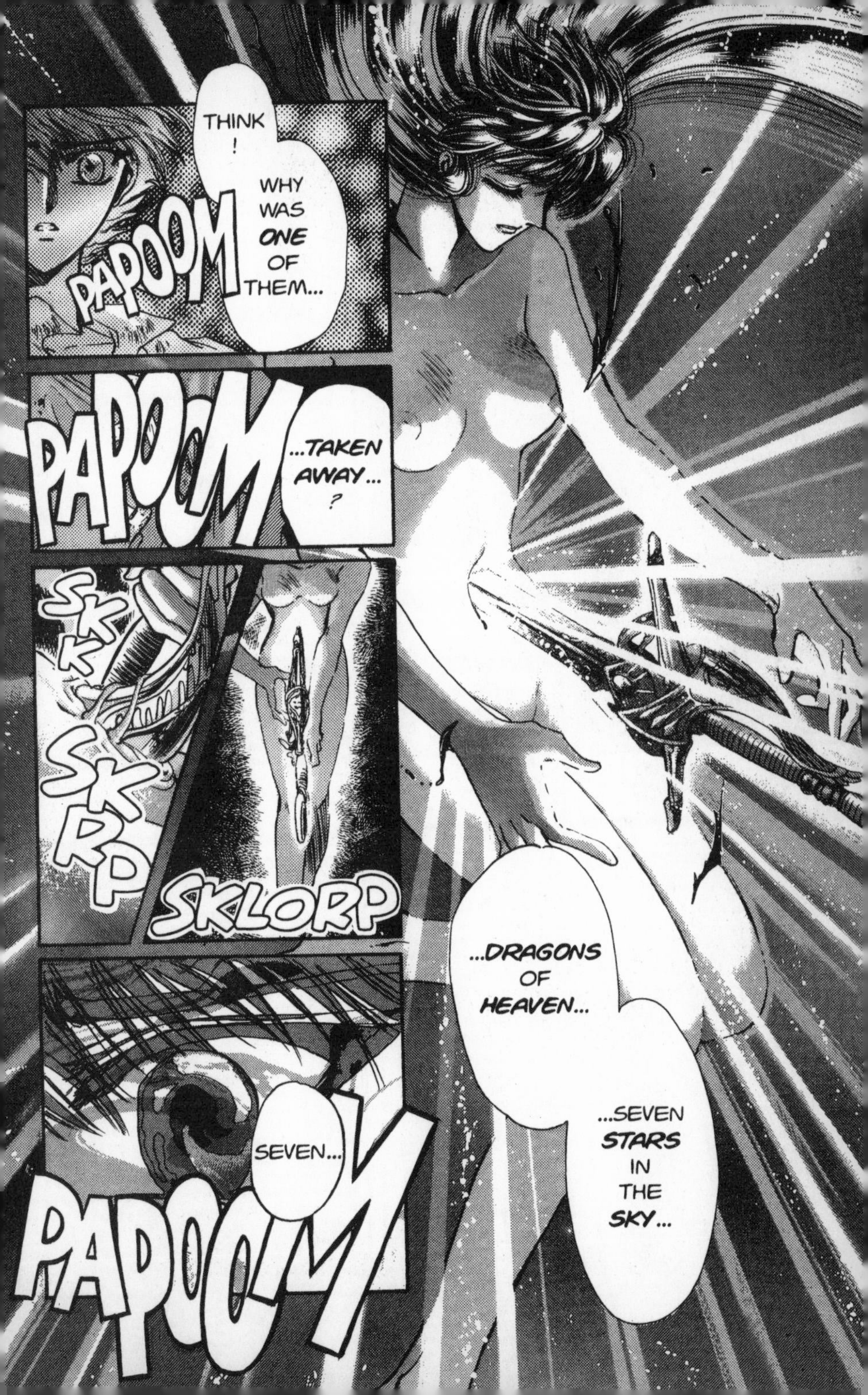
THINK! WHY WAS ONE OF THEM...
PAPOOM
PAPOOM
...TAKEN AWAY...?
SKK
SKRP
SKLORP
SEVEN...
PAPOOM
...DRAGONS OF HEAVEN...
...SEVEN STARS IN THE SKY...

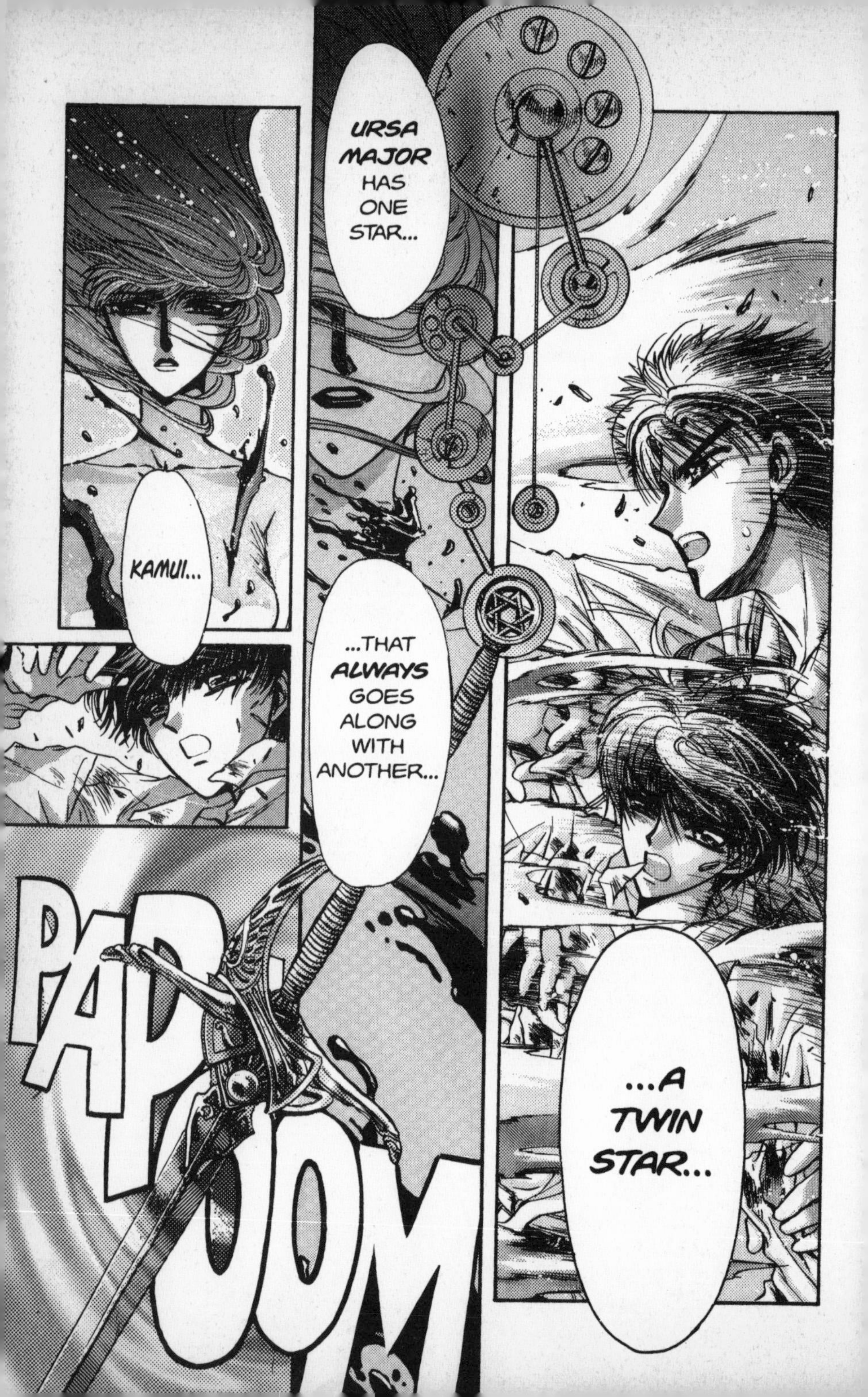
KAMUI...
URSA MAJOR HAS ONE STAR...
...THAT ALWAYS GOES ALONG WITH ANOTHER...
PADOOM
...A TWIN STAR...

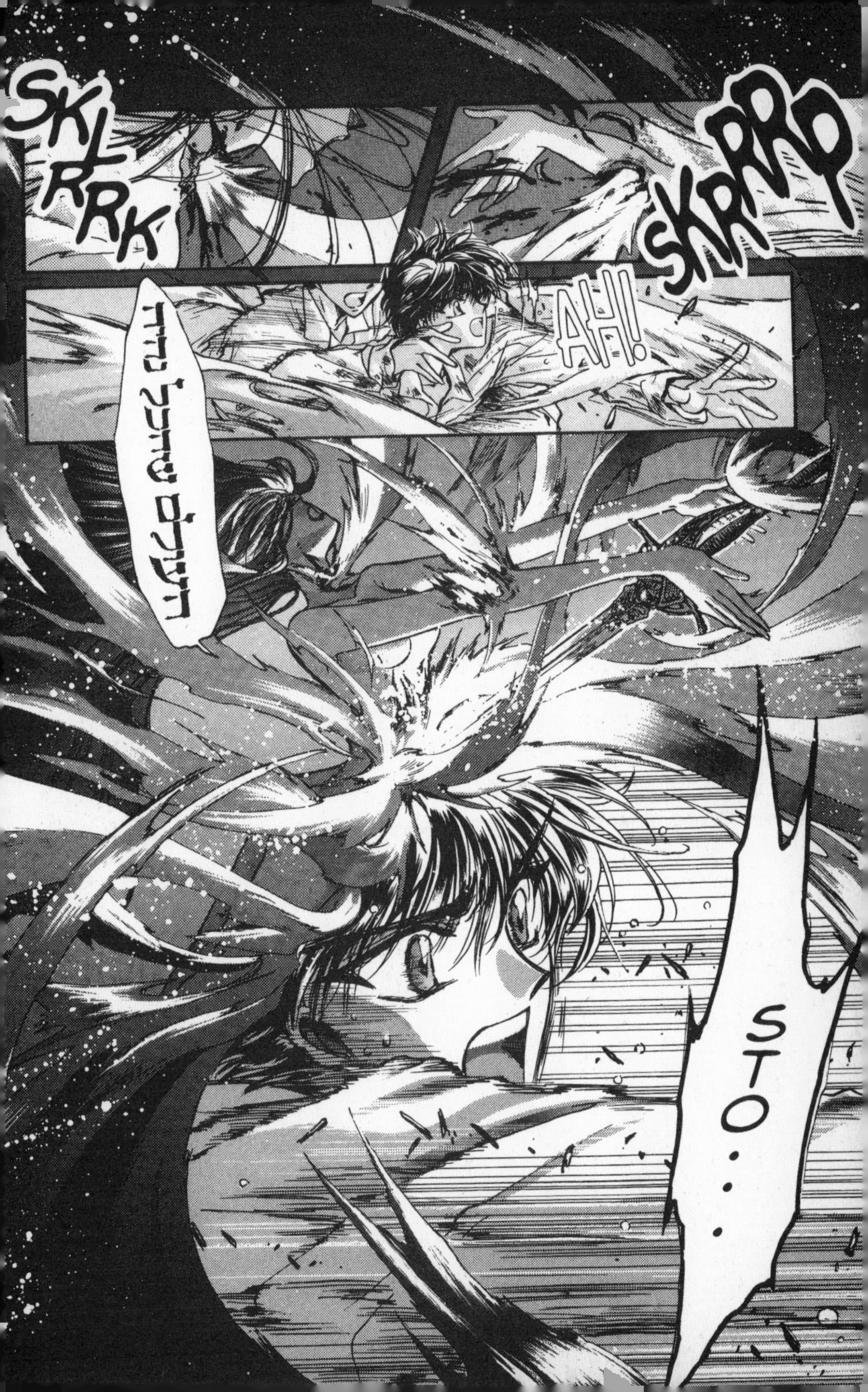
SKLRRK
SKRRRD
AH!
STO...

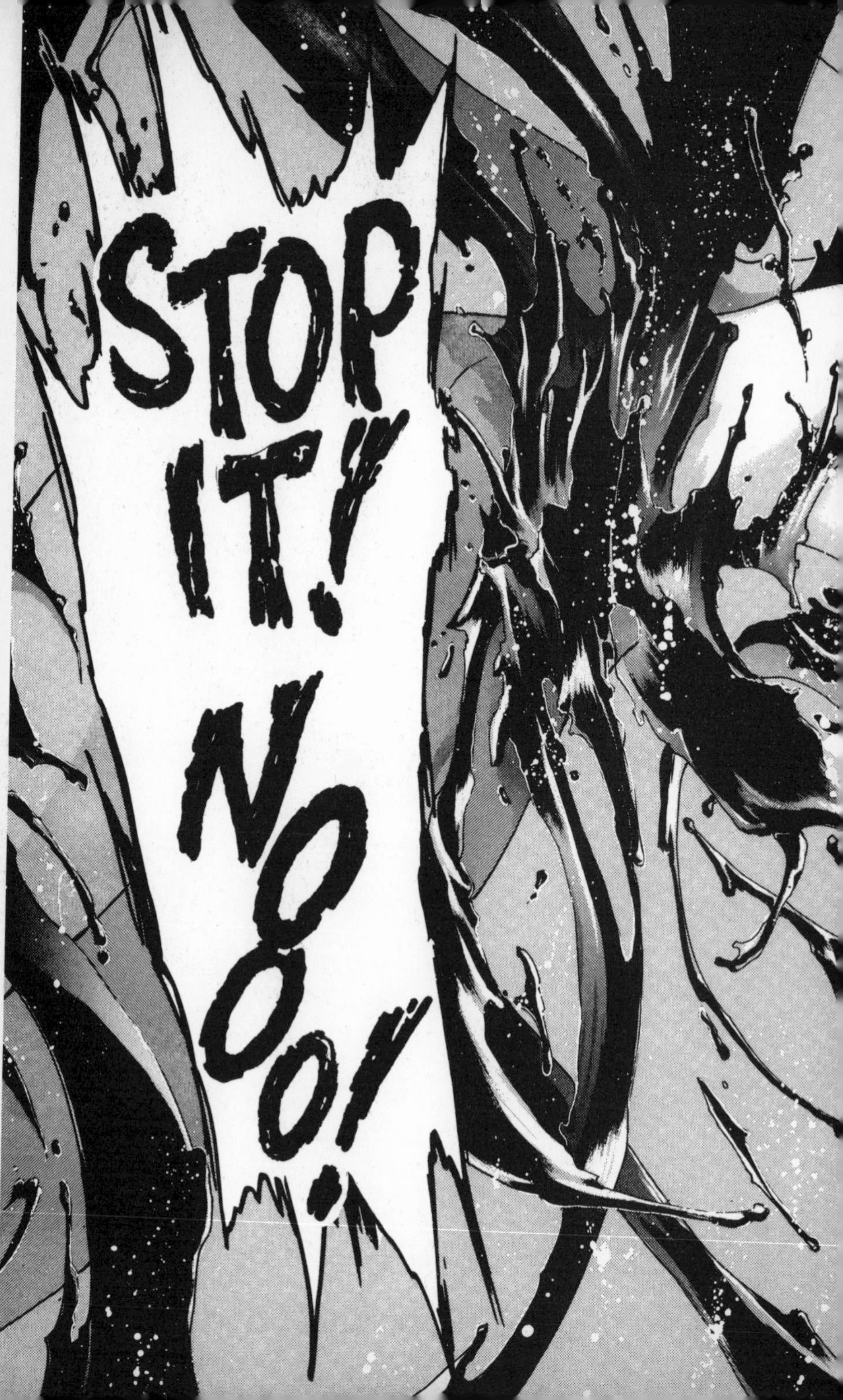
STOP IT!!
NOOO!!

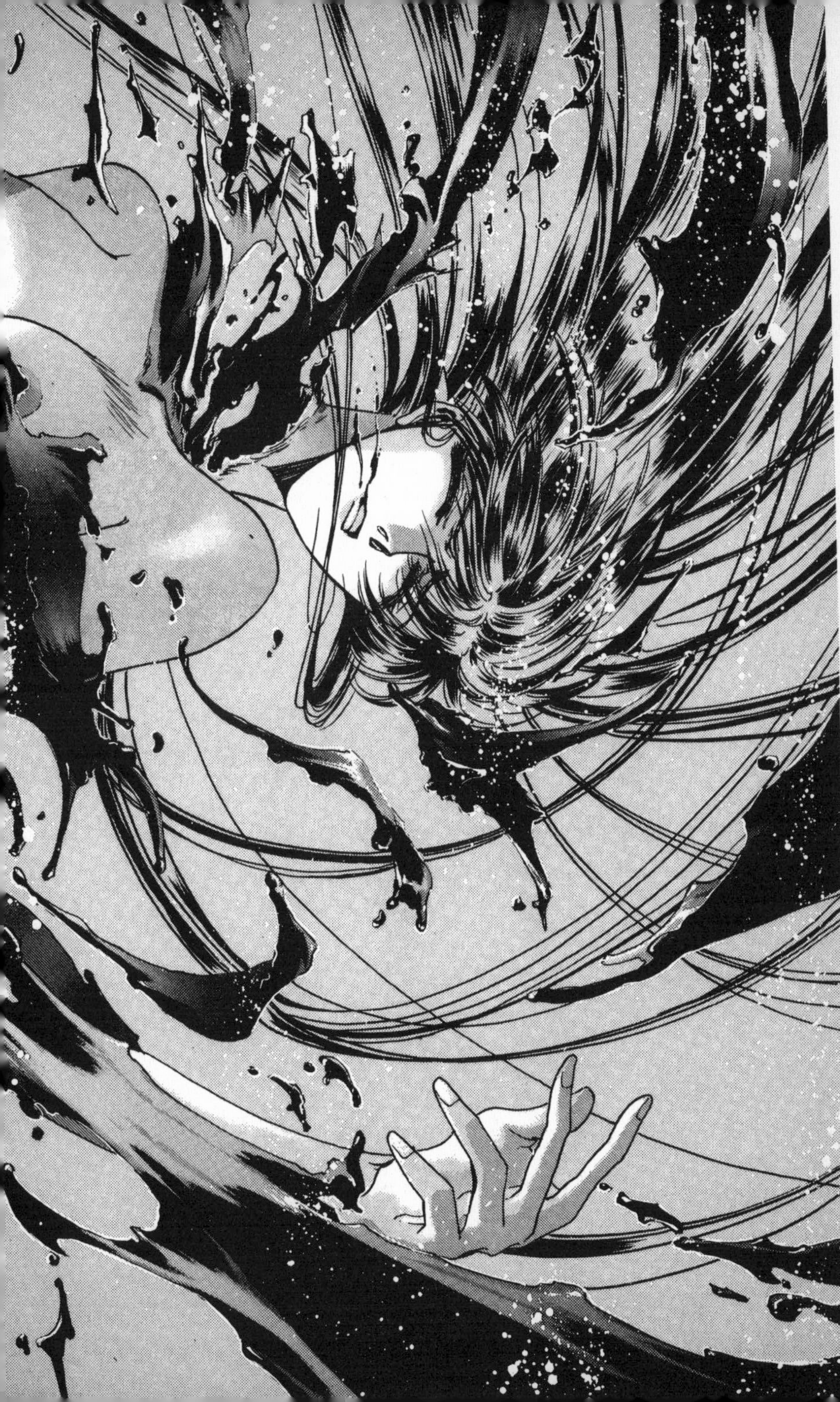

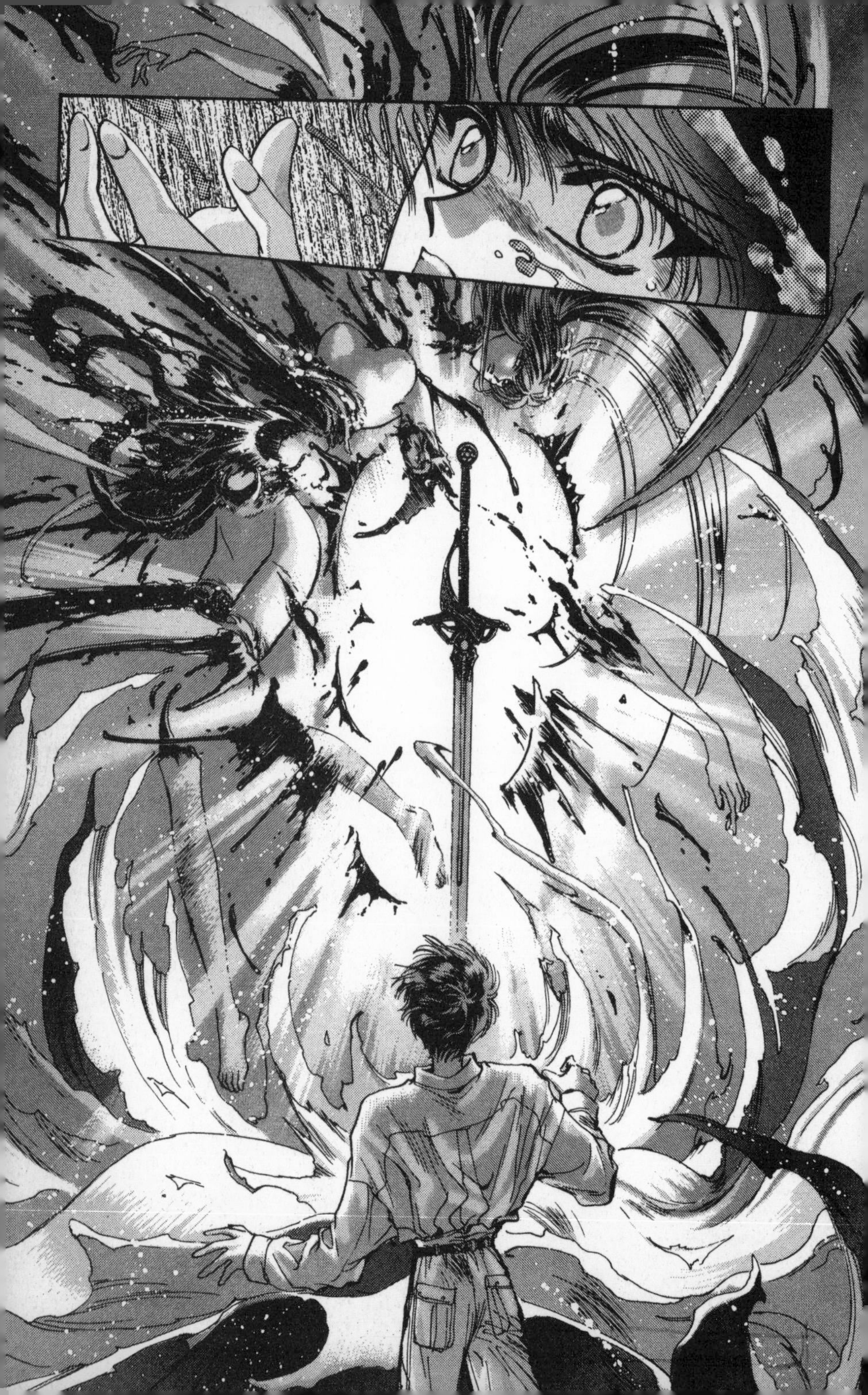

X

YUZURIHA NEKOI

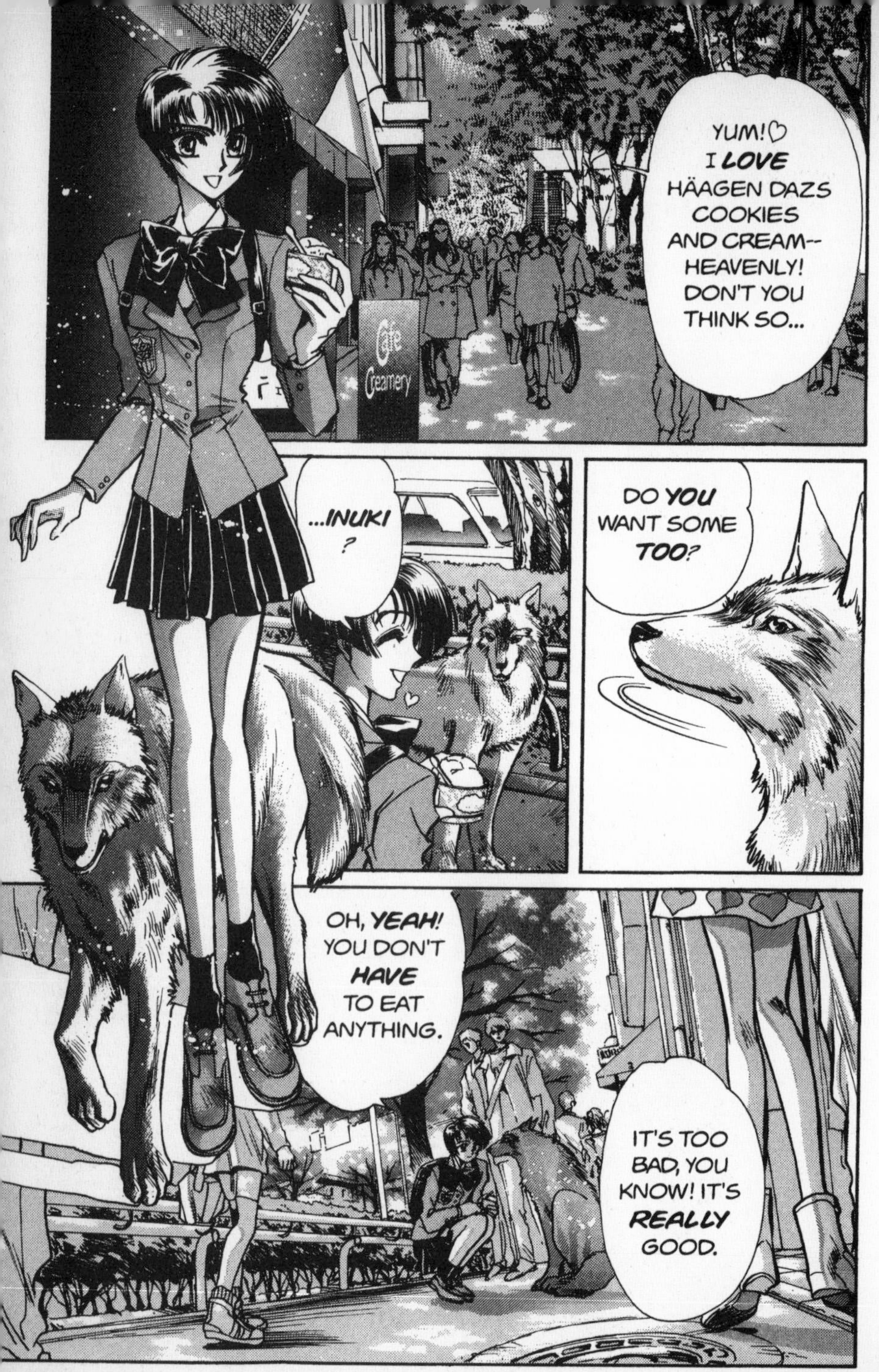
YUM!♡ I **LOVE** HÄAGEN DAZS COOKIES AND CREAM-- HEAVENLY! DON'T YOU THINK SO...
Cafe Creamery
...**INUKI** ?
DO **YOU** WANT SOME **TOO**?
OH, **YEAH**! YOU DON'T **HAVE** TO EAT ANYTHING.
IT'S TOO BAD, YOU KNOW! IT'S **REALLY** GOOD.

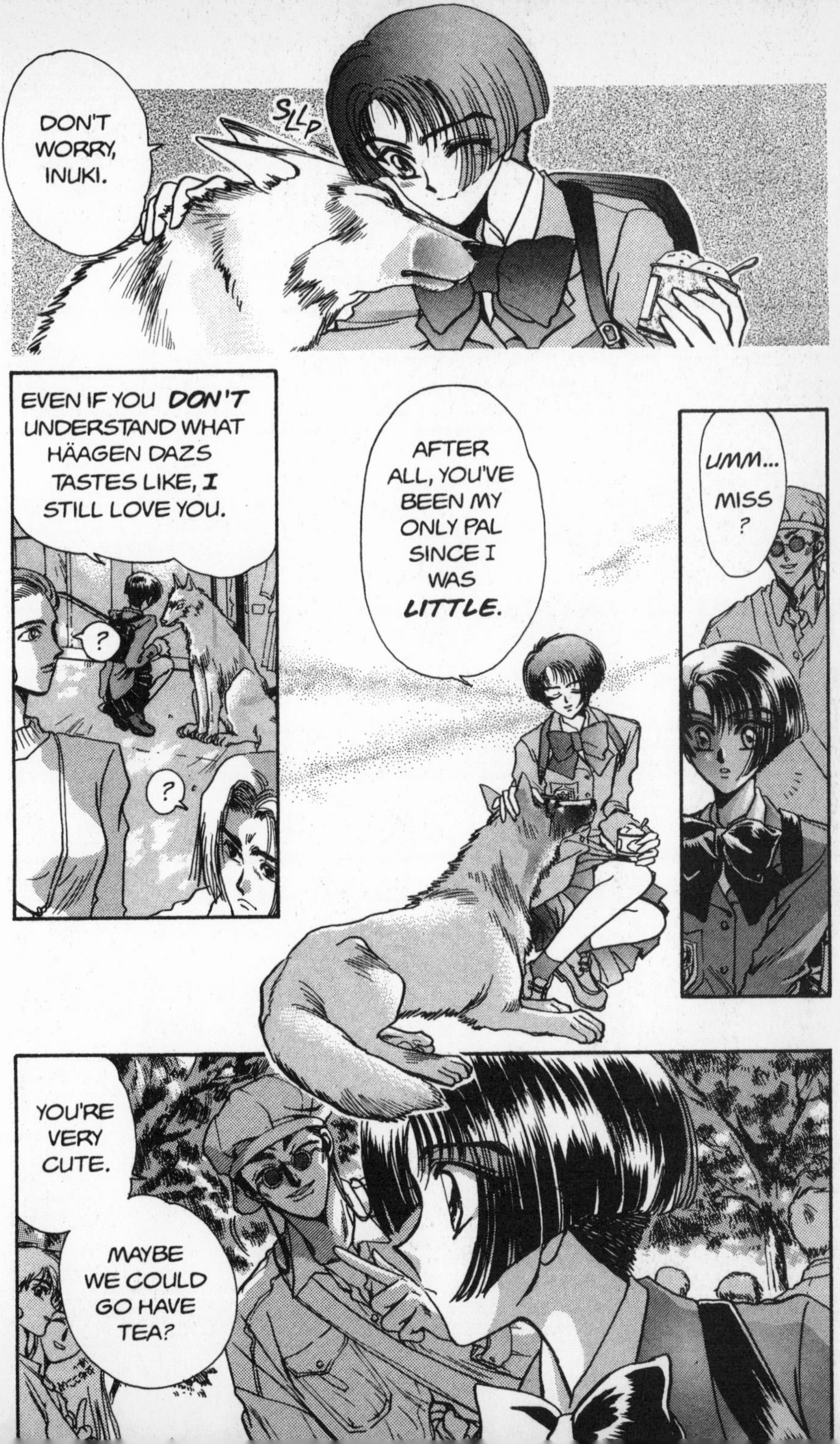
DON'T WORRY, INUKI.
SLLP
EVEN IF YOU **DON'T** UNDERSTAND WHAT HÄAGEN DAZS TASTES LIKE, **I** STILL LOVE YOU.
?
?
AFTER ALL, YOU'VE BEEN MY ONLY PAL SINCE I WAS **LITTLE**.
UMM... MISS?
YOU'RE VERY CUTE.
MAYBE WE COULD GO HAVE TEA?

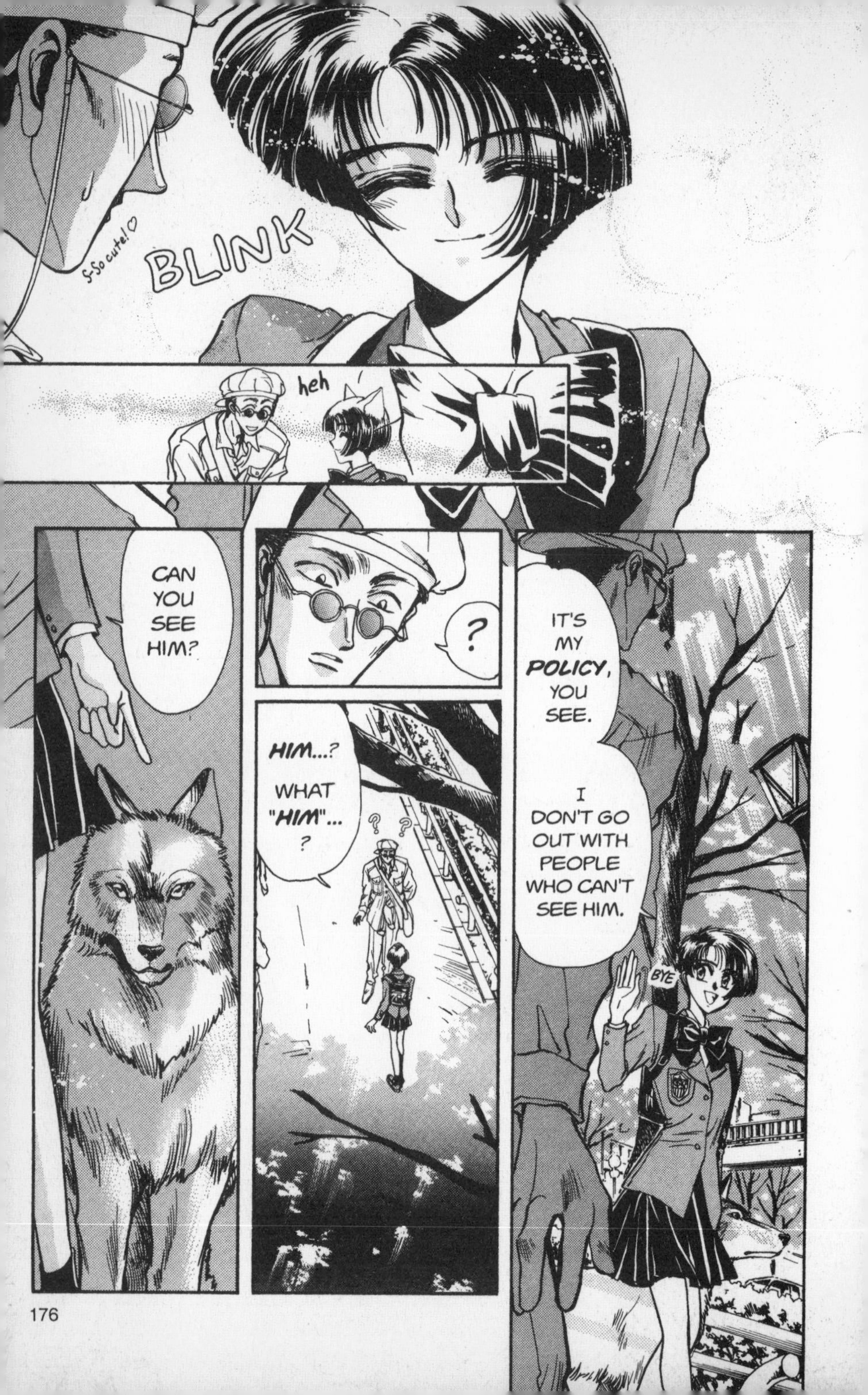
S-So cute!♡
BLINK
heh
CAN YOU SEE HIM?
?
HIM...?
WHAT "*HIM*"...?
IT'S MY *POLICY*, YOU SEE.
I DON'T GO OUT WITH PEOPLE WHO CAN'T SEE HIM.
BYE

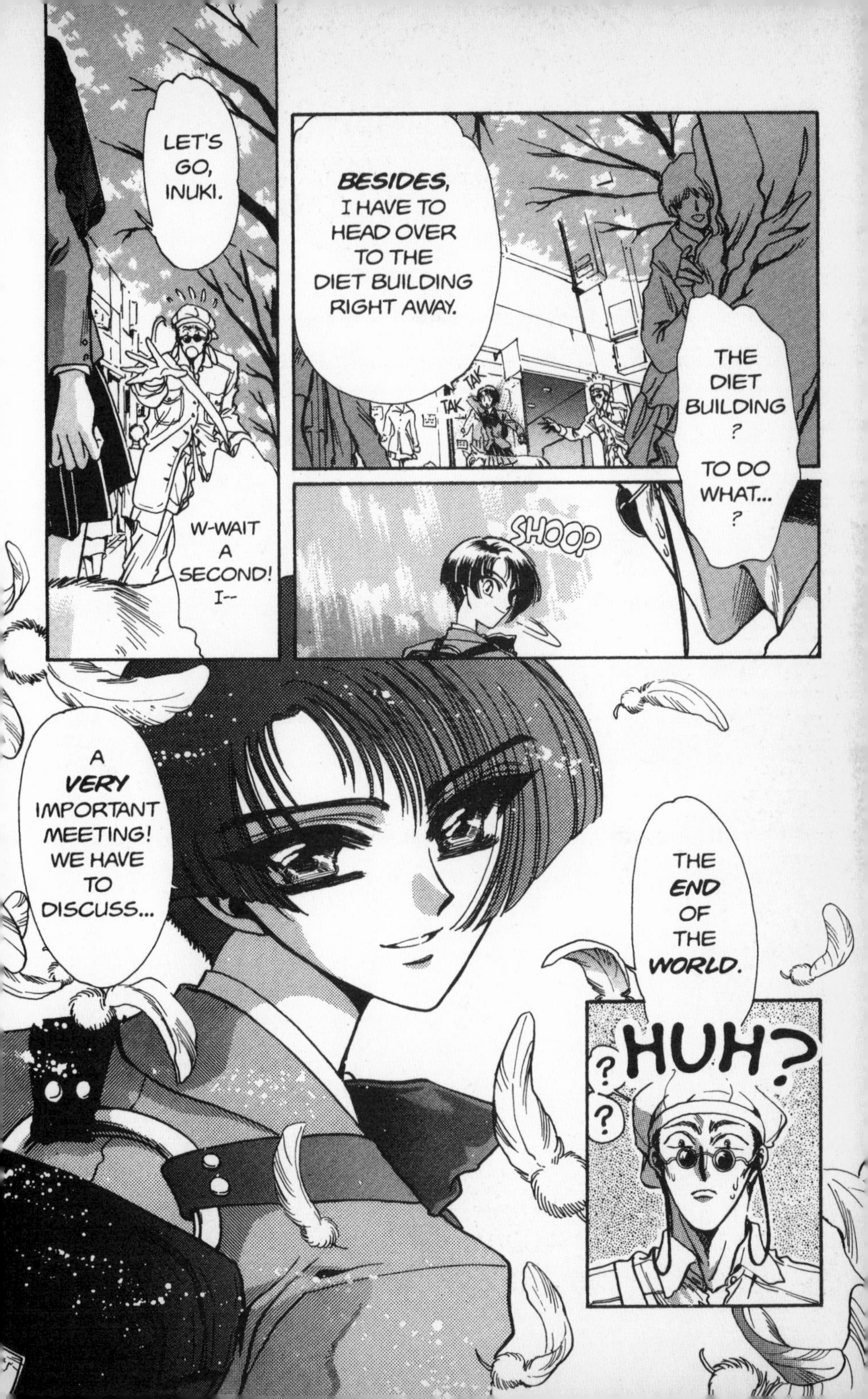
LET'S GO, INUKI.
W-WAIT A SECOND! I--
BESIDES, I HAVE TO HEAD OVER TO THE DIET BUILDING RIGHT AWAY.
TAK
TAK
THE DIET BUILDING? TO DO WHAT...?
SHOOP
A VERY IMPORTANT MEETING! WE HAVE TO DISCUSS...
THE END OF THE WORLD.
HUH?
?
?

GRAND-MA!

Tmp
Tmp

THEY SAY THEY CAN'T SEE INUKI...

...EVEN THOUGH HE'S *RIGHT* HERE.

IT'S NOT FAIR!

EVERY-ONE CALLS ME A *LIAR*.

THEY ALL SAY THAT I'M LYING.

IT'S ALL RIGHT, DEAR. INUKI IS RIGHT BY YOUR SIDE.

BUT OTHER PEOPLE CANNOT SEE HIM.

WHY NOT? WHY *CAN'T* THEY SEE HIM?

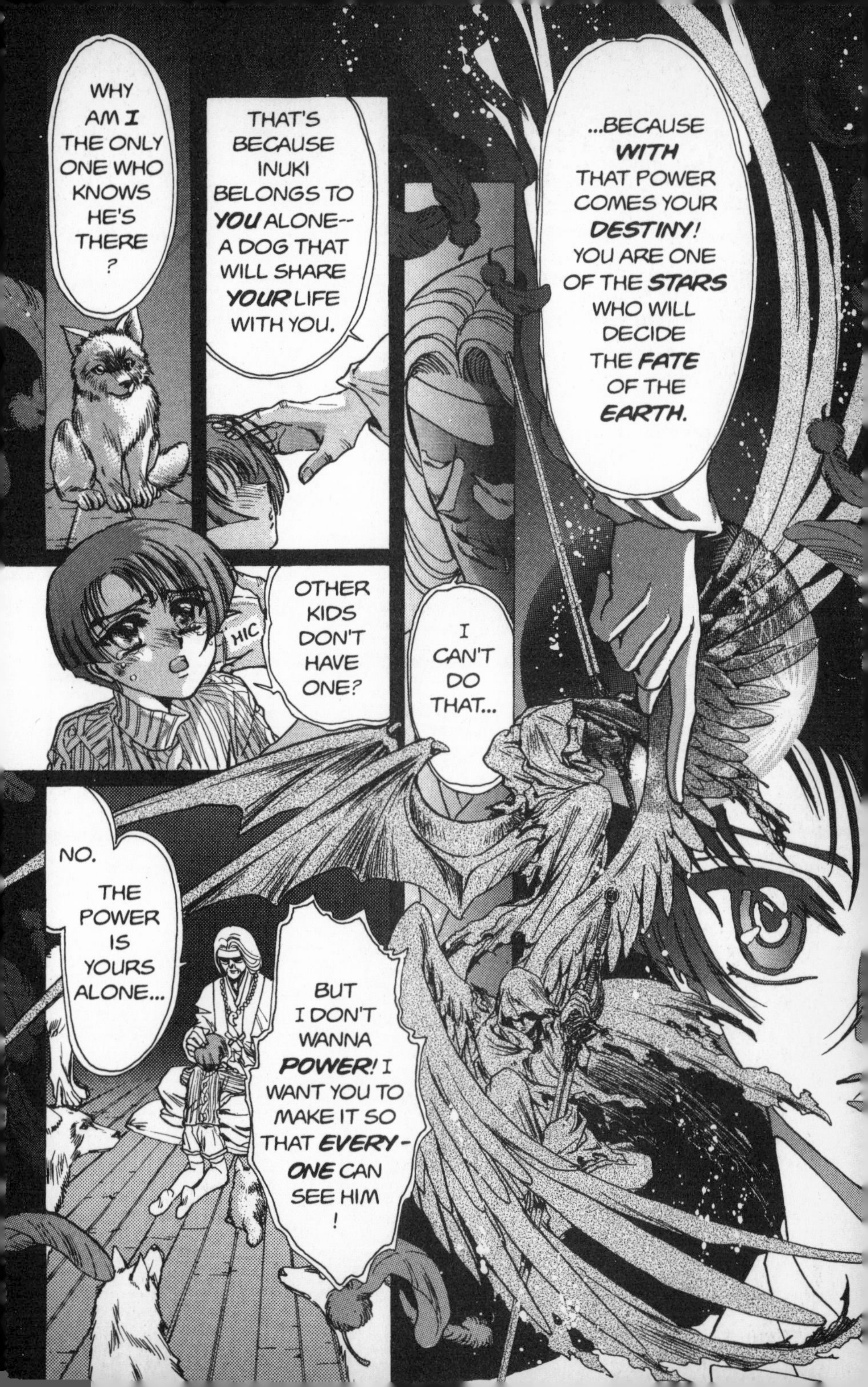

WHY AM I THE ONLY ONE WHO KNOWS HE'S THERE?
THAT'S BECAUSE INUKI BELONGS TO YOU ALONE-- A DOG THAT WILL SHARE YOUR LIFE WITH YOU.
OTHER KIDS DON'T HAVE ONE?
HIC
NO.
THE POWER IS YOURS ALONE...
...BECAUSE WITH THAT POWER COMES YOUR DESTINY! YOU ARE ONE OF THE STARS WHO WILL DECIDE THE FATE OF THE EARTH.
I CAN'T DO THAT...
BUT I DON'T WANNA POWER! I WANT YOU TO MAKE IT SO THAT EVERY-ONE CAN SEE HIM!

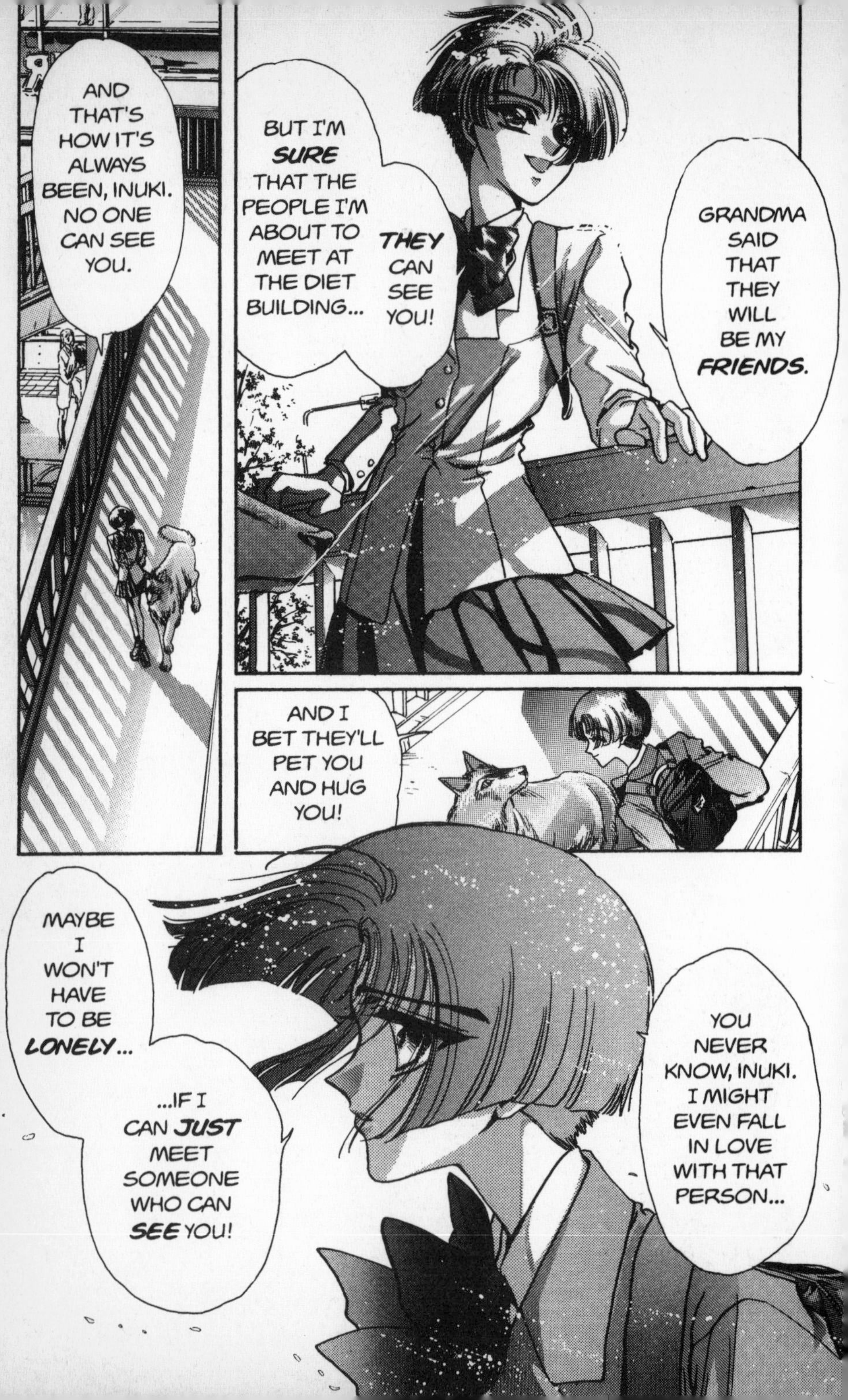
AND THAT'S HOW IT'S ALWAYS BEEN, INUKI. NO ONE CAN SEE YOU.
BUT I'M SURE THAT THE PEOPLE I'M ABOUT TO MEET AT THE DIET BUILDING...
THEY CAN SEE YOU!
GRANDMA SAID THAT THEY WILL BE MY FRIENDS.
AND I BET THEY'LL PET YOU AND HUG YOU!
MAYBE I WON'T HAVE TO BE LONELY...
...IF I CAN JUST MEET SOMEONE WHO CAN SEE YOU!
YOU NEVER KNOW, INUKI. I MIGHT EVEN FALL IN LOVE WITH THAT PERSON...

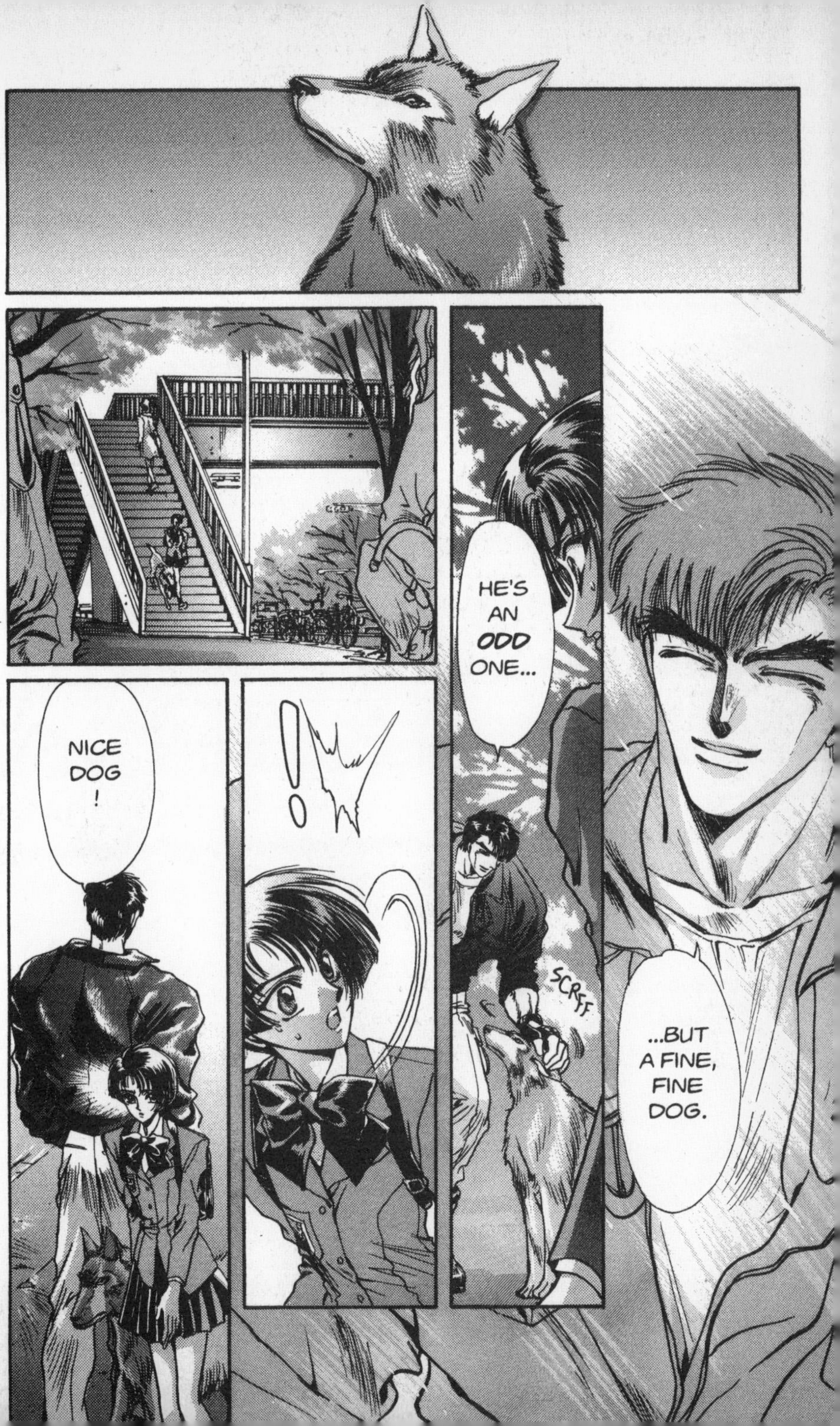
NICE DOG !
!
HE'S AN ODD ONE...
SCRFF
...BUT A FINE, FINE DOG.

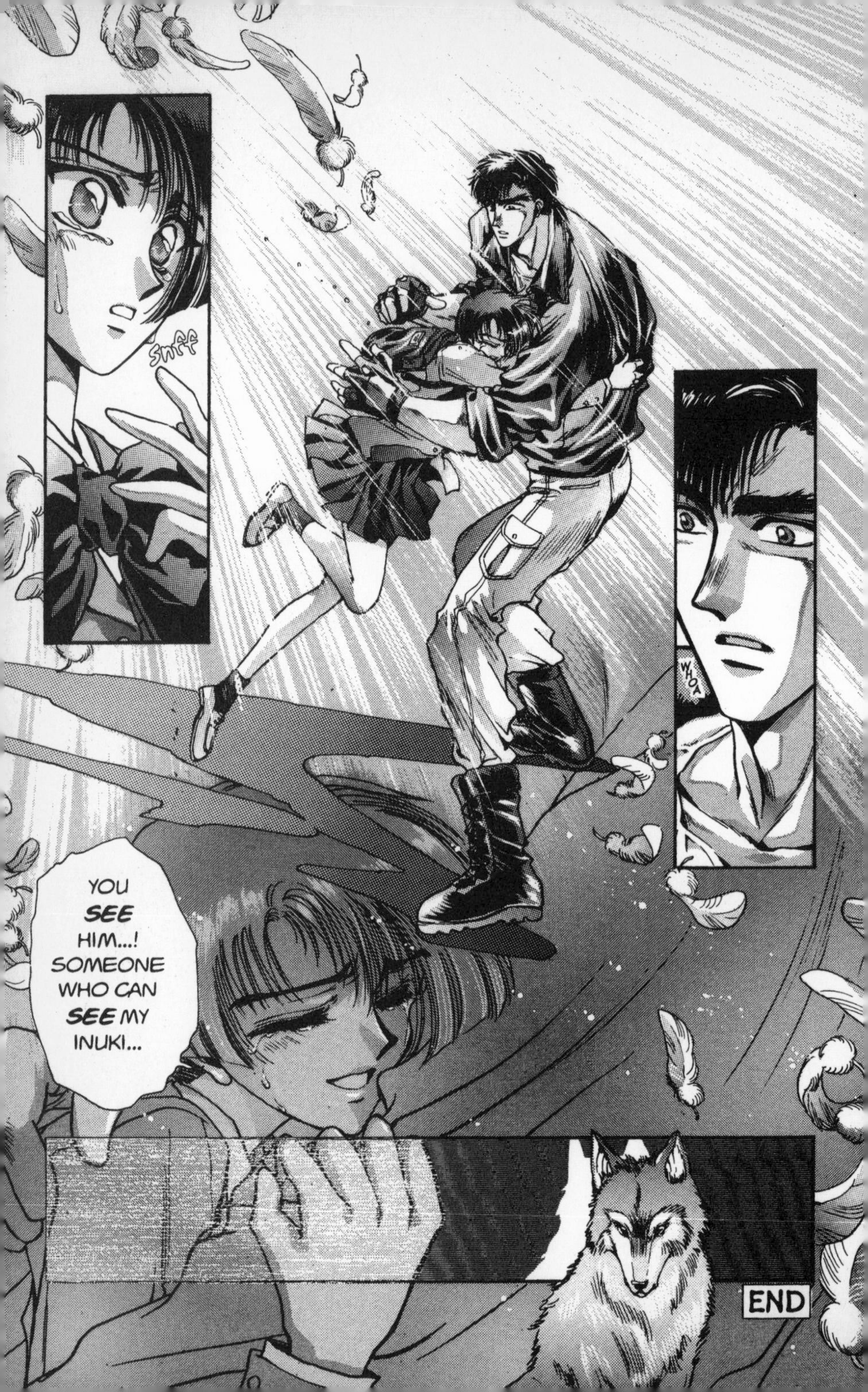
SNIFF
WHOA
YOU SEE HIM...! SOMEONE WHO CAN SEE MY INUKI...
END

THE MANGA
IDOLS O
YOUR
DREAMS!

an's comic magazine

RICA
EXTRA
™

Fantasy, science fiction, romance,
shôjo manga and more! Each issue of
America's #1 monthly manga anthology
contains 5-6 manga stories, plus exclu-
sive anime & manga news, fan art and
prize giveaway

- VIDEO GIRL AI
- FUSHIGI YÛGI
- X/1999
- STEAM DETECTIVE
- MARIONETTE GEN

monthly, b&w. 128 pa

SUBSCRIPTION RATES

ONE YEAR (12 issues)